Birds *of* Europe

with North Africa and the Middle East

Lars Jonsson

Translated by David Christie
Distribution maps by Magnus Ullman

Christopher Helm
A & C Black · London

English-language edition first published 1992
by Christopher Helm (Publishers) Limited,
a subsidiary of A & C Black (Publishers) Limited,
35 Bedford Row, London WC1R 4JH

ISBN 0–7136–8096–2

© 1992 Lars Jonsson
Translation © 1992 Christopher Helm (Publishers) Limited
Reprinted 1993

A CIP catalogue record for this book
is available from the British Library.

Original Swedish edition entitled *Lars Jonssons Fåglar*
published by Wahlström & Widstrand
Tysta Gatan 10, 11524 Stockholm, Sweden

Typeset by Falcon Graphic Art Ltd,
Wallington, Surrey

Contents

Foreword   4
Introduction   5
Birds' feathers   6
Topography   7
Head   8
Bill, legs and feet   9
Wings and tail   10
Wing and tail shape   11
Silhouette and actions   12
Shape and size   13
Moult, different plumages   14
Plumage terminology   15
Calendar-year terminology   17
Colour variation   18
Light   19
Voice   20
Behaviour and food   21
Distribution, with explanation of maps   22
Migration   23
Vagrants   24
Systematics   25
Review of the different families   26-31
Species accounts   32-545
Bibliography   546
Base references for maps   548
Sound recordings   549
Ornithological journals and societies   550
Index   551

Foreword

This book is born of a task which I started on as long ago as autumn 1973. During 1976-80 five volumes appeared in Swedish under the title *Fåglar i Naturen* ('Birds in the wild'); these books, later translated into English, dealt with European birds, including a few species from Turkey and N Africa. The material in the five books was split into different habitats and geographical regions. At the start of the 1980s an idea arose to put these together in a single volume, combining the existing works, with just a few additions and amendments. Through several stages, however, the project evolved to become what is largely a completely new book.

During the 1970s and 1980s interest in field identification of birds has grown, and a mass of specialist literature and articles has been published. The knowledge of today's birdwatcher is considerably broader than 20 years ago. When I started the illustrations for my second voume, 'Sea and Coast', in the mid 1970s, there were no pictures of juvenile waders in the available field guides, and this perplexed me as half of all waders I saw in the field were in fact juveniles. Today it is hard to imagine a 'Birds of Europe' without a juvenile Dunlin or Little Stint.

Birds are living creatures; their appearance changes not only with age, season and light conditions, but also with our own knowledge and experience. For me it is as enjoyable and exciting to look for subtle differences and characteristics in the seemingly commonplace species as in the more uncommon ones. In the foreword to the first volume I wrote of the difficulty of gaining a 'definitive' knowledge of the appearance of common species such as House and Tree Sparrows, despite almost daily studies. I can verify, with some thankfulness, that this impression has only been reinforced with the years. Each new contact with a species often provides some small detail or a deeper insight. The moment I have completed a plate I have often seen its shortcomings and/or inadequacy in conveying the species' appearance. It is probably the case that every depiction of a bird is basically an interpretation and that it can convey only a certain part of the complex reality, no matter how intimately the bird has been studied.

My aim has been to try to put across the field impression, and therefore I have so far as possible based the pictures on my own field observations and field sketches. Photographs and studies of museum skins, however, are in practice an important and for some species indispensable complement. Discussions and exchange of experiences with other ornithologists have also added substantial content to this book and I am grateful to all who have helped me, in various ways, over the years.

Special thanks are due to my friends Per Alström, Håkan Delin, Lasse Laine, Killian Mullarney, Hadoram Shirihai, Lars Svensson, Dan Zetterström and the late Peter Grant for their commitment, inspiring discussion and detailed comments. Special thanks also to Magnus Ullman, who has very knowledgeably and accurately prepared the maps and made various suggestions and comments on text and content. Many other people have also contributed considerably to this book's development: my thanks to Pe-Ge Bentz, Michael Averland, Tord Fransson and all others in the Sundregruppen, Peter Barthel, Lars Blomquist, Dick Forsman, Stellan Hedgren, Urban Olsson, Jan Olsson, Jan Pettersson, Krister Mild, Göran Wallinder, Nils Kjellen, Klaus-Malling Olsen, Göran Frisk and other staff at Naturhistoriska Riksmuséet in Stockholm, and many more.

Mart Marend at Calidris AB has had a major hand in the book as designer and computer wizard. Thanks to Ellinor Adolfsson and Anna-Lena Hansson, who have at various times recast the text.

Finally, I thank Ragnhild, Martin, Viktor and Rebecka, who have all too many times these last years been told 'We'll do that when the book's finished'.

Lars Jonsson, Hamra, November 1991

Introduction

This book treats all bird species which occur regularly in Europe and also the majority of those found in the parts of N Africa (including Madeira) and the Middle East shown on the maps. The emphasis is on Europe; species found only in the neighbouring continents have in some cases been given less space. Departures from this have been influenced both by the existing material from earlier publications and by the total space available. For vagrants, those species recorded in Europe more than five times this century up to 1989 are included (though a few are not illustrated). Species with fewer than five records are in some cases described, perhaps because particular confusion risks exist, or the records have attracted great interest, or quite simply because space permitted.

The illustrations are based in part on the series of five books which appeared in 1976-80 (see Foreword). Of the 300 or so plates within the species accounts, about 140 are entirely new, 40 revised and 120 from earlier books; of about 100 small pictures which e.g. head the text pages, 60 are new. The introductory text and 25 illustrations are entirely new. Maps are completely redone, based on census and atlas projects carried out in many countries in the last two decades.

Looking at birds

Birdwatching can be approached from many angles, from enjoying listening to the Blackbird during a walk in the park to long-term scientific research within a narrow field of the birds' lives. Being so mobile, birds are present in almost every environment: high-arctic regions, the very centre of cities, and right out on the open oceans. What is needed is a pair of binoculars and a notebook. The more active will perhaps get themselves a telescope and a stable tripod to find and identify birds at longer ranges. With increased knowledge often comes a need to document one's observations. Notes on different birds' arrival in spring, species seen on a trip or the date an uncommon species was found are examples of what most birdwatchers put down in a notebook. A deeper interest may lead one to specialise, e.g. study the migration at a particular site over a lengthy period, pursue rare species, photograph birds, do a local breeding-bird census, or work to protect certain habitats or sites from exploitation or destruction. Birdwatching is in all forms positive, so long as the birds are not disturbed, consideration is shown for the environment, and the interests of landowners and other people respected.

Identifying birds

Every observation and attempt at a field identification has intrinsic conditions, possibilities and limitations. The person on familiar home territory often sums up probabilities, and perhaps makes a reliable guess at a bird which to the uninitiated appears totally impossible to identify. Shape, movement and general habits, usually summed up in the term 'jizz', are important to the experienced birdwatcher. One who knows his/her birds knows what to look for and therefore sees more. With experience and perhaps an ear for music, calls play a major part. Some of the basics for identifying birds are given in the introductory pages. A simple key word is to *look*, really observe birds, common as well as uncommon ones. A way of training one's powers of observation — and one which to me of course seems natural — is to draw birds in the field. The important thing is not to produce good sketches but to practise seeing, to get the eye and the brain to 'decide on' what is seen and then formulate impressions; one is then compelled in an active way to observe the appearance of the whole bird.

Birds' feathers

Are mainly of two types: **down** and **contour feathers**. On most non-passerines the young are already covered in an insulating layer of down on hatching. On the full-grown bird the outward shape is formed by contour feathers, which conceal the underlying down; commonly the contour feathers have a down-like lower section. In some families, e.g. those in the order Galliformes, there is also a secondary down attached to the shaft base of the contour feather. There is also a feather type intermediate between down and contour feathers, known as a semiplume.

With contour feathers a distinction is usually made between **body feathers**, incl. head and wing-coverts, and **flight feathers**, i.e. **wing** and **tail feathers**.

Body feathers, having various functions, have acquired a number of different appearances. Extremes are the whisker-like **bristles** at the gape of nightjars or the long ornamental scapular feathers on drake dabbling ducks.

A further type of feather, known as a **filoplume**, occurs on e.g. cormorants and egrets/herons. These are long ornamental hairs which grow out around the ordinary feather follicle.

In detailed descriptions of plumage, a part of the feather is often mentioned in combination with a marking, e.g. shaft streak, diffuse dark centre etc. Some of these feather markings are shown here.

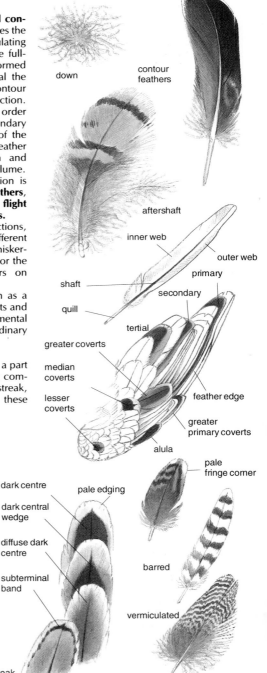

down

contour feathers

aftershaft

inner web

outer web

primary

secondary

shaft

tertial

quill

greater coverts

median coverts

lesser coverts

feather edge

greater primary coverts

alula

pale fringe corner

pale tipped

spot tip

dark centre

pale edging

dark central wedge

diffuse dark centre

subterminal band

barred

drop-shaped spot

vermiculated

large pale tip

dark shaft-streak

Topography

Birds' feathers lie in certain zones or tracts which form more or less discernible parts of the bird's outward shape. These tracts are very similarly located on the various bird species and the terms can, with minor additions or modifications, be used for all bird orders. They are the starting point when describing a bird's appearance.

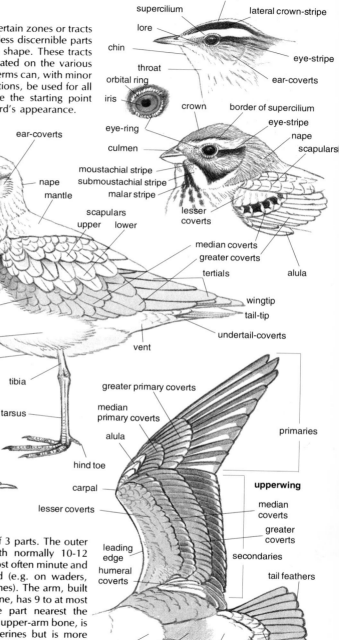

The wing consists of 3 parts. The outer part is the hand, with normally 10-12 **primaries**, the outermost often minute and not visible in the field (e.g. on waders, gulls and most passerines). The arm, built around the forearm bone, has 9 to at most c30 **secondaries**. The part nearest the body, built around the upper-arm bone, is barely visible on passerines but is more developed on e.g. seabirds and pelicans.

7

Head

Often we seek the eye of a bird and the appearance of the head is the first thing we note. On many species, stripes and markings provide distinguishing features between closely related species.

Which species? Compare p. 413

Song Thrush

Redwing

Redwing has bold supercilium and submoustachial stripe, Song Thrush variegated ear-coverts and distinct eye-ring.

Bonelli's Warbler

Even relatively unmarked birds can have a distinctive facial expression created by a number of subtle characters.

In species groups with highly patterned heads it is harder to memorise details, leaving only the impression of e.g. spottiness or that the bird was highly variegated. Previous knowledge of which details of pattern contain crucial distinguishing features enables one to check these quickly.

Heads of ad. and juv. Great Spotted Woodpecker and ad. Middle Spotted.

Chiffchaff

The 'clean' face with pale lores and complete eye-ring of Bonelli's Warbler give it a 'peering' and 'inquisitive' expression, while the Chiffchaff is always slightly dingier and 'tougher'.

♂ Great Spotted   juv   Middle Spotted

8

Bill length and shape are adapted to the bird's food. They therefore reveal its lifestyle and tell which family or genus a bird belongs to. In some species, however, great individual variations can be seen. Differences between the sexes are not uncommon, an adaptation enabling exploitation of a wider feeding niche in one and the same territory. In many waders, e.g. godwits and curlews, the female is bigger and has a noticeably longer bill than the male, while the situation is reversed in gulls. In some species, juvs. at first have a less developed bill than full ads., e.g. Razorbill and Curlew. Bill size can also vary geographically; in e.g. Dunlin this difference is obvious in the field.

Curlew, ad. female and juv. male (Jul). Whimbrel for comparison.

Legs and feet can be useful features. Bar-tailed Godwit has clearly shorter legs than Black-tailed. Rough-legged Buzzard has feathered tarsi, unlike Buzzard and Long-legged Buzzard.

Marsh Sandpiper can be told in flight from Wood Sandpiper by its long legs.

Comparison between southern and northern Dunlins.

Little Ringed Plover

Ringed Plover

Colours of bare parts, i.e. **iris, orbital ring, bill, cere** and **legs,** often identify a species and sometimes its sex and age. Buzzards have a paler iris as imms., while eagles acquire a paler iris as ads. 1st-cal-year Lesser Whitethroat (see p.17) has a greyer and generally paler iris than ad. which has more brown with a light crescent on upper half of iris, while reverse applies to Whitethroat. Many species have seasonal changes in bill colour, e.g. divers, and some herons and egrets have a change in colour of the skin around the bill base and on the legs for a brief period during courtship.

1st-cal autumn

1st-cal autumn

ad

ad ♂

Lesser Whitethroat

Whitethroat

9

Wing and tail

The term **wingbar** is used in a wide sense for dark or pale bands on the wing. Depending on their position other terms may be used. The pale wingbar can e.g. on many waders be formed by white tips to greater coverts together with pale colour on shaft and at base of inner primaries. Wingbars visible on perched passerines are usually formed by pale tips to greater coverts. **Double wingbar** is often formed by pale tips to both median and greater coverts, as on Two-barred Crossbill.

double wingbar

Terminal band runs along the rear edge of the wing or tail.

If a greater part of the rear wing is pale, as e.g. on Terek Sandpiper and Kittiwake, the term **pale panel** or **trailing edge** may be used.

Diagonal band or **panel across inner wing** is a contrasting band across the median secondary coverts and the lesser coverts in front of them, as on e.g. Booted Eagle (pale) or juv. Kittiwake (black). On latter, it forms a zigzag pattern with the dark leading edge of the outer wing.

A contrasting marking along the fore edge of the wing is usually called pale or dark **leading edge to wing.**

Speculum refers to the often lustrous marking on the secondaries of dabbling ducks. It is often framed by a pale terminal band and a pale wingbar along the greater coverts.

The **axillaries** are the feathers in the 'armpit'. On e.g. the *Pluvialis* plovers they reveal diagnostic differences.

Tail markings are often a signal to conspecifics. They are easy to see and remember and are often valuable field characters. Many bright markings become visible only when the tail is spread e.g. on take-off. **Back, rump** and **uppertail-coverts** also conceal signals at rest which are revealed in flight, e.g. on waders and finches.

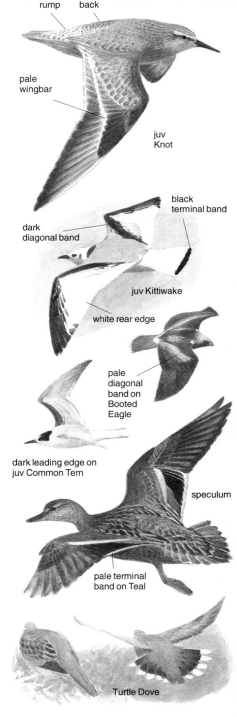

rump back

pale wingbar

juv Knot

black terminal band

dark diagonal band

juv Kittiwake

white rear edge

pale diagonal band on Booted Eagle

dark leading edge on juv Common Tern

speculum

pale terminal band on Teal

Turtle Dove

Wing shape

Primary projection is the part of the wing-tip that is visible beyond the longest tertial. It is important in separating several very similar species in the field.

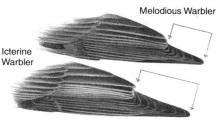

Melodious Warbler

Icterine Warbler

Icterine Warbler (lower) has longer primary projection and more prominent pale secondary panel than Melodious.

American Golden Plover

Pacific Golden Plover

In the **wing formula** small differences in wing shape and measurements between different species can be compared, in connection with ringing or when examining skins in museums. Several very similar species can be separated by differences in **primary emargination** (or 'notch') on inner and outer web and by the **primaries' relative length.** These differences are sometimes visible in the field or on photographs. In descriptions of wing formulae and plumage characters, ringers normally number feathers from the outer one inwards; on most passerines the 1st primary is vestigial and very short. In descriptions of moult patterns, the primaries are usually numbered from innermost outwards.

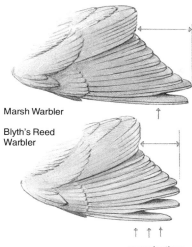

Marsh Warbler

Blyth's Reed Warbler

emarginations

forked tail

Blyth's Reed Warbler

Reed Warbler

Icterine Warbler

Tail shape

Tail shape and length as well as length of the undertail-coverts can differ between very similar species.

Tail shape and length of undertail-coverts in three different warblers.

River Warbler

11

Sooty Shearwater

Lesser
Black-backed
Gull

Pomarine Skua

Cory's
Shearwater

Sooty Shearwater

Silhouette and actions

The bird's **flight silhouette** and **pattern of actions** are often sufficient for identification. When studying birds in flight at long range, e.g. raptors and seabirds, differences in shape, attitude and movement pattern are of critical importance.

With birds of prey one can often practise one's skills in observing wing attitude. Various postures produce distinctive silhouettes from various angles. Eagles which **droop the hand** have, in a certain situation, e.g. only the arm visible on the forewing.

A buzzard soars above the forest: common Buzzard or Honey Buzzard? Wing posture decides it.

Moult and abnormal wear can in some cases alter silhouette and overall impression. Tail projections and other visual signals used in pair-forming and during breeding are developed with onset of breeding condition, and in e.g. skuas and some ducks the ornamental feathers are shed after breeding.

Black Kite and dark-phase Booted Eagle can be separated by tail shape.

Seabirds alter their flight pattern above a certain wind strength; in about force 7 shearwaters change to simply riding on the wind and their wings are angled back to reduce the area exposed to the wind.

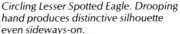

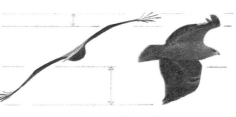

Circling Lesser Spotted Eagle. Drooping hand produces distinctive silhouette even sideways-on.

Goshawk with broad, more blunted wings, Peregrine with pointed wings.

Booted Eagle with damaged tail

Booted Eagle

Black Kite

Shape

The outward shape varies with the bird's mood and activity. Many species look e.g. more rounded, more plump, in cold weather. Long-necked waders in strong wind look short-necked etc. Many species, however, consistently have an outward shape and posture which reveals their identity.

juv Ruff

Nightingale

L 13.5 cm

Robin

WS 135—150 cm

Size

Total length is given after each species name and refers to the bird in stretched posture. Normally any elongated tail feathers are included.

Wingspan is also given for non-passerines. This refers to the distance between the wingtips when the bird has wings spread to the maximum under natural conditions. In scientific publications **wing length** refers to the length from carpal to wingtip, i.e. only the outer-wing measurement; this is not given in this book.

Judging size in the field is often difficult other than in direct comparisons. The impression is also influenced by light conditions. In mist, objects often appear larger than they really are. Birds seen through magnifying lenses, i.e. telephoto lenses or telescopes, can be misjudged owing to **optical size illusion**: with two same-sized birds, the eye will see the one farther away as bigger than the one in front. This can be important e.g. if observing through strong magnification a flock of gulls or waders on a bank.

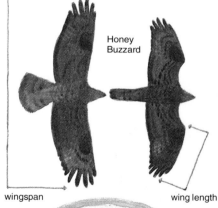

Honey Buzzard

wingspan

wing length

Optical size illusion: two equal-sized plovers seen through a telescope.

13

Moult

All birds must renew their plumage regularly, since it becomes worn and loses its function. Some assume a more colourful **summer plumage** before the breeding season and a more modest **winter plumage** after completing breeding. Differences in moult cycles can be considerable: some species manage up to three changes per year, while for others it takes three years before a complete plumage change is achieved. Some species, e.g. larks, reach full-adult plumage with their first non-juv. plumage; others can take five years.

Each species has developed a moult strategy so as best to cope with this energy-exacting transformation. Birds of prey e.g. are totally dependent on retaining good powers of flight and change the feathers successively so that there are never more than two or three flight feathers missing in each wing. Divers and ducks can stand a period of flightlessness and shed their flight feathers simultaneously. Some species have an interrupted cycle, changing some flight feathers before migration and then continuing the moult on arrival in winter quarters. In northern latitudes it is most common for change of flight feathers to take place in summer after the breeding season and before autumn migration. Within certain limits individuals can control the moult to adjust it best to their own breeding and migration; failed breeding can e.g. lead to the moult being brought forward.

Complete moult — wing and tail feathers are changed at the same time or in association with moult of body feathers.

Partial moult — only body feathers and parts of wing-coverts are changed, on some also tertials and 1−2 inner secondaries. This can include almost all or only limited parts of head and body.

Loss of fringes — acquiring summer plumage without moulting. The bright summer plumage is hidden by pale feather fringes, but appears gradually through wear and loss of these.

Different plumages

All species have at least two different plumages, and up to ten plumages distinguishable in the field occur, e.g. in Herring Gull. In species descriptions and illustrations terms for these plumages are regularly used following two alternative principles. The **plumage terminology** shown opposite is that most used in Europe. In N America the terms **definitive plumage** for winter and **alternate plumage** for summer are often used in order to avoid the problem that summer and winter have a different significance in the S Hemisphere. Besides describing which plumage the bird is in, one can also classify it from a **calendar-year terminology** (see p. 17) based on which calendar-year it has reached. The systems complement each other and both are used as and where practical. The first down plumage, i.e. any downy coat the bird may have on hatching, has been omitted in the following.

The black bib that the House Sparrow has in spring and summer appears through loss of feather fringes.

Plumage terminology

Juv. − juvenile plumage. The bird's first proper plumage in which it fledges. It can be retained for a period of about one month up to one year.

Change to subsequent plumage takes place through a post-juvenile moult.

1st-winter − 1st-winter plumage, used for those species, e.g. most passerines, waders and gulls, which undergo a partial moult in late summer−autumn (winter). Recognised by retained juvenile feathers on wings and tail. Some species, e.g. Galliformes and larks, undergo a complete moult in their 1st autumn.

Change to subsequent plumage occurs via a spring moult or through loss of fringes.

1st-summer − refers to the plumage acquired before first breeding season, i.e. spring/summer of year after hatching. Degree of adult-type coloration varies; some are winter-like, while many in this plumage are very like ad. summer. Some are recognisable in the field by all or parts of the wing still being juv.

Moult before the bird's 2nd winter is often complete, whereby the juv. wing and tail feathers are changed.

2nd-winter − 2nd-winter plumage, can be distinguished in some genera, while in e.g. most passerines it is identical with that of ads. In species whose plumage development extends over several years, e.g. large gulls and larger birds of prey, subsequent plumages are described − **2nd-summer**, **3rd-winter** etc. Some passerines, too, e.g. buntings and many *Sylvia* warblers, do not attain full coloration before their 2nd-summer plumage.

Immature birds and those which have failed in their breeding attempt often moult earlier than breeding adults.

Ad. winter − adult winter plumage. See also p.16.

Little Gull

juv

1st-winter
dark-winged
individual

1st-
summer

2nd-winter

ad winter

Ad. – adult: the bird is sexually mature and has full plumage coloration.

Ad. winter – adult winter plumage. Worn for a period during the winter months. *In most species is acquired through a complete moult towards end of or after breeding season.*

Ad. summer – adult summer plumage. The plumage in which the bird breeds. *Acquired via a partial moult (in a few cases complete) or loss of feather fringes.*

Drakes of ducks mate and carry out their part of breeding duties in a plumage worn from late autumn to early summer of the following year. Their breeding plumage is here called **full or winter plumage.** In late summer–autumn they have a female-like **eclipse plumage** corresponding more to other species' winter plumage. Other transitional plumages with partial moults also occur, e.g. in Long-tailed Duck and Ruff.

♂ winter

Whinchat

♂ summer

full plumage

eclipse plumage

Jan   Feb   Mar   Apr   May   Jun   Jul   Aug   Sep   Oct   Nov   Dec

subad Imperial Eagle

Subad. – subadult: a bird which is not juvenile but is not yet adult.

Imm. – immature, a non-adult bird, i.e. juvenile or subadult.

Full-plumaged – a bird which has reached its optimum plumage; thus, Great Black-backed Gulls are not full-plumaged until four or five years old, whereas the Willow Warbler is in its first year.

16

Calendar-year terminology

1st cal-year – 1st calendar-year, i.e. from when the bird hatches until 31 Dec of same year, regardless of whether it has two different plumages.

2nd cal-year – 2nd calendar-year, i.e. from 1 Jan to 31 Dec of following year. During this year up to three plumage changes may take place.

3rd cal-year, 4th cal-year etc – subsequent years as per the above principle.

For species which have a slow plumage development and wear transitional plumages for lengthy periods, identification to calendar-year may be preferable. Some raptors can have three generations of feathers at the same time and show no obvious difference between winter and summer. A seasonal label can be added to specify a species' plumage appearance at a certain time of the year, e.g. 2nd cal-year autumn. An Arctic Skua in Jul moulting from 1st-summer to 2nd-winter can be termed 'Arctic Skua, 2nd cal-year.

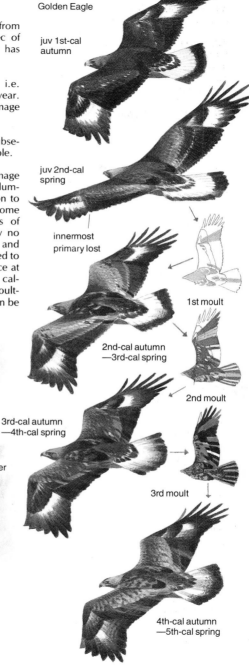

Golden Eagle

juv 1st-cal autumn

juv 2nd-cal spring

innermost primary lost

1st moult

2nd-cal autumn —3rd-cal spring

2nd moult

3rd-cal autumn —4th-cal spring

ad (6th-cal)—older

3rd moult

4th-cal autumn —5th-cal spring

5th—6th-cal

Colour variation

Birds vary in colour. In some species, e.g. Buzzard or Ruff, this is obvious. Others have more subtle variations, but given time anyone will discover that all species vary in colour and patterning. **Colour phase** or **form** is used in those cases where two or more well-defined colour types appear within a species without being connected with a geographical race. The ratios between various colour phases can, however, differ geographically: e.g. pale-phase Arctic Skuas are commoner in arctic regions than in the southern part of the range. Disorders in colour pigmentation also occur rarely and can be partial or total.

Albinism – lack of colour pigment

Leucism – absence of dark pigments

Melanism – dominance of black pigment

Discoloration – mainly because of oil, can sometimes create odd appearances which are easily misconstrued as natural markings. Legs of waders can sometimes be stained by surrounding mud so that dark legs look muddy-coloured.

Bleaching and wear – light, water and wind greatly affect the general plumage impression. Paler parts fade and wear faster than dark areas as dark pigment (melanin) hardens the feather. The juv. plumage is sometimes of poorer quality than that of ads. in this respect: e.g. juv. larks fade more quickly than ads. Some pale gulls and seabirds in southern latitudes often show individual variations due to bleaching.

Cosmetic coloration – of pale pink or ochre, as seen on certain gull species, comes from yellow and red pigments (carotenoid) in the oil secreted by a gland at the very rear of the back. The oil is used when preening the feathers, as a lubricant so that the interlocking barbule hooklets between the barbs of the vane function properly.

Arctic Skua

pale phase

dark phase

partial albino Starling

leucistic Teal

wear of one outer scapular feather on Curlew Sandpiper in summer plumage

pale juv Skylark

Black-headed Gull in fresh winter plumage with pink flush

Light

Lighting of course affects the general impression a bird gives, and the ability of the light to create illusions is infinite. The contrast between upperparts and paler underparts which most birds have is often neutralised in the field by the normally stronger light from the sky. Sun, however, can both strengthen and reduce existing contrasts. Delicate tinting on a pale background often shows best in overcast weather. Strong underlighting from snow or desert sand changes the impression of the underpart markings on e.g. birds of prey.

Southern birds which the widely travelled birdwatcher has got used to seeing in strong light may give a different impression as vagrants on a chilly October day in northern latitudes. A pale gull over open sea can look surprisingly dark in cloud shadow, and so on.

Short-toed Lark

summer,
in strong sunlight

autumn,
in dull weather

Rough-legged Buzzard ♂ backlit

Buzzard backlit

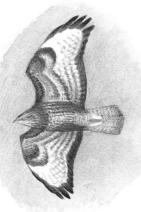

Buzzard, lit from below

Yelkouan Shearwater
in strong sunlight and
in cloudy weather

Voice

Song and calls are among birds' most obvious attributes. Various calls often have a specific meaning: they communicate something. The breadth of repertoire and the use of voice vary between different genera. Some types of calls or functions do not have well-defined borderlines: different simple calls and alarm calls can e.g. be run together according to mood.

Song or **display call** is used by males to claim territory and attract a female or alternatively to strengthen the bond between a pair. In some cases females sing, too. Song is associated with passerines and display usually with non-passerines.

Call (simple call) is used for calling to a member of the same species, in some cases also for claiming territory. In flocking birds a sharp distinction can sometimes be perceived between call and contact call.

Contact call is used for keeping contact within the flock and is often shorter than the simple call. In e.g. Siskin the gravelly call is the contact and the more insistent 'tseelü' the simple call.

Flight call is often the same as the simple or contact calls or a variant of either. The term is used for e.g. the Greenshank's 'tchew-tew-tew' as it normally is not given until the bird takes off or is in flight, but for this species it is synonymous with simple call.

Alarm call is given near the nest or in the presence of a presumptive enemy. Many species may show agitation or stress in the intonation by simply sharpening the tone of the simple call, while others have specific alarm calls.

Begging call is the call used by fledged young to beg for food. In some species the ad. female may also use a similar call to beg for food from the male.

Other calls when foraging, bickering among their own species, mating etc are specified in the text so far as they occur.

Voice is at least as important as appearance for identifying birds in the field. The principal method of learning calls, apart from through field experience, is to listen to various recordings. A list of such recordings is given on p. 547. Describing calls in words is difficult and in some cases virtually impossible. Sonagrams are a scientific way of representing pitches and time intervals in birds' voices, but it is hard to envisage a sound picture from a sonagram. It can, however, be seen that the character of certain sounds is created by a broad range of both low and high sounds. Three well-known calls are shown below in sonagram form, somewhat simplified.

Green Sandpiper's flight call

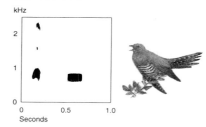

Cuckoo's display call

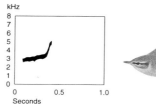

Willow Warbler's call

Behaviour

Birds' behaviour in the wild normally follows an hereditary pattern. Choice of songpost, habitat selection, method of foraging or formations of flocks provide more or less important information on the species or genus to which a bird belongs. The Snipe's 'sawing' movements with the bill in mud, the Greenshank's dashing runs after fish in shallow water, the Common Sandpiper's habitually rocking rear body are a few examples among the waders. A grouse on bare mountain above the tree line is in all probability a Ptarmigan; down on the heather moor it can only be a Red Grouse. The Tree Pipit often perches on a branch in the middle of an open tree, the Meadow Pipit always on top of the bush or on the ground. Choice of singing position can provide clues to identification of passerines: a Grasshopper or Marsh Warbler hardly perches more than 3 m up, though this is common for River and Blyth's Reed Warblers. Hobby and Merlin only rarely hover, while this is a regular hunting technique of Kestrel and Red-footed Falcon.

Strange and unexpected behaviour can on the other hand create identification problems: e.g. a flycatcher hopping on the ground or a Reed Warbler on passage singing from shrubbery.

Food

Much of a bird's behaviour and choice of habitat is of course linked with its food. Some species are highly specialised and appear only in specific biotopes, while others have a broader food spectrum and are at home in fairly widely differing types of habitat. Bill shape often reveals the bird's diet. A passerine with a small thin bill indicates an insect diet, while a thicker, conical bill points to seeds as a major food source.

Greenshank running after small fish

Meadow Pipit

Tree Pipit

hovering Kestrel

typical songposts of:

River Warbler
Blyth's Reed Warbler

Grasshopper Warbler
Marsh Warbler

Willow Warbler
insects

Robin
insects/berries

Scarlet Rosefinch
seeds

Hawfinch
seeds

21

Distribution

The different species' geographical distributions are shown on maps. Individual density within a given breeding or wintering area can vary greatly from species to species.

Yellow-green: *breeds, but migrates out for a period during the winter.*

Dark green: *breeds, and is present in all months of the year.*

Blue: *winters but does not breed.*

Most species appear more or less regularly during the migration periods in the plain areas situated between winter and summer ranges.

Distribution of Short-eared Owl

Breeding presence is governed by food supply, availability of suitable nest sites and for certain species by competition from other species. For many hole-nesters, e.g. Stock Dove and Pied Flycatcher, the number of individuals can fluctuate greatly between comparable biotopes owing to supply of nest holes. Many species are site-faithful and return each year to the same breeding area. A few species which are dependent on small rodents, e.g. Long-tailed and Pomarine Skuas and most northern-breeding owls, can fluctuate enormously between different years.

Residents and short-distance migrants can show seasonal changes in habitat choice and local occurrence. Several species change for instance from the summer's insect food to a diet of berries. Forest birds may move out to open fields, inland breeders may resort to the coast etc. Areas marked in dark green can hold both local breeders and winter visitors from relatively far away.

Wintering area shows regular occurrence during winter. There are often wintering records outside these areas. For seabirds that winter near the coast, the distribution is marked on the inside of the coastline; only species with predominantly pelagic wintering habits are shown outside the land areas. Within a species' wintering area non-breeders may be found oversummering (this is common in e.g. waders).

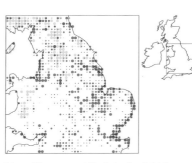

Many Short-eared Owls in the British Isles migrate in winter from inland bogs to coastal meadows. Winter populations in particularly the eastern coastal districts are made up also of Scandinavian and to some extent Continental Short-eared Owls. Some have migrated from N Finland, more than 2000 km away, while others have moved only a few tens of km.

Migration

Through their mobility and ability to migrate birds have been able uniquely to adapt to northern and more isolated parts of the earth. Migration research has opened our eyes more and more to this unparalleled phenomenon, but many questions still remain to be answered.

An extreme long-distance migrant is the Arctic Tern, which migrates between the Arctic and the Antarctic: it breeds at the earth's northernmost land area in N Greenland and is found again during the winter months in the drift-ice zone 3000 km south of the southern tip of Africa. Only a few species in N Europe totally lack migratory instinct, e.g. Grey Partridge, Green Woodpecker and Crested Tit. Species that we think of as residents in Europe, such as Bullfinch, Great Tit and Carrion Crow, are in fact migrants in parts of their range. Migratory activity can be periodic and in some years is triggered by food shortage and large production of young, and then perhaps consists only of birds of the year.

Many passerines navigate using star constellations, the sun and the earth's magnetic field, following an hereditary pattern. Others, e.g. cranes and geese, follow leading lines in the landscape; young must therefore accompany their parents and learn the migration routes.

Migratory birds have evolved a number of different strategies to cope with the dangers and stresses of migration. Many passerines and several waders migrate mainly at night in order to avoid predators. Some migrate shorter distances at a time and slowly work their way forward, others cover long distances without stopping. Fat reserves are put on before migration, and in some passerines and waders these can in extreme cases represent 50% of the total body weight.

For most migratory species **migration times** (for Britain unless otherwise stated) are given at the end of the accounts.

Heavier species with a large wing area use warm upwinds over land during migration, avoiding open areas of water. Birds of prey, storks and pelicans therefore concentrate at certain bottlenecks in Europe and the Middle East.

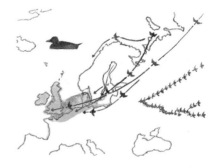

Large numbers of geese, ducks and waders move in a southwesterly direction in autumn towards the ice-free waters of S Scandinavia and W Europe.

There are many indications that a Sedge Warbler which has stored fat reserves from an aphid diet in reedbeds in southern England can fly without foraging 4300 km to tropical W Africa in just over three days.

Vagrants

Species which appear accidentally within a region outside their actual range. In this book most species are included which regularly stray to Europe from breeding sites in N America and Asia. The majority occur according to a fixed pattern dependent on the distance to the normal winter or summer quarters, the times of migration and weather situations. It is almost exclusively species with long migration routes that reach us from neighbouring continents.

The degree of uncommonness or the concept of rarity is of course relative. It can be harder to see a White-backed Woodpecker a few dozen km from a known breeding site than a new species for Europe in the Isles of Scilly off Cornwall, England. It is probably easier to see a Siberian *Phylloscopus* warbler than a Willow Warbler in Nov in Scandinavia, yet the Willow Warbler is the most numerous bird species there during summer.

The **transatlantic species**, gulls, waders, cuckoos, thrushes, wood-warblers etc, consist mainly of those species which in autumn migrate between northern N America and S America. Many of these first migrate eastwards and then, leaving the Atlantic coast of NE America behind them, pass over the W Atlantic to the Caribbean Islands or direct to S America. They get caught up by the periodic cyclones with their poor weather and strong west winds in the N Atlantic westerlies zone. They turn up mainly at the end of Sep and in Oct, and the few spring records in all probability represent birds that have overwintered in Europe and W Africa. A certain percent take refuge on ships out at sea and have assisted passage over to W Europe. Iceland, the westernmost parts of Ireland and England, the Azores and other strategic outposts in the west naturally receive transatlantic visitors more often than other parts of Europe.

Asiatic passerines which are regularly seen in Europe in autumn by contrast actively migrate in the wrong direction. Pallas's and Yellow-browed Warblers have their breeding centre c6000 km to the east in the Siberian taiga, and their wintering areas are in S Asia. Yet they regularly appear during Sep–Nov in NW Europe. These species probably navigate wrongly in all directions and the records

reflect as much the degree of ornithological activity. Their occurrences in western Europe show their easterly origin and the number of records is always greater in autumns with easterly winds.

Vagrants to N Europe involving birds with a **southerly and easterly origin in spring** are usually the result of overshooting migration. Long-distance migrants fly too far in spring and are seen within an extension of the migration direction to the north. Alpine Swift, Lesser Grey Shrike and Black-eared Wheatear are examples of such species.

Records of Desert Warbler in Europe. The northern records originate from breeding areas in C Asia, while those in the Mediterranean probably have a N African origin.

Records of Black-and-White Warbler in Europe. The westerly distribution of the records indicates the species' N American origin.

Systematics

In recent centuries man has sought to bring some rules into nature's enormous diversity. A systematic or taxonomic classification will reflect our existing understanding of the evolutionary lines and reciprocal generic relationships among birds. New knowledge, however, leads to a re-examining of species concepts and generic relationships.

Using tests with DNA molecules, i.e. the birds' hereditary factors, Sibley & Ahlquist (1990, Phylogeny and Classification of Birds) have created a new systematics which differs essentially from the one used in modern handbooks. In this book, however, taxonomy and scientific nomenclature mostly follow Voous (1977, *List of Recent Holarctic Bird Species*). Some races have been given species status in the light of recent findings.

Pp. 26−31 give a brief presentation of the bird families represented in this book, their systematic arrangement and also the pages on which they are treated.

family	**Crows**	Corvidae
genus	**Crows, jays etc.**	*Corvus*
species	**Carrion Crow**	*Corvus corone*
race	**Hooded Crow**	*Corvus corone cornix*

Carrion Crow *Corvus corone corone*

Hooded Crow *Corvus corone cornix*

Species − The definition of a full species is traditionally that it is so genetically different that it cannot produce a fertile offspring with another species. In some cases two populations of the same species are so geographically isolated that they no longer have any contact with one another; the species concept then becomes more hypothetical. Rarely, hybrids between two 'species' may produce fertile offspring within a restricted geographical area, Glaucous × Herring Gull in Iceland and Pied × Collared Flycatcher on Gotland (Sweden). Differences in morphology, voice and behaviour, however, mean that they are nevertheless regarded as separate species.

Race − is a geographically isolated population below species level which differs in outward structure, shape or colour from other races of the same species. Some can be distinguished in the field. Often a gradual transition is noticeable between two races. The racial name, in Latin, is placed after the specific name. **Nominate race** is the first described race of a species and racial name is identical with the Latin specific name.

Evolution is a highly complex process and many species, e.g. gulls, have reached intermediate positions between species and race. The concept of species is thus largely relative, to be seen as a tool in our study of birds.

25

Divers Gaviidae p.32
Large elongated waterbirds totally adapted to life in the water. Dive for fish. Neck and legs extended in flight.

Grebes Podicipedidae p.40
Small to duck-sized waterbirds which dive for food. Diagnostic head markings in summer plumage.

Albatrosses Diomedeidae p.52
Huge seabirds from the S Hemisphere.

Fulmars, shearwaters and petrels p.44
Procellariidae
Gull-sized seabirds associated with the open sea. Nest on cliff ledges or in holes on islands. Characteristic ways of flying.

Storm-petrels Hydrobatidae p.50
Small black seabirds with white rump markings. Tied to open sea. Nest in holes on rocky islands.

Gannets and boobies Sulidae p.52
Large spool-shaped seabirds which dive steeply for fish.

Cormorants Phalacrocoracidae p.54
Goose-sized blackish waterbirds which dive for fish. Stand upright on rocks etc, sometimes with extended wings.

Pelicans Pelecanidae p.58
Very big and heavy whitish birds with conspicuous bill. Swim in flocks. Adept at soaring flight.

Frigatebirds Fregatidae p.52

Herons and egrets Ardeidae p.60
Medium-sized to very large, long-necked and long-legged marshland birds. Fly with neck retracted.

Storks Ciconiidae p.70
Very big, long-legged birds with black-and-white markings. Fly with neck extended and have eagle-like wing silhouette. Expert soaring birds.

Ibises and spoonbills Threskiornithidae p.72
Have rapid series of wingbeats alternating with gliding. Extended necks in flight.

Flamingos Phoenicopteridae p.75
Extremely long-legged and long-necked waterbirds.

Wildfowl Anatidae   p.76
Swimming birds with webbed feet; include:
Swans: very big long-necked and white birds;
Geese: brown and black-and-white birds which graze on fields and shores;
Dabbling ducks: forage at water's surface or 'upend'; rise vertically from water;
Diving ducks: dive for food and run across surface to take off;
Sawbills: have slender bills with 'teeth', dive for fish.

Vultures and hawk-type raptors   p.121
Accipitridae
Heterogeneous group of birds of prey; includes Honey Buzzard, kites, vultures, Short-toed Eagle, harriers, hawks, buzzards and eagles. Generally broader- and blunter-winged than falcons. Build own nest.

Osprey Pandionidae   p.155
Pale bird of prey which hovers and plunges steeply for fish.

Falcons Falconidae   p.156
Pointed-winged and relatively long-tailed birds of prey. Breed in nests built by other birds and on rock ledges.

Grouse Tetraonidae   p.168
Mainly northern or alpine gamebirds with feathered tarsi. Include grouse and Capercaillie.

Partridges and pheasants Phasianidae
                                              p.176
Gamebirds with bare tarsi and more southerly distribution. Include Grey Partridge, Quail and pheasants.

Button quails Turnicidae   p.188
Small Quail-like birds with several representatives in the tropics.

Rails and crakes Rallidae   p.(182) 184
Small to medium-sized chicken-like swampland birds. Many have secretive habits. Very vocal at night.

Cranes Gruidae   p.190
Very big and tall birds. Fly with neck extended.

Bustards Otididae   p.(190) 192
Big, long-legged birds. Live in open dry terrain. Peculiar displays.

Oystercatchers Haematopodidae p.194
Large, mostly pied waders with thick red bill.

Avocets and stilts Recurvirostridae p.196
Elegant long-legged waders with black-and-white pattern.

Stone-curlews Burhinidae p.194
Nocturnal brown-streaked waders with short thick bills and big hawk-like eyes.

Pratincoles and coursers Glareolidae
p.198
Short-billed, long-winged, on the ground rather plover-like waders. Elegant flight.

Lapwings and plovers Charadriidae p.200
Short-billed waders, often with variegated markings. Vocal. Characteristic feeding behaviour: stand dead still, run a few steps, freeze again etc.

Sandpipers and allies Scolopacidae p.214
Heterogeneous appearance, from small short-billed waders to large long-billed ones. Most are tied to wetlands. Include sandpipers of genus *Calidris*, snipes, Ruff, godwits and curlews, genus *Tringa* (Redshank, Wood Sandpiper etc) and phalaropes. Most are very vocal.

Skuas Stercorariidae p.256
Fast and powerful seabirds which rob gulls, terns and auks of their prey. Have dark mantles and in some species dimorphic dark or light belly.

Gulls Laridae p.262
Associated with water. Mostly pale birds with grey or black mantle and yellow or red bill. Imms. usually mottled brown.

Terns Sternidae p.282
Elegant, long-winged and often long-tailed birds of sea and coast. Pale plumage with black crown typical for *Sterna* species. Marsh terns *Chlidonias* darker, snatch prey from surface.

Auks Alcidae p.294
Black-and-white birds living at sea. Nest in colonies on coastal cliffs. Whirring flight on small wings.

Sandgrouse Pteroclididae   p.299
Pigeon-like flocking birds associated with steppe and desert. Fast flyers with pointed wings.

Pigeons and doves Columbidae   p.302
Medium-sized, often round-headed birds. Form flocks outside breeding season. Have gloomy cooing calls.

Cuckoos Cuculidae   p.308
Long-tailed birds, solitary, and nest parasites.

Parakeets Psittacula   p.311

Barn owls Tytonidae   p.312
Pale heart-shaped face. Nest in buildings and rock crevices.

Typical owls Strigidae   p.312
Birds of varying size, active at dusk or night. Plumage often cryptically coloured, with brown or grey streaks. Startling calls at night.

Nightjars Caprimulgidae   p.328
Nocturnal, long wings and long tail. Characteristic continuous and monotonous songs.

Swifts Apodidae   p.331
Adapted in the extreme to a life in the air, with scythe-shaped wings and large mouth with which they rake in airborne insects and spiders.

Kingfishers Alcedinidae   p.334
Strikingly patterned birds with very large bill, usually found at wetlands.

Bee-eaters Meropidae   p.336
Elegant long-tailed and gaudy birds which take large insects in the air. Nest in tunnels excavated in earth embankments and steep banks.

Rollers Coraciidae   p.338
Shimmering-blue Jackdaw-sized birds.

Hoopoe Upupidae   p.338
Unique species, pied wing pattern, can raise crown feathers.

Woodpeckers Picidae   p.340
Specialists in climbing on tree trunks, hack at bark and wood for insects. Chisel out nest hole in tree trunk. Includes Wryneck.

Passerines

Larks Alaudidae   p.350
Ground-dwelling birds, mostly brown-streaked, often with large bill. Sing in flight.

Swallows and martins Hirundinidae p.362
Aerial birds, take flying insects. Build distinctive nests.

Pipits and wagtails Motacillidae   p.366
Elegant, mostly ground-dwelling birds with long tail.

Bulbuls Pycnonotidae   p.476
Brown thrush-sized birds associated mainly with tropical regions.

Waxwings Bombycillidae   p.378
Short-tailed, in flight starling-like.

Dippers Cinclidae   p.378
Black with white breast, dive in fast-flowing water.

Wrens Troglodytidae   p.380
Very small brown bird with short upward-angled tail.

Accentors Prunellidae   p.380
Small sparrow-like birds with relatively thin and pointed bill, live in bushes or in alpine environment.

Thrushes Turdidae   p.384
Include thrushes, Robin, redstarts, wheatears, chats and nightingales. All hop on the ground.

Warblers Sylviidae   p.420
Relatively small, simply patterned birds. Chiefly insectivorous but some also take berries. Pronounced migrants.

Flycatchers Muscicapidae   p.456
Short-legged birds, perch motionless on branches and sally after flying insects.

Babblers and Bearded Tit Timaliidae
                              (460) p.475
Long-tailed, very social birds.

Long-tailed Tit Aegithalidae   p.468

Tits Paridae   p.462
Small woodland birds, cling to branches. Seed- and insect-eaters.

Nuthatches Sittidae   p.470
Short-tailed, creep along trunks and rocks.

Wallcreeper Tichodromadidae   p.474

Treecreepers Certhiidae   p.472
Small brownish birds, creep on trunks and branches.

Penduline Tit Remizidae   p.460

Sunbirds Nectariniidae   p.476
Small, richly coloured nectar-feeders.

Orioles Oriolidae   p.486

Shrikes Laniidae   p.478
Long-tailed birds with powerful raptor-like bill. Take prey up to thrush size.

Crows Corvidae   p.487
The largest passerines. Powerful bills, walk on ground.

Starlings Sturnidae   p.484
Short-tailed birds with plumage wholly or partly black.

Sparrows Passeridae   p.496
Thick-billed seed-eaters, most with terrestrial habits.

Waxbills Estrildidae   p.502
Small seed-eating birds.

Vireos Vireonidae   p.540
Vagrants from N America.

Finches Fringillidae   p.502
Often brightly patterned, with pronounced wing markings. Seed-eaters, often with large bills.

Wood-warblers Parulidae   p.542
Vagrants from N America. Warbler-like.

Tanagers Thraupidae   p.544
Vagrants from America.

Buntings Emberizidae   p.522
Longer-tailed than finches, have short conical bills. Many have distinctive head markings.

Troupials Icteridae   p.544
Vagrants from America.

Red-throated Diver *Gavia stellata* L 53–69 cm, WS 106–116 cm

Somewhat smaller than Black-throated Diver, with straighter neck, more angular nape and smaller head with flatter forehead. Bill more slender, usually points slightly upwards. In summer plumage has dark brown-red neck patch, which at distance often looks simply dark. In winter plumage always paler above than Black-throated, at close range bestrewn with small white elliptical spots, and has more white on neck and head; eye always isolated within white oval around eye. Young in autumn often have wholly grey-brown neck with only throat pale, and back is bestrewn with small pale grey-buff to dirty white V marks. The front and sides of neck gradually become paler during winter but are retained on some birds until Mar. In very first summer acquires an almost complete summer plumage, though often not before Jun–Jul, so imms. on spring passage often have dark-marked neck and paler throat. In flight has shorter rear end with straight, uniformly thick feet, and neck often sags slightly while head tends upwards; often looks somewhat hunched and wings seem to be placed farther back than on Black-throated. Has curious habit of regularly tossing its head, which Black-throated does only sporadically. Gives goose-like cackling 'kak-kak-kak' in flight, in rhythm with wingbeats. On water also a drawn-out wailing 'eeaaooh'; song a repeated 'koor-koorruee, koor-koorruee, koor-koorruee…'. Nests on lakes and pools on bogs, moors and tundra. Winters mainly on coasts. Spring migration Apr–May, southward return Oct–Dec; often migrates and winters in small flocks.

Black-throated Diver *Gavia arctica* L 58–73 cm, WS 110–130 cm

Slightly larger than Red-throated Diver, with a uniformly thick neck often held in a graceful S curve. Summer plumage characteristic, but in other plumages harder to tell from other divers (see also Cormorant p. 54). In winter plumage blackish above with slate-grey nape and sharp contrast with white underparts, pale grey bill with dark culmen and tip. Juv. paler and with slight brown tone to nape, has regular pattern of pale feather edges on scapulars though this difficult to see at distance; juv. has dirty-grey foreneck to varying degree and in flight can look wholly dark-necked, when often hard to tell from juv. Red-throated. 1st-summer and 2nd-winter like ad. winter, but lacks white spots on leading secondary coverts (hidden at rest). On rear flanks white reaches farther up than in Red-throated, which on birds resting on water produces a white stern patch (like male Eider), a very useful distinguishing mark. In flight, elongated profile with long, narrow wings; wingbeats shallow and stiff but with typically springy wingtips. Flight silhouette differs from Red-throated's in longer feet (stern area) horizontally held bill, and different neck markings. Spring song a series of desolate calls, sonorous and far-ringing, 'klowee, kok-klowee, kok-klowee'. Also gives loud, howling 'oo-aaoh' and deep rumbling calls. Breeds on deep clear lakes of medium to large size. On migration and in winter on sea coasts, often gathers in small loose groups. Migration peaks Apr−May and Sep−Oct.

Red-throated Diver

Black-throated Diver

Red-throated Diver

juv/1st-winter

2nd-cal spring

summer

ad winter

juv

Black-throated Diver

juv

ad winter

1st-summer

summer

Great Northern Diver juv

Black-throated Diver juv

Great Northern Diver   *Gavia immer*   *L 68–91 cm, WS 127–147 cm*

Generally considerably bigger than Black-throated Diver (though some overlap occurs), with larger head, steeper forehead and clearly heavier bill. The Great Northern is slightly smaller than the White-billed Diver, and at rest on the water head and bill are held horizontal and body appears more elongated with highest point farther forward. In summer plumage characteristic, with black bill, head and neck and a broad band of white stripes on neck-side. In winter plumage very dark above, slate-grey, with blackish half-collar, nape and crown contrasting sharply with white foreneck; typical of this species is that the border between the dark and light on the neck cuts in in a white wedge above the dark half-collar, a diagnostic character vis à vis Black-throated Diver both on the water and in flight. Juv. is browner on neck and head, with darker ear-coverts, dirty-toned foreneck and with less bright pale eye-ring. The body is also generally paler, with a regular scaly pattern of pale feather edges. On adults the slightly paler scapular markings form a squarer block pattern. In winter–spring, 2nd-cal-years moult into a plumage more like that of ad. winter. The bill of 'winter-marked' birds is pale blue-grey to dirty-white with dark culmen and tip. Before the transition to summer plumage in late winter, ad. can look almost wholly whitish on bill-tip, which combined with the then paler and worn neck markings produces a risk of confusion with White-billed Diver. With its less contrasting neck markings, juv. in autumn (especially in flight) can easily be taken for juv. Black-throated. In flight Great Northern usually gives a 'more solid' impression than Black-throated, with longer and broader wings, clearly longer and bigger feet and also heavier head and bill. Great Northern is a mainly N American breeding bird but also breeds commonly in Iceland (and Greenland). It winters regularly off western and northern parts of the British Isles (in smaller numbers elsewhere), along the Norwegian coast and uncommonly in other parts of the North Sea. Noisy at breeding sites, with various desolate calls, mainly a drawn-out, ghost-like

howling (like wolf) 'aaooooh' and a clearer vibrating tremolo call. Feeds on fish and shellfish. Arrives in W Europe (in summer plumage) from latter part of Oct and into Dec, returning north again in Apr–May.

Great Northern Diver

juv

worn juv

ad winter

juv

2nd-cal spring

2nd winter

ad winter (Mar, moulting)

ad winter

summer

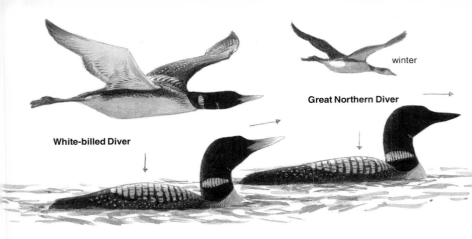

winter

Great Northern Diver

White-billed Diver

White-billed Diver   *Gavia adamsii*   L 75–100 cm, WS 137–152 cm

The giant among divers and somewhat bigger than Great Northern, with thicker neck and paler bill in all plumages. On the water head is held so that bill points obliquely upwards, which amplifies bill's slightly more upward-angled shape compared with Great Northern's. In summer plumage yellowish-white bill is diagnostic; also has sparser and larger spots on back as well as fewer stripes in the 'white' neck-band, which also narrows towards the rear (on Great Northern it is broadest towards the nape). In winter and imm. plumages usually relatively easy to recognise by paler and smudgy brownish-grey neck-sides, paler face and characteristic elliptical vertical dark patch on cheek down towards neck-side. Half-collar is paler, often bisected, and foreneck is always dirty-white in contrast to dark white breast. Bill is grey at base and bone-coloured or yellowish-white towards the tip; area around nostrils and outwards to maximum of two-thirds of culmen length is darker, but tip is never dark. Juv. paler than ad., with obvious broad pale feather edges on back forming regular scaly pattern; on juv. the dark half-collar is often not very prominent. In spring and early summer, imm. moults and then acquires a darker base of neck and darker brown-grey back; a variegated light and dark impression to the back in May–Jun is characteristic. 2nd-cal-year bird from midsummer through 2nd winter resembles ad. but lacks white markings on the wing-coverts. In 2nd-summer plumage White-billed Diver's coloration is less full-adult than Great Northern's, often having drab sooty-grey neck and scattered sprinkling of white spots over back. In flight very elongated, with uniformly thick neck and long feet; distinguished from Great Northern by generally paler neck which is smudgily marked without clear white wedge above half-collar, and paler, often whitish face with the dark eye standing out like a currant in the pale area. 2nd-cal-year birds in spring often show a very pale face in which the forehead and the base of upper mandible are the darkest part. Calls are like Great Northern's. A high-arctic breeder which winters regularly

along Norwegian Atlantic coast and sparsely in Baltic and rest of North Sea area. Rare but regular off Scandinavian coasts, mostly end Apr to first few days Jun at migration watchpoints and in Sep–Dec (peak in Oct through southern Baltic). Rare in Britain and Ireland, mostly on east coast and in Scotland between Oct and mid Jun. Feeds on fish and often seen on shallow waters near the shore.

White-billed Diver

2nd-cal spring, worn

juv

juv

ad winter

2nd-cal May

3rd-cal summer

surnmer

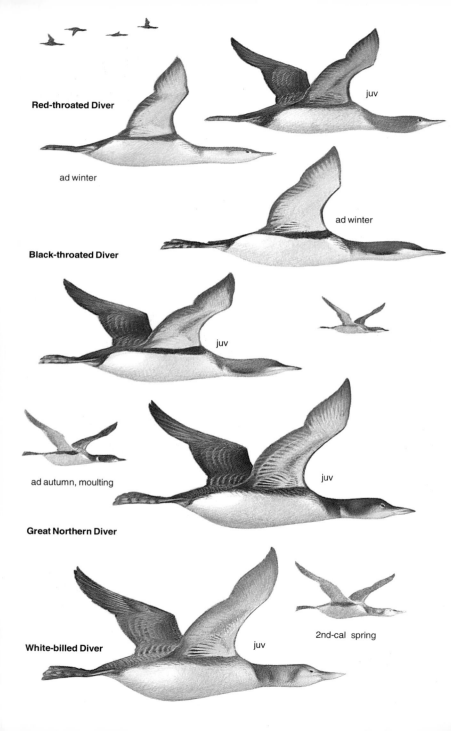

Red-throated Diver

ad winter

juv

Black-throated Diver

ad winter

juv

ad autumn, moulting

juv

Great Northern Diver

White-billed Diver

juv

2nd-cal spring

winter

Great Crested Grebe

winter

1st-cal autumn

summer

Red-necked Grebe

winter

1st-cal autumn

Slavonian Grebe

winter

1st-cal autumn

winter

summer

Black-necked Grebe

winter

Little Grebe

winter

summer

Great Crested Grebe   *Podiceps cristatus*   L 46–51 cm, WS 85–90 cm

In summer unmistakable with its brownish-red and black tippets. In winter always appears paler than Red-necked Grebe, has longer neck, brilliant white in front and with more white on cheeks, and dark crown does not reach down to eye. Juv. much like ad. winter, but traces of down plumage, especially dark stripes on head, can be seen until Dec. In flight Great Crested Grebes are often a surprising sight: very elongated, have rapid, almost whirring wingbeats which are characteristic of all grebe species and produce a very pale-variegated impression. In spring the adult pair performs a number of striking pairing ceremonies: float breast to breast with tippets erected and perform head-waggling, mock-preening etc. Quite noisy in spring, uttering various grating and loud calls, including a rolling heron-like 'aoorr' and during displays a repeated, slightly chattering 'kek-kek-kek...'. In late summer young often attract attention by their persistent whistling 'wee-e wee-e wee-e...' begging calls. Common on shallow lakes. Nests in reedbeds or other aquatic vegetation next to open water, seldom on smaller ponds. In winter resorts to larger lakes, reservoirs, sheltered sea bays. Feeds mainly on fish, but also on other small aquatic animals, at sea e.g. shrimps. Most northernmost breeders move south (Sep–Nov) for winter, returning Mar–Apr.

Red-necked Grebe   *Podiceps grisegena*   L 40–50 cm, WS 77–85 cm

Smaller and more compact than Great Crested. In summer plumage easily recognised by its dark rust-brown neck, grey cheeks, and black bill with characteristic bright yellow 'clown-face' gape. Mainly on sea coasts in winter, when differs from Great Crested in shorter, more thickset neck, which is grey in contrast to white throat and breast; dark of crown extends below eye and bill is dark with yellow base. Juv. retains remnants of head stripes until late in Oct, when it begins moult to 1st-winter plumage. In flight shows less white on wings and has shorter and darker neck. Breeds on shallow well-vegetated lakes and ponds. In breeding season more secretive than Great Crested Grebe but often reveals its presence by its calls, including very loud, squealing, Water Rail-like 'aaek' or 'ooa-ehk'. Also makes cackling and grunting sounds. Feeds on fish and aquatic insects. Mainly winter visitor to Britain, especially to east coast, Aug–Apr (most in Oct–Mar); increasingly recorded also in summer.

Pied-billed Grebe   *Podilymbus podiceps*   L 31–38 cm, WS 56–64 cm

Very rare visitor from N America. Size of Slavonian Grebe, coloration like winter-plumaged Little Grebe. Distinguished by its short and thick bill, which is horn-coloured in imm. and winter plumages and bluish-white with a black central band in summer plumage. Shows all-dark wings in flight.

Great Crested Grebe

Red-necked Grebe

1st-winter

summer

Pied-billed Grebe

winter

summer

Great Crested Grebe

Great Crested Grebe
juv *c* 2 months

juv *c* 2 months

Red-necked Grebe

winter

summer

Little Grebe   *Tachybaptus ruficollis*   *L 25–29 cm, WS 40–45 cm*

A very small, dumpy and dark grebe with bright yellow gape. In winter plumage paler: yellow-brown on sides, neck and cheeks, with whitish throat. Often fluffs up its pale stern. In juv. plumage breast and neck are tinged reddish-brown and head is comparatively dark; stripy markings are formed by down remaining on tips of growing feathers, these being gradually worn away during autumn. Acquires 1st-winter plumage in Oct–Dec, like ad. winter but often with smudgy mark on cheek below eye. In flight lacks white in wings (sometimes a little white on base of secondaries). Breeds on well-vegetated lakes, rivers and ponds; shy and often difficult to observe. In autumn and winter appears more in open, on lakes, quiet bays, reservoirs etc. Call a bubbling or vibrating trill (like female Cuckoo), which often betrays its presence. Contact call a clear whistling 'veeht veeht'. Feeds on insects, small molluscs and small fish. Scandinavian populations mostly migratory.

Black-necked Grebe   *Podiceps nigricollis*   *L 28–34 cm, WS 56–60 cm*

Like Slavonian Grebe, but with steeper forehead and distinctly 'retroussé' bill giving it a characteristic profile. In summer plumage dark, at a distance often blackish with 'unkempt' oily and straggly brush-like plumes of golden-yellow on cheeks. In winter plumage has darker ear-coverts and dirty-grey foreneck compared with Slavonian. Rear body often looks more fluffed out. In flight, white on rear wing also includes inner primaries, and pale marking on forewing lacking or poorly developed. Call is a plaintive and squeaky 'yoorr-eep', also short whistles, 'peep' or 'psheep-chee'. Breeds on food-rich lakes, often in small colonies. Feeds mostly on aquatic insects, which it also snatches up in dabbling-duck fashion. Winters, often in flocks, on lakes, lagoons and sea bays.

Slavonian Grebe   *Podiceps auritus*   *L 31–38 cm, WS 59–65 cm*

Differs from Black-necked Grebe in red neck (though can look black at distance), fuller and more orange head plumes, and also profile: lower forehead and flatter crown. In winter has purer white cheeks and foreneck, border between dark crown and white cheek often appears straight and regular; has a pale line of bare skin between eye and bill and a pale round spot on lores. Juv. in autumn often still with pale stripe above/behind eye and sometimes rusty-coloured neck, can be confused with young Red-necked. White on rear wing (secondaries) and white 'thumbmark' where forewing joins body (absent or reduced in some from eastern populations). Noisy at nest site, incl. at night, commonest call a rolling, shrill but quite melodious 'heeaarr' in short series, and drawn-out screams like Water Rail. Breeds on lakes and ponds with bulrushes, sedge or other densely vegetated margins, around Baltic also in sea bays. Winters mostly on sheltered coasts and estuaries. Food: aquatic insects, molluscs, tadpoles etc.

Little Grebe

Black-necked Grebe

Slavonian Grebe

summer

Little Grebe

winter

winter

Black-necked Grebe

summer

1st-cal autumn

winter

Slavonian Grebe

summer

Fulmar   *Fulmarus glacialis*   *L 45–50 cm, WS 102–112 cm*

Common in N Atlantic and often follows ships. Immediately told from a gull by its stiff wings and rapid wingbeats alternating with long periods of gliding low over the water. Wings appear shorter and narrower than those of gulls. Typically has greyish mantle with pale patches at bases of primaries. Occurs in different colour phases: the darkest in W Europe are mid-grey on mantle and ash-grey on head and underparts (in Pacific, types which are almost as dark as Sooty Shearwater are common). Nests in exposed site on ledges on bird cliffs and on near-inaccessible cliff faces near coast. At breeding sites utters nasal grunting and chuckling sounds. Feeds on animals floating on sea surface, often takes fish offal and carrion and gathers in large flocks where food supply plentiful. Present all year along coastal cliffs of Britain.   *Map p. 46.*

Gon-gon (Soft-plumaged Petrel)
Pterodroma (mollis) feae   *L 33–36 cm, WS 84–91 cm*

Size of Manx Shearwater but larger-headed and longer-tailed and in flight wings more angled. The two *Pterodroma* species have a colour pattern unique for these waters: above, grey on mantle with darker primaries and secondaries and pale grey tail; pale below, with dark markings on underwings (often look all-dark from distance) and dark shading on sides of breast and neck. Head shows dark eye-mask and darker crown. Breeds on Bugio, southernmost of Desertas Islands off Madeira, and on Cape Verde Islands. Nests in rock crevices at 300–400 m, in autumn on Bugio and in winter on Cape Verdes. Found in proximity of breeding sites throughout year. Possibly a race of Soft-plumaged Petrel *Pterodroma mollis*, an abundant breeder in S Atlantic, but probably genetically isolated from latter.

Freira (Soft-plumaged Petrel)
Pterodroma (mollis) madeira   *L 32–33 cm, WS 78–83 cm*

Very closely related to Gon-gon (the two may be races of same species). Probably difficult to distinguish from latter in field, though weighs one-third less and is 5–10% smaller in length. Bill is much slimmer and crown and forehead possibly paler. A highly endangered species, breeding only on main island of Madeira (about 30 pairs). Nests high in the mountains (c1600 m); breeding begins in May.

Bulwer's Petrel   *Bulweria bulwerii*   *L 26–28 cm, WS 68–73 cm*

A very distinctive seabird, like a huge attenuated storm-petrel with extremely long wings and long tail. Flight light and springy. Wings are often pressed forward, held slightly bowed with hand slightly drooping. Tail is strikingly long and narrow and is often held slightly raised, and is fanned only briefly. At a distance looks all-dark but has brownish band on secondary coverts (as Leach's Storm-petrel), and at close range a paler bar along greater underwing-coverts is visible. Breeds on Desertas Islands off Madeira, the southernmost of the Azores, on Canaries and Cape Verdes. Migrates south in winter.

Fulmar   **Gon-gon**   **Freira**
              (Soft-plumaged Petrel)   **(Soft-plumaged Petrel)**

Fulmar

dark phase

Gon-gon

Bulwer's Petrel

Freira

Cory's Shearwater   *Calonectris diomedea*   L 45–56 cm, WS 100–125 cm

Slightly bigger than Great Shearwater, looks larger-headed and more front-heavy. Long wings are normally held slightly pressed forward and gently arched, more so in strong winds. Upperparts relatively pale, variegated grey-brown, often with darker band over secondary coverts and paler area on tail base. Head uniformly grey, with dark area around eye and lores. Bill large and pale, yellow, and at closer range shows a darker area towards tip. Below, purer white on underwings than Great Shearwater but with proportionally more dark at tips. Common in Mediterranean Sea and off W Africa up to Bay of Biscay. After breeding season the birds partly move west and north in autumn and occur regularly off SW Ireland and SW England; much rarer in North Sea. Breeds colonially in cavities and on ledges on islands. Feeds on fish, cephalopods, shrimps etc. Follows larger ships for short distances and also appears in numbers around trawlers and other larger fishing boats where food is made available.

Great Shearwater   *Puffinus gravis*   L 43–51 cm, WS 100–118 cm

Much bigger than Manx Shearwater. Dark cap, pale neck-collar and brown-grey upperparts are best field characters. Pale tips of uppertail-coverts are often obvious, especially in strong lighting. Most easily confused with Cory's, but head/neck markings and dark mark on underwing are important characters (cf also skuas). Breeds in N Hemisphere's winter on Tristan da Cunha and Gough Island in S Atlantic. After breeding season migrates north along the American continents and spends summer at the food-rich banks off coast of New England and eastern Canada up to S Greenland; in late summer moves into E Atlantic in association with southward migration, and then appears off W European coasts, though relatively uncommonly and irregularly from year to year. Annual SW England/Ireland, mainly Jul–Oct. Feeds mostly on cephalopods and fish.

Sooty Shearwater   *Puffinus griseus*   L 40–51 cm, WS 94–109 cm

The dark sooty-grey or grey-brown coloration, spool- or cigar-shaped body and comparatively narrow wings make the Sooty Shearwater fairly easy to identify. It can be confused with dark phases of Arctic Skua, though latter have longer tail and pale flash at base of primaries. Pale panel on underwing, variable in extent, is usually visible only at closer range; at distance bird looks uniformly dark. Feeds on shrimps, cephalopods and small fish. Nearest breeding areas in southernmost S America, and 'winters' in spring–summer in N Atlantic. Regular in E Atlantic and North Sea, seen mainly in Jul–Oct (Nov) in association with southward passage.

Fulmar

Cory's Shearwater

46

Cory's
Shearwater

Great
Shearwater

Sooty
Shearwater

Little Shearwater *Puffinus assimilis* *L 25–30 cm, WS 58–67 cm*

Much smaller, more compact and shorter-winged than Manx Shearwater. Flight as latter's, but flight path is more direct, less twisting and slightly unsteady. Wings stiff and straight, but are held slightly downward-angled when gliding. Does not ride the waves in high arcs like the larger shearwaters. Looks white-faced, has narrower black trailing edge to underwing with only a narrow black 'peg' at wing join, compared with Manx. Legs/feet blue. Voice higher-pitched than Manx. Nearest breeding sites on Azores, Desertas Islands off Madeira and on Canaries, as race *baroli*. On Cape Verdes race *boydi*, with dark undertail-coverts and more dark on side of head. Seen very rarely in NW Europe (only *baroli*), mainly in Apr–Oct.

Manx Shearwater *Puffinus puffinus* *L 30–35 cm, WS 76–82 cm*

The commonest shearwater in N Atlantic and North Sea. Smaller than Great and Cory's, with sharp contrast between blackish upperparts and white underparts. Has typical shearwater flight, series of rapid wingbeats followed by long glides on straight stiff wings. In higher wind speeds, the hand is angled back and birds ride on upwinds of wave crests in high bounding arcs. Often appears in small flocks, fishes far out to sea and is seen relatively rarely from land during breeding period. Nests in excavated burrows on steep grassy slopes on marine islands, sometimes far from the shore. Visits nest holes at dusk; very noisy at night, with chuckling and mewing calls. Food mainly fish. Migrates to seas off S America in Jul–Sep (Oct), returning in Mar–Apr.

Yelkouan Shearwater *Puffinus yelkouan* *L 32–38 cm, WS 78–89 cm*

Previously considered a race of Manx Shearwater. Breeds in Mediterranean in two races: both with proportionally shorter tail, longer bill and bigger feet (at close range feet can be seen extending beyond tip of tail), brown instead of black above, and to varying degree more marked below than Manx. Forages closer to land and is easy to see from many shores around Mediterranean. Slightly smaller race *yelkouan* is more widely distributed and breeds in C and E Mediterranean; it is more contrastingly patterned than *mauretanicus*, underparts mostly showing dusky vent and dark axillaries and a band across the secondary coverts. Race *mauretanicus* breeds in Balearic Islands; outside breeding season it moves out towards Atlantic and in part northwards up to British Isles, more rarely reaching North Sea. In field, *mauretanicus* is visibly larger than Manx in direct comparison: border between upperparts and underparts is diffuse and the pale areas are dirty grey-buff with dark vent and axillaries; varies in strength of colouring below, darkest individuals almost matching Sooty Shearwater in field impression.

Manx Shearwater

Yelkouan Shearwater

Little Shearwater

baroli

Manx Shearwater

Yelkouan Shearwater

yelkouan

mauretanicus

British Storm-petrel   *Hydrobates pelagicus*   L 14–17 cm, WS 36–39 cm

Smaller than Leach's, with shorter, more rounded and stiffly held wings, and also has a shorter and square-ended tail. At distance looks all-black, apart from rectangular snow-white rump which 'wraps around' and reaches a bit onto vent. At close range a narrow pale bar on secondary coverts is sometimes visible. Has a diagnostic white band on underwing. Flight path rather straight, close above water surface, with fast, bat-like fluttering wingbeats interrupted by short glides. Nests in cavities on isolated Atlantic islands (also in Mediterranean), visited only in breeding season and under cover of darkness of night. At night, series of purring 'ooarrrrr' sounds interrupted by loud hiccups are heard from nest holes. Very numerous as breeding bird in W Europe. Migrates south to waters off S Africa in Sep–Nov, returning in Apr. Occasionally seen inshore after storms.   *Map p. 52*

Leach's Storm-petrel   *Oceanodroma leucorhoa*   L 19–22 cm, WS 45–48 cm

Bigger than British Storm-petrel, and with longer and more pointed wings and forked tail. Flight path slightly jerky and dancing with continual direction changes, wings are held angled with marked bend at carpal, and wingbeats are deep and somewhat Black Tern-like. Paler than other storm-petrels, and pale band on secondary coverts visible at long distance. White rump is less conspicuous than British Storm-petrel's, somewhat V-shaped and bisected by grey mid line. Wings are often held with inner half slightly raised and outer angled downwards, like a flattened M. Breeding habits as British Storm-petrel. From and near nest holes birds utter drawn-out, slightly wavering purring sound interrupted every 3–4 seconds by short sharp whistled 'chwee'; also has an odd cackling call. Migrates south in Sep–Nov, returning in Apr–May (though Lofoten, Norway, population breeds only when nights have become dark, in Aug, so some young not fledged until Dec). Seen from coast mainly after westerly storms, sometimes in large numbers. Food various zooplankton and small fish.   *Map p. 52*

Wilson's Storm-petrel   *Oceanites oceanicus*   L 15–19 cm, WS 38–42 cm

Most like British Storm-petrel in silhouette, with wings held out straighter, though rounded in shape and without sharp angle at carpal. Flight is more direct, with longer glides and short series of shallow wingbeats. Differs further from British Storm-petrel in clear pale band across secondary coverts, lack of or only faintly marked pale band on underwing, and also longer legs which project behind tail. When feeding, it hangs above sea surface on raised wings and trips across surface. Has yellowish webs between toes, visible only at very close range. Breeds in S Atlantic. Found regularly in summer–autumn northward to coasts of SW Europe, very rarely farther north.

Madeiran Storm-petrel   *Oceanodroma castro*   L 19–21 cm, WS 42–45 cm

Gives an impression midway between Leach's and Wilson's Storm-petrels. Is darker and has less conspicuous pale band across secondary coverts than both these species. Has more striking and more rectangular white rump than Leach's, with broader and slightly shorter wings. Wings are held more horizontal, less downward-angled at carpal joint, but are usually angled backwards more than on Wilson's. Small numbers breed in N Atlantic on islands off Madeira and possibly also on Azores, on Tenerife and Lanzarote in Canaries and on Cape Verde Islands.

White-faced Storm-petrel   *Pelagodroma marina*   L 20–21 cm, WS 41–43 cm

Unmistakable. Rather large grey-brown storm-petrel with whitish underparts and patterned head. Feet project beyond slightly forked tail. Breeds colonially, in N Atlantic on Selvagens and Cape Verde Islands. Accidental in W Europe, possibly regular in waters off Portugal.   *Not illustrated*

**British
Storm-petrel**

**Leach's
Storm-petrel**

**Wilson's
Storm-petrel**

**Madeiran
Storm-petrel**

Black-browed Albatross   *Diomedea melanophris*   *L 80–90 cm, WS 213–246 cm*

The only albatross species that appears off coast of NW Europe with some regularity. Solitary birds have turned up periodically in Gannet colonies in Scotland and returned annually thereafter. Nearest breeders are in S Atlantic. Bigger than a Gannet, in plumage coloration it resembles a huge Great Black-backed Gull but with broad black frame to underwings. Imms. have more dark on underwings, grey rear head/nape and darker bill.

Wandering Albatross   *Diomedea exulans*   *L 110–135 cm, WS 275–305 cm*

Extremely rare in N Atlantic. Gigantic and clearly bigger than Black-browed. Juv. has wholly dark brown underbody and mantle with white face and underwings, becomes gradually paler over several years, and in the final stage is predominantly white with dark primary tips and a few scattered dark greater coverts.   *Not illustrated*

Gannet   *Sula bassana*   *L 87–100 cm, WS 165–180 cm*

A powerful, long cigar-shaped seabird with long, strikingly narrow wings. Adults are unmistakable, in size, coloration and patterning. Juv. can at first sight resemble a large shearwater, but its long, pointed head/bill area and pointed tail together with its movements give it away. Compare also Black-browed Albatross. Ad. plumage is assumed in successive stages and is not fully completed until 4–6 years of age. Yellow-ochre colour of head is paler during non-breeding season. The Gannets' actions and overall impression are majestic, and they perform impressive vertical dives from at times considerable height. Silent at sea, but at breeding colonies makes loud, grating calls. Breeds locally in N Atlantic, in colonies on rocky islands and ledges along vertical bird cliffs. Relatively common in North Sea (breeds N Humberside), but much more numerous in west Britain. Many birds, and majority of imms., migrate south in autumn to coasts of W Africa, but ads. return early to colonies, often in Jan. Often seen migrating in small parties, which fly in a line.

Brown Booby   *Sula leucogaster*   *L 64–74 cm, WS 132–150 cm*

Smaller than Gannet, entirely chocolate-brown above with white belly and white underwing-coverts. A tropical species with nearest regular occurrence around Cape Verde Islands and in Red Sea.   *Not illustrated*

Magnificent Frigatebird   *Fregata magnificens*   *L 95–110 cm, WS 215–245 cm*

Extremely rare visitor from tropical seas, nearest breeders Cape Verdes. Clearly bigger than Gannet, extremely long-winged and with long, deeply forked tail. Mainly black; female and subad. male have white breast girdle, juv. also has white head. At distance difficult to separate from other species of frigatebird, but this species is the only one recorded with certainty in Europe.   *Not illustrated*

British Storm-petrel

Leach's Storm-petrel

Gannet

Great Black-backed Gull

Black-browed Albatross

juv

Gannet

juv

2nd-cal autumn

3rd-cal

winter

juv

Cormorant juv

Shag juv

Cormorant *Phalacrocorax carbo* L 80–100 cm, WS 130–160 cm

A large dark waterbird with a somewhat reptilian appearance. Perches upright, often in small groups on rocks or posts out in the water; has a habit of perching with wings open, a behaviour for which the reasons are not entirely clear. It swims low in the water, with straight neck and slightly uptilted head. Differs from Shag in larger size and heavier neck, head and bill. In summer plumage has large white patch on rear flanks and in spring shows white filoplumes on nape and neck. Two races occur in N Europe: one (*carbo*) breeds on bird cliffs on N Atlantic coasts, and one (*sinensis*) nests in trees in the Baltic and south through the Continent. Latter has more white on neck in breeding plumage and more greenish gloss on neck and breast. Young slightly variable, but typically have a white belly bestrewn to varying extent with dark patches; occasionally has wholly white underparts. In Moroccan race *maroccanus*, young with wholly white underparts are commonly seen and ad. has white breast and foreneck at all seasons. In flight, compared with Shag, has more elongated profile with flatter belly, longer tail and heavier head and neck area; usually shows slight kink at neck-join, and whole of fore area inclines slightly upwards. Further, wings are not raised so high, are more angled and appear more pointed. Partial migrant in Britain, also winter visitor; disperses to coasts in winter, also inland (sometimes seen soaring). Takes fish. *Map p. 56*

Shag *Phalacrocorax aristotelis* L 65–80 cm, WS 90–105 cm

Smaller than Cormorant, greenish-black, and has curved crown-tuft in breeding season. Neck is thinner, head more rounded and bill more slender. Generally less pale colour on throat. Young usually appear all-brown with paler whitish throat; their underparts vary but are usually somewhat lighter brown, especially on foreneck, and with darker thighs, and they also have paler secondary coverts which in flight produce paler secondary panel (especially in worn and faded plumage), big rounded belly, small tail and long narrow neck and 'nobbly' head. In flight, wings appear straighter and stiffer, more rounded, and are beaten at faster rate and with higher upstroke compared with Cormorant. Often flies close above water and is never seen flying in over land. Quite common on NW European coasts, breeds on cliff ledges. Relatively common in Mediterranean as race *desmarestii*, in which juv. has generally more white below. *Map p. 56*

Shag

juv

winter

breeding

juv

winter

Cormorant

breeding
sinensis

sinensis
juv
(pale)

maroccanus

Cormorant

maroccanus
ad winter

Pygmy Cormorant *Phalacrocorax pygmeus* L 45−55 cm, WS 80−90 cm

Considerably smaller than Cormorant and Shag and in almost all plumages has characteristically brown neck and crown. For a short period at start of breeding season has varying amount of white 'hairs' on mainly head and neck. Flight silhouette is characterised by proportionately short head/neck and long tail. Wingbeats noticeably faster than in the larger species, but gliding phase is Cormorant-like with slightly bowed wings; also soars in good thermals. Nests in colonies at reedy lakes and river areas, often together with Cormorants and herons/egrets in trees. Locally numerous at shallow fish-rich lakes in Balkans and in Turkey. Also fishes on quite small rivers and ponds, but never in Mediterranean Sea like the larger species. Food mainly fish, caught by diving in shallow water. Flocks may sometimes drive fish shoals towards edge of reeds in Goosander fashion.

Shag

Cormorant

Pygmy Cormorant

breeding

Pygmy Cormorant

Cormorant
ad winter

Shag
ad winter

Pygmy Cormorant
ad winter

juv

ad winter

Pygmy Cormorant

breeding

White Pelican   ad   juv   juv   subad   ad   Dalmatian Pelican

Dalmatian Pelican   *Pelecanus crispus*   *L 160–180 cm, WS 280–295 cm*

Slightly bigger than White Pelican, and has a steel-grey tinge to plumage and in spring a deep reddish-orange (mango-coloured) throat-sac. Imms. and ads. in winter have yellow-pink throat-sac. Legs grey in all plumages. Has curly, untidy mane in spring and vestige of this during rest of year; first-years also have 'baby curls' on nape (cf White Pelican). In flight shows black only on upperside of primaries, giving it less contrasty appearance than White Pelican. Subad. has dark grey flight feathers, looks especially plain. The odd one or few birds seen during breeding season at lakes and river deltas outside the breeding lakes are usually these drab dirty-white imms. Behaviour and food as for White Pelican, with which it sometimes associates.

White Pelican   *Pelecanus onocrotalus*   *L 140–175 cm, WS 235–310 cm*

A very striking bird, the size of a swan. White plumage has a distinct orange-coloured tinge, resting birds at long distance and through heat haze can be taken for Flamingos. Yellow (at darkest orange-coloured) throat-sac, size and yellow-pink face-mask with dark eye, together with pinky legs, also distinguish it from Dalmatian Pelican. Juv. darker than juv. Dalmatian and with pinkish legs. In flight differs from Dalmatian in underwing showing black flight feathers (dark brown on imms., which also have dark leading edge). Accomplished soaring/gliding birds, often seen circling in thermals. Migrate in flocks, sometimes of considerable size, and at distance can recall White Storks. Regularly passes through Egypt autumn and spring. Nests colonially on islands and in reedbeds at shallow, fish-rich lowland lakes and river deltas. Owing to draining of habitat and persecution, numbers have declined during 1800s and 1900s.

Pink-backed Pelican   *Pelecanus rufescens*   *L 125–132 cm, WS 265-290 cm*

Vagrant to Europe and N Africa (regular Egypt) from Africa south of Sahara. Smaller than Dalmatian Pelican, which closest to in colour and structure; ad. has blackish ring around the orbital ring and black loral mark, ad. and juv. have darker iris than Dalmatian.

Dalmatian Pelican

White Pelican

White Pelican

Dalmatian Pelican

breeding

juv

juv

ad

Pink-backed Pelican

juv

breeding

White Pelican

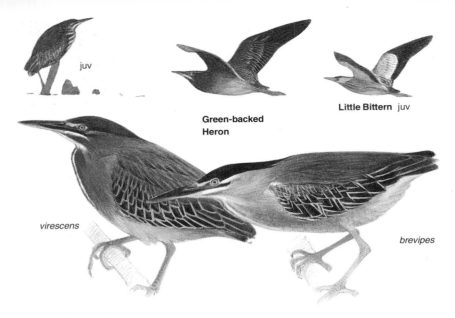

juv

Little Bittern juv

Green-backed
Heron

virescens

brevipes

Green-backed Heron   *Butorides striatus*   L 40–48 cm, WS 52–60 cm

A small dark heron with wide distribution in tropics. Represented by several races. The African race *brevipes* has grey neck-sides; nearest breeders in Red Sea. The N American *virescens* has been recorded 3 times in Britain (Oct-Dec): has wine-red neck-sides, juv. has streaked neck and small drop-shaped spots on wing-coverts.

Bittern   *Botaurus stellaris*   L 70–80 cm, WS 125–135 cm

The Bittern is seldom seen, as it leads a retiring life under cover of extensive reedbeds. Its presence, however, is revealed in spring by a conspicuous call. Male's foghorn booms, which in tone are close to the sound produced by blowing across the mouth of an empty bottle, are given most intensively at night. The booms are repeated at intervals of c2 seconds in short series and the sound can be heard at over 5 km. At closer range each boom is heard to be preceded by a heavy intake of breath, 'uh-BOOH'. If the bird is seen in flight, one may react (as often with well-known but rarely seen birds) first with surprise but then with an 'of course it is' reaction. It then resembles a cross between an owl and a heron. When flying low over reeds the neck is not uncommonly half extended, but over longer distances it is retracted. Flight call a short, Grey Heron-like 'aurr'. Adopts camouflage posture when approached. Feeds on fish, frogs and other small animals. Very local in Britain, with some dispersal in winter, when also a few immigrants arrive from the Continent (Nov−Feb).   Map p. 62

American Bittern   *Botaurus lentiginosus*   L 60−75 cm, WS 105−125 cm

Somewhat smaller than Bittern, with more uniformly brown-coloured back lacking latter's contrasty pattern. In flight resembles Bittern, but with darker and more uniform flight feathers. Seen more in open than Bittern. A very rare vagrant from N America, with most records from Britain and Ireland in Sep−Dec.

Bittern

American Bittern

Little Bittern
juv

2nd-cal

ad winter

juv

Night Heron

Little Bittern   *Ixobrychus minutus*   L 33–38 cm, WS 52–58 cm

Often common in bird-rich wetlands with dense vegetation, especially in reedbeds. Most active at dusk, and unobtrusive but more mobile and easier to see than its larger relative the Bittern. Is not uncommonly flushed along rivers and canal banks, when its small size and contrasting pale panels on secondary coverts identify it. Usually flies away a short distance and before long dives a little clumsily back into reeds. On long flights looks odd, with slightly front-heavy profile and with fast jerky wingbeats alternating with glides. Where common it often reveals itself at dusk by a short 'kuk' or 'kek', though this easily drowned by the calls of the Moorhens and Coots. Also has (when excited) fairly loud and insistent call in slow staccato, 'keck eck eck eck eck eck'. Courtship call at night 'kock', repeated at 2-second intervals, though usually drowned by frog chorus. Feeds on fish, frogs, insects and small animals. Migrates to mainly tropical Africa Aug–Sep, returning end Mar to beginning May. Vagrant to Britain, mainly spring (has bred).

Night Heron   *Nycticorax nycticorax*   L 58–65 cm, WS 105–112 cm

A characteristic heron, with stocky body, soft curves and soft grey colour tones with velvety-black crown and mantle. The white head plumes are present only in spring. Legs raspberry-red at start of breeding period but more yellowish during rest of year. Juv. has partial moult in winter, acquiring dark grey-brown mantle/scapulars (can breed in this plumage). 2nd-summer resembles ad. Fairly common but has nocturnal habits; easiest to see at dusk, when it flies to sheltered shores and reedbeds to forage. Flight path a trifle unsteady, strongly rounded wings are beaten relatively slowly and rigidly (mechanical). Colour often looks uniform grey in flight. Flight call a rather Raven-like 'kwark'. Migrates mainly at night in small flocks which fly in single file. Rests by day in clumps of trees and bushes: often they do not take off until one is really close, so are encountered usually very suddenly. Nests in trees or tall bushes, often in heron/egret colonies. Takes frogs, fish, insects etc. Migrates Oct–Nov to tropical Africa (few winter around Mediterranean), returning Mar–Apr. Vagrant to Britain.

Bittern

Little Bittern

Night Heron

Little Bittern

♀

♂

2nd-cal
♂ spring

juv

subad

breeding

Night Heron

Cattle Egret *Bubulcus ibis*   L 48–53 cm, WS 90–96 cm

A small heron, striking because of its white plumage and habit of occurring on most types of meadowland. Hunts on altogether drier ground than other herons and egrets and preferably on grass fields and pasturelands. Runs about energetically, often follows cattle and tractors in pursuit of insects, reptiles and other small animals. Very sociable. Seen mainly morning and evening in small, neat 'string of beads' flying to and from roosts (usually in tree clumps). Shorter bill and legs and stockier body with less sagging neck distinguish flight silhouette from Little Egret's. Commonest call a short 'ark' and a rather duck-Mallard-like 'ag-ag-ag'. Locally common in open cultivated country, especially in Andalusia and Alentejo regions of Iberia. Resident, but non-breeders and imms. often disperse far from breeding sites. Species seems also to be increasing its range in Europe.

Squacco Heron *Ardeola ralloides*   L 44–47 cm, WS 80–92 cm

Ad. in breeding plumage a beautiful golden-ochre and slightly purple-tinted on mantle and with elongated nape feathers, bill base greenish-blue. In winter plumage loses long nape plumes, acquires streaked neck-sides and yellowish bill bass. Juv. drab brownish-buff above with streaked fore parts. In flight predominantly white, a surprising transformation since in particular imms. are well camouflaged on ground. Flight faster and wingbeats more clipping than in e.g. Cattle Egret. Flight call a short straight 'karr' with typical heron-like harsh throaty sound. Common but seldom abundant in well-vegetated wetlands, also found on small ditches and rivers. Solitary hunter, stands and waits for prey, usually among vegetation cover but, mainly in early morning, also out in open on fields and wet meadows. Nests in trees, often with other herons/egrets. Migrates to tropical Africa Aug–Sep, returning Mar–Apr. Avoids salt water but on passage sometimes found on rocks and islands along Mediterranean coast. Very rare vagrant to Britain.

Western Reef Heron *Egretta gularis*   L 55–65 cm, WS 86–104 cm

Size of Little Egret but less elegant, with thicker bill which appears slightly curved on culmen. Occurs in a dark grey and a white phase, rarely in intermediate forms. Juv. white phase shows isolated dark grey feathers on wing (greater coverts and flight feathers) and tail. In summer plumage has long nape plumes and back plumes. Bill yellow to brownish-yellow with irregularly darker brown elements. Legs dark with greenish-yellow to yellow tones. Along Red Sea eastern race *schistacea*, often with whole foot and whole tarsus (or patchily) pale yellow; the pale areas become red during courtship. Along W African coast race *gularis*, which is darker grey, has dark brown bill and legs and yellow only on toes. Strongly coastal; odd records in Mediterranean.

Map and ill. next spread

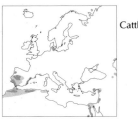

Cattle Egret

Squacco Heron

breeding

Cattle Egret

Cattle Egret

winter/juv

**Squacco
Heron**

breeding

winter/juv

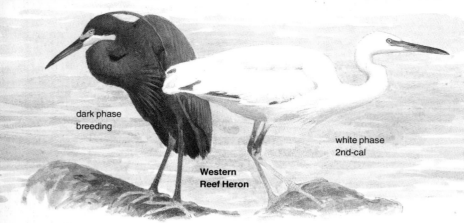

dark phase
breeding

white phase
2nd-cal

**Western
Reef Heron**

Little Egret   *Egretta garzetta*   *L 55–65 cm, WS 88–95 cm*

The most widespread of the white herons in Europe. Differs from Cattle Egret in lack of ochre tones in plumage, blacker legs and bill and also (in breeding plumage) the long nape plumes. During courtship in spring ad. has yellow or almost reddish lores, green-blue/grey-blue during rest of year. Young imms. have brown-green legs, grey lores and pinkish base to lower mandible. Very rare dark grey form, with or without white throat, can be confused with Western Reef Heron. Occurs relatively commonly at shallow lakes, ponds and river deltas but also at saltpans and lagoons on coast, though only exceptionally on dry pastures like Cattle Egret. Sociable and nests colonially with other herons in trees. Usually silent in flight but sometimes utters a straight and nasal 'ksheeh', higher in tone than Grey Heron's; also short, soft, grunting 'raaak' or 'owkr'. Feeds mostly on fish and small shore-dwelling animals. Winters relatively uncommonly around Mediterranean, though most migrate to Africa. Increasing visitor to Britain (a few winter).

Great White Egret   *Egretta alba*   *L 85–102 cm, WS 140–170 cm*

Almost as big as Grey Heron and easily told from Little Egret by size alone. Imms. and winter ads. have dirty yellowish or mud-coloured legs and yellowish bill; in breeding season ad. acquires black bill and darker tarsus with yellow or pinkish-yellow tibia. In flight very big, with more composed wingbeats than Little Egret. Breeds at reedy lakes in C and SE Europe. Seen in small numbers but relatively commonly in E Mediterranean region, mainly in non-breeding season, but solitary imms. often linger during summer months at fish-rich wetlands. Rare vagrant to Britain (increasingly recorded), mainly late spring to summer.

Western Reef Heron

Little Egret

Great White Egret

Little Egret

breeding

non-breeding

breeding

Great White Egret

non-breeding

Grey Heron   *Ardea cinerea*   *L 90–98 cm, WS 150–175 cm*

The commonest and most widespread heron species in Europe and the only one commonly occurring in Britain. In flight looks huge, with heavy flight on solidly dark and deeply bowed wings. Crane and Black Stork fly with neck straight, wings less bowed and primary tips spread. Despite its size, it is easy to overlook when resting absolutely still at edge of reeds, in a field or in a tree. Call usually a raucous 'krowrnk', and at nest site several grating calls. Found at all types of watercourse and in agricultural country. Nests locally in colonies in trees, in reedbeds and on Atlantic coast partly on cliffs. Disperses from colonies towards late summer and then appears relatively commonly at fish-rich waters outside actual breeding areas. Mostly resident in Britain, with some winter immigration from east. Feeds on fish, small animals and insects.

Purple Heron   *Ardea purpurea*   *L 78–90 cm, WS 120–140 cm*

Looks darker and somewhat smaller than Grey Heron. Head and neck appear narrow and reptilian, long and angular. In flight at distance can be confused with Grey, but has squarer-edged 'throat-pouch' and longer, more jutting hindclaws (adaptation to living among reeds). Imms. take c2 years to reach full adult plumage, and on most Purple Herons wing-coverts look dull red-buff to purple-brown in flight. Stands out in open much less often, and is often flushed from the reeds and other dense vegetation which it prefers. On rising often gives a Grey Heron-like but less throaty, rather Caspian Tern-like call, otherwise usually silent. Breeds mostly in colonies in reedbeds on previous year's reeds or in low bushes. Migrates to tropical Africa Sep–Oct (Nov), returning end Mar–May. Food as Grey Heron's. Breeds in Holland and rare but regularly seen in southern and eastern parts of England.

Grey Heron

Purple Heron

Grey Heron

juv

Purple Heron

juv

Black Stork   *Ciconia nigra*   L 95–100 cm, WS 185–205 cm

Less numerous than its white relative and often shyer and difficult to observe. Nests in undisturbed older forest but seeks its food, fish, batrachians, insects etc, in shallow water, in marshes and on damp meadowland. In E Europe sometimes side by side with White Stork. Imms. dark brown with olive-green to grey-pink tone on legs and bill. At nest makes soft plaintive and bill-clattering sounds. Like White Stork, has decreased during 1900s, but some increase has occurred recently in several countries. Seen in larger numbers only on migration. Often migrates in family parties, generally about a month later than White Stork. Occasional visitor to Britain, mostly in Apr–Aug.

White Stork   *Ciconia ciconia*   L 100–115 cm, WS 195–215 cm

Common and a typical bird of open cultivated country over large parts of its range, but has decreased drastically and disappeared completely in several regions in W and N Europe since end of 1800s. Climatic changes, draining of marshlands and agricultural pesticides are major reasons for decline. Feeds on all kinds of smaller animals such as frogs, snakes, fish, rodents, worms, young birds etc. Often walks imposingly in low marsh vegetation, along ditch banks and on meadowlands. Breeds in big stick nest in trees and on specially fitted platforms on house roofs, telegraph poles etc. Bill-clatters loudly on contact with conspecifics. Migrates in Aug–Sep to Africa, huge numbers concentrating at Strait of Gibraltar and Bosporus. Annual visitor to Britain, mostly Apr–Aug.

Black Stork

White Stork

Black
Stork

White
Stork

ad

juv

Black Stork

White Stork

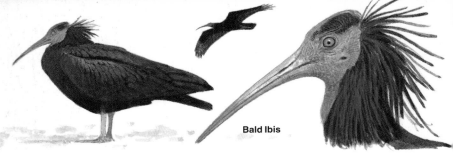

Bald Ibis

Spoonbill *Platalea leucorodia* L 80–90 cm, WS 115–130 cm

Unmistakable, usually flies in groups in single file with necks extended and with fast shallow wingbeats interspersed with short glides. Imms. have black wingtips. Ads. lack yellow neck-ring and nape plumes in non-breeding season. Rather scarce and local at shallow lowland lakes, river deltas and coastal lagoons. Nests colonially in reedbeds, bushes or trees. Feeds on small fish, insects, tadpoles and other small aquatic animals, sifted out in rhythmic side-to-side sweeps of bill. Can be told from white egrets at several km range, as feeding birds keep together in tight groups in constant slow movement. In Europe threatened by e.g. marsh-draining, pesticides; sensitive to disturbances when breeding.

Glossy Ibis *Plegadis falcinellus* L 55–65 cm, WS 80–95 cm

Characteristic wetland species of SE Europe. At distance looks entirely brownish-black, but at closer range shows beautiful glossy green and pink highlights. Juv. plumage much duller. In winter plumage has muddy-brown bill, indistinct white loral streak and pale streaks on neck and head. Often performs long flights between feeding sites and roosting/breeding sites. Flight behaviour resembles Spoonbill's: in trim 'string of beads' which undulates neatly as birds lose height in gliding phase. Fairly common in SE Europe, mainly on floodlands and in shallow marshes. Has decreased in 1900s. Nests colonially in reedbeds, bushes or trees, sometimes with egrets/herons, storks and Pygmy Cormorants. Takes small water- or bottom-dwelling animals. Most migrate south of Sahara but odd ones winter around Mediterranean. Call slightly guttural, crow-like 'kraa kra kra'; short grunting calls often heard from feeding flocks.

Bald Ibis *Geronticus eremita* L 70–80 cm, WS 125–135 cm

Shorter-legged than Glossy Ibis, all-dark with red legs, red bare head and bill and straggly elongated nape feathers. An endangered species with only a few known colonies in Morocco and at one site in SE Turkey (only odd birds left in 1989); observed in winter at Ta'izz in N Yemen. Nests on rock ledges and feeds mainly in dry open country.

Spoonbill

Glossy Ibis

Greater Flamingo

Spoonbill juv breeding

Glossy Ibis

breeding

juv

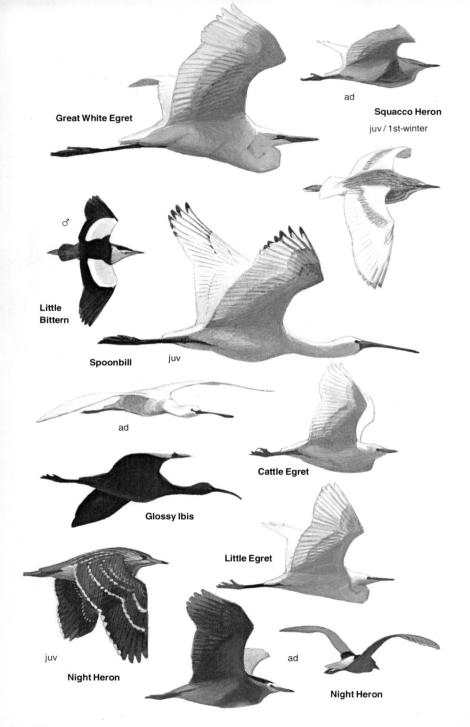

Great White Egret

ad

Squacco Heron

juv / 1st-winter

♂

**Little
Bittern**

Spoonbill   juv

ad

Cattle Egret

Glossy Ibis

Little Egret

juv

Night Heron

ad

Night Heron

juv

Greater Flamingo

Greater Flamingo *Phoenicopterus ruber* L 125–145 cm, WS 140–165 cm

Breeds very locally in large colonies on shallow saline lakes and coastal lagoons. Feeds on small water-dwelling invertebrates, plankton and algae, which it extracts by sucking in water and then squeezing it out with its tongue through a system of fine lamellae in the bill. Feeds in dense flocks which move slowly forwards. The head is either immersed or held above frothy water surface and moved in scything motions from side to side; can also swim. Large flocks in distance resemble pink ribbons. Fully fledged juvs. have legs and neck two-thirds adult length. In addition, males are noticeably larger than females. Amount of dark brown markings varies. Becomes successively whiter and gradually acquires pink hue and red wing-coverts. Imms. swimming can be taken for young swans at distance. Call a short, nasal grunting double note, sometimes cracked, 'gagg-agg', 'gegg-egg' etc. Large flocks create a wall of sound recalling a goose flock.

Map p. 72

Whooper Swan   *Cygnus cygnus*   L 145−160 cm, WS 218−243 cm

Differs from Bewick's Swan in larger size, longer neck, more elongated head shape, more yellow on bill and also call. Extent of yellow on bill varies slightly but always shows more than Bewick's. Juv. more uniformly grey-toned than juv. Mute Swan and has paler bill base which contrasts with darker face. Whooper Swan has loud, nasal trumpeting calls at different pitches, 'hwang, klong' etc. Flies in V formation or in oblique line. Migrants stop off at freshwater lakes, rivers or shallow sea bays. Breeds on boggy lakes and river deltas; has in recent decades also begun to breed sparsely in C and S Sweden. Feeds mostly on various aquatic plants but also grazes on shore meadows and fields in goose fashion. Migrates north in Mar-Apr and south in Oct-Nov. Northern limit of wintering range depends on ice situation.

Bewick's Swan   *Cygnus columbianus*   L 115−127 cm, WS 180−211 cm

In direct comparison appreciably smaller than Whooper Swan, with shorter neck, less elongated head shape and less yellow on bill, yellow being more oblong in shape. Young accompany their parents on autumn migration. Shape of the 'yellow' at bill base is indicated at an early age by a slightly paler pink tone. Outer part of bill darkens gradually and is usually black towards midwinter. Breeds on arctic tundra and migrates in autumn via southern Baltic to wintering areas in W Europe. Migration periods Mar−Apr and Oct−Nov, but more concentrated than in Whooper Swan. Stops off on sea coasts and adjacent fields and wetlands. In Britain and Ireland winters mainly at traditional sites on floodlands and lakes.

Mute Swan   *Cygnus olor*   L 145−160 cm, WS 208−238 cm

The commonest of the swans and a familiar breeding bird on many lakes and rivers. Recognised at distance by its more curved neck/nape and in certain situations by higher rear end and longer tail; at closer range by its red bill with black knob. Imms. are browner, often with paler breast, and have dark marking around bill base which contrasts with face. In flight wings produce a throbbing whine, lacking in Whooper Swan. Feeds on aquatic plants, which are grazed from bottom in shallow water. Winters also on sea coasts and estuaries.

Whooper Swan

Bewick's Swan

Mute Swan

Whooper Swan

Bewick's Swan

Bewick's Swan
juv

juv

Whooper Swan

juv

Mute Swan

Bean Goose

Greylag Goose

Pink-footed Goose   **White-fronted Goose**   **Lesser White-fronted Goose**

Pink-footed Goose *Anser brachyrhynchus*   *L 60–75 cm, WS 135–170 cm*

Smaller than Bean Goose, has pink and slightly shorter legs, shorter neck and more compact head profile with short black bill with pink band close to nail. It produces a paler, more grey and buff-pink impression, with belly-sides the darkest part of body. In flight, wings, mantle and back are distinctly paler than on Bean and tail has broader white border. Juv. drabber and often has buffish legs. As in Bean, ad. often has white edging or small patch at bill base. Call resembles Bean's but is higher and shriller. Breeds only in E Greenland, Svalbard and interior of Iceland. Birds from Svalbard migrate along Norwegian coast down to Denmark and North Sea coasts, while the western populations have their main winter quarters in E Scotland and in lesser numbers farther south. Winters on pasturelands, stubble and crop fields and locally saltmarshes, roosting on nearby lakes and estuaries.

Bean Goose *Anser fabalis*   *L 66–88 cm, WS 147–175 cm*

Differs from Greylag Goose in generally browner overall impression and contrasting dark brown head and neck, together with dark markings on bill. Bill pattern and shape vary: nominate *fabalis* breeding in taiga region has somewhat larger neck and bill, which shows less black than on tundra geese *rossicus*, which often have just an orange band near tip. Sometimes has a narrow white 'halter' around bill base. In flight shows darker wings, both above and below, than Greylag and darker lower back. Call is a varied nasal, quite lively cackle, 'kayakak' or 'kayak'. Breeds on tundra and in upper coniferous region on bogs and in river deltas. Migrates in Sep–Nov, returning Mar to beginning of May. Wintering habits much as those of Pink-footed. Most winter on Continent, with very few in Britain.

Pink-footed Goose

Bean Goose

Pink-footed Goose

juv

Bean Goose

rossicus

fabalis

juv
fabalis

Lesser White-fronted Goose   *Anser erythropus*   L 53–66 cm, WS 120–135 cm

Smaller than White-fronted Goose, on the whole darker, shorter-necked, with smaller bill and steeper forehead. White 'blaze' reaches higher up on forehead, and at close range the diagnostic yellow eye-ring is also visible. Juv. lacks blaze but has pale eye-ring. In flight very hard to tell from White-front. Flight call higher-pitched than White-fronted's, a fast bouncing 'dyee-yeek' or 'dyee-yik'. Breeds by lakes on tundra and in willow and birch regions of mountains. In Scandinavian mountains has decreased in numbers in recent decades and is very rare. Shy and difficult to find at nest sites. Migrates southeast and returns in May. Appears rarely in Britain and W Europe, often in flocks of other goose species.

White-fronted Goose   *Anser albifrons*   L 65–78 cm, WS 130–165 cm

White forehead blaze, unmarked pink or yellow bill and tar-black irregular bars on belly distinguish White-fronted Goose from other geese apart from Lessere White-front. Juvs. lacks forehead blaze and dark belly markings and have black nail to duller bill. Migrates in family parties, so imms. often seen together with parents. White blaze is often acquired as early as first winter, dark belly markings in second autumn. Greenland race *flavirostris*, which winters in Ireland, W Scotland and W Wales, has orange-yellow, slightly longer and heavier bill than Siberian *albifrons*, which winters in S England and other parts of Europe. In flight comparatively longer-winged and shorter-necked than Bean Goose. Call a varied 'kow-yoo' and fairly musical 'kyo-kyok', markedly clearer and shriller in tone than Bean, rather reminiscent of barking dogs. Imms. have higher and slightly hoarser voice, 'kick-elick'. In Britain, Siberian race present mainly Dec–Mar; Greenland race arrives Oct, leaving Apr.

Greylag Goose   *Anser anser*   L 75–90 cm, WS 147–180 cm

Gives a rather uniform brown-grey impression, with large pale bill and pink legs. Eastern race *rubrirostris*, breeding in E Europe and farther eastward, has pink bill and somewhat paler upperparts. Western race *anser* has more orange-yellow bill. Most Baltic breeders are pink-billed. In flight, striking silver-grey panel on wings and shows paler underwing-coverts than other *Anser* geese. Loud-voiced and noisy, with nasal sonorous sounds like those of domestic geese, from flying birds typically a 'krang-ung-ung'. In flight looks heavy, with big neck-and-head area. For nesting prefers undisturbed islands and peninsulas along seashores or at lakes. In Britain mostly resident in north, with many feral flocks elsewhere to south; also winter visitor Oct–Apr, mostly from Iceland, but there are occasional records of eastern race.

Lesser White-fronted Goose

White-fronted Goose

Greylag Goose

Lesser White-fronted Goose

juv

White-fronted Goose
juv

White-fronted Goose

Siberian race

White-fronted Goose
Greenland race

Greylag Goose

Canada Goose

Bar-headed Goose

Snow Goose   *Anser caerulescens*   *L 65–78 cm, WS 130–160 cm*

A N American species which breeds on the arctic tundra. Seen regularly but rarely in NW Europe and Scandinavia, usually among other *Anser* geese. In most cases escapes or specially 'put-down' birds are involved, but genuine wild accidentals are also assumed to occur within the region. Generally somewhat smaller than White-fronted Goose, all-white with black wingtips. Young birds are slightly dirty in plumage, with faint brown-grey markings. In N America also occurs in a dark phase, the 'Blue Goose', which is dark grey with white head and silver-grey wing-coverts. Gives a cackling monosyllabic 'keck' in flight.

Bar-headed Goose   *Anser indicus*   *L 70–82 cms, WS 140–160 cm*

Size of Bean Goose, looks very pale in the field, with characteristic head markings. Native to C Asia. Escapes from zoos and parks. Breeds ferally in Norway.

Canada Goose   *Branta canadensis*   *L 90–110 cm, WS 150–180 cm*

Our largest goose. Big brown body and long black neck with white cheek, unlike Barnacle Goose, which has almost whole head white. Introduced into Europe, but true range includes whole of N America. Occurs on lakes, marshes and sheltered sea bays, also on fields and farmland. In flight the long narrow neck is rather striking, which creates a somewhat swan-like profile. In the air gives itself away at long distance by trumpeting 'ah-honk', second syllable higher, shrill and very penetrating.

Red-breasted Goose   *Branta ruficollis*   *L 53–56 cm, WS 116–135 cm*

Breeds on Siberian tundra from River Ob eastwards across Taymyr Peninsula. Nearest wintering area SE Europe, above all in Romania and in smaller numbers in Bulgaria and NE Greece. Seen rarely but fairly regularly in company of the Barnacle Geese which winter in Holland and which stop off in the Baltic (Öland and Gotland) on spring and autumn migration, very rarely at other sites (e.g. S Britain). Unmistakable, but surprisingly hard to pick out among the motley Barnacle Geese. In flight it is first and foremost the dark belly and also the shorter and plumper neck that catch the eye at a distance.

Canada Goose

Red-breasted Goose

dark phase, 'Blue Goose'

Snow Goose

Canada Goose

juv

Red-breasted Goose

Brent Goose

juv

Barnacle Goose

Red-breasted Goose

Brent Goose   *Branta bernicla*   *L 56–61 cm, WS 110–120 cm*

A small, stocky goose which is mostly tied to sea coasts. Occurs in Europe in two races. The race *bernicla* with dark belly, which breeds in W Siberia, winters in large numbers in southern North Sea area, including E and S Britain, mainly Oct–Mar. Western race *hrota*, breeding in Greenland and Svalbard, has paler grey-buff belly and winters mainly in Ireland, NE England and Denmark. (Race *nigricans*, breeding in E Siberia east to Canada, has brownish-black belly with contrasting paler flanks; odd vagrants recorded annually W Europe, incl. England.) Juvs./1st-winters have pale-edged wing-coverts (wing looks striped), with neck patch only poorly indicated or lacking. Looks all-dark in flight, with white stern, and compared with Barnacle flies faster with Eider-like wingbeats. Large flocks fly in less well-ordered formations than other geese. In flight gives a nasal muttering 'kr-rop'. Feeds largely on eelgrass and other seaweed, but also grazes grass.

Barnacle Goose   *Branta leucopsis*   *L 58–70 cm, WS 132–145 cm*

A small parti-coloured goose, with black, grey and white plumage. In flight at long range can be confused with Brent Geese, but Barnacles have longer wings and slower wing action. Noisy in the air, with short vocal barks which often tell of their approach (see also Canada Goose). Has a limited distribution, breeding in Novaya Zemlya, Svalbard and parts of E Greenland. The eastern populations migrate through Baltic and winter mainly in Netherlands; Svalbard birds move along coastal Norway and across North Sea to winter on Solway Firth (NW England/SW Scotland); Greenland population migrates via Iceland to Ireland and W Scotland. A small population has recently started to breed in the Baltic, on Gotland. Winters on coastal pastures and grassy areas, feeding on grass, clover and seeds of marsh plants.

Brent Goose

Barnacle Goose

juv

bernicla

Brent Goose

Barnacle Goose

juv

juv   ♀

Shelduck

Shelduck   *Tadorna tadorna*   *L 58–71 cm, WS 110–133 cm*

A boldly marked and often conspicuous duck. Female, which is slightly smaller than male, lacks bill knob and usually has white markings around eye and bill base. Juv. lacks bright brownish-red tones of ads. Juvenile especially can be puzzling in flight at long distance because of its white throat and white band along rear edge of wing. During spring courtship male gives a squeaky whistling call and female a louder cackling 'ga-ga-ga-ga-ga-ga-gak'. Occurs mainly along flat sandy shores, bays and estuaries but also on lakes near the sea as well as on fields. In early mornings from late Mar can often be seen looking for nest sites: nests in holes, from rabbit burrows to cavities under buildings, in haystacks and even old dog-kennels. Many birds leave breeding sites as early as Jun−Jul to moult in Waddenzee area (much smaller numbers, mostly from Ireland, go to Bridgwater Bay, Somerset, to moult).

Ruddy Shelduck   *Tadorna ferruginea*   *L 61−67 cm, WS 121−145 cm*

Size of Shelduck and with distinctive uniformly rust-coloured plumage. Male has black neck-ring only during breeding season. Very striking in flight. Rather noisy, in flight utters a rolling 'rrowl' and Greylag-like 'gag-ag'; male also gives low muffled pumping 'wooh', not unlike spring call of drake Eider. Occurs locally at lakes and swamplands, particularly those with wide surrounding delta areas and sandbanks. Relatively common in ornamental parks.

Egyptian Goose   *Alopochen aegyptiacus·*   *L 63−73 cm, WS 134−154 cm*

Somewhat bigger than Shelduck, longer-legged and with characteristic colour markings. Generally brownish-red above, buffish-grey below and with dark brown-red patch on belly. Head pale, with distinctive dark mask around eye. Wing pattern as Ruddy Shelduck's. A tropical African species introduced to East Anglia, where it breeds in the wild. Breeds naturally in Egypt from Lake Nasser southwards, wintering along Nile north almost to Cairo.   *Not illustrated*

Shelduck

Ruddy Shelduck

juv

♂

Shelduck

♀

♂

Ruddy Shelduck

Wigeon ♂

American Wigeon ♀

Wigeon   *Anas penelope*   *L 45−51 cm, WS 75−86 cm*

Differs somewhat from other dabbling ducks in more diving-duck-like shape. Male has striking yellowish forehead and crown in full plumage, and brilliant white secondary coverts in all plumages, though 1st-summer males have greyish coverts. Female is rather drab brown-grey with more or less rusty flanks, dark shade around eye and comparatively short lead-grey bill. Migrants from north begin to appear in Britain from early Sep onwards; they are then in eclipse plumage and coloration varies from young females' brown-grey to ad. males' deep wine-red. Ad. females can be told from young birds by more rounded median and lesser coverts with prominent whitish fringes. 1st-cal-year females have drab grey coverts lacking obvious fringes; 1st-cal-year males have lighter grey coverts and black speculum mostly showing glossy green. Only a few females have a green gloss to dark speculum. In flight looks long-winged with pointed tail and relatively small and 'bulbous' head, below has pronounced white belly and grey axillaries. Males give melodious whistling 'wheeoh' and female has a growling Goldeneye-like 'warr, warr, warr…'. Breeds by northern lakes surrounded by bogs and grasslands, wintering on lowland lakes and floodlands as well as on muddy sea coasts. Feeds on plant matter and often grazes on land like geese. Returns north in Mar−May.

American Wigeon   *Anas americana*   *L 45−56 cm, WS 76−89 cm*

In every respect very like Wigeon and, especially in female-type plumage, very difficult to separate. In all plumages has white axillaries and more contrastingly marked underwings. Male has whole body pinkish and behind eye a diagnostic dark band with a metallic green sheen. Females and both sexes in eclipse have contrast between greyish head and rusty flanks (never pronounced on Wigeon). On upperwing the greater coverts are mainly white with black tips, showing as a broad white wingbar in flight, and on some females white panels are formed almost as on males. Call of male resembles Wigeon's but is given more as two syllables, 'wheeoh-woh'. Rare vagrant from N America, mainly in late autumn to winter; rare breeder in Iceland.

Wigeon

Wigeon

♂ eclipse

♂

♀

American Wigeon

♀

♂ eclipse, moulting

♂

Mallard ♀   Gadwall ♀

Mallard *Anas platyrhynchos* L 51–62 cm, WS 81–98 cm

The most abundant and widespread of the dabbling ducks. Male in full plumage unmistakable; in eclipse plumage differs from female in e.g. uniformly green-yellow bill. Female varies considerably in coloration and markings, in eclipse appearing darker overall; bill yellow to reddish-orange with dark markings on inner part of culmen and usually in an irregular band over middle, sometimes uniformly dark grey. Female gives loud quacking, varying in tone and number of syllables according to mood, shrill and insistent when agitated. Male's call is a quiet, nasal and rather frog-like 'vaehp', heard on spring nights; during late-autumn courtship a high-pitched whistle, 'pyee'. Mallards breed on most types of fresh water, often occurring quite fearlessly on park lakes and at feeding stations; city duck flocks in winter also include wild-breeding Mallards. Food very variable: seeds, fruits, plants, insects and other small aquatic animals. Forages also on land far from water, e.g. stubble fields. Males begin migration to moulting sites as early as May−Jun and females and young in Jul−Aug, but northern migrants often do not move to final wintering areas until later, in Oct−Dec.

Gadwall *Anas strepera* L 46−56 cm, WS 84−95 cm

Slightly smaller, slimmer and 'more lithe' than Mallard. In all plumages recognised by white in speculum, like a white rectangle on rear inner wing (though *cf* Wigeon). On the water full-plumaged male's black rear characteristic; with birds in all other plumages colour pattern of bill decisive, showing yellow-orange band along lower side. In flight Wigeon-like white belly characteristic. Often noisy. Female's call differs from Mallard's in slightly higher and shriller tone and in more even 'articulation'; alarm call at breeding site a mechanically repeated 'ehk', uttered persistently. Male has a lower, more grating 'errp', to a certain degree recalling Garganey's. Often sparse in occurrence, but locally common on fresh and brackish waters with dense shore vegetation. Lives readily on small ponds and flooded marshy shore meadows, but in breeding area needs open areas of water. Most winter in W Europe, Aug−Apr. Food mainly plant material.

Mallard

Gadwall

♂ eclipse

♂

Mallard

♀

juv

Gadwall

♀

♂

Pintail ♀

Shoveler ♀

Pintail   *Anas acuta*   L male 61–76 cm, female 51–57 cm, WS 80–95 cm

A big and long-bodied dabbling duck. Male unmistakable; female and imms. have long neck, rounded head shape, and a rather long, narrow, all-grey bill. Male in eclipse plumage appears in Jul-Oct; like female, varies in colour, but is usually greyer in tone and more finely patterned. Flight silhouette characteristic with long fore and rear areas, and has broad white trailing edge to speculum and comparatively variegated, banded underwing pattern. At distance mantle and scapulars look darker, creating slight contrast with paler flanks; at closer range darker saddle on bluish-grey bill is diagnostic for ad. male. Male has a mellow rolling, almost Teal-like 'kreel', female a Mallard-like but lower quack and also a Wigeon-like growling call. Mainly a northern duck, but also breeds sparsely and irregularly at a few scattered sites in Britain and Ireland. Not uncommon, though rather local, winter visitor to Britain from N Europe and Iceland, mostly Sep–Apr, wintering mainly on estuaries, coastal wetlands and flooded fens, often in company of Wigeon. A large part of the Siberian populations, however, winter in Sahel region of Africa.

Shoveler   *Anas clypeata*   L 49–52 cm, WS 70–84 cm

The large bill with broad tip makes the Shoveler a characteristic duck in all plumages. Looks front-heavy on the water and in flight. Flying birds are dark on belly and have all-white underwing-coverts, unlike e.g. Pintail and Garganey. Ad. male has beautiful blue-grey secondary-covert panel above; on female this is a rather more subdued grey, especially on imms., which can have very plain wing markings. On spring evenings Shovelers are often seen in pairs or small tight groups performing courtship flights at tremendous speed and with sudden twists and turns over the breeding lake; males then utter a double, abruptly clipped 'vack-ack' and the female a more Mallard-like and drawn-out 'vaek-aek'. Occurs commonly on food-rich lowland lakes, marshy meadows and flooded grasslands (also on seashores in Baltic), in winter also on more open shallow lakes. Food mainly plankton, crustaceans, insects and seeds, filtered from the water with the large lamellae-equipped bill. In Britain most breeders migrate to Mediterranean in Jul–Oct, returning Mar–Apr, being replaced by winter visitors from N and E Europe.

Pintail

Shoveler

♀

Pintail

♂

♂ eclipse

♀

Shoveler

♂

Teal ♀

Garganey ♀

Teal *Anas crecca*   *L 34–38 cm, WS 58–64 cm*

Our smallest duck and one of the most common. At a distance male looks dark with bright yellow stern patch. In Aug–Sep all birds have a female-like plumage: they differ from Garganey in pale oblong patch at tail base, yellow-orange bill base and less well-marked head, at distance appear to have dark skull-cap on rear head. Quite often a little nervous and quickly takes wing. Swerves in flight. Juv., however, often not shy. Compared with Garganey, wing is darker above and the front pale wingbar is broader than rear one, on ad. males more like an oblong patch. Often active at night and noisy. Male has a short, bell-like ringing 'krick' or 'kreek' like a house-cricket. Female has clear, nasal quacks and on rising a low growling 'trrr'. As breeding bird commonest in north, often on moorland and forest pools with surrounding vegetation, also lowland lakes. In winter widespread on shallow lakes, reservoirs, marshes, estuaries. In Britain partial migrant, also abundant winter visitor from N Europe Sep–Apr.

Garganey *Anas querquedula*   *L 37–41 cm, WS 63–69 cm*

Slightly bigger than Teal, has longer and stouter bill and more front-heavy profile on water. Male has dazzling white supercilium. Female and juv. are recognised by their contrasting head markings with dark cheek-bar and a pale spot at bill base, and also by lack of Teal's pale mark at side of tail base. Ground colour varies, especially in autumn when head can be cinnamon-coloured and less contrasty. In flight somewhat more elongated than Teal; males have bright grey-blue coverts and grey webs to primaries (wing looks pale), and females also have paler wings than Teal. White trailing edge is broader than wingbar (reverse applies in Teal). Male has a dry crackling call, like scratching one's fingernail across a comb. Female gives Teal-like quacks. Relatively shy and unobtrusive. Far less numerous than Teal in W Europe. Prefers shallow food-rich lakes surrounded by boggy meadows and small pools. Migrates to tropical Africa in Aug–Sep (Oct), returning in Feb–Apr.

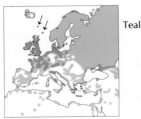

Teal

Garganey

Teal

♂

♀

juv

Garganey

♀

♂

♂ eclipse

Wood Duck   *Aix sponsa*   L 41–50 cm, WS 68-74 cm

A N American duck often kept in collections, not recorded naturally in Europe, but female is easily confused with female Mandarin.

Mandarin   *Aix galericulata*   L 41–49 cm, WS 68-74 cm

An E Asian duck which has, through introductions and escapes, established a permanent population in England. Male unmistakable. Female very like female Wood Duck, though latter slightly darker, has larger white patch around eye, dark nail to bill, smaller flank spots and less pointed tail. Female Mandarin has fuller 'mane' covering neck, on Wood Duck more like a nape crest. Breeds in tree holes.

Falcated Duck   *Anas falcata*   L 48–54 cm, WS 78-82 cm

An Asiatic species recorded a few times in Europe, incl. Britain. Size of Gadwall. Female darker in ground colour than most other dabbling ducks, rather plainly patterned and with full nape. On male secondary coverts are grey, speculum glossy green bordered at front by broad white wingbar but terminal band absent or only faintly indicated. Female's wing is similar but less contrasty, with brown-grey secondary coverts and a buff-coloured wingbar.

Baikal Teal   *Anas formosa*   L 36–40 cm, WS 60-66 cm

An E Asiatic species which has occurred as a genuine vagrant a few times in Europe; escapes have also been reported. Size of Garganey, male unmistakable. Female and imms. also fairly characteristic owing to their striking head markings, in which pale spot at base of bill is very distinctive. In both sexes nape is fuller than in Teal or Garganey. Wing pattern differs from Teal's in having a rusty band along greater coverts and a very broad white trailing edge.

Blue-winged Teal   *Anas discors*   L 37–41 cm, WS 63-69 cm

Rare vagrant from N America. Size of Garganey. Male brownish-yellow, black-speckled, and with dark violet-blue head with conspicuous white crescent mark in front of eye and also white patch at sides of stern. Female brownish-buff and with less contrasty head than female Garganey; has paler spot at bill base like female Garganey, but never a pronounced dark cheek-bar. In flight, both sexes have blue secondary coverts and they lack pale trailing edge to secondaries typical of both Garganey and Teal; female in addition lacks or has only faint suggestion of greater-covert band. Male has clear single or repeated 'pying' or 'peehp' like young chicken.

Cinnamon Teal   *Anas cyanoptera*   L 37–43 cm, WS 64-70 cm

Occurs in W and C N America. Has not been recorded in wild in Europe, but included here as escapes can be confused with Blue-winged Teal. Obviously long-billed. Female has less contrastingly marked head than female Blue-winged.

Green-winged Teal   *Anas crecca carolinensis*   L 34–38 cm, WS 58-64 cm

Vagrant from N America. Male in full plumage differs from Teal in having vertical white stripe on breast-side and no horizontal line along folded wing; also appears slightly darker overall. Female resembles Teal.

American Black Duck   *Anas rubripes*   L 53–61 cm, WS 85–96 cm

N American relative of, or colour variant of, Mallard. Has declined in numbers in breeding range in eastern USA. Recorded a few times in W Europe. Male blackish-brown at distance, female like a dingy female Mallard but with olive-green bill. Also has more glossy purple speculum than Mallard and lacks white wingbar on greater coverts.

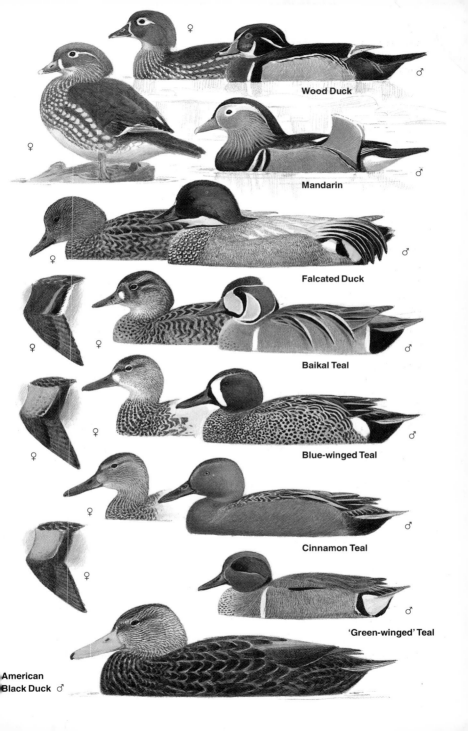

Wood Duck ♀ ♀ ♂ ♂

Mandarin ♀ ♂

Falcated Duck ♀ ♂

Baikal Teal ♀ ♀ ♂

Blue-winged Teal ♀ ♀ ♂

Cinnamon Teal ♀ ♂

'Green-winged' Teal ♀ ♂

American Black Duck ♂

Marbled Duck with Pintails ♀ ♂

White-headed Duck ♂   **Marbled Duck**

White-headed Duck *Oxyura leucocophala* L 43−48 cm, WS 62−70 cm

A peculiar diving duck, size of Tufted Duck, with a long tail held cocked at rest. Together with Ruddy Duck belongs to a subfamily known as 'stifftails'. Male in full plumage has white head and a bright blue, almost grotesquely swollen bill, which is smaller and greyer in summer−autumn. Males have chestnut-brown and females and imms. more buffish-brown plumage and rather variable head markings. Submerges for long periods when foraging and when danger threatens. Flies rarely, and then low with long run at take-off. Rare and very local. Has declined considerably in Europe during 1900s, with some recovery in Spain in recent years. Prefers shallow lakes with open water surrounded by extensive vegetation, in winter occurring also on open lakes and saline lagoons.

Ruddy Duck *Oxyura jamaicensis* L 35−43 cm, WS 53−62 cm

A N American relative of the White-headed Duck. Introduced into Britain, where it has established feral populations and is locally common (e.g. W Midlands). A characteristic duck, size of a Teal, with long tail and long bill. Never has swollen bill base. Behaviour reminiscent more of a grebe.

Marbled Duck *Marmaronetta angustirostris* L 39−42 cm, WS 63−67 cm

A very pale dabbling duck with dark eye patch, long neck and long wings, recalling, especially in flight, a female Pintail. Relatively shy and difficult to observe, as it often keeps concealed in rank vegetation. Mostly silent but has a 'gick gick' call like a hoarse Kestrel. Occurs rarely in S Spain. Has decreased greatly during 1900s, but some recovery has taken place in recent years. Lives on shallow well-vegetated lakes, on passage and in winter sometimes also on saltpans and river mouths at coast. Migrates irregularly, majority wintering north of Sahara.

White-headed Duck

Ruddy Duck

Marbled Duck

subad ♂

White-headed
Duck
♀

Ruddy
Duck

♀

juv

♂

Marbled
Duck

♂

Red-crested Pochard   *Netta rufina*   L 53–57 cm, WS 84–88 cm

Size of a Mallard. Male's pale red bill very striking, as also are crown feathers, which are ruffled up according to mood. Female most resembles a female Common Scoter, with pale grey cheeks and contrasting dark cap. Male in eclipse is more like female, uniform grey-brown with pale grey cheeks but with straggly remnants of the fox-red comb and with red bill. In flight looks very big, male with broad, brilliant white wingbar and narrow white leading edge to wing; female has buffish-white wingbar. Commonest call a short mechanical 'gick'. When courting female, male gives a call similar in tone, 'keuvik', nasal and like a sneeze. Like some dabbling ducks, performs pursuit flights over breeding lake in spring, when 2–7 males chase one female. Occurs locally and irregularly in Europe on shallow secluded sea bays, saltpans, lowland lakes and river deltas with dense vegetation. Some increase has taken place in recent years, is most numerous in Spain. Feeding behaviour more like dabbling ducks', upends and picks but also dives for plants and other food.

Pochard   *Aythya ferina*   L 42–49 cm, WS 72–82 cm

Male unmistakable. Female rather insipid, but peaked head and elongated bill characteristic, as also to varying degree are head markings. In winter females have grey vermiculated body with dark brown breast and head, in breeding season becoming more uniformly brown. Juv. resembles ad. summer female but lacks pale markings on head. In flight both sexes differ from other *Aythya* ducks in grey, not white, duck (but see Ring-necked Duck). Female's call is a growling 'krrrak', courting male's a soft whistled 'pee, pee, pee...' and a quiet, rather drawn-out mechanical 'aish-chong' (bellows drawing air in and out). Breeds on well-vegetated lakes with larger areas of open water. Males much more numerous than females. Food mainly seeds and plant matter but also small aquatic animals. Scarce breeder in Britain, but many winter immigrants Sep–Apr.

Ferruginous Duck   *Aythya nyroca*   L 38–42 cm, WS 63–67 cm

Smaller and with large peaked head and characteristically long forehead and long bill compared with Tufted Duck. Looks very dark, chestnut-coloured, with bright white undertail and, on male, white iris. Female is browner, with brown iris. In flight contrasting white belly and undertail, though these are grey-buff and indistinct on juvs. and less obvious on female in eclipse. White wingbar very conspicuous, extending onto outermost primaries on male. Female in spring very noisy in flight, with Tufted Duck-like but slightly higher 'err, err, err...'. Male has short 'chuk' or 'chuk-chuk'. Fairly common on shallow lowland lakes with rich vegetation, in E Europe often on carp ponds. Unobtrusive, unlike other diving ducks seldom sits out on open water. Food mainly seeds and plants, fewer aquatic animals. In Britain scarce winter visitor, mainly to SE England.

Red-crested Pochard

Pochard

Ferruginous Duck

Red-crested Pochard ♀ ♂

Pochard ♀ winter ♂

♀ ♂ juv **Ferruginous Duck**

Scaup

♂ 1st-winter

♂

Tufted Duck ♀

♀ ad winter

Tufted Duck *Aythya fuligula* *L 40–47 cm, WS 67–73 cm*

Male black with white belly and long drooping crest. Female dark brown, can be confused with females of Ferruginous Duck and Scaup. Has somewhat squarish yet nevertheless rounded head shape and slight indication of crest on nape. Some females have white around bill base but never as extensive as on Scaup, moreover is never grey-frosted on body like winter-plumaged female Scaup. Male's display call is a quiet vibrant whistle, 'pee-yee-peep peep', like a duckling. Female gives angry growl, 'err...err...err...'. Common on lakes and ponds with some shore vegetation, also on coasts in Baltic. Winters on open waters in large flocks, locally also on sheltered sea bays and in harbours. Takes molluscs etc and plant matter.

Scaup *Aythya marila* *L 42–51 cm, WS 72–84 cm*

Male easily told from Tufted by pale grey-vermiculated back. Head more rounded in shape than Tufted's and has green gloss. Female in winter is paler on body than female Tufted, with grey-vermiculated flanks and large white patch around bill-join; in breeding season she assumes a browner plumage, often with rusty-brown flanks and with white spot (varying in size) on cheek. Autumn juvs. are often all dark brown with rust-brown flanks and sometimes have less conspicuous white area around base of bill, distinguished from Tufted by rounder head shape and broader bill. From Oct young males gradually acquire elements of grey and vermiculated feathering on flanks and back; some look completely adult around midwinter but have duller, less green-glossed head and darker tertials. Male's display call is a deep whistle, 'peAoo'. Female's call resembles Tufted Duck's but slightly lower-pitched, more like 'arr...arr...'. Breeds on mountain lakes and on coasts in Scandinavia and Iceland (also very rarely in N Britain). Winters mostly on relatively shallow coasts, especially in sheltered bays, sometimes in large mixed flocks with Tufted, rarely inland. In Britain and Ireland mainly passage and winter visitor, Oct–Mar.

Tufted Duck

Scaup

Tufted Duck

♂

Scaup

♂

Scaup

breeding ♀

breeding ♀

♀

Tufted Duck

♀

Pochard × Tufted hybrid

Lesser Scaup ♂

Ring-necked Duck

♂

♀

Lesser Scaup   *Aythya affinis*   L 38-45 cm, WS 65-70 cm

A N American duck recorded a few times in W Europe. Smaller than Scaup and with more pointed head profile and purple-glossed head on male, somewhat more coarsely vermiculated above than Scaup and with faint (difficult to see) vermiculations on fore flanks. In flight shows white wingbar on secondaries only.

Ring-necked Duck   *Aythya collaris*   L 37–46 cm, WS 61–75 cm

A N American diving duck, like Pochard in habits and behaviour. Male has grey flanks and a contrasting white wedge in front which cuts up in front of wing. Head profile most like Pochard's, with peaked crown and long, sloping bill. Bill dark grey, with narrow pale grey band around base and a broader one just inside nail. Gets its vernacular name from the dark rusty-purple neck-band, though this is not conspicuous in the field. Female like female Pochard, but has more peaked crown and bill is 'dipped in black' with a paler band behind tip. Head often looks quite pale but with a dark 'pixie cap', has pale band around bill base but lacks female Pochard's dark 'gape extension'; also, breast is more rusty-toned and back darker. Both sexes have grey wingband, not white as on Tufted Duck. Can easily be confused with hybrids between (among others) Pochard and Tufted, something which occurs very rarely but regularly. Occasional but regular visitor to Europe. Vagrants have habit of returning to same wintering site from year to year. Exclusively a freshwater duck, seen in similar habitats to Tufted.

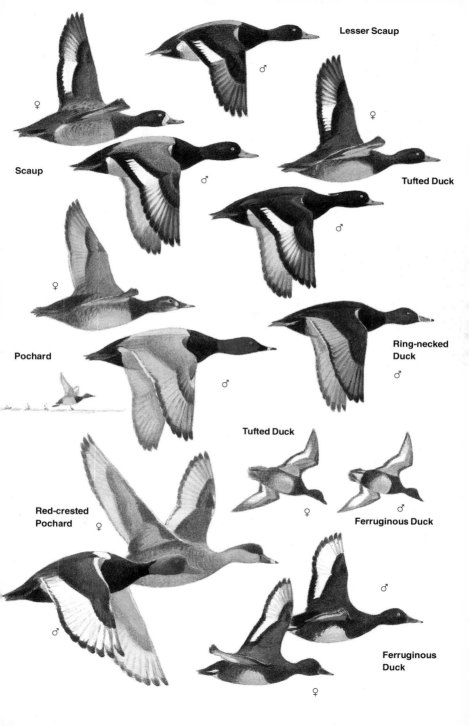

Lesser Scaup ♂

Scaup ♀

Scaup ♂

Tufted Duck ♀

Tufted Duck ♂

Pochard ♀

Pochard ♂

Ring-necked Duck ♂

Tufted Duck

Ferruginous Duck ♀

Ferruginous Duck ♂

Red-crested Pochard ♀

Red-crested Pochard ♂

Ferruginous Duck ♂

Ferruginous Duck ♀

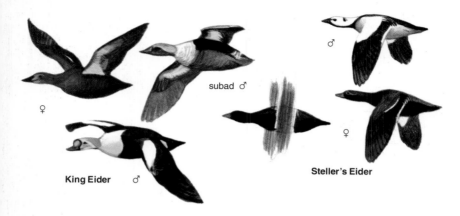

subad ♂

♀

King Eider ♂

Steller's Eider

♀

King Eider *Somateria spectabilis* *L 55–62 cm, WS 86–102 cm*

Slightly smaller than Eider. Ad. male unmistakable. In eclipse predominantly black with brown on breast and head and white wing coverts. Males in 1st-winter plumage vary in appearance: body blackish-brown with buff-grey to white patch on stern, brownish-grey or white breast (also with pink tone), head brown-grey, darker towards bill and with varying amount of pale on throat. Bill in 1st winter with suggestion of yellow-orange knob. 2nd-winter plumage adult-like but with slightly less inflated bill. Female like female Eider but smaller, not so 'long-nosed', bill is shorter and wholly dark grey and contrasts with paler cheeks; has a well visible and 'happy-looking' gape line. Ad. female usually brownish-red. A high-arctic breeder which winters along coast of northern Norway and in E Iceland. Rare but regular in varying numbers in Britain and North Sea, mostly in Scotland, mainly in winter and on passage.

Steller's Eider *Polysticta stelleri* *L 43–47 cm, WS 70–76 cm*

Barely half the size of Eider. Ad. male unmistakable; in eclipse plumage all-black with brown vermiculations on breast, but with white secondary coverts. 1st-winter males are, unlike the bigger eiders, entirely brown and female-like but with faint suggestion of ad. male's head and neck markings, sometimes showing traces of white on side of breast and scapulars. Ad. females are very dark red-brown, have dull blue tertials and greyish-white inner webs (see illustration) and, when wing exposed, show two conspicuous white wingbars. Head shape more squarish and bill as it were 'fitted on' with vertical bill-join. 1st-winter females have entirely brown tertials; a clear pale eye-ring is characteristic of all female-type plumages (missing on a few individuals). Often keeps together in tight flocks, all dive simultaneously; flight fast with rapid wingbeats. Breeds on Russian arctic tundra east of Taymyr Peninsula, sporadically perhaps also in N Norway, where it is found in large numbers throughout year. Rare in rest of W Europe but regular winter visitor to Baltic Sea in small numbers.

King Eider

Steller's Eider

Eider ♂ 1st-winter

♀ 1st-winter

♂ 1st-winter

King Eider

♂ 1st-winter

♀

♂

ad ♂ eclipse

♂ 1st-winter

♀

Steller's Eider

♂

Spectacled Eider — *Somateria fischeri* — L 52–57 cm, WS 85–93 cm

Size of King Eider (i.e. smaller than Eider), with characteristic 'spectacle markings'. Male has distinctive blackish breast which gives it away at long range, even in flight. On distant female the dark shadow on lores is the most striking feature. Very rare vagrant from arctic coast of E Siberia and W Alaska.

Eider — *Somateria mollissima* — L 50–71 cm, WS 80–108 cm

A very common coastal bird in N Europe. Male unmistakable, but after breeding assumes an almost all-black eclipse plumage with white secondary coverts. Juv. male moults towards late summer-autumn into fresh blackish plumage and then becomes very dark, almost wholly blackish-brown. 1st-winter plumage is acquired towards late autumn, shows much individual variation. 2nd-winter plumage is in the main adult-like, but with a sprinkling of darker tips to upperpart feathers. In spring, 3rd-cal-year male normally as ad.; dark tips to tertials and paler green colour on nape are the only visible differences in the field. Ground colour of female varies from buff-grey to rich red-brown, red-brown individuals being commoner in Iceland and farther north. Also wintering in Iceland are birds from Greenland/Canada with more orange-toned bill base, odd ones also having short white 'sail' on back (like King Eider). Courting male gives far-carrying and crooning 'ah-haoo', female answers with low chuckling 'kok-ok-ok'. Feeds largely on mussels and crustaceans, dives but also upends like dabbling ducks in shallow water. A prominent passage bird in the Baltic. In Britain and Ireland most breeders sedentary but imms. move farther south, also winter visitor from Continent.

Eider

Harlequin Duck

Long-tailed Duck

Eider

♂

♀

ad ♂ eclipse

1st-winter (spring)

1st-winter (autumn)

1st-winter

1st-winter

♀

♀

♂

Harlequin Duck *Histrionicus histrionicus*   *L 38–45 cm, WS 63–69 cm*

A N American and E Siberian species with nearest breeders in Iceland and southern Greenland. In breeding season closely tied to fast-flowing water, occurring even along quite small streams. After breeding migrates to sea coasts, where it lives around cliffs and rocky shores. Males migrate as early as Jun, and after that adopt a more female-like eclipse plumage. 1st-winter male like ad. but less marked on fore parts and without white on scapulars and tertials. Female and juv. very uniform and alike in appearance. Always flies low over water, typically with very fast wingbeats and head erect. Calls include an odd, quiet high-pitched squeaking as from Turkey chicks. Feeds on various small aquatic animals which cling fast to bottom of streams and to rocks in sea. Vagrant to NW Europe outside Iceland.   *Map p. 108*

Long-tailed Duck *Clangula hyemalis*   *L male 58–60 cm, female 37–41 cm, WS 73–79 cm*

A mountain and tundra species which winters at sea. Male in winter unmistakable. Female very variable in pattern, but owing to its small size, short bill and dark cheek markings hardly like any other European duck except possibly Harlequin. Odd individuals are very pale, with only faint shading on cheeks and with drab grey-brown upperparts. In flight, the combination of pale underbody and all-dark, long, slightly arched wings is characteristic. Acquires summer plumage from Apr, male then becoming mostly dark brownish-black. 1st-winter male generally like female but with bicoloured bill, slightly elongated tail point and scattered pale grey elongated scapulars. Male has a far-carrying mellow 'ow-OW-lee', which is heard frequently on calm days in late winter. Feeds mainly on molluscs and crustaceans in winter. Winters in large flocks in Baltic, usually far out from land, though smaller groups closer to shore; fewer in North Sea and around Britain (and rarely inland). Restless, small groups of males often seen chasing one female, make horizon appear to 'be boiling' where they are abundant. Often threatened by oil spills. Large spring passage in Baltic, with majority passing in third week of May along Gulf of Finland and east overland to Siberian tundra.   *Map p. 108*

Long-tailed Duck

♂ winter

♀ winter

♂ winter

♂ summer

♀ summer

♂ winter

♀ winter

♀ winter

♀ winter

♂ winter

migrating Common Scoters

Velvet Scoter ♀

Common Scoter ♀

♀ ad

Surf Scoter

Common Scoter   *Melanitta nigra*   L 44–54 cm, WS 79–90 cm

Slightly smaller than Velvet Scoter and without white speculum, though flight feathers obviously paler than rest of bird when in flight. Male often looks all-black at distance. Female has characteristic pale cheeks, visible at long range. Otherwise looks more rounded, swims higher in the water and has more rounded forehead than Velvet Scoter. Breeds commonly to sparsely on lakes on upland moors and tundra. Winters at sea, huge numbers (millions) in southern Baltic and North Sea countries (large concentrations around Danish islands) with small flocks locally elsewhere in W Europe. Males migrate to moulting areas in midsummer, but females and young move later, up to Nov (with peak in Oct). Majority of return passage through English Channel and North Sea takes place in Apr and beginning of May. Migrating Common Scoters often assume the shape of a large 'blob' with a bushy tail at the back. Males in flight have short fluting whistles, 'pyee' or 'pyew-pyew', which sometimes give away northward-migrating flocks on still spring nights when the route also passes overland. Female's call is a loud deep 'how(howrr)…how…how…'. On take-off a whirring sound (like chinking ice) is heard from the wings, created by the first visible primary on the males being strongly emarginated on inner web. Feeds mainly on sea mussels but diet also includes other molluscs, crustaceans and bristleworms.

Velvet Scoter   *Melanitta fusca*   L 51–58 cm, WS 90–99 cm

Almost size of Eider. Male raven-black, female blackish-brown, both with characteristic large white wing patch though this is often hidden when bird is on the water. Female usually has white patches on head but sometimes wholly dark-headed (probably older females). A late breeder, in Baltic young hatch in first half of Jul. Nest often placed far from shoreline. 'Rings in' nest site by making circular flights in pairs over intended breeding place at dawn and dusk. Females then give nasal rolling 'arr-ha', and then whistling call is also heard from male. Food as Common Scoter's. Males migrate to moulting areas in summer, females and young through Sep–Nov, seldom in large flocks like Common Scoter. Winter visitor to Britain on open coasts, often with Common Scoters.

Common Scoter

Velvet Scoter

Common Scoter

Velvet Scoter

Surf Scoter

♂   ♀

younger ♀

ad ♀

Surf Scoter   *Melanitta perspicillata*   *L 45–56 cm, WS 78–82 cm*

A N American species, very rare in Europe but regular N Britain (mostly Sep–Apr). Size of Common Scoter and with all-dark wings, lacks Common's paler colour to flight feathers. Male unmistakable. Female can be confused with Common but has stronger neck and characteristic angular head profile: crown is straight but with marked peak at forehead and sharp angle with straight nape, and feathering extends far down onto culmen. Has two pale patches on side of head separated by a dark mark beneath eye. Older females have dark belly and less pale on face, often only poorly indicated cheek markings but with a pale patch on nape. Young female has pale belly and always distinct white cheek patches. 1st-winter male has wholly black head apart from a pale patch on nape, and a moderately swollen bill but with the species-characteristic blackish spot on bill-side.

Bufflehead   *Bucephala albeola*   *L 32–39 cm, WS 54–61 cm*

Slightly smaller than a Smew. Like Goldeneye in behaviour and build, also in bill shape though bill somewhat narrower at base. Male unmistakable, white body with black 'cloak' over back, green-glossed black head with large white 'clasp' over rear head running right down to eye in a rounded curve. Female has grey underparts, greyish-black back and dark brown head with an elliptical white patch behind eye; can be confused with Goldeneye x Smew hybrids. Vagrant from N America, recorded a few times in Europe.

Bufflehead

♀

♂

♂

♀

young ♂ moulting

♀ moulting

♀ winter

♂

Barrow's Goldeneye

Barrow's Goldeneye   *Bucephala islandica*   *L 42–53 cm, WS 67–84 cm*

Has its main distribution in N America but is also found commonly in Iceland. Slightly bigger than Goldeneye and solid-looking, with steep forehead and short but very deep bill. Male has purple-glossed head, elongated white patch behind bill and more black on upperparts and looks generally darker than Goldeneye. Bill-and-head shape also distinguish female and juv. from Goldeneye. In winter–spring female has an orange-yellow band on bill. In flight shows less white on wings and upperparts than Goldeneye. Resident throughout year in Iceland and has been recorded only a few times in rest of Europe. Breeds commonly on clear small lakes and river systems. Numerous in Myvatn area, where the fields of solidified lava provide hollows for nest sites (in N America also nests in tree holes).   *Map p. 116*

Goldeneye   *Bucephala clangula*   *L 42–50 cm, WS 65–80 cm*

Male is very pale at distance and characteristically marked. Female in full plumage grey, with distinctive and 'triangular' brown head as if pressed on to the white neck like a young cep fungus. 1st-winter female is very nondescript grey-brown with wholly dark bill and dark eye. In flight show large white wing panels and dark underwings. Have rapid wingbeats and male produces a characteristic whistling wing noise. In display, male utters loud fast 'be-baeeek' (like Mallard quack played at too fast a speed) followed by quiet Garganey-like rattle. Female has fast grating 'berr, berr, berr'. Common on wooded lakes and watercourses, nests in tree holes, often in Black Woodpecker holes, and readily accepts nestboxes. Winters on lakes, reservoirs, large rivers and sheltered coasts. Feeds mainly on molluscs, crustaceans and insect larvae, but also seeds. Breeds in increasing numbers in N Britain, but mainly passage and winter visitor to Britain and Ireland in Oct–Apr.

Smew   *Mergus albellus*   *L 38–44 cm, WS 55–69 cm*

Male in full plumage very pale at distance, whitish and distinctively marked. Female can be taken for Goldeneye at quick glance, but the white cheeks give her away. Male in eclipse resembles female and full plumage is not acquired again until late autumn. In flight differs clearly from dabbling and non-sawbill ducks in its long slender shape and fast agile flight. Male's dazzling white and female's grey-white wing patches on median coverts (as on Wigeon) are also conspicuous in flight. Habitat requirements and breeding biology very like Goldeneye's; the two are sometimes seen side by side and can even interbreed. The Smew is an uncommon breeder within its range and usually appears in lesser numbers at passage and wintering sites: lakes, reservoirs and sheltered bays and estuaries. Feeds mostly on fish and insect larvae.

Barrow's Goldeneye

Goldeneye

Smew

116

Goldeneye ♀

♂

Smew

♂

♀

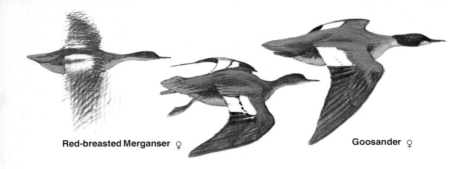

Red-breasted Merganser ♀ **Goosander ♀**

Red-breasted Merganser *Mergus serrator* L 51–62 cm, WS 70–86 cm

Male easy to distinguish from Goosander, appearing darker overall and with black-marked rusty-brown breast. In Britain male loses full plumage as early as latter part of May and in eclipse plumage is more like female, though recognised by white secondary coverts, darker and browner mantle and red eye. Female differs from female Goosander in even merging of colour between head and neck; she also has more straggly crest and more uniformly narrow bill. In flight, female's white speculum is divided by a black cross-line and the wing is also darker on lesser/median coverts. Female's call a muffled gruff 'ahrrk, ahrrk, ahrrk…', usually uttered on rising and in flight. Starts nesting late, often not until around midsummer. Males display in winter and spring by making strange mechanical movements, but are often overlooked as they often just gather in small groups with no obvious calling. Fairly common on coasts and on clear inland lakes and rivers in N Britain/Ireland, moving to coasts in winter; also winter visitor to most coasts from N Europe, Sep–May. Feeds mainly on fish.

Goosander *Mergus merganser* L 58–66 cm, WS 82–97 cm

Size of Eider. Male very pale, with greenish-black bushy head and black back. Female like female Red-breasted Merganser, but recognised by greyer back and sharply demarcated dark brown head. On both sexes the palest, white areas are tinted with a beautiful orange-pink, though this fades towards spring. Males in summer wear very female-like eclipse plumage, but recognised then by their all-white wing-coverts. Arrives early at nesting sites, with break-up of ice. Nests in tree holes and nestboxes, mostly by clear lakes and rivers. In autumn big flocks gather locally at fish-rich lakes, forming large driving cordons to hunt fish. Migration often coincides with freeze-up. Among winter flocks males often seen facing each other with 'inflated' crowns and stretching neck and head while giving faint frog-like 'kuorr kuorr' calls. In early spring male also utters a pleasant ringing double sound (echoing), in tone like a distant duet call from a pair of Cranes. Female has loud rolling 'skrrak, skrrak, skrrak'. Feeds mainly on fish.

Red-breasted Merganser

Goosander

Red-breasted
Merganser

♂

♀

Goosander

♀

♂

Black Vulture

ad

subad
Lammergeier

juv
Egyptian Vulture

juv
Bonelli's Eagle

Booted Eagle

Booted Eagle

Black Kite

juv

Long-legged Buzzard

N Africa

Buzzard

Booted Eagle

Lesser Spotted Eagle

juv

Short-toed Eagle

Black-shouldered Kite

display

juv

Black-shouldered Kite   *Elanus caeruleus*   *L 31–34 cm, WS 75–83 cm*

Body as small as Kestrel's, pale as Common Gull, with black lesser/median secondary coverts. Often perches on telegraph poles, fences or in a treetop. Looks lightweight in flight and glides long stretches with wings raised in V. Has triangular wings and short tail. Often hovers. In display flight spirals upwards with fast wingbeats, and then dives or glides away on V-held wings like a paper swallow, at times with dangling legs and rhythmic whistling. Call a soft whistle, 'kyuit' or 'kuee', not unlike Little Owl's call. Alarm when raptor present a drawn-out low, gravelly 'kreeay'. Rare breeder in open savanna-type country with scattered trees. Feeds on insects, reptiles, small rodents, with a few birds. Resident.

Black Kites
gathering to roost

Black Kite   *Milvus migrans*   L 55–60 cm, WS 135–155 cm

Buzzard-sized but with more uniformly broad wings and a longer and shallowly forked tail, has neat flight silhouette. Like Marsh Harrier, but above shows characteristic pale diagonal bands on secondary coverts and so is easy to confuse with dark-phase Booted Eagle. Flight light and slightly swaying and tail is used as a rudder and frequently twisted. Circles on flat wings, not as Marsh Harrier and Buzzard with wings held in V. Juvs. have heavy pale markings on underparts, neck and head and are also paler on primary bases below. Calls include a vibrant 'kuee ee ee ee ee' like young gull, sometimes followed by a chatter, and also a mewing like Buzzard or Common Gull. Black Kite is distributed in various races almost throughout the Old World and is common in many places in Europe. Occurs in various open or semi-open terrain with element of forest or clumps of trees, usually near lakes, rivers and other watercourses. Lives on fish, smaller animals, insects and often carrion and refuse. Rare visitor to Britain, mainly in Apr–Aug.

Red Kite   *Milvus milvus*   L 60–66 cm, WS 145–165 cm

A 'refined' form of the Black Kite. The long, deeply forked tail which is arbitrarily steered at different angles together with the slender wings give the Red Kite a strikingly elegant flight. Circles on flat or slightly arched wings. Tail's rust-red colour and deep fork make it unique. The general rusty-red coloration, pale diagonal bands on secondary coverts above and contrasting white patches on underwings are often striking features. Juv. has shallower tail fork and more sandy-coloured underparts and tail. In gliding flight the translucent inner primaries make wings often look more angled than on Black Kite. At nest site gives a varied, rather wailing 'heeah-hee-hee-hee-hee-hee-heeah'. Also has a soft mewing call, weaker, more feeble than Buzzard's. Found in hilly regions, typically in landscape with areas of old deciduous wood mixed with open fields and meadows. In winter often gathers in flocks at dusk to roost together in clumps of trees or sections of forest. Hunts over open terrain and lives on small rodents, smaller birds, insects etc, but also takes dead animals and refuse; steals prey from other birds, e.g. Rook and Carrion Crow. Predominantly resident, but many 1st-years migrate south or west.

Black Kite

Red Kite

Black Kite

ad

Black Kite juv

Red Kite juv

Red Kite

ad

Egyptian Vulture
subad

Egyptian Vulture

Lammergeier

Lammergeier *Gypaetus barbatus* L 100–115 cm, WS 245–272 cm

Usually appears singly or in pairs. Mostly seen circling around top of a mountain or leisurely patrolling a mountainside. The sight of it is majestic and often overwhelming. Its size is reinforced by fact that it often moves along a mountainside in slow motion with few movements. Wings and tail droop slightly and as it were trail on the upwinds, which, together with the usually groundwards-pointing head, gives it a characteristic profile. Tail looks sometimes long and falcon-like, sometimes shorter and broad. Subad. has varying extent of whitish markings on back and wing-coverts. Occurs in small numbers and very locally in mountainous tracts in S Europe and N Africa, more commonly in Turkey. Nests on mountain precipices. Other vultures are sometimes driven away from vicinity of nest ledge or cave. Lives on carrion, mainly deer, sheep and goat casualties, whose presence is probably a prerequisite for the species' occurrence. An important food source is bone marrow, which it gets at by dropping larger bones from the air on to hard rock surfaces so that the bone shatters. Has decreased in many areas in Europe in 1800s and 1900s as a result of direct hunting, deliberate poisoning and changes in domestic-animal husbandry.

Egyptian Vulture *Neophron percnopterus* L 60–70 cm, WS 158–163 cm

Ad. unmistakable, but can be taken for White Stork at long distance. Juv. dark brown and recalling Lammergeier in silhouette, but has shorter, more pointed tail and blunter and stiffer wings. Soars on flat wings. Acquires ad. plumage successively over about 5 years. Relatively common and dispersed over most habitats, even deserts, but seen mostly in mountainous regions as well as at refuse tips and slaughter-sites. During 1800s was common in S Europe and even nested on outskirts of towns. Has decreased in 1900s, partly as result of rationalisation of waste-disposal methods. Omnivorous, diet includes carrion, household waste, excrement, insects, eggs and young of birds. Usually migrates in smaller flocks, mostly in Sep, and returns in Apr–May. Resident in Canaries.

Lammergeier

Egyptian Vulture

juv
Egyptian Vulture

juv

Lammergeier

4th–5th-cal

2nd–3rd-cal

Egyptian Vulture

Black Vulture

juv   ad

Griffon Vulture

juv

ad   ad

Black Vulture *Aegypius monachus* L 100–110 cm, WS 250–295 cm

Europe's biggest bird of prey. Usually appears quite different from Griffon owing to more uniformly broad wings, wedge-shaped tail and dark, brownish-black overall impression. Also, wings held perfectly flat when soaring and with drooping hand when gliding. Often looks uniformly coloured, older birds dark chocolate-brown, younger ones black-brown, and with the pale bare parts on head and legs conspicuous at reasonable distance. On older birds paler bands can be seen on lesser coverts and they also have paler dirty-brown collar. Bare parts are pink on juvs., pale blue-grey on older birds. Rare and few in number, mainly in wooded and hilly or mountainous country. Breeds in small loose colonies in large stick nests in trees. Often seen soaring in leisurely manner high up, but also patrols hills and mountainsides at low level. Lives on carrion and can tear holes in skin and sinews with its strong and powerful bill. Higher in pecking order than Griffon at corpses. Resident.

Griffon Vulture *Gyps fulvus* L 95–105 cm, WS 255–280 cm

The Griffon Vulture immediately betrays itself by its size and characteristic flight silhouette. Wings are long, broad and bulging in the arm and with a narrowing hand with deep splaying fingers. Tail is conspicuously short and more square-ended than on Black Vulture. In soaring flight, wings are held slightly pressed forward and raised in a distinct V. At a distance ads. look dark below and pale above; at closer range paler bands are visible along coverts and body colour is mid-brown. Juvs. show contrast below between cinnamon-brown body and mostly pale sandy-coloured underwing-coverts, and are darker above. Griffons live mostly on carrion, which they search for while circling high up or gliding slowly along mountain ridges and hills. They leave their nest ledges in the colony after sunrise and return towards afternoon and evening. At corpses they gather in flocks. Like other vultures has decreased in numbers during 1900s, but is still common locally in some areas in Spain, rarer towards E Mediterranean region. Mainly resident, but imms. move south in Sep–Nov, earlier in E Mediterranean region.

Black Vulture

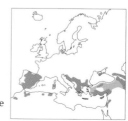

Griffon Vulture

Black Vulture

ad

Griffon Vulture

Griffon Vulture

ad

juv

Black Vulture

juv

Montagu's Harrier *Circus pygargus* *L 43–50 cm, WS 98–110 cm*

A long-winged and elegant raptor which glides solemnly over heaths and meadowland. Long pointed wings are held raised above the horizontal, often with a kink near body seen head on in gliding flight. Male has one black wingbar above and two below and faint rust-coloured streaking on belly and underwing-coverts. 2nd-summer (3rd-cal-year) males are relatively dark and shabby-grey on wings, while older ones are bright silvery-grey. Display song clearer than Hen Harrier's, a shrill 'nyack-nyeck-nyeck'; call a sharp 'knieck'. Female's begging call is a clear whistle, 'peeh-ee', alarm a rapid cackling, shrill 'check-eck-eck-eck...'. Nests on peatbogs, heaths, meadowlands and cornfields. Feeds on smaller animals and birds, e.g. lizards, rodents, larks and wader young. Migrates Aug–Sep/Oct, returns mid Apr–May (as early as Mar in S Europe). Rare in Britain. *See also p.130–132*

Pallid Harrier *Circus macrourus* *L 40–48 cm, WS 95–110 cm*

Male slightly smaller than Montagu's, with more pointed hand, shorter 1st and 2nd primaries. Often moves more quickly, at times almost falcon-like, over open heaths and meadows, and impression is often of shorter and more pointed wings than on Montagu's. Ad. male almost all-white below with sharply demarcated black wedge at wingtip, uniform grey above with diffusely marked wedge, reminiscent of a big gull and very different from Montagu's. Younger males, especially 2nd-cal autumn to 3rd-cal spring, have variable but always darker grey upperparts and at first rusty breast and more contrasting facial markings; field impression at distance is of contrast between pale belly and darker head/breast, like Hen Harrier. 1st-year Hen when moulting can show a Pallid-like wedge in late summer-autumn. Food mainly small rodents and ground-dwelling birds. Migrates Aug–Oct to E Africa and returns Apr–May, though odd birds may stay behind in E Mediterranean region and Middle East.
See also p.130–132

Hen Harrier *Circus cyaneus* *L 43–50 cm, WS 100–120 cm*

Bulkier and broader-winged than Pallid and Montagu's. Male blue-grey with darker head and breast. Often sails slowly and waveringly on V-held wings low over hunting grounds, but in migration flight usually surprisingly fast and in gliding flight often with flat or slightly arched wings. Nests on open bogs and moors, in Britain only in north and N Wales but also in Ireland. On passage and in winter in various open terrain, such as cultivated fields, downland, coastal meadows, river deltas etc. Roosts communally in groups (up to c20 individuals) in reedbeds, tall-grass meadows or like places. In display flight male utters a dry chattering 'chuck-uck-uck-uck-uck'. Female's alarm an excited 'theck-eck-eck-eck...', like Great Spotted Woodpecker. Feeds mainly on rodents and small birds. British breeders mainly resident, reinforced by passage/winter visitors from N/E Europe in Sep–Apr. *See also p.130–132*

Montagu's Harrier

Pallid Harrier

Hen Harrier

Montagu's Harrier

♂

♂

2nd-summer ♂

♂

2nd-cal ♂ autumn

Pallid Harrier

♂

♂

Hen Harrier ♂

♂

♂

Hen Harrier

♂

Montagu's Harrier, female and immatures

Ad. female very like Pallid but can be distinguished. Above, flight feathers are paler, more so on older females, with a usually distinct dark bar on secondaries close to greater coverts, something never seen on Pallid. Below, the secondary barring is more clearly defined: of the three dark bars, the two inner ones are darkest and are closer together, so that a broader pale area is formed between them and the terminal band; terminal band is of uniform thickness along entire length of secondaries (cf Pallid). On older females the head appears as pale and rather insipidly marked; at distance the dark oval on ear-coverts is most obvious and eye is enclosed in a large dirty-white area, at close range like a 'lobster-claw' clasping from the rear. Can show a pale neck-ring. Juv. a beautiful rusty colour on the pale areas and with more contrasting facial markings than ad. female, the dark on the cheek extends farther forward towards gape; some individuals show clear pale neck-collar, but this is always rusty-toned and the dark on neck-side is never broad and pronounced as on juv. Pallid. 2nd-cal-year female in spring/summer often retains rusty tones below, streaking breaks through first on breast, and as they lack dark secondary bar above they can be taken for Pallid. 2nd-cal-year male in spring acquires grey elements on head, breast and back, can show a pale neck-collar owing to retained faded feathers; when they have moulted some of the primaries towards late summer, the new black primaries can form a black wedge, recalling that of Pallid.

Pallid Harrier, female and immatures

Ad. female a little more robustly built and slightly more powerful in aerial progression, can recall Hen Harrier. Markings also bear the stamp of Hen, with darker secondaries below and some contrast between pale belly and darker-marked breast/head area. Field impression at long range is often that greater coverts and secondaries look smudgy-dark below, especially on younger females, apart from a pale wedge breaking in from primaries and to about halfway down on arm. At closer range three dark bars can be distinguished on the secondaries, as with Montagu's, but the inner two are clearly narrower and less distinct than the terminal band (on Montagu's, central one is broadest and most distinct); also, terminal band is usually broader towards wing base. Closed tail is patterned more like Hen Harrier below, with a dark terminal band and an inner bar defined more as a dark central patch. On upperwing, flight feathers are generally darker, without dark bar towards coverts. Can, however, be confused with 1st-year female Montagu's with retained uniformly dark juv. secondaries. Facial markings generally more contrasting than on Montagu's, more so with younger females. Eyes encircled by narrower pale zones, especially above eye, and these are separated behind eye by a dark eye-stripe; dark of ear-coverts extends farther forwards towards bill base. Pallid has paler, more sharply defined neck-collar, though this feature not conspicuous on older females. Juv. told from juv. Montagu's by its contrasting head-and-neck markings: bright pale, usually whitish neck-collar is most important character, usually emphasised at rear by a broad dark neck-boa; underparts generally paler, more rusty-yellow, but variation considerable.

Hen Harrier, female and immatures

Ad. female and juv. often very difficult to separate. Ad. females, however, often have paler ground colour below, paler secondaries and coverts and also more washed-out facial markings, though variation considerable. Compared with the two smaller species, Hen is always broader-winged with more rounded wingtip, but its markings are close to Pallid's in overall impression.

Montagu's Harrier

♀

juv ♀

Pallid Harrier

juv ♀

♀

Hen Harrier

♀

juv ♀

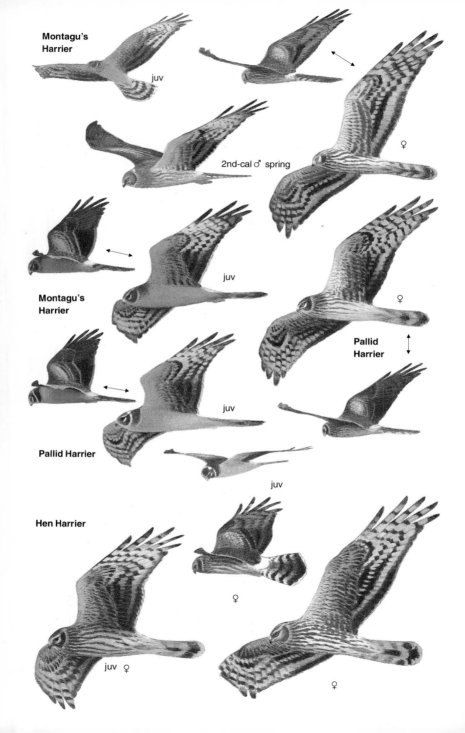

Montagu's Harrier juv

2nd-cal ♂ spring

♀

Montagu's Harrier juv

♀

juv

Pallid Harrier

♀

Pallid Harrier

Pallid Harrier

juv

Hen Harrier

♀

juv ♀

♀

♀

♂

Marsh Harrier   *Circus aeruginosus*   L 48–55 cm, WS 110–125 cm

Immediately recognised as a harrier from its light flight with wings held in shallow V and its long tail. Size and coloration distinguish it from other harriers. Male acquires the pale areas of plumage successively over at least 3 years, and breeds when 2 years old with grey of primaries not very prominent. Female brown with yellow-buff crown, throat and leading edge of wing. Imms. dark chocolate-brown with to varying degree reddish-ochre head markings (fading to yellow-buff), though latter can be entirely absent, probably mainly on eastern populations. Often seen flying back and forth 'suspended' above reedbed, now and then dropping down and disappearing for a while. Male displays high in air with a few Lapwing-like 'way-oo' calls and also utters rather

Magpie-like 'kyepp epp epp epp'. Females, like young off nest, beg with drawn-out, mewing, high whistles, 'pee-wyuu', and also have a 'keesh' and a 'kye ki ki ki' in pair-flight with male. Tied to larger reedbeds but hunts also over marsh and meadowlands. Common in suitable habitats, rare and local in Britain. Feeds on all kinds of small animals and birds, nestlings, frogs etc. Migrates Aug–Oct, most return Apr; odd ones seen in winter.

Sparrowhawk   *Accipiter nisus*   *L 28−38 cm, WS 60−75 cm*

A small, commonly seen raptor with broad blunt wings and long tail. Flies with series of rapid wingbeats (at distance flickers in the sun) alternating with glides with wings half pulled-in. Female considerably bigger than male and can be confused with male Goshawk, though body slimmer and tail appears longer with narrower tail base and square-ended tip. Fully adult male is blue-grey above and to varying extent rust-red on cheeks and flanks. Juv. at distance very like female, above has rufous fringes and below broader wavy barring with rusty-brown elements and heart-shaped, more longitudinal spots on breast. Large white spots are often seen at bases of scapulars on the perched bird. At nest site a monotonously repeated 'kyi-kyi-kyi…' is frequently heard, and during aerial displays also a tern-like ringing call. Common in most types of woodland, open country with isolated groups of trees, also at home near human habitation and readily nests in city parks. Feeds mainly on small birds. Predominantly a resident in Britain and Ireland, but juvs. disperse widely from Aug on; also a passage and winter visitor from Continent, Sep−Apr.

Goshawk   *Accipiter gentilis*   *L 48−61 cm, WS 98−117 cm*

Larger than Sparrowhawk. Female is size of a Buzzard, while smaller male can be confused with female Sparrowhawk; male Goshawk is c25% bigger than female Sparrowhawk in length but 3−4 times as heavy. Flight silhouette is characterised by longer and broader arm, narrower hand and, especially on male, shorter tail which is more uniform in width and has slightly more rounded tip. In active flight, wingbeats slower and more powerful than Sparrowhawk's, body keeps a steadier, more rectilinear course and it sometimes recalls Gyrfalcon. Soars with its wings held level or raised slightly above horizontal. Sometimes flies with stiff, slow wingbeats almost like Short-eared Owl, especially when near nest. Male is lead-grey above and at distance looks uniform pale grey below with pronounced blackish crown and ear-coverts and brilliant white supercilium. Female is more brown-grey above and with less contrast on head. Juv. is clearly streaked below on rusty-buff to pale yellow ground colour, brown above and usually with pale-mottled area on secondary coverts. Becomes successively smaller and darker towards S Europe and conversely larger and paler northeastwards. Ad. of Siberian race *buteoides*, seen rarely in N Europe, looks almost all-white below and juv. has reduced and narrower streaking below on creamy-white ground and is heavily marked with pale above. Alarm call at nest site a powerful and piercing 'kyee kyee kyee…'. Call a melancholy, slightly vibrant 'peee-yeh'. Tied to unbroken wooded areas but also hunts low over open fields and meadows. Feeds mostly on medium-sized birds, rabbits and hares. Causes consternation among crows, which give shrill screams and mob it with great respect and always keeping a line of retreat open. Ad. resident, but many juvs. in nothernmost regions move south in Oct–Nov.

Sparrowhawk   Goshawk   Levant Sparrowhawk

Sparrowhawk

juv ♂

♂

♀

Goshawk

juv ♂

♂

♀ 2nd-cal/
3rd-cal

Levant Sparrowhawk *Accipiter brevipes*   *L 33–38 cm, WS 64–80 cm*

A shade larger and has a slimmer flight silhouette than Sparrowhawk. Difference in size between sexes is less than in Sparrowhawk. Characteristic in flight, with pale (on male almost white) underwings with contrasting black wingtips. Juv. has heavy drop-shaped spotting below (juv. Sparrowhawk has drop markings only in crop area and sometimes on breast). Upperparts dull blue-grey on male. When perched, differs from Sparrowhawk in dark red eye, grey cheeks, unbarred central tail feathers and shorter and more powerful toes. Occurs relatively sparsely in areas with elements of deciduous wood, mainly in low-lying, dry cultivated country; in S Europe Sparrowhawk is found mostly in mountainous districts. Migrates to E Africa mainly in Sep and then appears in dense flocks, does not return until latter part of Apr. Food mainly ground-dwelling animals such as small rodents, reptiles, some birds and insects.   *Map p.134*

Dark Chanting Goshawk *Melierax metabates*   *L 38–48 cm, WS 95–110 cm*

An African species with isolated presence in Sous Valley in Morocco. Pale ash-grey above, with finely barred belly and bright red bill base and legs. Wings broad and hawk-like and tail long. Juv. dark brown above, with bold rusty-brown barring below and dirty-yellow bill and legs. Occurs in savanna-type country, perches upright on top of acacia, bush or lower lookout post.

Sparrowhawk

♀

juv ♂

Goshawk ♂

juv
buteoides

juv

juv ♂

Goshawk

juv ♀

**Dark Chanting
Goshawk**

Honey Buzzard   *Pernis apivorus*   *L 52−60 cm, WS 135−150 cm*

Almost always seen only in flight, circling over woodland or migrating. Like Buzzard, but has narrower neck and Cuckoo-like projecting head as well as longer tail with more rounded corners. Soars on flat wings, slightly arched in gliding flight. Straight rear edge of wing and well-projecting carpal joints are characteristic in gliding flight. Wingbeats flexible and slightly swinging. Dull grey (male) to grey-brown (female) above, usually paler on primaries, and very variable below from almost entirely dark brown to almost pure white. Barring on tail is diagnostic: one broad outer band and two narrower ones towards base. Underpart markings are formed by coarsely defined transverse blotching which forms bars along wings. Males have greyer head and generally less barring on flight feathers below than females. Juv. very variable, commonest type dark brown and, owing to more regular barring on wings and tail, very like Buzzard. In addition to silhouette, the darker secondaries, bright yellow bare parts and (on pale-headed individuals) dark eye-mask are distinguishing features. Never has Buzzard's pale area on midriff. Eye yellow in ad., dark in juv. Call a clear, slightly piteous 'peee-lu'. Feeds mainly on wasp larvae, which it digs out; hardly ever seen perched in open. Migrates to tropical Africa in latter part of Aug−Sep, returns in May.

Buzzard   *Buteo buteo*   *L 51−57 cm, WS 113−128 cm*

A medium-sized, predominantly dark brown raptor, in flight with broad rounded wings with distinct pale patches at primary bases. Soars with wings raised in shallow V, glides with flat or slightly arched wings. Hovers only rarely, but often hangs motionless in wind. Coloration variable, usually dark brown with pale band over 'midriff', intermediate types whitish-buff and richly patterned brown below. Ad. has a broad blackish terminal band on wing and tail, juv. is slimmer-winged and generally more streaked below than ad. Usually wholly dark above or with a somewhat paler panel over median coverts, sometimes paler at tail base. Confused with Honey Buzzard, but has broader head, shorter tail with pointed corners, V-held wings when soaring, and appears stiffer-winged and more compact. Very pale individuals are rare in Britain. Eastern races (*vulpinus* in Russia, *menetriesi* in Middle East) have overall more rusty-coloured plumage. The race *vulpinus* is possibly a full species, the Steppe Buzzard, which is a long-distance migrant to E Africa: noticeably smaller than Buzzard and often has rusty tail (see also Long-legged Buzzard). Call a more or less drawn-out plaintive or mewing whistle, 'peee-ay'. The Buzzard is one of the most widespread and abundant raptors in Europe, common in cultivated country with groups of trees or wooded regions bordering pastureland, arable land, bogs, clearings and other open terrain for hunting. Often perches on exposed telegraph poles and in trees. Feeds on rodents, young birds, snakes, frogs, worms, insects etc. Most Scandinavian breeders migrate southwest in Sep−Nov, returning Mar−Apr.

Honey Buzzard

Buzzard

138

Honey Buzzard

juv

♂

♀

♂

Buzzard

juv

ad

pale juv

ad

pale juv

Long-legged Buzzard *Buteo rufinus* L 50−65 cm, WS 126−155 cm

A big, long-winged and usually pale buzzard, very like Rough-legged in proportions, wing attitude and actions but with predominantly buff and rusty-red coloration. Does not hover so frequently as latter, but often hangs motionless in wind. Colour pattern variable; typical is pale, almost unmarked head and breast with rusty-brown belly-sides and 'trousers', underwing-coverts pale buff to pale brown-red contrasting with darker belly-sides and a dark carpal patch. Tail pale, rusty-tinted with paler, often whitish, base and rust-coloured rump, on juv. more buff-grey with faint barring; rarely with narrow dark terminal band. Upperwing shows characteristic paler area on leading primaries, most marked on imms., and also rust-coloured lesser coverts contrasting with brown secondaries. Head markings often reduced to merely a darker line behind eye, faint moustachial stripe and dark triangle on nape. Also occurs, above all in easternmost areas, in a dark phase, which is predominantly dark brown with whitish tail showing darker barring, though with paler inner primaries. In N Africa race *cirtensis* (possibly a full species), which is smaller and more Buzzard-like in silhouette and often paler. Long-legged is never barred on belly like ad. Buzzards. Most easily confused with Steppe Buzzard (see under Buzzard), though latter is smaller, shorter-winged, with entire tail pale buff to rust-coloured and faintly barred. When perched, more elongated, with longer tarsus and bigger bill than Buzzard. Call Buzzard-like but fuller and less plaintive. Occurs in open, often mountainous country, on dry steppes and in desert, in winter often in cultivated areas. Regularly sits on look-out on posts and low vantage points, also walks on ground. Feeds on various smaller mammals, mainly rodents. Partial migrant in Europe and C Asia.

Rough-legged Buzzard *Buteo lagopus* L 50−60 cm, WS 120−150 cm

Slightly larger than Buzzard, longer-winged, usually paler, and always recognised by white tail with dark terminal band. Regularly hovers. Soars with wings held in V; glides with inner part of arm raised and hand bent flat, producing characteristic kink. White leading edge of wing and carpal often well visible in head-on views. Juv. very pale below with contrasting solid brown-black belly and dark carpal patches, and above has pale markings over primaries. Older birds have more barred belly and more-intense dark markings on breast, head and underwing-coverts. Males darker than females, with one broad and 2−4 narrower bands at tail-tip; females have more ochre and buff above, paler breast and head, and only 2−3 tail bands which merge together and at distance look like a single broad terminal band. Dark males sometimes resemble Buzzard, but tail markings and combination of dark throat and pale forehead, weaker bill and feathered tarsi diagnostic. A predominantly tundra species which is dependent on small rodents for breeding, in some years also nests down into the taiga of Fennoscandia. In winter on fields and meadows in open cultivated country. Migrates Sep−Oct, returns Apr−May. Scarce winter visitor to Britain, mainly Oct−Apr.

Long-legged Buzzard

Rough-legged Buzzard

typical

ad typical

ad brown-red

juv

Long-legged Buzzard

ad

juv

ad

juv

ad

Rough-legged Buzzard

ad ♂

juv

ad ♂

ad ♂ typical

ad ♀ typical

ad ♂ dark

juv
pale

juv
rusty

ad ♂ pale

**Honey
Buzzard**

juv dark

juv

ad ♂

Buzzard ad
typical

ad pale

2nd-cal autumn/
3rd-cal spring

**Rough-legged
Buzzard**

juv

ad

**Long-legged
Buzzard**

juv

ad
typical

juv dark

Steppe Buzzard

ad
red

ad
brown

juv

ad dark

White-tailed Eagle

White-tailed Eagle   *Haliaeetus albicilla*   L 77–92 cm, WS 200–245 cm

The largest N European raptor, always an overwhelming sight in the field. Wings rectangular and uniformly broad and dominate the silhouette compared with the short wedge-shaped tail. When soaring, wings held flat or faintly raised and slightly arched. When gliding, wings are pressed forward with relatively jutting carpals and often with drooping hand, the long 'fingers' splayed and conspicuous. Active flight with series of shallow wingbeats and short glides, sometimes beats wings surprisingly quickly. Ads. are easily identified by their white tail and their pale head with huge, pale yellow bill. Imms. can be confused with other eagles, mainly Spotted. It takes c5 years for White-tailed to acquire ad. plumage; entirely pale buff head and pale yellow iris are typical only from 8–10 years old. A specific feature of younger birds is the pale feather bases to the axillaries, pale buff on 1st-years, whiter in subsequent plumages, an important character compared with Spotted Eagle. Subad. consistently has a very variegated plumage, feathers of belly, greater and median underwing-coverts and back being whitish with dark brown tips. White-tailed Eagle hunts mainly along sea coasts, at lakes and other wetlands. Builds stick nest in trees, along Norwegian coast more commonly on cliff ledges. Most ads. resident, but imms. roam about and are found at lowland lakes outside breeding range (e.g. regular in winter NE France); reintroduced W Scotland in 1975, now breeds regularly in small numbers. Call consists of a series of stuttering yelps, 'kyick, kyick, kyick…', like Black Woodpecker's spring territorial call. Takes fish, seabirds and all kinds of carrion.

Pallas's Fish Eagle
Haliaeetus leucoryphus   L 70–84 cm, WS 180–205 cm

Somewhat smaller than White-tailed Eagle and with slimmer build. Ad. distinctive, with black band on tip of white tail. Juv. like subad. White-tailed, but more uniform and paler brown and with pale panel on inner primaries below. A C Asiatic species, tied to fish-rich lakes. Rare visitor to Caspian and Black Seas. Recorded a few times in Europe outside the Soviet Union.

White-tailed Eagle

ad

juv

Pallas's Fish Eagle

2nd-winter

2nd-winter

juv

White-tailed Eagle

juv

ad

juv

ad

ad *heliaca*

ad

Golden Eagle   **Imperial Eagle**   **Steppe Eagle**

Golden Eagle   *Aquila chrysaetos*   *L 76–89 cm, WS 190–227 cm*

A huge raptor, having nicely balanced silhouette with long tail and long supple and elastic wings. In gliding or soaring flight wings are held in a flat V, which is characteristic of the species. In the field older birds often look all-dark below and rather variegated buff, grey and dark brown above. Juv. dark chocolate-brown with white wing patches and inner part of tail, markings which stand out at long range. Juv.-like flight and tail feathers in both 2nd and 3rd winters, secondary coverts more pale-mottled than on juv. Pale tail with dark terminal band not lost until in 5th or 6th cal-year (see also p.17). Golden Eagles farther south, mainly in N Africa and Asia Minor, are darker overall than in N Europe: ad. has less pale on secondary coverts above and a more brown-red than golden-yellow nape-shawl; imms. have the species-characteristic white or pale wing and tail markings but they are often reduced. Builds big nest of twigs on cliff ledges or in big sturdy pines. Older pairs usually remain within breeding area in winter. Hunts hares, small rodents and birds and also takes dead game. Dives from high up or surprises prey in low-level flight like Hen Harrier. From late autumn performs aerial displays, when male makes mock attacks at female whereupon the two cartwheel while dropping towards ground; may then utter a sonorous 'kluee'. Some imms. from N Europe move southwards in winter.

Golden Eagle

Imperial Eagle

Tawny Eagle   Steppe Eagle

146

Golden Eagle

juv

subad (4th-cal/ 5th-cal)

ad

ad

juv

Imperial Eagle   *Aquila heliaca*   *L 75–84 cm, WS 180–215 cm*

Two races in Europe: in Iberia *adalberti*, with white scapular patches and white leading edge to wing; in east *heliaca*, with white only on scapulars. Ad. tar-black with creamy shawl and pale grey to grey tail with black terminal band. In flight, ad. almost always has closed tail of uniform width which looks small and narrow. Wings long and narrow, flat when soaring, in gliding flight not uncommonly with slightly raised arm and with hand more level. Juv. has a more rounded, less angular flight silhouette and soars with tail spread. Juv. brown-red (*adalberti*) to brown (*heliaca*), but fades and acquires a pale milky-tea colour: lacks Steppe Eagle's white bar on underwing and is often clearly streaked on breast/upper belly; lower back, rump and uppertail-coverts are more uniformly pale, without contrastingly pale uppertail-coverts. Subad. often becomes checkered as dark feathers appear first on head and then here and there on body. Call a deep and slightly goose-like 'gahk', at nest site repeated in well-spaced series. Hunts in open, flat or slightly hilly cultivated country, on steppe or around river deltas. Usually nests on wooded ridges or mountain hillocks. Rare and local in Spain (only c60 pairs), more widespread in east. Takes sousliks and other small rodents, young birds, some waterfowl and carrion. Resident or short-distance migrant; older birds less inclined to migrate. Only few at passage sites in Middle East, mostly imms. in Sep–Oct and mid Feb–Mar.   *Map p. 146*

Steppe Eagle   *Aquila nipalensis*   *L 67–86 cm, WS 175–230 cm*

Size of Imperial Eagle. Soars on level wings and often with hand slightly lowered. Wings often held straight out from body and slightly bent back at carpal, wings appear very long and narrow at 'wrist', they often look markedly bulging; tail longer and more rounded than on Imperial and sometimes looks a trifle wedge-shaped. Bill smaller than Imperial's but stronger than on the spotted eagles and with long bright yellow gape-line. Ad. fairly uniformly dark tobacco-brown below on body and lesser wing-coverts, often with visibly paler throat; flight and tail feathers are normally paler and greyer, typically with dark barring and with a broader terminal band. All-dark above, with paler bases to primaries and on c75% of birds a pale patch on back and sometimes a mid-brown or rusty-brown patch on nape, though head looks all-dark at distance (*cf* Imperial Eagle). Varies in darkness, however, and often difficult to tell from spotted eagles. Some subads. are pale 'milk-coffee'-coloured. Juv. has characteristic broad white band on underwing, which is partly retained until at least a couple of years of age. Imms. have darker back than Imperial, with pronounced whitish half-moon on uppertail-coverts. Relatively common on steppe and in semi-desert. In Europe and east to Altai Mountains race *orientalis*, winters mainly in E Africa. Farther east and in Tibet/Mongolia race *nipalensis*, somewhat bigger and winters mainly in Indian subcontinent. Migrates in large numbers through Middle East, ads. mainly mid Feb to mid Mar, imms. later, up to mid Apr, and southwards end Sep to mid Nov. Very rare in Europe outside Soviet Union, though imms. recorded several times in Scandinavia and NE Europe. Takes mostly sousliks in breeding season.   *Map p. 146*

Tawny Eagle   *Aquila rapax*   *L 65–77 cm, WS 170–205 cm*

Very like Steppe Eagle, formerly considered conspecific. Nominate race breeds in large parts of tropical Africa and *vindhiana* in Indian peninsula. In N Africa *belisarius*, rare, mainly in Sous Valley in Morocco in low-lying savanna with acacias (also Djelfa region in N Algeria and in southwesternmost part of Arabian Peninsula). Varies in colour, ads. of N Africa race often paler, more grey-brown than Steppe Eagle. Juv. differs from Steppe in lack of white band on underwing.   *Map p.146*

ad *adalberti*

Imperial Eagle

juv

ad *adalberti*

juv

heliaca subad/ad

Imperial Eagle subad

Steppe Eagle juv

Tawny Eagle subad

ad

juv

Steppe Eagle

Spotted Eagle   *Aquila clanga*   L 62–74 cm, WS 158–182 cm

Often difficult to distinguish from Lesser Spotted Eagle. Is generally somewhat bigger, broader-winged and gives a more compact impression, and to a certain extent recalls White-tailed Eagle. Both spotted eagles have characteristic habit of depressing hand in flight, most pronounced when gliding. When soaring, Spotted has more level wings, arm may occasionally even be slightly raised but hand always droops a little. On subad. and ad. colours are generally darker brown than on Lesser Spotted, often look all-dark with pale only on primary shafts and as an edging to tail-coverts. Older birds often have a slightly paler chocolate-brown tone to wing-coverts and body. Imms. have a black-brown ground colour with conspicuous pale drop-shaped spots on secondary coverts and white rump. Below, contrast between dark wing-coverts and slightly paler flight feathers is a good character compared with Lesser Spotted. Spotted is less migratory than Lesser Spotted and is virtually the only one of the two that is found in Europe in winter. Most, however, move south in Sep–Nov to Middle East and E Mediterranean. Call at nest site resembles Lesser Spotted's. Nests in woodland near water and often perches for long periods low down, often on ground, on look-out for frogs and water voles. Smaller mammals, young birds and carrion are also included in diet.

Lesser Spotted Eagle   *Aquila pomarina*   L 57–64 cm, WS 134–160 cm

A small, well-proportioned eagle with long wings of uniform width. In soaring and gliding flight wings are held angled downwards or slightly arched from carpal outwards. Generally smaller, lighter and a shade more slender in build than Spotted Eagle, but these two species should be separated by plumage characters. Variations in colour, patterning, moult phases and observation conditions, however, make some examples of both species very difficult to identify specifically. At distance in the field often looks all-dark below, but wings have chocolate-brown to buff coverts contrasting faintly with slightly darker flight feathers compared with the reverse in Spotted Eagle — an important identification feature. Above, has pale patches at bases of inner primaries which are more distinct than on Spotted Eagle and are also restricted to the inner primaries. The lesser coverts on upperwing are, especially on older birds, clearly paler, camel-hair-coloured, contrasting with darker flight feathers and a darker scapular/ mantle region. Can also be confused with subad. Steppe Eagle, but has weaker bill and more constantly 'drooping' hand. Often perches like Buzzard and watches for prey from fenceposts and similar lookouts, often from small elevations directly on ground. At nest site announces itself with series of slightly squeaky but loud 'kyeek, kyeek…' calls. Relatively common in larger forested areas bordering open meadows and wetlands. Feeds on small mammals, frogs and insects. Migrates to E Africa at end of Aug–Sep. Annual in Scandinavia, mostly in south in Aug–Sep.

Spotted Eagle

Lesser Spotted Eagle

Spotted Eagle

ad

juv 'fulvescens'

juv

juv

juv

ad

ad

juv

Lesser Spotted Eagle

ad

ad

juv

ad

Pair of Bonelli's Eagles hunting

Bonelli's Eagle *Hieraaetus fasciatus*   *L 70–74 cm, WS 150–170 cm*

A medium-sized eagle, looks powerful and a bit hawk-like. Soars with level wing posture, often with wings straight out from body but also slightly pressed forward. Glides with slightly arched wings and typically with straight rear edge. Ad. characteristically marked, though extent of white on underwing-coverts and back varies. Juv. pale brownish-pink to rich rusty-red below on body and wing-coverts, palest on belly and in a band over median coverts, and with variably narrow dark band framing underwing-coverts; inner primaries often translucent, producing pale panel against the light. Subad. darker brown and with broader dark band along greater coverts. Patrols mountainsides and hills when hunting, often in pairs. Uncommon and local, in N Africa more common in mountainous regions. Hunts also over plains, river deltas and wetlands. Feeds on birds and small mammals. Strongly resident, but imms. occasionally seen at migration watchpoints.

Booted Eagle *Hieraaetus pennatus*   *L 45–50 cm, WS 110–132 cm*

Smallest eagle, size of a buzzard. Occurs in a pale and a dark form. At distance, pale form is dirty-white with dark flight feathers, grey tail and grey-buff head and breast. Dark form easily confused with Black Kite and subad. Bonelli's Eagle: varies in ground colour from cinnamon-brown to black-brown, from below often looks all-dark with a slight translucency of inner primaries and a paler warm-toned tail, which is diffusely darker towards tip; greater underwing-coverts are darker, blackish, forming slight contrast with median/lesser coverts. Pale upperpart markings and white 'position lights' at wing-join characteristic on both forms. When soaring, wings are held slightly pressed forward while hand tends backwards in a highly characteristic gentle curve, giving impression that wing is not completely extended. Noisy at nest site. Calls rather wader-like, include a 'heeup', quite like Ringed Plover, and in display flight a short 'chee-dee', sometimes vibrant and drawn out in long series. Scarce to relatively common around wooded mountains and hilly country. Takes rodents, young birds, reptiles and insects. Migrates south mainly in Sep and returns Mar–Apr. Resident in Menorca.

Bonelli's Eagle

Booted Eagle

Short-toed Eagle

Bonelli's Eagle

subad

ad

Booted Eagle

dark

pale

pale

Short-toed Eagle   *Circaetus gallicus*   L 62–67 cm, WS 170–185 cm

Usually found singly or in pairs, regularly hovers or hangs on upwinds. A big pale raptor with broad, quite flexible wings, relatively small body and narrow, square-ended tail. Soars with wings held level and has for its size a 'compact' hand, the relatively pale primary tips often being held well together. Markings below variable: some individuals almost all-white, while others are densely and coarsely patterned dark, majority having darker breast/head area. Lacks dark carpal patches typical of pale buzzards and Osprey and has 3–4 well-visible bands on tail. Above, usually has pale grey-buff secondary coverts and bright white markings at base of outer tail feathers (conspicuous only when tail spread). The big, rather owl-like head is most obvious when bird perched or in display flight; feet washed-out grey to blue-grey. Usually silent but in display gives repeated soft mewing 'giup'. Relatively common in Mediterranean countries, scarce in C Europe, in open, often hilly country with wooded elements. Feeds mainly on reptiles and often hunts over sun-warmed hillsides. Migrates mostly in Sep and returns from end of Feb to Apr.   *Map p. 152*

Osprey

juv

♂

Osprey   *Pandion haliaetus*   L 55–69 cm, WS 145–160 cm

A big narrow-winged raptor, pale below with dark secondaries and dark carpal patch, pale head with dark eye-band. Female and juv. have more pronounced breast-band on buff background. Fishes rivers and fish ponds and larger lakes and sea bays. When circling or gliding above water is easily taken for immature large gull on account of silhouette, characterised by rather projecting carpals and narrow hand with latter drooping. Fairly soon it rises up and hovers with deep wingbeats and dangling legs, and gull impression completely disappears. On sighting suitable prey it often descends in stages and then dives at good speed, often disappearing completely beneath surface. Male's display call over territory is a piteous 'ueelp...ueelp...ueelp...'. Contact call a loud ricocheting 'pyeepp', at nest repeated 'pyew, pyew, pyew...'. Builds big stick nest at top of tall pine, often exposed on e.g. an islet, occasionally far from water. Winters in tropical W Africa, some in W Mediterranean; migrates Aug–Sep, returning Apr–May.

Red-footed Falcon   *Falco vespertinus*   L 28−31 cm, WS 65−75 cm

A small falcon, less powerful than Hobby and for most part recalls a short-tailed Kestrel. Both sexes fairly unmistakable. Female has rusty-orange to pale yellow crown and abdomen, in contrast to grey dark-barred upperparts. Female and juv. have black 'highwayman's mask', always with paler forehead than juv. Hobby. 1st-summer males variable, often like ad. but with elements of paler rufous feathers on head (usually paler cheeks) and underparts. Flight and tail feathers (though central pair replaced) are juvenile in 1st-summer, i.e. barred below. Often perches on telegraph wires and posts. Hovers regularly and catches dragonflies and other insects in air like Hobby, often late at dusk. Sociable, breeds mostly in colonies in Rook nests. Occurs on open heath and cultivated steppe, often adjoining wetlands. Also takes young birds and frogs during breeding season. Rare but annual visitor to Britain in association with high pressure to the east, mainly in May−Jun (Apr−Oct).

Kestrel   *Falco tinnunculus*   L 33−39 cm, WS 65−80 cm

Often seen hovering or perched on wires and posts beside roads, when its long-tailed silhouette is characteristic. Sexes often alike at distance. Male has grey head, grey tail lacking narrow bars, and is more brick-red and less marked on back. Female and juv. alike, but ad. female more distinctly marked above and has more heart-shaped spots which are also repeated on belly-sides, juv. being more streaked below. Noisy at nest site, gives sharp piercing, sometimes somewhat rasping 'kee kee kee kee...' in rapid series or single 'kee' calls. Begs with drawn-out whining trill, 'kree'e'e'e'e'. Common in cultivated country with fields and meadows, on heaths, moors and bogs up to willow zone in mountains. Breeds in old crow nests, tree holes or on cliff or building ledge, locally sometimes in small colonies like Lesser Kestrel. Takes rodents, terrestrial birds, frogs and insects. Mainly resident in Britain, but northern/eastern populations migratory.

Hobby   *Falco subbuteo*   L 28−35 cm, WS 70−84 cm

More 'muscular' than Kestrel and Red-footed Falcon, speedier and more powerful in its actions, and at distance can be confused with Peregrine. Flight silhouette marked by long pointed wings and short tail, looks dark below with prominent white cheeks. Ad. has red 'trousers' and vent, lacking on juv. which also has slightly paler crown and narrow pale feather edges above. Captures its prey, birds and insects, almost exclusively in the air. Often hunts dragonflies over marshes and reedbeds on summer evenings, when flight slow and more like Red-footed's. Call at nest site 'kew-kew-kew...', very varied, sometimes almost like Lesser Spotted Woodpecker, or 'ki-ki-ki...'. Breeds in crow nest in tree clumps or open woodland. Winters in Africa south of equator. Migrates Aug–Sep, returning end Apr–May.

Red-footed Falcon

Kestrel

Hobby

2nd-cal
♂

juv

**Red-footed
Falcon**

♀

♂

Kestrel
juv

Kestrel ♂

Hobby

juv

♂

Sooty Falcon

♀

juv

Lesser Kestrel   *Falco naumanni*   L 29−32 cm, WS 58−72 cm

Ad. male differs from Kestrel in blue-grey greater secondary coverts and unmarked rusty-red mantle and in less patterned underwings. 2nd-cal-year male lacks the blue-grey above and has juv. flight feathers and parts of tail (barred feathers). Female very like Kestrel, but has shorter tail, usually with slightly projecting central feathers, and also paler underwings. Claws white (black on Kestrel). Calls more frail and often hoarse in tone compared with Kestrel's: a hoarse 'kye-kye' or 'kye-kiki'. Female begs with a piercing high vibrating call. Scarce to locally common in cultivated country, hunts mostly over pastures. Has declined greatly in S Europe. Nests colonially on rock faces, ruins and buildings. Feeds mainly on insects. Migrates in Aug−Sep and returns in Mar−Apr (end of Feb in N Africa).

Sooty Falcon   *Falco concolor*   L 33−36 cm, WS 78−90 cm

Between Hobby and Eleonora's Falcon in size. Direct and powerful in flight, gliding on level wings. Slim and long-winged; long tail has longer central feathers, often looks pointed. Ad. grey-blue with darker primaries and tail-tip. Male has yellow-orange cere, eye-ring and legs, on female more lemon-yellow. Juv. like juv. Hobby but dirtier, more yellow-brown on cheeks and underparts and less distinctly marked below. Has dark extension on rear end of ear-coverts like juv. Hobby and unlike Eleonora's. Catches migrating passerines, arrives Apr−May, nests Aug−Sep on coral islands in Red Sea and on cliffs in desert. Migrates Oct.

Eleonora's Falcon   *Falco eleonorae*   L 36−42 cm, WS 90−105 cm

Very slim and delicate with conspicuously longer tail than Hobby and Peregrine. Two colour phases (with intermediates), the dark one in the minority. In the field looks a dark bird; pale phase rusty-tinted below with contrasting pale throat and cheeks. Underwing shows contrast between darker coverts and paler bases to flight feathers (absent on juv. Sooty Falcon and Hobby). Juv. paler below and barred on flight feathers. Nests colonially on cliff precipices by the sea and mainly on islands. Often glides effortlessly along coast or soars, several together, around a cliff summit. Playful and acrobatic in the air. Nests in Aug−Sep, when hunts migrating passerines over open sea; also takes insects. Calls slightly creaky 'kye-kye-kye-kye-kye-kye'. Migrates in Oct, mostly to Madagascar, returns in Apr.

Lesser Kestrel

Sooty Falcon

Eleonora's Falcon

♀

♂

♂ 2nd-cal spring

♂

♂

♀

Lesser Kestrel

♀

Eleonora's Falcon

pale phase

dark phase

♀

♂

Peregrine   *Falco peregrinus*   L 39−50 cm, WS 95−115 cm

Most widespread of the larger falcons, compact and deep-chested with broad-based pointed wings. Flies with shallow elastic wingbeats in which tips very springy (characteristic of the larger falcons). Ad. steel-grey above with paler blue-grey rump and tail base; below with dark bars on belly, at distance often looks grey with contrasting pale breast. Broad conspicuous black moustachial stripe. Juv. slightly slimmer in profile and browner above, tone varying from buff-grey to blackish-brown, yellow-buff to whitish below with longitudinal streaking; moustachial stripe is generally narrower, has paler forehead and pale supercilium and also grey-blue to greenish-blue cere. Around Mediterranean and in Middle East race *brookei*, which is smaller, more buff below and more heavily marked. Strikes medium-sized birds in the air, either by outflying them or with stooping dives from high up with closed wings. Creates great alarm among resting birds. Breeds mostly on cliff ledges, in N Finland also on tussocks in middle of bogs. At nest gives stuttering 'ka-yack' calls and shrill 'kek-kek-kek-kek' in alarm. Following catastrophic decline during 1900s has increased in parts of N Europe, common in e.g. Scotland. Winters in open terrain where bird prey common, often on coasts. Migrant in N Europe, from where some visit Britain in winter.

Barbary Falcon   *Falco pelegrinoides*   L 34−40 cm, WS 90−100 cm

Slightly smaller than Peregrine, but closely similar and possibly a race of latter. Ad. somewhat paler grey above and more finely patterned below. Cheeks and underparts often buffish-pink. Rusty-red (male) or buffish (female) across nape and has narrower moustachial stripe and paler ear-coverts than Peregrine of race *brookei*. Differs from ad. Lanner in paler mantle, finer more vermiculated markings below and less clearly barred tail above. Juv. like Peregrine, but has buff band across nape. Replaces Peregrine in desert regions.

Merlin   *Falco columbarius*   L 25−30 cm, WS 60−65 cm

Our smallest raptor, has markedly compact flight silhouette. Wings short and broad at base, though tail long and conspicuously square-ended. Can be taken for Peregrine when size comparison not possible. Often sweeps low over the ground and surprises small birds, makes prolonged aerial pursuits. Wingbeats powerful and shearing, in final advance upon prey with Mistle Thrush-like flight, possibly a camouflage ploy. Male clearly smaller than female, with greyish-blue and rusty tones. Female dark brown above and heavily patterned below, sometimes with ash-grey feather bases above and then relatively pale. Alarm call at nest a persistent, very rapid 'kikikiki...'. Nests beside open terrain with plenty of small birds, e.g. upland moors, bogs and swamps, in Britain often on grouse moors. In Britain and Ireland mostly resident, moving to lower areas in winter; also passage and winter visitor in small numbers from Iceland and perhaps N Europe.

Peregrine

Barbary Falcon

Merlin

Peregrine

Merlin

♂

♂

juv

♂

♀

Peregrine

Saker

Lanner

Lanner   *Falco biarmicus*   L 43–52 cm, WS 95–115 cm

Size of a Peregrine, flight silhouette somewhat slimmer with uniformly broad and longer wings and tail, ad. with more rounded wingtip. In Europe represented by race *feldeggi*. Ad. brown-grey above with darker barring, male with rusty and female with buff nape and supercilium from eye backwards. Often paler than Peregrine below, ad. male especially often has barring reduced to belly-sides, in flight often looks all-pale below with only wingtips darker; female more coarsely marked on underparts, more so on younger birds. Ad. of N African *erlangeri* is smaller and more Peregrine-like in flight silhouette, less spotted below, and paler, more grey above. Juv. of both races is noticeably slimmer than ad., is browner above and heavily streaked dark below. Upperparts seldom with distinct pale feather edges, and these more concentrated at tips than on Saker. As in Saker, in flight shows sharp contrast between pale flight feathers and dark-marked belly and greater coverts below. Head pattern very like juv. Saker's: dark eye-stripe and moustachial stripe join at the dark eye and make the pale orbital ring stand out more clearly; also, dark streaking often forms a 'diadem' over forehead which cuts off eyebrow band at front edge of eye. Rare in Europe, rather more common in N Africa, mainly in dry, mountainous regions inland. Resident and nomadic. European race feeds mostly on birds, N African race more on ground-dwelling animals.

Map p. 164

Saker   *Falco cherrug*   L 48–57 cm, WS 110–125 cm

Size of Gyrfalcon and normally appears bigger than Lanner. In flight slimmer than Gyrfalcon, with narrower tail base and more pointed wings. Often circles high up with level wings and closed tail. Active flight, powerful with springy wingtips. Ad. grey-brown above with paler, warmer-toned feather edges, in worn plumage whole upperparts appear warm brown. C Asian populations generally more red-brown above. In W Palearctic normally lacks barring on mantle, though a rare variant has greyer ground colour above and with dark barring. Head strikingly pale with whitish-buff crown. Dark markings below variable, ad. always streaked (never barred) and most intensely on belly-sides and 'trousers'. On underwing, contrast between pale flight feathers and dark-marked coverts characteristic, but can be absent on very pale individuals. Juv. more heavily streaked below, is very like juv. Lanner: mantle is often warmer brown and a shade paler than the dark markings on flanks; head markings vary in intensity, often more streaked on crown than ad.; supercilium extends forward to and partly joins with pale forehead, area in front of eye is paler and moustache very faint or lacking under eye, making orbital ring less obvious. Feet and cere yellow or nondescript greyish-yellow on ad., more grey-blue on juv. Rare in open steppe and cultivated country with wooded elements or groups of trees. Often perches on telegraph poles in flatlands. Partly resident in Europe, but some migrate south or southeast. Feeds largely on sousliks and other rodents, but also on birds in winter.

Map p. 164

Barbary Falcon
juv ♂

Lanner

♀

♂

Lanner ♂

Saker

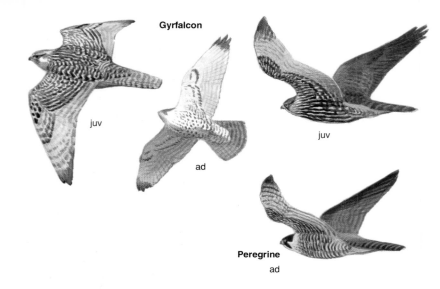

Gyrfalcon

juv

ad

juv

Peregrine
ad

Gyrfalcon   *Falco rusticolus*   *L 55–60 cm, WS 125–135 cm*

Size of female Goshawk, but in every respect a falcon with long pointed wings. Differs from Peregrine in larger size, broader wing bases and tail and slower wing action. Varies in coloration, some can be almost entirely lead-grey, and some in high-arctic regions (the closest in Greenland) are wholly white with a few dark spots; averages paler in Iceland than in Scandinavia. Ad. has yellowish cere and legs and is barred on flanks. Juv. streaked below and with blue-grey to greenish cere and feet. Typical juv. in Scandinavia dark brown-grey above, with dense dark streaking below; normally has less prominent moustachial stripe and is more streaked on cheeks than juv. Peregrine, at distance looks very dark. Underwing on juv. shows contrast between dark coverts and lighter flight feathers. Wing action at times like Goshawk's, but latter has shorter wings and fuller, more rounded wingtips. In fast flight, more supple and slimmer-winged and can look very like Peregrine. Alarm call a coarse and urgent 'kerreh-kerreh-kerreh…'. Very much an arctic raptor, breeding on tundra and high mountain around the whole N Hemisphere. Feeds on grouse and ptarmigan and eats dead animals, so able to remain all year in arctic regions; waders, ducks and lemmings are other important prey in breeding season. Many juvs. move south in late autumn, and winter along shores and on inland plains, occasionally reach Britain. Often hunts close to ground and regularly perches on low lookout.

Lanner

Saker

Gyrfalcon

164

Gyrfalcon

juv

ad

ad

ad

Red-footed Falcon ♀ ♂

Kestrel juv ♂

Kestrel ♂

ad

juv

Hobby

Red-footed Falcon
juv

Hobby
juv

Eleonora's Falcon
juv

Merlin
juv/♀

Peregrine
juv

Lanner
♂ *erlangeri*

Lanner
juv

Saker
juv

display
flight ♂

Willow Grouse ♂ summer

Ptarmigan ♂ summer

Ptarmigan   *Lagopus mutus*   L 34–36 cm, WS 54–60 cm

The two *Lagopus* species are difficult to separate in certain plumages. In winter they are usually seen in single-species flocks and black lores of cock Ptarmigan (absent on female) are then a good character. In both species male has as many as four plumage changes a year and female three, all so as to merge into the changing colours and snow patterns of their surroundings. Male in summer and autumn is more grey than Willow Grouse. Female in summer plumage variable, but more pale yellow-grey and with more irregularly spotted markings (big dark spots on mantle, uneven change-over to paler belly and so on) than Willow Grouse; in autumn, female resembles autumn-plumaged male. Male's call on rising is a dry crackling 'hurr-hurrrrr', like a male Garganey, with similar calls in display. Female has a low 'kuk'. During breeding season mostly high above the tree line in boulder zone, where often relatively tame and even inquisitive if it has young nearby. Occurs on rocky and gravelly slopes and plateaux in the Alps as race *helveticus* and in Pyrenees as race *pyrenaicus*, usually at 2000–3500 m, where it is the only gallinaceous bird with white wings. Feeds on insects, berries, shoots and leaf buds. Chicks are dependent on insects as food, so species is severely hit by persistent rain and cold in early summer.   Map p. 170

Willow Grouse   *Lagopus lagopus*   L 37–42 cm, WS 55–66 cm

In spring and autumn cock is recognised by its liver-red to greyish brown-red plumage colours. During spring in the most intensive period of display cock has liver-red head, neck and breast area, rest of body being all-white (dark feathers gradually break through in the white). Hen differs from hen Ptarmigan during summer months in heavier, more uniform patterning and deeper buff, in part brick-coloured tones, but variation is great. Male's slightly hysterical laughing call, which often issues suddenly from within the birch forest or willow scrub, has a weird, almost human character and not infrequently startles fell-walkers. It is a nasal, clamorous and slightly frog-like 'ke-uk kehehuhuhuhuhu', and display call is a similarly-toned but evenly accelerating series of 'frog croaks'. Hen has a softer 'vehk'. Occurs in mixed forested land up to willow region in mountains. Food as Ptarmigan's.   Map p. 170

♂ summer

♂ spring

Ptarmigan

♂ winter

♂ winter

Willow Grouse

♂ spring

♀ winter

Red Grouse   *Lagopus lagopus scoticus*   *L 37–42 cm, WS 55–66 cm*

Race of Willow Grouse confined to heather moors of Britain and Ireland. Both in flight and on ground appears very dark, with wholly dark grey-brown wings. Cock liver-brown, hen a shade paler, more buff, and both sexes relatively more buff in summer. Call as that of nominate race. Occurs commonly on large treeless heather moors, in winter uncommonly on cultivated fields. Feeds chiefly on heather throughout the year. Habits otherwise as Willow Grouse.

Ptarmigan

Willow Grouse

Red Grouse

♂ autumn

♀ summer

Ptarmigan

♂ autumn

♀ summer

Willow Grouse

Capercaillie

Capercaillie   *Tetrao urogallus*   L 60−87 cm, WS 87−125 cm

Our largest grouse, male c40% bigger than female and large as a goose. Female is bigger than hen Black Grouse, identified by big rust-red patch on breast and longer more rounded tail, which is conspicuously rufous brown. During courtship period from end Mar to May, cocks gather at special sites in the forest to display at dawn. Display 'song', which is roughly 7 seconds long, consists of bill-clicking followed by a gulp and finally a saw-whetting call. Droppings (thickness of little finger) on the ground often reveal Capercaillie's presence in an area. Very much a forest bird, it prefers older coniferous forest, especially pine with elements of deciduous trees and small bogs with plenty of berry-bearing shrubs. Feeds largely on pine needles but also eats aspen leaves and berries. Swallows gravel for digesting pine needles and often seen walking on forest paths at dawn. Capercaillies may exceptionally hybridise with other gallinaceous birds: this occurs most commonly with Black Grouse, and offspring then go by German name of 'Rackelhahn'.

Black Grouse   *Tetrao tetrix*   L 40−55 cm, WS 65−80 cm

Size of domestic hen. Cock black with conspicuous white wingbar and lyre-shaped tail. Hen ('Greyhen') smaller and darker than hen Capercaillie and has a narrow white wingbar and shorter, more shallowly forked tail. In spring and occasionally at other times of year cocks gather in larger or smaller groups on bogs, fields and ice-covered lakes to display at dawn. After sunrise they often perch in treetops. At this time the cocks' cooing calls sound like a distant surging wall of sound. The cooing is mixed with an explosive 'tshoo-eesh'. In winter often seen returning to a favourite group of birches to eat buds; seeds and buds from other trees as well as various berries and shoots are also included in the diet. The chicks feed largely on insects. More common than Capercaillie and prefers woodlands bordering clearings, bogs or fields; seriously declining in Britain.

Capercaillie

Black Grouse

Caucasian Black Grouse

displaying ♂

♂

♀

Capercaillie

♀

♂

Black Grouse

Capercaillie ♀

Black Grouse ♂

♀

♂

♀

♂

♀

Hazel Grouse

Hazel Grouse   *Bonasa bonasia*   L 35–37 cm, WS 48–54 cm

Very much a forest bird, which throughout the year appears in small groups in dark woodland, both in dense spruce forest and in pure deciduous forest but most often in luxuriant mixed forest. Particularly favoured are damp depressions and stream gullies with alder, birch and *Vaccinium* scrub. Grey tail with black-and-white band at tip characteristic. Male has black chin patch and is greyer than female, which is more brownish. In C Europe more brown-red in colour. Rhythmic noise heard from wings on take-off. Unlike Black Grouse and Capercaillie does not fly away very far when flushed, and when approached again is observed perched in a tree. Sometimes perches in open in a tall birch in a forest glade. Throughout the year reveals itself by its pin-sharp whistles, not unlike song phrase of a Goldcrest or Treecreeper

Caucasian
Black Grouse

♀

Caucasian
Snowcock
♂

Caspian Snowcock   Caucasian Snowcock   Caspian Snowcock

♂

♂

♂

Caucasian Black Grouse *Tetrao mlokosiewiczi*   L 38–52 cm, WS 58–62 cm
Slightly smaller than Black Grouse, lacks white wingbar and has black vent and longer tail with shorter lyres. Display is silent, though during flutter-jumps male produces whistling wing noise audible to c150 m. More terrestrial and reluctant to fly than Black Grouse. Endemic in Caucasus at 1500–3000m on alpine meadows, often in rhododendron and willow scrub. In winter also in lower regions.   *Map p. 172*

Caucasian Snowcock *Tetraogallus caucasicus*   L 54–56 cm, WS 80–95 cm
Large as female Capercaillie, greyish with rusty-red and buff tones together with white markings on neck and wings. Male gives long series of whistling or fluting notes, audible at 1 km. Found throughout year above tree line in Caucasus.

Caspian Snowcock   *Tetraogallus caspius*   L 58–62 cm, WS 80–95 cm
Larger than Caucasian Snowcock, more uniformly grey in flight with darker tail feathers and tips to primaries. Call resembles Caucasian Snowcock's. Found in high rocky mountainous regions, locally in Taurus Mountains and easternmost Turkey and also in southern Caucasus, N Iran and Iraq.

175

Black Francolin

Sand Partridge

♀ ♂ ♂

Sand Partridge
Ammoperdix heyi   L 22–25 cm

A small, desert-dwelling partridge. Female wholly sandy-coloured with mixed shades of grey. Occurs in desert tracts, often in dried-out riverbeds, around Red Sea.

See-see   *Ammoperdix griseogularis*   L 22–25 cm

Southeasternmost Turkey and Iraq. Like Sand Partridge except black supercilium and white lores.   *Not illustrated*

Black Francolin   *Francolinus francolinus*   L 33–36 cm, WS 50–55 cm

Slightly bigger than Grey Partridge. On rising, both sexes have striking dark outer tail feathers and warm brown or cinnamon-coloured wings (dark-barred). Difficult to see or flush and noticed mostly by call, a far-carrying, sharp and shrill series of usually 7–8 syllables, 'kek, keek keek-kek-kik ki-keek', uttered mostly mornings and evenings from a low mound or bush. Occurs in low-lying terrain with dense shrub vegetation, often beside water, e.g. river deltas, riverbeds and cultivations with canals. Introduced in Tuscany region of Italy.

Chukar   *Alectoris chukar*   L 32–34 cm, WS 47–52 cm

Distinguished from Rock Partridge, besides their separate ranges, by cream-coloured throat, pale lores together with more brown on ear-coverts and broader white band behind/above eye. Call short chucks, 'kvak (chuk)...kvak..kvak.. kvak', followed by 'chuck, chuckcheper...chuck, chuckcheper', on rising a loud jolting 'pitch pitch pitch..k'trr k'trr k'trr'. Common on dry rocky mountain slopes with or without scrub vegetation up to at least 2800 m. Often very shy and only heard or is flushed, when glides down mountain at high speed. Often kept in captivity.

Rock Partridge   *Alectoris graeca*   L 32–35 cm, WS 46–53 cm

More tied to higher mountain regions than Chukar, mainly on south-facing rocky and craggy alpine slopes with or without bushes or trees. Seen mostly when rising, and then difficult to distinguish from Chukar. Has snow-white chin, with more regular and more sharply demarcated black frame which at bill-join reaches gape. Range differs from Chukar's. Call a 4-syllable 'chair tsirittchee, chair tsirittchee...', a clear 'vitt...vitt...vitt' and a sharp 'pitch-ee, pitch-ee'. Food as Chukar's.

Black Francolin

Chukar

Rock Partridge

Rock Partridge

Ptarmigan
♂ summer

Chukar

**Rock
Partridge**

Red-legged Partridge

Double-spurred Francolin

Barbary Partridge

Double-spurred Francolin *Francolinus bicalcaratus*

L 30–33 cm, WS 45–50 cm

Size of Barbary Partridge, but pattern of streaking and rust-red crown/nape unique for the region. Lacks contrasting dark rusty outer tail of *Alectoris* species. Main distribution in W Africa. Rare and isolated in occurrence in Morocco, chiefly in Forest of Mamora and around Essaouira, mostly in open woodland with taller undergrowth and preferably near water. Very shy, easiest to see at dawn, when male calls from a bough, wall or mound. Call a grating 'kwarr-kwarr'.

Barbary Partridge *Alectoris barbara*

L 32–34 cm, WS 46–49 cm

On take-off as well as on ground the dark crown, 'Sioux hair-style', is the most striking character. In level gliding flight wings often held just above the horizontal, unlike in other *Alectoris* partridges. Display call repetitive series of e.g. 'kchek kchek...kchek kchek...' or 'prr...prr...prr' like a poor car engine. Also has a low Curlew-like 'kyew'. On take-off 'pekyew...pekyew...', when alarmed/flushed a shorter 'psi...pchee...p-chee'. Occurs in various dry habitats such as maquis, cultivations, euphorbia steppe etc, in low-lying terrain as well as in mountains to above 3000 m; common in N Africa. In Europe only on Corsica and Gibraltar. Often keeps well concealed and runs away when danger threatens; sometimes perches in bushes or low down in trees.

Red-legged Partridge *Alectoris rufa*

L 32–34 cm, WS 45–50 cm

Easy to separate from Grey Partridge by its contrastingly marked head and wholly grey-brown back. Juv. rarely appears unaccompanied by adults, is rather similar to juv. Grey Partridge. Juvs., however, have traces of adults' dark 'necklace' and flank barring (unlike juv. Grey, which has pale longitudinal shaft streaks). More often heard than seen. Calls variable, hoarse and mechanically repeated series, often beginning with 'kcho kcho..kcho kcho..' followed by e.g. 'kochoko-koke..kochoko-koke'. Common, in open country, on farmland, heaths or lower mountain slopes (not in higher mountains). Eats seeds, plant matter and insects.

Barbary Partridge

Red-legged Partridge

Grey Partridge

178

Barbary Partridge

Red-legged Partridge

Grey Partridge   *Perdix perdix*   *L 29–31 cm, WS 45–48 cm*

Usually easy to recognise by its shape, pale brick-red head and, on take-off, its short, distinctly rusty outer tail feathers. Male acquires a visible red bare spot behind eye in spring and has brighter coloration than female. In addition, female has clearly reduced belly patch, paler and more prominent supercilium and her back markings are neutral dark brown (partially rusty-brown on male). Juv. buff-grey with clear pale shaft streaks and dull brown and grey head. Common in open cultivated areas, during greater part of year occurs in coveys which keep close together, usually families, in spring in pairs. They follow patches of arable, pathsides, hedgerows and similar 'edge' areas where weed seeds such as *Polygonum* and *Silene* are plentiful. When surprised, they all take wing one after the other with a loud wing noise and excited 'pitter-pattering' calls, 'pitt, pitt…pik…pitt…prr, pik…' etc; when agitated they run away. Often dusts and sun-bathes. Song an explosive, metallic, creaking throaty sound, 'kierr-ik, kierr-ik…', given at all times of day but especially at night. In summer–autumn eats mainly seeds, in winter–spring green plants, but also insects and other small animals in summer (applies particularly to chicks).   *Map p. 178*

Lady Amherst's Pheasant

Golden Pheasant ♀

Golden Pheasant

Golden Pheasant   *Chrysolophus pictus* *L 60−115 cm, male ⟩ 80 cm, WS 65−75 cm*

A mountain bird from C China which was introduced into Britain and now breeds in the wild in at least a couple of areas: Galloway in SW Scotland and East Anglia in E England. Thrives particularly in younger coniferous plantations, is unobtrusive and its presence is not always conspicuous. Also fairly common in captivity.

Lady Amherst's Pheasant
Chrysolophus amherstiae   *L 60−120 cm, male ⟩ 105 cm, WS 70−85 cm*

Introduced to SE England, where it has established viable and independent populations; originates from mountain districts in China. Occurs in various semi-open or wooded terrain with dense undergrowth. Runs rather than flying.

Pheasant   *Phasianus colchicus*   *L 53−89 cm, male ⟩66 cm, WS 70−90 cm*

Introduced into Europe from various parts of Asia, into Greece as many as 2000 years ago and into N Europe c200 years ago. Captive-bred birds are released annually. Cock varies in colour depending on race, several of which (with variants) occur in Britain. The *torquatus* type from China has a clear white neck-ring. Nominate *colchicus*, which also occurs naturally between Caspian and Black Seas, lacks neck-ring and has brownish-red rump and brownish-buff wing-coverts. Size and tail shape distinguish species from other gamebirds. Usually occurs in small groups in cultivated country with elements of woodland, clumps of trees, hedges or large gardens, in winter often in reeds. Male displays with a 2-syllable loud crowing call followed by a rapid series of noisy wingbeats. Wings also make a loud whirr when flying, and a metallic loud and hoarse clucking 'eg' is heard in flight. Food very varied, chiefly vegetable matter: seeds, fruits, nuts, roots, plants, but chicks also take insects and other small animals. Often visits feeding stations in winter.

Quail   *Coturnix coturnix*   *L 16−18 cm, WS 32−35 cm*

Usually announces its presence by the 'Quail call', male's song, a fast and rhythmically repeated trisyllabic and 'dripping' whistle, 'pit pil-it'. The persistent 'machine' is heard most intensively at dusk, echoing from the clover pastures, potato fields, cornfields or other fields and meadows, preferably with low-growing crops, where the birds live. Female has a low 'preet-peet', sometimes synchronised with final syllable of male's song. Flight distinctive, wingbeats shallow and very fast, it sweeps just above the vegetation and soon alights in or rather falls down into it again; on rising, a slightly ringing 'pik-kreee' is sometimes heard. Generally, however, very difficult to flush and prefers to run away or to squat. Long-distance migrant, mainly to Africa south of Sahara. Migrates at night in groups or flocks. On passage can appear in larger numbers and in rather odd habitats, especially in S Europe. Numbers in Britain vary annually, in some years very scarce; present May−Oct.

Corncrake   *Crex crex*   *L 27−30 cm, WS 46−53 cm*

Noticed mainly by its call, a remarkably far-carrying disyllabic, loud rasping 'crex crex' or 'errp-errp', mostly at night and in the morning hours. Often two, sometimes three males are heard close to each other. Difficult to catch sight of, if flushed it flies away clumsily to the nearest cover with limp wingbeats and dangling legs; the rusty-brown wings are then characteristic. Most closely related to *Porzana* crakes but occurs in drier terrain: rank meadowland, fodder-fields, ditched marshes or in drier parts of marsh-lands etc. Migrant, arriving mid Apr−May and flying to Africa Sep−Oct. Now very scarce in Britain, with most in N and W Scotland; more in Ireland.

Pheasant

Quail

Corncrake

♀

♂

Pheasant

♀

juv *c* 15 days

♀

♂

Quail

Corncrake

Baillon's Crake   *Porzana pusilla*   L 17–19 cm, WS 33–37 cm

Size of a House Sparrow, overall impression darker than Little Crake, with more irregular white spots above and barring extending farther forward on flanks. Bill wholly olive-green without red at base, eye reddish and stands out pale against dark grey cheeks, legs vary from brownish-pink to olive-green. Female as male but slightly duller in coloration and with brown ear-coverts. Song not so loud as Little Crake's, audible at 200–250 m at most: a dry, scratching call 2–3 seconds long, which fluctuates or alternates in intensity, recalling drake Garganey. Easy to confuse with call of Edible Frog. Occurs in streamsides, marsh, beside ponds and in other, even quite small, swampy areas with profuse vegetation, especially sedge, and with low water level. Food as Little Crake's. Rare vagrant to Britain.

Little Crake   *Porzana parva*   L 18–20 cm, WS 34–39 cm

Slightly bigger, with paler grey underparts and more muddy-brown than red-brown upperparts with fewer white spots, though some individuals give a very pale-spotted impression (probably mostly 2nd cal-year). Also, shows less barring on flanks and has green legs and red bill base. Juv. similar to Baillon's, though pale spots above solid (not ring-shaped) and arranged in rows which form pale bands. Has longer primaries than Baillon's. Male's song is leisurely croaking at low pitch which accelerates towards the end into a rapidly stammering, but never rolling, component: 'kwak (kwek)…kwak…k-wak…kwak, kwak, kwak, kwa, kwa, kva-kva-kva-kva-kva-kva'. Female's call has a more rapidly accelerating, more vibrant terminal trill, 'kwek, kwek, kverrrrr', is somewhat variable in pitch and sometimes very like Water Rail's song. Occurs, to a degree unlike other crakes, in reedbeds with rather deeper water, above all in bulrush and reedmace; also swims freely. Comes out into open more at edge of reeds or shore in mornings and evenings. Feeds on small aquatic animals such as water-beetles, fly larvae, spiders, snails etc. Rare vagrant to Britain, mostly in Mar–May and Aug–Nov.

Spotted Crake   *Porzana porzana*   L 22–24 cm, WS 37–42 cm

Slightly bigger than Little Crake but smaller than Water Rail, usually looks dark but with reasonable views easily recognisable by its spotted plumage and pale ventral region. Song a very far-carrying and rhythmically repeated, whiplashing whistle, 'hwitt', at distance like dripping tap. Does not normally sing until after dark has set in. Occurs in marshes, around lakes, ponds and small rivers with low water level and rich vegetation, preferably of rush and sedge. Locally common on Continent. Migrates at end of Aug–Sep (Oct) to tropical Africa. Rare and isolated breeder in Britain, mainly in north (Scotland), also passage migrant Mar–May and Sep–Nov and occasional winterer.

Sora   *Porzana carolina*   L 20–23 cm, WS 35–40 cm

Rare vagrant from N America. Size and overall impression as Spotted Crake but has black mask around bill and lacks spots on head and breast. Song distinctive, a plaintive 'ker-veep'.   *Not illustrated*

Baillon's Crake

Little Crake

Spotted Crake

Baillon's Crake

juv

juv

Little Crake

♀

2nd-cal ♂

♂

Spotted Crake

juv

Water Rail *Rallus aquaticus*   *L 22−28 cm, WS 38−45 cm*

A small, dark, retiring bird. When flushed, it flies away a short distance on loosely fluttering wings and with dangling legs. Difficult to see but sometimes stands in open at very edge of reeds and suns or preens itself. Usually, however, shows its presence by peculiar grunting and groaning sound from within vegetation, as e.g. sudden, almost explosive onslaught of shrill squeals which rapidly become strangulated and dissipate into grunts, whining 'kweerrr' notes and other stomach-churning sounds. On spring nights male utters rhythmic 'kipp...kipp...' and so on, occasionally with a vibrant final flourish, such as '...kipp...kipp, keerrrl' (not unlike female Little Crake, but high-pitched and more metallic), also a similar, fast rolling 'keerrl', usually in high-level flight during spring. Common in reeds, marshes, boggy sedge meadows and similar dense aquatic vegetation, also with element of willow. Mainly a resident in Britain, with immigrants from Continent in Sep−Apr (notable influxes in hard winters). Feeds on invertebrates, seeds and plant material.

Moorhen *Gallinula chloropus*   *L 32−35 cm, WS 50−55 cm*

Unmistakable. Frequently demonstrates its characteristic stern with incessant tail jerks, swims with body stooped forward hen-like. Juv. paler, more grey-brown and with muddy-coloured bill. Very varied calls, several of which can be bewildering on spring nights. Often gives a varied, often sudden, gurgling 'kurrl', or 'kurruk', sometimes a loud, almost Grey Partridge-like 'kr-r-eck', a repeated 'kek', 'kik' or 'kikik'. Sings at night with persistent clucking 'kreck-kreck-kreck...', incl. during extensive nocturnal aerial excursions. During breeding season more retiring than Coot, but on e.g. park lakes and in winter often quite bold. Nests relatively commonly in reedbeds, on rivers, ponds etc with sheltering vegetation of reeds, bulrushes, willow etc. Has a broad diet of plants, seeds, fruits and various small animals. Mainly resident in Britain, but some immigration from Scandinavia and Low Countries during Sep−Apr.

Coot *Fulica atra*   *L 36−38 cm, WS 70−80 cm*

A familiar waterbird, rounded and sooty-black with brilliant white bill and frontal shield. Establishes a territory early in spring and defends it aggressively against encroachment by other waterbirds. Takes off in characteristic fashion in tripping run across water surface with beating wings. Most typical calls are a loud, repeated, often varied 'kowk' and an explosive, at times incredibly high 'pitts' as if a light bulb had been dropped on to a stone inside the reeds. During nocturnal aerial excursions also a trumpeting, rather hollow and desolate 'pay-ow'. In autumn and winter often seen in close-packed flocks which graze or dive for water plants and plant stalks; diet also includes small animal matter. Mainly resident in Britain, but many visit in winter from Continent, Oct−Apr.

Water Rail

Moorhen

Coot

juv

Water Rail

Moorhen

juv

juv

Coot

Andalusian Hemipode ♀   **Crested Coot** winter   **Coot** winter

Crested Coot   *Fulica cristata*   *L 38−42 cm, WS 75−85 cm*

Occurs in same habitat as Coot and often together with it. A mainly E and S African species, occurring locally and very rarely as relict population in SW Andalucia and locally more commonly in N Morocco. Usually difficult to pick out in mixed flocks, especially during non-breeding season when the red 'horns' are small and insignificant. In the field appears to have a shade longer neck (stiffer nape) and more angular head profile and does not have Coot's pointed 'lobe' of black loral feathers which cuts in between bill and frontal shield. Lacks white terminal band on secondaries. Calls Coot-like, but also has a species-specific groaning or 'mooing' call.

Purple Gallinule   *Porphyrio porphyrio* **porphyrio** 45−50 cm, WS 90−100 cm

Unmistakable, as big as a domestic chicken. Behaves like Moorhen, jerks tail up and exposes the white ventral region when nervous. Outside breeding season bill less bright and with dark patches. In Egypt race *madagascariensis*, green on scapulars and back; in Turkey and Middle East *caspius*, which is paler blue and has greenish head. Calls many and varied, in form not unlike Moorhen's, but most are gruffer and very deep in pitch, incl. dull mooing; contact call a low 'chock-chock'. Very local in occurrence. Nests in marsh and dense shore vegetation. Not infrequently shows itself in the open, mostly evenings and mornings. Feeds on plant material, largely pith from rush and bulrush, which it exposes dexterously using foot and bill.

Andalusian Hemipode   *Turnix sylvatica*   *L 15−16 cm, WS 25−30 cm*

Resembles a Quail, but has rust-red breast and black-spotted body-sides. Female brighter in coloration. Is extremely retiring and very difficult to flush. At night has a characteristic song like the lowing of a distant cow, also a pigeon-like call. Rare in N Africa in low-lying dry sandy or grass-covered terrain with low bushy vegetation, especially dwarf palm. Was locally common in S Spain and in Sicily during 1800s, but today is very rare and local in Andalucia. Belongs to the family Turnicidae, with several species in tropical Africa. Male takes care of eggs and young.

Crested Coot

Purple Gallinule

Andalusian Hemipode

188

juv

Purple Gallinule

Crested Coot

Crane   *Grus grus*   *L 114–130 cm, WS 200–230 cm*

Big and stately, on ground moves with slow, markedly dignified steps. Huge in flight, with long wings of uniform width, narrow extended neck (cf herons) and long projecting legs. Migrating birds often noticed by their very far-carrying calls consisting of nasal and grating trumpet blasts. At nest site the pair often calls in duet, 'krruee-krro, krruee-krro', most actively at dawn. Very shy at nest site. In spring performs a dance in which the birds leap up with raised wings, make deep bows, trumpet and erect the 'tail plumes' (formed by elongated inner secondaries). Breeds sparsely on open or semi-open bog or marshland. Migrates in families in groups and larger flocks, which fly in a V or a diagonal line. Stops off on open farmland, heaths and marshes. Feeds on insects, smaller animals, young of birds, seeds and fruits. Rare on passage in Britain, mostly Mar–Jun and Aug–Nov, has wintered.

Demoiselle Crane   *Anthropoides virgo*   *L 90–100 cm, WS 165–185 cm*

Smaller than Crane, appears more elegant with more slender and more attenuated tail area, shorter neck and bill. More uniformly toned above and the black on neck continues down over breast as plumes. Remarkably similar to Crane in flight, but shorter-necked, steeper forehead and shorter bill, with less pale on neck and with grey (not black) tone on inner primaries and coverts. Call Crane-like but higher in pitch. A steppe species of C Asia which also breeds rarely in easternmost Turkey and north of Black Sea. Earlier in 1900s bred in N Africa, and a small population remains in N Morocco. European birds winter in Africa, seen regularly on passage only in Cyprus. Passage in Aug to early Sep and end Mar to mid Apr.

Great Bustard   *Otis tarda*   *L 75–105 cm, WS 190–260 cm*

Europe's heaviest bird, can weigh up to 18 kg. Male twice as big as female. Size as well as male's long throat whiskers (only in breeding plumage) and the brown-red breast-band develop successively with age. Very shy. Walks, or rather struts, with dignified strides and with upright neck. At a distance the feeding flock can be taken for sheep or suchlike. Flight powerful, with regular eagle-like wingbeats, but without tendency to glide. Males have a striking display in which they perform an amazing transformation: they appear to turn themselves inside out and take on the form of a big bundle of white feathers. Usually occurs in smaller flocks in extensive open terrain such as heaths and arable land. Most often stands in open, frequently on mounds with a clear view but sometimes in among cork oaks or olive trees (Iberian peninsula). Pesticides and agricultural mechanisation have contributed to a severe reduction in the species' numbers, now very local. Food mostly plants and seeds, but also, especially in summer, insects, rodents and other smaller animals, which can, when in good supply, make up the main diet. Resident, but may wander in winter (mainly imms.) and be found outside normal range.   *Illustration and map on next spread.*

Crane

Demoiselle Crane

Crane

juv

Crane

Demoiselle Crane

lek display ♂

Houbara Bustard

♀

Great Bustard

Houbara Bustard   *Chlamydotis undulata*   *L 55–65 cm, WS 135–170 cm*

Size of female Great Bustard. Has long tail and slender neck. Warm sandy-coloured with dark spots above, well camouflaged. Black 'mane' on neck most conspicuous. In flight, long, slightly bowed wings are beaten in slow Crane-like tempo. Flight feathers blackish with bright white patch at primary bases. Rare and local on dry steppe and semi-desert, with or without low scrub. Migrant in C Asia (recorded a few times in Europe in late autumn), resident in N Africa and Middle East. Endangered in many regions owing to disturbance and hunting.

Little Bustard   *Tetrax tetrax*   *L 40–45 cm, WS 105–115 cm*

Considerably smaller than Great Bustard and in winter the flocks are like gallinaceous birds. In spring the males stand out on fields and meadows like oddly marked posts. They then display with inflated neck and give short 'knerr' calls like a quick stroke with a coarse file, and also make brief leaps in the air. Flight fast and gamebird-like, and wings show much white. At distance flocks give impression of white-mottled racing pigeons. In flight male's wings make a fast whistling noise as from an unoiled cycle hub; the noise is produced by the 4th primary, which is shorter and narrower than the rest. Locally common in SW Europe, scarcer in other parts, usually on extensive cornfields, cultivations and grass steppes. Feeds on insects and smaller animals, also seeds, shoots and other plant material. Gathers in large flocks in winter.

Great Bustard

Houbara Bustard

Little Bustard

Great Bustard

♂

♀

juv

Houbara Bustard

♂ winter

♂ lek display

Little Bustard

♀

♂

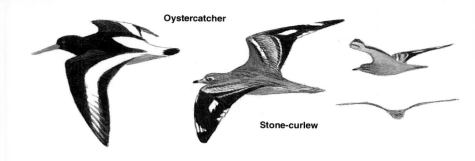

Oystercatcher

Stone-curlew

Oystercatcher   *Haematopus ostralegus*   L 40–45 cm, WS 80–86 cm

Unmistakable. In winter ad. has white chin-stripe; juv. acquires this in autumn (1st winter) and often retains it until summer of 2nd cal-year. Occurs on most types of seashore and locally inland, in N Britain on river shingle and even grassy areas near inland waters. Very noisy, often also at night on arriving in breeding area. Has high loud 'kubeek, kubeek...' and 'pik, pik...', gives alarm call persistently and chases crows, gulls and others encroaching near eggs and young. Males often gather in peculiar assemblies, when they walk around in troops with heads bent down and utter vocal poundings, castanet clappering and drawn-out trills. Different individuals or pairs are tied either to the shoreline, where they feed on molluscs and bristleworms, or alternatively to areas a bit away from the water, when worms form the staple food. Partial migrant in Britain, also passage and winter visitor Jul–May from N Europe.

Stone-curlew   *Burhinus oedicnemus*   L 40–44 cm, WS 77–85 cm

An oddity among European birds. Somewhat Curlew-like, but its big head, Sparrowhawk-like eye and often completely motionless posture produce reptilian associations. Male has a more prominent black bar above the whitish one on the wing-coverts, and juv. is less contrastingly marked overall. Occurs sparsely in semi-desert, on heaths, pasture fields and arable land, in non-breeding season often in small parties or flocks. Most active at dusk and at night, during the day usually found resting on cryptically coloured, rather parched and stony ground. Relatively common in Mediterranean countries. When flushed, it usually flies off a short distance low over the ground and with fast shallow wingbeats. The variegated wing markings are unmistakable in flight, which is curlew-like over longer distances. Its calls recall Curlew's: flight call 'ke-e-uhw', varying in strength, 'krruee-leee' or suchlike. At night a number of startling calls, incl. a repeated 'kurr-ee', a vibrating 'puee-vee-vee' recalling alarm of Oystercatcher, an initially hissing then heart-rending high 'ksh ee'ee'ee'tt', a high clear 'weep' and so on. Feeds on snails and slugs, insects, worms etc and may even take such large animals as mice, young birds and frogs.

Oystercatcher

Stone-curlew

194

1st-winter

Oystercatcher

juv

♂

Stone-curlew

Black-winged Stilt

1st-winter

Avocet

Black-winged Stilt   *Himantopus himantopus*   L 35−40 cm, WS 67−83 cm

Looks rickety, with extremely long legs which in flight stick out behind like long streamers. Dark markings on head variable: both sexes can show wholly white head or varying degrees of black on crown and nape in breeding plumage. Slightly larger male, however, identified by its blacker and more glossy green mantle. In autumn and winter both sexes have grey crown and ear-coverts. Juv. brown on mantle and with pale trailing edge to wing. Calls varied, 'kiu', 'kek' or 'kyepp' but with a very particular nasal ring, tinny and slightly bleating. Occurs mostly on coastal lagoons and shallow lakes, typically in river mouths and saltpans around the Mediterranean. Migrates to Africa south of Sahara in Aug−Nov, returning in Mar−Apr; winters locally around Mediterranean. Rare visitor to Britain, where it has bred several times.

Avocet   *Recurvirostra avosetta*   L 42−46 cm, WS 77−80 cm

Few birds radiate such elegance as the Avocet. With its splendid black-and-white plumage and upcurved bill it is like no other wader. Female often has pale area around bill base and suggestion of an eye-ring. Juv. has brown-buff vermiculation on parts of upperparts. Along flat marshy shore meadows, shallow seashores and estuaries where it nests it nevertheless is not infrequently lost among the throng of gulls and other shorebirds. It is, however, immediately located if one recognises the particular Avocet ring in its calls, usually agitated 'pleet, pleet' notes. Alarm a croaking 'kweht' and slightly cackling calls. When feeding it swings its head from side to side and with its recurved bill skims off the surface-water invertebrates. Prefers to wade in water about 10 cm deep, but can also swim (has webbed toes). Concentrates in large numbers in Waddenzee area to moult in late Jul−Sep; most move southwest in Sep−Oct to Iberian peninsula and W Africa. In mild winters many stay in W Europe and return to breeding grounds in Mar−Apr.

Black-winged Stilt

Avocet

♂ summer

♂ winter

♀ summer

1st-winter

♂ summer

Black-winged Stilt

Avocet

♂

juv

♀

Collared Pratincole

Black-winged Pratincole

Black-winged Pratincole   *Glareola nordmanni*   L 23−26 cm, WS 60−68 cm

Very difficult to distinguish from Collared Pratincole. Darker above, lacking sharp contrast between upperwing-coverts and flight feathers, lacks white trailing edge to secondaries and has shorter tail streamers. Has less red at bill base. Underwing-coverts and axillaries are black (not brown-red as on Collared), though this is difficult to assess in the field, and underwing often appears black on Collared, too. In winter and juv. plumages perched birds seem almost impossible to identify specifically. Calls resemble Collared's, but in flight has a sharper call, like the squeak of a rubber, 'keye…kiche'. Behaviour and habitat very like Collared Pratincole's, but more tied to steppe. Has been found a few times in Britain during May−Sep.

Collared Pratincole   *Glareola pratincola*   L 24−27 cm, WS 60−65 cm

Pratincoles have a character all of their own, like *Charadrius* plovers on the ground and like terns in flight. Very gregarious, usually found in flocks which catch insects in the air in fast easy flight or pass by in loose formation, often high up. Often reveals itself by its tern-like but more nasal calls: tone like that of Black-tailed Godwit but higher, 'keuw…kerreu', often in rhythmic sequence, as well as 'kerreu…kewuk…kek'. Occurs on large flat expanses with some shallow pools and marsh, often dried-out flood areas, grazed shore meadows and salt steppe adjoining coastal lagoons and deltas, locally relatively commonly. Feeds on insects and other smaller animals. Migrates in Aug−Sep and returns in Apr. Rare vagrant to Britain, mostly in May−Jul.

Cream-coloured Courser   *Cursorius cursor*   L 19−21 cm, WS 51−57 cm

Unmistakable. Flight very fast, profile deep-breasted with striking sooty-black under-wings. Occurs on steppe and in semi-desert, often on extensive gravelly plains. Rare in winter in Morocco and Tunisia. Very rare vagrant to Europe.

Black-winged Pratincole

Collared Pratincole

Cream-coloured Courser

Black-winged Pratincole

summer

summer

Collared Pratincole

Collared Pratincole

juv

winter

Cream-coloured Courser

Ringed Plover   *Charadrius hiaticula*   L 18–20 cm, WS 48–57 cm

A robust wader with short bill and characteristic facial and breast markings. In summer plumage has orange legs and bill base, female often with brown feathers mixed in with the black. Has striking white wingbars in flight (*cf* Little Ringed Plover). Juv. in fresh plumage has scaly pattern above, but the pale feather edges are worn away towards autumn. Ad. in winter plumage has dark brown mask and breast-band and dark bill with yellowish base to lower mandible. Arctic race *tundrae* smaller than southern *hiaticula*, with darker brown upperparts, moults only on reaching winter quarters (from Nov), with further, partial moult Feb–Mar (spring migrants in full breeding plumage); *hiaticula* has one moult, in Jul–Oct. Call a soft 2-syllable whistle, 'tooip'. Noisy in spring, when males fly back and forth with stiff wingbeats while giving continuous yodelling 'tack-alü, tack-alü, tack-alü...'. Common on shallow shores, nests especially on sandy or gravelly ground, locally on heaths, river shores etc. In Britain mainly resident, but many passage and winter visitors from Scandinavia and Arctic during Aug–May.

Little Ringed Plover   *Charadrius dubius*   L 14–15 cm, WS 42–48 cm

Smaller, slimmer and more attenuated in body shape than Ringed Plover. Muddy-coloured legs, yellow eye-ring, dark bill (though base to lower mandible often yellow), call and absence of wingbar are best distinguishing marks compared with Ringed Plover. Juv. has 'faded' head lacking contrasts and without white mark behind eye, and with pale half eye-ring (base), usually a yellow-buff tinge to throat and forehead patch (which varies in extent and can extend in a wedge above/behind eye). On rising gives a loud 'kiu', characteristic in tone. Territorial calls at nest site are loud in volume and have a desolate ring; often begin with a rolling, tern-like and excited 'krre-u krre-u...'. Nests mostly inland on open terrain such as gravel-pits, sandy fields, refuse tips and other sites with similar ground structure, though often beside water, e.g. lakeshores or sewage-ponds. On passage at lakeshores, muddy sea bays, estuaries etc. Arrives in Britain end of Mar and in Apr, migrates Jul–Sep (Oct); local breeder.

Kentish Plover   *Charadrius alexandrinus*   L 15–17 cm, WS 42–58 cm

Overall impression always paler than that of other ringed-plovers, often looks large-headed and rather short-tailed, with incomplete breast-band (breast patches) and grey to blackish legs. Male has reddish-ochre crown only during breeding season. In flight shows broad white wingbar. Call an insignificant short, dripping 'pweep' or 'kip', not unlike Little Stint. At nest site also has grating, more drawn-out rolling calls. Common around Mediterranean, mostly at river deltas, lagoons and saltpans. Rare and local in NW Europe on shallow sandy shores. Small numbers formerly bred in S Britain, where now scarce migrant in spring (Apr–May) and autumn (Aug–Oct).

Ringed Plover

Little Ringed Plover

Kentish Plover

Ringed Plover

♂ summer

winter

juv

Little Ringed Plover

juv

♂ summer

juv

♂ summer

Kentish Plover

Lesser Sand Plover   *Charadrius mongolus*   L 19–21 cm, WS 45–58 cm

Like Ringed Plover in size and shape, but with longer legs and bill. Compared with Greater Sand Plover, generally has smaller bill and shorter and darker legs (more neutral grey), also often has a more upright stance. Represented by 5 races from C Asia to northernmost Siberia. The C Asiatic birds (*atrifrons* group) generally have longer bill and tarsus, shorter wing and also less white on forehead. Females are duller than males, especially in the C Asian populations. In winter plumage very like Greater Sand Plover and best separated by shape and size of bill and by darker legs. Juv. has narrow grey-buff or dirty-white fringes above, and in fresh plumage has a warm rusty tone over breast, neck and side of head. In flight, little or nothing of the feet is visible beyond the tail. Call a clear 'kiripp' or 'kurrip' sometimes reminiscent of drake Pintail. Westernmost race *pamirensis* winters in E and S Africa and in Arabian Peninsula, the other races in S Asia and Australia. Recorded only a few times in Europe. On passage on muddy and sandy shores.

Greater Sand Plover   *Charadrius leschenaultii*   L 22–25 cm, WS 53–60 cm

Larger, longer-legged and with longer and heavier bill than Lesser Sand Plover. Bill, however, shows obvious variation and is not always strikingly big, especially on the westernmost race *columbinus* which breeds in Turkey (C Anatolia) and Jordan. Those in C Asia often have a markedly heavy bill and correspondingly enlarged head, sometimes look slightly disproportionate and front-heavy. Legs longer and paler than on Lesser Sand Plover, often with a more muddy or greenish-buff tone. In summer plumage variable with regard to extent of black on head and rusty feathers on breast and sides of body, female often lacking black facial markings (especially in race *columbinus*). Mantle and scapulars often have some rusty-tinted feathers, a feature occurring more rarely on Lesser Sand Plover. In winter plumage the larger size and differences in bill and legs are the best field characters. Juv. has broader rusty-yellow fringes than juv. Lesser, usually most obvious on secondary coverts (form pale panel) and on forehead. In flight shows markings like Ringed Plover, but with paler tail base and with legs visible a centimetre beyond tail. Call somewhat variable, often a nasal three-part rolling 'pirrirrüp' or 'krüp krüp krüp', sometimes ricocheting and Turnstone-like; also a shorter 'krreeu' or 'krruk'. Flight and contact calls have a deeper ring than those of Lesser. Nests on dry, desert-type flats, often low-lying steppe with seasonal pools. During non-breeding season on shores and mudflats on or near coast. Very rare but annual visitor to Europe.

Map p. 204

Caspian Plover   *Charadrius asiaticus*   L 18–20 cm, WS 55–61 cm

Compared with Greater Sand Plover more elegant in build, with longer neck and long pointed rear end (long wings). In summer plumage lacks black facial mask and has dark lower border to breast-band. Female is duller and often has only slight rusty tinge to breast. In flight shows grey underwings, darker tail and less prominent wingbar. In winter plumage has broader breast-band and more yellowish-buff tint over pale areas of face compared with above two species. Juv. grey-brown above with broad rusty-buff fringes, also found in 1st-winter plumage (like Dotterel). Legs usually have a grey-buff tone. Feet project a centimetre behind tail-tip in flight. Call a loud sharp 'kuwit' or 'quit'. Breeds in C Asia in similar habitats to Greater Sand Plover, wintering in E and S Africa, more of an inland bird which stops off on passage on short-grass fields. Rare but regular in Middle East, mostly during spring passage. Recorded a few times in Europe.

Map p. 204

juv

Lesser Sand Plover

♂ summer

mongolus
group

Greater Sand Plover

♂ summer
eastern

juv

winter
Greater Sand Plover

♂ summer western

♀ summer

♂ summer

juv

Caspian Plover

juv

♂

♀

♀

Dotterel

Dotterel *Charadrius morinellus*   L 20–22 cm, WS 57–64 cm

Clearly smaller than Golden Plover, with distinctive colour pattern. At distance, broad supercilium and narrow breast-band conspicuous. In flight deep-chested, long-tailed and with pointed wings, lacks wingbar but white quill of outermost primary is often conspicuous; underwing plain grey or buffish-grey. Ad. winter resembles juv. but has less contrasting and more yellow-grey coloration. The male, slightly more subdued in colour, takes charge of incubation and care of the young, while the female is responsible for courtship and display. Display flight like Ringed Plover's, accompanied by rhythmic, clear 'weet-weeh' calls, heard also when alarmed. In flight gives rolling 'brrüt', with rather deep and far-carrying ring. Very fearless. Nests on dry mountain moor, often on small plateaux in the lichen region. Sparse and local in occurrence. Sporadic breeding records in Pyrenees, Italian and French Alps, Poland and Czechoslovakia. On passage and in winter on dry heath- or steppe-type terrain, often on poor arable land. Food mostly insects and their larvae.

Greater Sand Plover

Caspian Plover

Dotterel

Lesser Sand Plover winter

juv

Ringed Plover

winter

Kentish Plover

Greater Sand Plover
winter

juv

Little Ringed Plover

Caspian Plover
juv

Dotterel
juv

juv

Golden Plover
juv

American Golden Plover

juv

Grey Plover

Pacific Golden Plover

Killdeer   *Charadrius vociferus*   L 23−26 cm, WS 59−63 cm

A very rare vagrant from N America, where common in various kinds of open terrain, shores, fields, grassland etc and usually near water. Unmistakable, clearly bigger and more elongated than Ringed Plover and with double breast-band. In flight shows very long tail, brownish-red rump and broad white wingbar. Very noisy, with shrill, almost yelling tone in the voice, on rising a drawn-out loud 'cheee-et', sometimes trisyllabic; in display, repetitive series of 'kill-deeay' calls.

American Golden Plover   *Pluvialis dominica*   L 24−28 cm, WS 65−72 cm

Breeds on tundra in Alaska and Canada, winters in S America. Very rare vagrant to mainly W Europe. Daintier and more slightly built than Golden Plover. Has longer and dark grey legs, longer neck and longer wings which on standing bird reach well beyond tail. In flight the silhouette is fairly well separated from Golden Plover's by long uniformly narrow wings and slimmer body, with feet barely visible beyond tail. Axillaries, as well as entire underwing and also the narrow bar on upperwing, have a grey tone (not white as on Golden Plover). In summer plumage has all-black underparts incl. flanks and vent, females with browner ear-coverts and sometimes some grey feathers mixed in the black. Upperparts darker than on Pacific Golden Plover owing to smaller size of greenish-yellow spots, and with wing/scapulars the same shade. In winter plumage shows brownish-grey tones throughout, without greenish elements. Typical juvs. have rather drab grey or brownish-grey markings with often darker mantle and with grey-vermiculated flanks (like juv. Spotted Redshank); head is characterised by dark crown and clear dirty-white supercilium, upperpart spots are small, greenish-yellow to dirty-white and generally less greenish-yellow than on Pacific Golden, and ground colour on wing-coverts is also obviously darker. Call in flight a clear, somewhat vibrating whistle, 'kluilip' or 'kuee-eep', rather variable, on the ground also shorter 'kweep', though never sharp and Spotted Redshank-like as in Pacific Golden.

Pacific Golden Plover   *Pluvialis fulva*   L 23−26 cm, WS 60−67 cm

Breeds on tundra in Siberia, from Yamal Peninsula eastwards to W Alaska. Very rare vagrant from the east above all in summer−autumn. Very like American Golden Plover but looks even longer-legged, more round-bodied with shorter rear end, longer neck and generally longer and heavier bill. Colour markings are more like Golden Plover's, with the black underparts in summer plumage flanked by a white band mixed with dark. Vent pale with dark markings but males can be all-black at the sides of vent. Often a colour contrast is evident between greenish-yellow spots on mantle and white ones on wing-coverts. Females lack or have restricted black markings on head and some 2nd-cal-years lack black also on belly. In winter plumage has more greenish brown-yellow elements on mantle and overall warmer, more dirty-buff tone below and on head. Compared with American Golden, juv. is paler and more greenish-yellow or buff-yellow in tone, has bigger spots on mantle and different facial markings (more like Golden Plover's); head is dominated by big dark eye on pale background, diagonal loral streak in front of eye and a dark patch on rear ear-coverts. Facial markings vary, however, and certain individuals are extremely difficult to identify in the field. Pacific Golden has a shorter primary projection, the longest tertial leaving three primary tips exposed whereas American Golden shows four: a reliable character on non-moulting birds. In flight told from Golden Plover by long slender wings and grey underwings and wingbar. Compared with American Golden slightly shorter-winged and longer-legged with legs projecting well behind. Call a diagnostic sharp, Spotted Redshank-like 'chüwit', also 'chooit' or softer 'klüee'.

Killdeer

Golden Plover juv

juv

American Golden Plover

juv

♂ summer

American Golden Plover

juv

♂ summer

Pacific Golden Plover

juv

winter

Grey Plover ♀ Pacific Golden Plover ♀ American Golden Plover ♀

Golden Plover ♀

Golden Plover   *Pluvialis apricaria*   L 26–29 cm, WS 67–76 cm

Is confused mainly with Grey Plover, but in all plumages has greenish-yellow tones above and white armpits (axillaries). The black on the underparts is usually more restricted on females, particularly in the southern populations. In winter and juv. plumages more anonymous and camouflaged against the arable land, fields and coastal pastures where flocks live during non-breeding season. Flight fast and powerful, profile rather compact and deep-breasted, wings relatively short and broad-based. Flight call, which often gives away the species, is a short melancholy whistle, 'pyüh' or 'pyeek', at times repeated 'pyü-pü' or a higher, slightly cracked 'kuee'. At nest site, when agitated, constantly utters a melancholy and mournful 'plu-ee-wee', drawn out and dying away at the end; in display flight this is rhythmically repeated and followed by a drier and rolling 'pre-kwirreeoo... pre-kwirreeoo'. Nests on open moors and upland bogs and pastures. Feeds on beetles, worms and other small ground-dwelling animals, as well as some berries and seeds. British breeders mostly resident, moving to lower ground in winter (Sep–Feb/Mar); also, many passage and winter visitors to Britain from Iceland and Scandinavia during Aug–May, and during freeze-ups may occur on coastal shores.

Grey Plover   *Pluvialis squatarola*   L 27–30 cm, WS 71–83 cm

Bigger and heavier-billed than Golden Plover, lacks obvious yellow and green elements and also has black armpits (axillaries). Summer male jet-black below and coarsely speckled black and white above; the white framing the black face terminates in a white patch on breast-sides. Female duller, with grey-brown cheeks and with upperpart markings more grey and brown. Juv. evenly patterned in dark slate-grey and often with a faint yellow-buff tinge to the pale areas. Winter plumage as juv., but with more diffuse and irregular markings above. In flight gives a characteristic indrawn whistle which often announces the arriving bird, usually a drawn-out 3-syllable 'pleeoo-wee' but sometimes shorter 'plooee'. A high-arctic wader, breeding on treeless tundra. On passage and in winter more coastal than Golden Plover, found mostly on extensive muddy and sandy shores. Common in winter on some British coasts, and with pronounced passage mainly in May and in Jul–Sep (ads.) and Sep–Nov (juvs.); some 1st-years remain through summer.

Golden Plover

Grey Plover

juv

Golden Plover

♀ summer

♂ summer

juv

Grey Plover

♂ summer

winter

White-tailed Plover

Red-wattled Plover

Sociable Plover winter

Red-wattled Plover *Hoplopterus indicus* L 32–35 cm, WS 80–81 cm

Bigger than Spur-winged Plover, with distinctive black pattern on head and breast, red bill (black-tipped) and loral wattle and yellow legs. At distance, is darker above than Spur-winged and has white (not black) belly. Noisy, calls also at night and is very loud in display flight. Call a loud, insistent, rather rhythmic 'did-he-do-it'. Occurs mainly in cultivated country on tilled land beside water, e.g. ponds, ditches and seasonally irrigated fields.

White-tailed Plover *Chettusia leucura* L 26–29 cm, WS 67–70 cm

Smaller in body but considerably longer-legged than Sociable Plover, with paler and more unmarked head, all-white tail and yellow legs. Juv. has dark brown subterminal lines or spots on mantle and wing-coverts. Forages mostly in shallow water around river deltas, on flooded meadows and other wetlands, in breeding range often together with Black-winged Stilt. Breeds very rarely and irregularly in Middle East, nearest real numbers in Euphrates and Tigris delta. Recorded a few times in Europe.

Sociable Plover *Chettusia gregaria* L 27–30 cm, WS 65–70 cm

Slightly smaller than Lapwing, longer-legged and with attractive and characteristic colour pattern somewhat recalling Dotterel's. In summer plumage has black-and-chestnut belly, contrasting black and white markings on head and yellow-buff cheeks. Female often has less black on belly and browner mantle. In winter plumage more anonymous, with grey-brown colours; mantle and wing-coverts acquire broad rusty-brown fringes, breast darker spots and belly becomes pale. Juv. resembles winter ad., but has paler crown, is more streaked on head and breast, and has more conspicuous pale fringes on mantle and secondary coverts reinforced by suggestion of dark subterminal lines. Variegated in flight, with black primaries and white secondaries and greater coverts. Legs and bill black. Appears in Europe often with Lapwings on short-grass fields. Very rare visitor from steppes of C Asia.

Red-wattled Plover

White-tailed Plover

Sociable Plover

White-tailed Plover

Red-wattled Plover

White-tailed Plover

♂ summer

Sociable Plover

winter

juv moulting to 1st-winter

juv ♀

♂

Spur-winged Plover

♂

Lapwing

Spur-winged Plover   *Hoplopterus spinosus*   L 25–27 cm, WS 65–70 cm

Unmistakable. Flies with fairly slow clipped wingbeats, and wings have Raven-black flight feathers and white 'Woodpigeon-band' on secondary coverts. Juv. lacks pointed scapular feathers, has brown fringes on crown and faint patterning on upperparts. Calls shrill like Lapwing's but with something of Oystercatcher's metallic ring, e.g. 'peeh' or 'veik', display call a repeated loud 'peeyk, peeyk, peeyk…peeyk…'. Occurs fairly commonly but locally beside lakes, marsh and river deltas, though often found on dry, sandy ground with additional elements of taller grass and low scrubby vegetation. Feeds on insects and other small animals, captured in soft sand or earth in Lapwing fashion. Returns end Mar−Apr, migrates Aug−Sep.

Lapwing   *Vanellus vanellus*   L 28−31 cm, WS 70−76 cm

A characteristic bird on coastal pastures and farmland. Unique among waders with its long wispy crest and green back. Female somewhat more subdued in coloration than male and merges into colours of its habitat; crest is shorter, chin often pale and wingband not glossy blue. Juv. has only insignificant crest and has scaly yellow-brown pattern on upperparts. In Aug−Nov ad. acquires winter plumage, with pale chin and throat and pale-scaled upperparts, more so on female. At nest site utters excited and shrill 'peoo-vit' or 'wee-oo-way', and performs aerial acrobatics. In display flight male calls continuously and a loud humming sound is heard from the rounded wings. Found in flocks in greater part of the year. Occurs on fields and meadowland, preferably short-grass slightly damp meadows, most abundantly next to wetlands. A migrant in north and east of range, where its early return is one of first signs of spring. Feeds on all kinds of terrestrial invertebrates, insects, worms etc. Partial migrant in Britain, where also a common passage and winter visitor from N and E Europe; in cold weather often huge movements to west/south.

Spur-winged Plover

Lapwing

Spur-winged Plover

displaying
males

Lapwing

♂ summer

♂ winter

♀ summer

Turnstone

♂ summer

winter

Turnstone   *Arenaria interpres*   *L 21–24 cm, WS 44–49 cm*

A robust and short-billed wader with characteristic facial markings and strikingly variegated pattern in flight. Female generally more subdued in coloration, and especially on wing-coverts and face has less defined markings. In winter plumage upperparts predominantly dark grey-brown with lighter edges and facial markings more diffuse. Juv. is grey-brown above with rusty-buff edges (scaly pattern). Calls nasal, short and ricocheting, but sonorous and very characteristic, 'kutt' or 'kut'ut'ut'. When alarmed, a typically vibrant 'te vut-te-vut-te-vut-te-dededede'. Nests on coastal tundra and in Scandinavia on outer islands of skerries and along rocky shores. Passage and winter also on open sandy and muddy tidal shores. Has broad food selection, often pokes among seaweed with its short conical bill and turns over pebbles in search of invertebrates. Passage and winter visitor to Britain, present mid Jul–May, with small numbers (imms.) oversummering.

Sanderling   *Calidris alba*   *L 20–21 cm, WS 36–39 cm*

Size of a large Dunlin but with shorter and straighter bill. In summer plumage breast and upperparts to varying degree rusty-red, though odd individuals lack or have only faint rusty elements. In all plumages shows broader and brighter white wingbar in flight than other *Calidris* species. Lacks hind toe. Can be confused with Little Stint and Red-necked Stint, which, however, are smaller. Transverse vermiculated breast markings and pale areas in the dark centres of wing-coverts and tertials characteristic and a distinguishing mark compared with Red-necked. Juv. very checkered black and white above and initially with creamy-buff tint on breast-side and parts of mantle. Call a loud liquid 'plit' or 'krit', not unlike Little Stint or Kentish Plover, sometimes 'tuk' like Turnstone. A high-arctic breeder regularly passing along European coasts. In winter lives mainly on extensive sandy shores, where feeds by dashing restlessly along water-line, parrying waves and picking up small animals thrown up by the sea. In Britain winters on sandy beaches Oct–Mar; passage migrants more widespread on coast, mainly in Apr–Jun and in Jul–Sep (ads.) and Sep–Oct (juvs.).

Turnstone

Sanderling

juv

Turnstone ♂ summer ♀

summer

duller individual
summer

juv

winter

Sanderling

Knot Sanderling Dunlin Curlew Sandpiper

Knot *Calidris canutus* L 23–25 cm, WS 47–54 cm

Largest *Calidris* species, robust and fairly stocky in build, with straight bill. In summer plumage characteristic, with a particular, slightly cold brick-red colour below. Juv. greyish, scaly-patterned above (each feather bordered with dark subterminal arc and pale outer fringe), and with V-shaped markings or spots on breast-sides and back onto flanks; initially has clear reddish-ochre wash on breast, though this soon fades. In winter plumage like juv., but upperparts more uniformly grey, feathers lack dark subterminal marks. Juv. moults mantle feathers in autumn and in 1st-winter plumage is similar to ad. Legs greenish-grey, slightly darker on ad. In flight long-winged with narrow white wingbar and characteristic pale grey rump with almost unmarked grey tail. Flight call a short 'wutt wutt' or 'kwet', not especially loud but with a particular, restrained nasal, slightly goose-like ring, most easily confused with Bar-tailed Godwit. High-arctic breeder, wintering on W European coasts and south to W Africa (also farther south), the majority on tidal shores around British Isles and in North Sea region. Not uncommon also on autumn passage Jul–Aug (ads.) and Sep (juvs.), fewer in spring (mostly May).

Curlew Sandpiper *Calidris ferruginea* L 18–23 cm, WS 38–41 cm

In summer plumage most easily mistaken for Knot, but is smaller, longer-legged and has long and distinctly curved bill. Body often markedly rounded. In summer plumage dark brick-red below, though females usually paler/duller and in fresh plumage with broad pale fringes and dark vermiculation on belly, look 'floury' and not very warm-toned. The attractive full-summer males are seen mostly within a short period in Jul and birds moving south in latter part of Jul and early Aug often have some grey winter feathers. In spring very rare in Britain and NW Europe, though large flocks stop off in E Mediterranean, mostly in May. Juvs. stop off fairly commonly at wader localities in Britain (incl. inland) in Aug–Sep: they are scaly-patterned above, initially with a beautiful orange-ochre wash across breast and upperparts, but in late summer most look rather yellowish-grey and they easily get lost among Dunlin flocks. In flight the wholly white rump is a good species character. Flight call a pleasing 'krillee' (kril'l'l'lee'), in voice not unlike Dunlin's but clearer and purer in tone, more like a deep-voiced Temminck's Stint. Stops off on shallow shores, often accompanied by Dunlins, on sandbanks and mudflats, also inland at reservoirs, lakesides etc. Winters in tropical Africa, rarely in Israel and Egypt, occasional winter records in other parts of Mediterranean and W Europe.

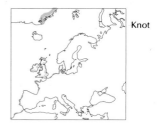

Knot

Curlew Sandpiper

Knot

winter

juv

summer

Curlew Sandpiper

1st-winter

summer
(worn)

summer
(fresh)

juv

Dunlin *Calidris alpina* *L 16–22 cm, WS 35–40 cm*

The commonest wader on passage and in winter along flat seashores. In autumn ads. migrate first (Jul–Aug) and are easy to identify by their black abdomen and brown-red back. Juvs. (Aug–Oct) vary somewhat in markings but typically have accumulation of dark spots on belly, echoing ad.'s black abdomen; rusty-yellow to red-brown fringes above. Grey winter feathers are acquired earlier than in ad., from as early as Aug, and these gradually give young birds a greyer overall impression. In winter plumage uniformly dirty-grey above. Compared with Curlew Sandpiper has shorter legs and straighter bill and in all plumages has dark centre to rump; in flight shows clear white wingbar. Chiefly two races in Europe. Northern/eastern *alpina* is longer-billed and with brighter, more contrasting coloration. Southern/western *schinzii* (Iceland, Britain and Ireland, S Scandinavia) breeds locally in British Isles on grassy, boggy moors and lowland marshes; has shorter bill and dingier coloration and the black belly patch is often reduced to dark patches on females. Juv. *schinzii* sometimes lack spotting on belly-sides. Flight call a harsh trilled 'krree' or 'kreeit'. Male displays in flight over nest site with long repetitive descending series of similar calls culminating in a drawn-out hum. Near nest or young a more vocal, nervous 'wut-wut-wut' also heard. Southern race returns to breeding areas in Mar–Apr, in Britain also common on passage; *alpina* is common on passage and abundant in winter; and some of NE Greenland race *arctica* (paler, duller) also migrate through British Isles.

Broad-billed Sandpiper *Limicola falcinellus* *L 16–18 cm, WS 34–37 cm*

Slightly smaller than Dunlin, with more elongated body shape and markedly kinked bill-tip. In summer and juv. plumages has conspicuous snipe-like crown-stripes. In fresh summer plumage fairly colourless (pale-dusted), but when worn remarkably dark, upperparts blackish-brown with pale fringes, dark breast and often coarse markings on flanks. Winter plumage like Dunlin's, but on some a suggestion of pale lateral crown-stripes, and has darker carpal area. Juvs. seen in Aug–Sep are paler than ad. in worn summer plumage, more regularly patterned (often with rather snipe-like stripes) and scarcely marked on flanks. Legs muddy-grey with greenish tinge. Call a buzzing 'chrrreeit', most like Dunlin's but more drawn-out and with clearer final upward inflection. Contact call also heard from groups, a short 'dritt' almost like Little Stint. In display flight it moves to and fro, sometimes quite high up, now and then pulls up, hanging on raised vibrating wings, all the time giving a mechanical buzzing 'swirr swirr swirr...' occasionally interspersed with a faster more whirring 'swirrirrirrirr...'. Nests sparsely on extensive bogs with sedge-covered quagmire. A relatively scarce wader with a southeasterly migration direction, often mingles with Dunlins at traditional wader sites but also stops off in 'snipe country' (e.g. muddy inland sites). Rare but annual migrant through Britain, mainly May–Sep, with most in May–early Jun.

Dunlin

Broad-billed Sandpiper

Purple Sandpiper

Dunlin

schinzii
♂ summer (May)

alpina
♀ summer (Jul)

ad winter

juv

Dunlin

summer (Jul)

Broad-billed Sandpiper

juv

summer (May)

ad winter

Purple Sandpiper

juv

summer

1st-winter

Purple Sandpiper   *Calidris maritima*   L 20–22 cm, WS 40–44 cm

Slightly bigger, stockier and more robust than Dunlin. In all plumages darker and, especially in winter plumage, which is dark grey with yellow legs, unlike Dunlin. In summer plumage crown, mantle and parts of breast-side acquire blackish-brown feathers with yellow-grey and rusty-brown fringes; legs darken and become greenish-brown, especially on feet and on 'knee-joint'. Juv. like ad. summer, but more uniform grey on face without prominent supercilium, is more 'daintily' patterned with narrow fringes above and more evenly streaked/spotted on breast. Secondary coverts on juv. have contrasting white fringes; they are more lacking in contrast on ad., a detail which distinguishes birds in 1st-winter plumage from ads. In flight obviously dark with a narrow pale wingbar. Call a varied liquid, usually nasal 'küt', keutt' or 'kewit'. Very tame at nest site, when agitated utters sharp 'keeit' calls or more excited 'krihihihihi'. Territorial song variable, includes a drawn-out buzzing 'kreuwirr' and 'hurr-ee' and series of other calls, usually with a deep and nasal ring. Nests on treeless tundra and upland moors. During non-breeding season on sea coasts. Winters farther north than any other wader, autumn passage often peaks in Oct–Nov. Winters locally in small numbers in Britain, where 1–3 pairs also breed annually in Scotland.   *Map p. 218*

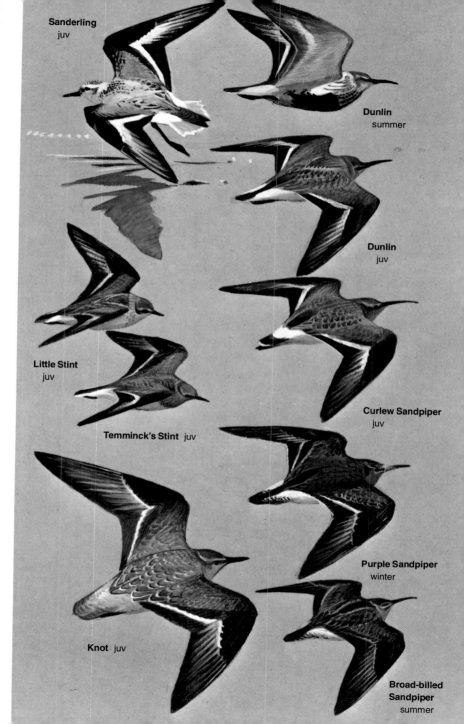

Sanderling juv

Dunlin summer

Dunlin juv

Little Stint juv

Curlew Sandpiper juv

Temminck's Stint juv

Purple Sandpiper winter

Knot juv

Broad-billed Sandpiper summer

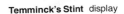

Temminck's Stint display

Little Stint   *Calidris minuta*   L 12–14 cm, WS 28–31 cm

Our smallest sandpiper. In summer plumage varies in intensity of colour from reddish-orange to rusty-buff, but all show a distinct yellowish V on mantle and a dark central crown 'ridge'. In winter plumage grey above, with or without clear dark shaft streaks. Juv. gives pale impression with plump snow-white abdomen and a rusty-orange tone above: markings are characterised by a prominent white V on mantle, a pale grey neck-boa, a rusty-tinted and streaked patch on breast-sides, and lateral crown-stripe bordering dark 'ridge' to crown. For differences compared with Red-necked Stint and Semipalmated Sandpiper see also next spread. During Jul to beginning of Aug mostly ads. are seen which, if size not obvious, can be mistaken for Sanderling. Call a short, clear 'tip' or 'tit', most like Sanderling's, and in interactions between foraging birds a 'ti hi hi ti hi hi' is sometimes heard. Breeds on tundra and seen in Britain and NW Europe mainly on autumn migration; majority of migrants are juvs. often making up a characteristic element among mixed *Calidris* flocks in Aug–Sep (Oct). Very few winter in Britain.

Temminck's Stint   *Calidris temminckii*   L 12–14 cm, WS 28.5–31.5 cm

A very small, often stocky-looking and short-legged wader, often with elongated body shape. In summer plumage looks grey-buff or brown-buff above, at most with cinnamon-brown fringes and never with Little Stint's rusty-orange tone; many have a sprinkling of dirty-grey winter-like feathers. Juv. has scaly upperparts and small dark patches on upper scapulars. In winter plumage uniform brown-grey above, with indistinct supercilium and pale eye-ring. In all plumages separated from Little Stint by paler clayey-coloured legs. Flight call a characteristic ringing 'tirr', often drawn out into a more or less prolonged trill. When flushed, it climbs rapidly and jerkily upwards. Nests relatively commonly in mountains, often on grassy areas with willow scrub beside various wetlands, e.g. along shores of Gulf of Bothnia; a few breed N Scotland. Less common than Little Stint on passage, often seen singly or in groups of 2–5 individuals. Stops off both at inland lakeshores and on coasts, not infrequently at quite small pools, but avoids exposed or rocky coast. Ads. seen mostly in May and Jul, juvs. in Aug–Sep. Has predominantly southerly and southeasterly migration direction and is seen at suitable localities throughout Europe, but is very scarce in Britain.

Little Stint

Temminck's Stint

1st-winter

winter

summer (Jul)

Little Stint

juv

juv

summer (worn, poorly marked)

winter

Temminck's Stint

summer (fresh, clearly marked)

Red-necked Stint *Calidris ruficollis* L 13–16 cm, WS 29–33 cm

Vagrant from easternmost Siberia. Recorded a few times in W Europe, all summer-plumaged ads. In all plumages much like Little Stint, but with shorter bill, slightly more thickset build with more attenuated rear end owing to long wings and tail; central tail feathers usually extend beyond wingtips. In summer plumage rusty-red on head and neck, throat and upper breast with pronounced border against whitish breast, latter dotted with prominent arrowhead spots; area around bill-join and supercilium behind eye usually pale. To varying degree shows rusty feather edges on mantle, rarely with pronounced pale lines on back. A difference compared with Little Stint is that all wing-coverts apart from the odd one are a washed-out grey without rust-tinted edges or distinct brownish-black centres, this often applying also to lowest row of scapulars and tertials. Juv. like juv. Little Stint, most important differences being: *1* tertials and greater secondary coverts have paler greyish centres and entire wing looks grey and lacking in contrast (Little has brown-black coverts and tertials with more distinctly defined rust-coloured fringes); *2* never shows broad, distinct pale bands on mantle; *3* more diffuse and smudgy streaking on breast-side; *4* plainer head markings in which lores stand out as darkest point, crown not markedly darker centrally. Call in flight like Little Stint but lower in pitch with 'l' sound, 'klüpp' or 'klürpp'. On breeding ground often with 'r' sound, 'kreep'.

Semipalmated Sandpiper *Calidris pusilla* L 13–15 cm, WS 28–31 cm

Vagrant from N America. Has short webbing between toes which can be observed in the field under good conditions. A shade bulkier than Little Stint; bill varies in length, is often strikingly stout at base and slightly blob-tipped. In summer plumage overall impression is grey-brown without Little Stint's bright rusty-orange elements. Juv. fairly well differentiated from juv. Little Stint by generally greyish impression with at most rusty yellow-brown fringes; often looks grey-brown with dirty-buff fringes fading to off-white, giving upperparts a scaly appearance. Distinguishing features are: *1* lack of distinct white lines on mantle; *2* darker ear-coverts and crown; *3* paler centres to tertials and wing-coverts; *4* dark anchor-shaped mark towards tip of feathers in the two lower rows of scapulars. Differs from Red-necked Stint in darker crown and ear-coverts. Most difficult to separate from Western Sandpiper (see below). Call variable, usually a coarse, slightly rolled 'chrrüp' or short 'kyet' or 'kyip', occasionally a trisyllabic 'ch-pi-lip' on rising. Recorded annually, majority in Britain and Ireland in Jul–Oct.

Western Sandpiper *Calidris mauri* L 14–17 cm, WS 28–31 cm

Extremely rare vagrant to Europe from western N America. Very like Semipalmated and similarly has small webbing between toes. Bill normally longer and slightly curved towards tip, but measurements overlap. Appears taller-legged, however, with centre of gravity located farther forward than in Semipalmated. In summer plumage normally easy to identify by profuse arrowhead spots on breast and along entire belly-side combined with rusty tone to ear-coverts and crown and also to scapulars. Juv. more difficult to identify, but compared with juv. Semipalmated has plainer head markings, greyer crown and rusty fringes to upper scapulars and centre of mantle; wing-coverts, tertials and lower scapulars often mid-grey without dark centres and lack obvious rusty tone to fringes. Combination of grey 'watered-down' crown and clear rusty tone to upper scapulars a good character compared with Semipalmated. Call a characteristic slightly drawn-out 'cheep', but also has more Semipalmated-like 'tchrrü'' or 'tchrree'.

summer

Red-necked
Stint

Red-necked
Stint
juv

Semipalmated juv   Western juv   Red-necked juv

Little Stint
juv

Semipalmated
Sandpiper
summer

Semipalmated
Sandpiper
juv

♂ summer

Western Sandpiper

Western
Sandpiper
juv moulting
to 1st-winter

Temminck's Stint juv   **Long-toed Stint** juv   **Least Sandpiper** juv

Long-toed Stint   *Calidris subminuta*   L 13–14 cm, WS 26.5–29.5 cm

Vagrant from E Asia; juvs. recorded a few times in W Europe. Pale greenish-grey to dirty-orange legs make confusion with Least Sandpiper most probable. Has long legs and toes and also longer neck than Least Sandpiper. Has slightly forward-leaning posture and sometimes stands upright more like Wood Sandpiper. In flight shows darker underwings and narrower wingbar than Little Stint and the long toes extend beyond tail-tip. Wingbeats clipped. Bill very short and fine-tipped, with paler area at base of lower mandible. Head with distinct supercilium, broadest in front of eye, bordering darker, usually rusty-brown crown-cap. Seen from in front, the dark on crown extends in a dusky band down over forehead, meets the bill base and joins with loral stripe at the side; loral stripe often less prominent and broken in centre. Breast has thinner streaks on sides which extend farther down on flank than in Least Sandpiper, summer-plumaged ad. often showing beautiful rusty-orange colour over breast and juv. a greyish-buff tone. Upperparts of juv. streaked, with black-brown centres with rusty-buff to red-brown and white fringes; normally has clear white V on back. Rusty-brown fringes to scapulars contrast with brown-grey overall impression of wing-coverts (on juv. Least wing-covert fringes are also rusty). Markings on wing-coverts also form a more obvious pattern and the dark colour on the feather shafts breaks the pale fringe at the tip. In summer plumage overall impression is much like summer-plumaged Little Stint. Call most like Curlew Sandpiper's, a loud and melodious 'chürrl', clearer and more vocal than Least's, lower in pitch than Temminck's.

Least Sandpiper   *Calidris minutilla*   L 11–12 cm, WS 26–29 cm

Very rare vagrant from N America. The smallest of the *Calidris* species and visibly smaller than Little Stint, often appears rather short-legged and crouched, looks podgy with short neck and angular head (steep forehead) and often is slightly abrupt in its movements. Legs pale, yellow-grey to yellow-green. Bill black and looks slightly curved, mainly because of concave lower edge. In the field often looks darker than the black-legged species, brownish with a characteristic 'Mongolian' expression, created by a broad dark loral stripe which dominates the facial markings. Has a paler area behind eye followed by a dark patch on rear ear-coverts. Juv. has rusty-brown fringes on mantle and wing-coverts, usually with a thin buff-white V mark on back; breast is often buffy-brown in tone and prominently streaked right across, with coarser spots on breast-sides. In summer plumage more variable, though few approach Long-toed Stint in intensity of coloration; certain individuals acquire pale markings in the dark centres to tertials and greater coverts, something never shown by Long-toed. In winter plumage obviously darker, more brown-grey than Little Stint, and typically with a dark shadowy area around base of shafts on mantle and scapular feathers. When flushed, it often climbs with sideways-tilting flight and clipping wingbeats recalling Temminck's Stint. Call a ringing 'chrreep' or 'krreeep', lower in tone than Temminck's and more drawn-out, also has shorter 'kleeep' or 'chueep' on rising.

226

Little Stint

juv

Least
juv

Long-toed
juv

mmer
sh)

Long-toed Stint

winter

summer
(fresh)

juv

Least Sandpiper

summer
(fresh)

juv

summer
(worn)

winter

White-rumped
Sandpiper

Baird's
Sandpiper

juv

winter

juv

juv

White-rumped Sandpiper   *Calidris fuscicollis*   L 15–17 cm, WS 36–38 cm

Size as that of a very small Dunlin: elongated body shape with long wings which extend a good bit beyond tertials and with relatively short legs. Bill fairly straight but has slight curve towards tip, most marked on underside; has paler area at base of lower mandible. In all plumages shows white rump like Curlew Sandpiper. Juv. has cinnamon to rusty fringes on centre of mantle and upper scapulars, with two double rather indistinct whitish V lines on back; crown rusty-toned with prominent whitish-grey supercilium. In summer plumage plain-looking, like Semipalmated Sandpiper above with pale yellowish-brown fringes to crown and mantle, breast is densely streaked and often (though not always) shows arrowhead spots on entire side of body. Winter plumage drab grey, acquired as early as Aug–Sep. Call characteristic, a drawn-out very high-pitched, squeaking 'tzeeeht', with an electrical character. Very rare but annual vagrant to Europe from N America, majority in Jul–Oct.

Baird's Sandpiper   *Calidris bairdii*   L 14–16 cm, WS 36–40 cm

Like White-rumped Sandpiper but with straighter and all-black bill. The protracted rear end (long projecting primaries) and the relatively short legs give it a distinctive profile. Juv. has an overall buff or grey-buff tone to upperparts, whole back looks scaly due to off-white fringes and it is somewhat reminiscent of upperparts of juv. Curlew Sandpiper; breast faintly streaked on a buff or greyish-yellow ground colour. Has distinctive facial expression, in part caused by e.g. shape of supercilium above lores (note that there is a pale spot formed above lores at forehead) and pale eye-ring. In flight strikingly long-winged, with poorly marked wingbar and without contrasting tail or rump markings. Call a rolling 'krrrü', lower in pitch and less ringing than Curlew Sandpiper. Occurrence in Europe much as that of White-rumped (but some may originate from breeding sites in NE Siberia).

Stilt Sandpiper   *Micropalama himantopus*   L 18–23 cm, WS 38–41 cm

Very rare vagrant from arctic N America, *Tringa*-like owing to its tall carriage; long greenish legs, long neck and long bill (straight with a slight droop at tip). Feeding behaviour like a dowitcher's, wades in belly-deep water and penetrates the bottom mud with a sawing snipe-like action. Plumage closest to that of *Calidris* waders. Juv. initially has rusty fringes to central upperparts on back and inner scapulars, but colour rapidly fades and it appears generally pale and yellow-grey. Acquires grey winter feathers early, usually in Sep. Both juv. and winter plumages show markings along flanks and on vent. In summer plumage heavily barred dark on entire underparts and with bright rusty-red cheeks and crown. In flight toes project at least 2cm beyond tail. Often silent, but has a slightly grating 'kcheeup'.

White-rumped Sandpiper

ad moulting to winter plumage

White-rumped

juv

summer

Baird's Sandpiper

summer

juv

Baird's

1st-winter

summer

Stilt Sandpiper

juv moulting to 1st-winter

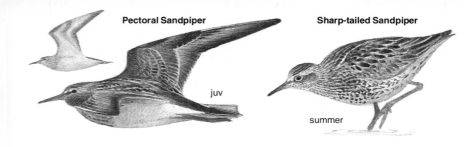

Pectoral Sandpiper   Sharp-tailed Sandpiper

juv

summer

Pectoral Sandpiper   *Calidris melanotos*   *L 19−23 cm, WS 38−45 cm*

Obviously bigger than Dunlin. Male c10% bigger than female. Solidly built with relatively long neck and small head. Legs and bill base greenish-buff to clay-coloured. Ad. summer looks generally brown and lacking in character, apart from, especially on male, the intensely dark-streaked neck and breast, which form a sharp edge against the dirty-white belly. Juv. at distance darker than a Dunlin, warm brown with pronounced border between streaked breast and white belly, upperparts with rather snipe-like longitudinal stripes; colours vary somewhat, some having brownish-yellow ground colour and others almost a rusty-orange ground. Winter plumage grey-brown and coarsely patterned with black-brown feather centres above. In all plumages shows narrow pale wingbar. Call a rolling 'chrrük'. Rare visitor from arctic America and E Siberia but the most frequent American wader in Europe, most being seen in Jul−Oct with peak in Sep−Oct. Stops off mostly on muddy and grass-covered shores.

Sharp-tailed Sandpiper   *Calidris acuminata*   *L 17−20 cm, WS 38−43 cm*

Like Pectoral Sandpiper, but taller-legged with shorter bill. Can give impression of a Wood Sandpiper. Juv. rusty-orange on parts of back, crown and breast, gives cleaner and more distinctive impression than Pectoral; also told from that species by the sharply demarcated dark crown, white supercilium and the breast which is ochre and unstreaked in the centre towards the white belly. In summer plumage prominent V-shaped marks on belly-sides and vent and prominent white eye-ring. Call very different from Pectoral's, clearer and more vocal 'peeip' and twittering Swallow-like 'trrree' or 'tree-trripp'. Prefers grassy freshwater shores. Breeds on tundra in E Siberia and is very rare vagrant to Europe, mostly in Aug−Oct.

Buff-breasted Sandpiper   *Tryngites subruficollis*   *L 18−20 cm, WS 43−47 cm*

A distinctive wader with round head and short straight bill. Ad. resembles juv. though mantle feathers have broader ochre fringes and their centres are entirely black-brown. Most easily confused with juv. female Ruff, but has shorter bill, yellower legs and is plainer around eye and with neat spots on breast-sides. In flight no obvious wingbar and lacks Ruff's conspicuous white ovals on rump. Usually silent in flight but occasionally utters a low soft 'gerk' on rising. Most often found foraging on short-grass fields or heathland. Very rare but annual vagrant to Europe from arctic N America, mostly Jul−Oct with a peak in Sep.

Upland Sandpiper   *Bartramia longicauda*   *L 28−32 cm, WS 47−52 cm*

Very rare vagrant from N American prairies, Jul−Dec, most in England. Distinctive long tail, curlew-like long neck and thin straight bill. Body appears large and head proportionately small. Legs yellow-buff. Prefers short-grass fields or arable land as habitats, moves like a plover and runs quickly. In flight, long-winged and long-tailed with dark, blackish rump and dark flight feathers. Call variable, on rising often a melodious loud 'kwip-eep-eep-ep' or 'kwee-leep'.   *Ill p.238*

♀ summer (worn)

Pectoral Sandpiper

juv

juv

**Sharp-tailed
Sandpiper**

Buff-breasted Sandpiper
juv

juv ♀

Ruff

**Buff-breasted
Sandpiper**

Ruff

winter

Ruff lek display

♀

♀

Ruff *Philomachus pugnax*   *L male 26–32 cm, female 20-25 cm, WS 46–58 cm*

A peculiar and distinctive wader. In May–Jun the appreciably larger males bear head tufts, ruffs and other variegated feathers and facial warts. This plumage is infinitely variable and at long distance e.g. entirely brown-red or black individuals can be taken for something completely different. The long neck and head feathers are grown during Apr and are shed as early as Jun. Female's amount of variegated feathering also varies considerably and birds can at times be predominantly blackish-brown. Leg colour of both sexes is orange-red or greenish-grey (partly age-related). Juvs. (p.231), which completely dominate the passage in late summer and autumn, vary in basic colour tone from buff-grey to distinctly rusty. Winter plumage as juv., but more drab grey and often with a prominent dirty-white patch around bill base. Flight is rather flicking and pigeon-like and birds show clear white wingbar as well as large white ovals on rump-sides. Males gather at breeding sites in spring at special arenas (leks), often returning to traditional sites to display: they dance, or rather joust, with each other with 'inflated' plumage, wing-flutters, leaps, bows and trailing wings, and the next second freeze like mechanical puppets. Breeds on sedge swamps in north and on flat coastal meadows in south. On passage and in winter occurs at muddy margins of lakes, rivers and ponds (occasionally coast) and on wet meadowland, but also on fields and ploughed areas. Silent, but a low 'wek' occasionally heard in flight, especially from females with young. In Britain local breeder (rare) and winterer, mostly seen on passage in Mar–Jun and particularly Jul–Oct.

Curlew   *Numenius arquata*   *L 50–60 cm, WS 80–100 cm*

Most easily confused with Whimbrel, but is bigger with longer and more evenly decurved bill and also different head markings. Female is bigger and has longer bill than male. Juv. males in late summer look conspicuously short-billed compared with ad. In winter often has pink tinge to base of lower mandible.Overall appearance similar all year round, but in spring partial moult gives variable extent of rich yellow-ochre colour to plumage. Has declined in many areas in southern part of range but is relatively common in the north on upland moors, bogs and on damp fields. On passage and in winter found largely on estuaries and other coastal habitats. In spring gives song of melodious fluting whistles which accelerate and merge into a bubbling trill, first uttered in climbing, then slowly descending song flight. Year round gives soft melancholy whistles, 'cour-lee', and various other, similar, calls. In Britain present on breeding grounds from Mar, partial migrant; also passage and winter visitor from N Europe during Jul–May. Females often migrate in Jun, leaving males to tend young.

Slender-billed Curlew   *Numenius tenuirostris*   *L 36–41 cm, WS 72–82 cm*

Obviously smaller than Curlew, with whiter ground colour and on ad. round or heart-shaped spots on flanks. Bill is shorter and distinctly tapering to a thin tip. In flight, inner primaries and secondaries paler and more heavily barred with sharp contrast against brownish-black outer primaries, underwings and axillaries are whiter and less patterned (but note that Curlews of race *orientalis* from C Siberia have more unmarked underwings than European breeders). Tail has fewer and darker bars on whiter background and meets virtually unmarked rump. Quiet; flight call Curlew-like but higher and faster. Extremely rare and highly endangered breeder in C Siberia. In 1800s common, migrated southwestwards to N Africa; now only odd individuals seen, mostly in winter in NW Morocco.

Whimbrel   *Numenius phaeopus*   *L 40–46 cm, WS 71–81 cm*

Smaller, shorter-legged and darker and less clearly patterned than Curlew. Bill appears more blunted and hooked owing to marked kink near tip. Crown has two dark lateral crown-stripes, which accentuate a more prominent supercilium. In flight obviously smaller, more like a Bar-tailed Godwit and with faster wingbeats than Curlew. Commonest flight call a somewhat stammering or laughing trill, 'pu hu hu hu hu hu', more mechanical and less fluting than Curlew's (like female Cuckoo). Song begins like Curlew's, but terminates in a similar straight 'stammering' trill. Breeds on tundra, upland moors, northern bogs and mosses, also beside sea on shores of Norwegian fjords and on the Atlantic islands. Stops off on passage on mudflats, rocky shores etc, but also to a large extent uses inland staging areas such as moorland, heath and fields. Seen on passage mainly Apr–Jun and Jul–Oct; winters along W African coasts.

Curlew

Slender-billed Curlew

Whimbrel

Curlew

♀ 1st-winter

♂ summer (fresh)

♂ summer

Slender-billed Curlew

summer

Whimbrel

Bar-tailed Godwit
♀ winter

Black-tailed Godwit   *Limosa limosa*   *L 36–44 cm, WS 62–70 cm*

Strikingly long-legged and slim with a long, straight bill. In summer plumage amount of brick-red varies, some females being predominantly grey. Race *islandica* in Iceland and on Lofoten and Shetland Islands is a deeper rusty-red, this extending onto belly, and has shorter bill. In winter plumage a uniform grey colour, with pink bill base. Juv. variable in shade, typically with reddish-ochre tint on neck and back. Chief distinguishing marks are the white wingbars and the white tail with black terminal band. Noisy at nest site, giving nasal and creaking notes; calls often repeated nervously in series, e.g. vibrating 'kew we we wu' or 'ke-weeku', more drawn-out 'krrreoo', very excited rapid 'kee-wee-wee-wee' and so on. Contact call a nasal, slightly metallic 'aip aip'. In flight display high in air gives creaking repetitive 'kevee'u-kevee'u…' during peculiar swaying or rocking flight. Nests locally on damp meadowland and bogs, often on drained marshes. On passage and in winter mostly on coastal estuaries, marshes and flood-lands. Rare breeder in Britain, more common (but rather local) on passage and in winter, Jul–May.

Bar-tailed Godwit   *Limosa lapponica*   *L 33–42 cm, WS 61–68 cm*

Shorter-legged and more robust than Black-tailed Godwit and without distinct wing and tail markings. In summer plumage the clearly smaller male is a deep rusty-red while female is buff or faintly rusty-tinted. In winter plumage buff-grey with dark shaft streaks above and on breast. Juv. buff-toned with rather Curlew-like markings above, but with unmarked breast, often with a dark dusky area around bill-join. Flight call nasal and similar to Knot's, 'ke-veu', sometimes slightly drawn-out 'ku-veayhk' or trisyllabic 'kew-wuh-wuh'. Song repetitive series with same nasal tone. Alarm a sharper 'kewik'. Nests on tundra and bogs in northernmost taiga. Bulk of W Palearctic birds winter in Mauretania but large numbers also in western Europe. Ads. arrive Jul–Aug, juvs. in Aug–Oct. In spring birds move north from mid March, with many staging in Waddenzee, but breeding areas are not occupied until late May–beginning of Jun. Winter on flat tidal mudflats and sandy shores, but also found on drier grassland.

Black-tailed Godwit

Bar-tailed Godwit

Black-tailed Godwit

winter

juv

♂ summer

♂ summer

juv

Bar-tailed Godwit

♂ summer

♀ summer

Whimbrel

Curlew

Bar-tailed Godwit
juv

Black-tailed Godwit
winter

Upland Sandpiper

juv

Green Sandpiper

Wood Sandpiper

Redshank

Spotted Redshank
juv

Greenshank

Ruff
juv

Redshank **Spotted Redshank** juv

Redshank *Tringa totanus* *L 27–29 cm, WS 45–52 cm*

A grey-brown and dark-spotted wader with bright orange-red legs and bill base. The dark markings vary and appear particularly heavy on northern populations. In winter plumage looks almost uniformly grey-brown above. Juv. lacks distinctively red bill base; it differs from juv. Spotted Redshank in having a more brown and buff colour tone, whiter and less patterned belly and also shorter bill without red at base. Characteristic in flight with brilliant white trailing edge to wing. Very alert and restless at nest site, gives persistent pounding 'klü-klü-klü…' in alarm. Flight call a usually disyllabic 'teu-hu', sometimes 'teu-hu-hu'. Displays in air in rising and falling flight with rapid, shallow vibrating wingbeats, uttering slow 'tyoo, tyoo, tyoo…'. In Britain nests on wet meadows, coastal grassland, boggy heaths and moors etc. On passage and in winter on most types of shallow shores, also locally at inland wetlands. Mostly resident in Britain, also passage Mar—Apr and Jul—Oct, with large immigration Oct—Mar.

Spotted Redshank *Tringa erythropus* *L 29–32 cm, WS 48–52 cm*

In summer plumage warm sooty-black with black legs, female often with more white fringes on belly. Subads. in summer of 2nd cal-year have intensely dark-barred underparts and dark-spotted neck and upperparts (oversummer south of breeding range). Females migrate as early as second week of Jun, males later. In winter plumage looks very pale, greyish above and white below with grey wash on breast; dark lores contrast with white supercilium in front of eye. Juvs. have long orange-red legs (occasionally ochre-coloured), a character shared only with Redshank and ad. Ruff; compared with juv. Redshank, colder grey and with vermiculations over entire belly. Bill markedly long and narrow, with slight but often obvious downward kink at tip. Slim build and long neck, but in flight, which is fast, straight and purposeful, appears a rather plump, spool-shaped bird. On migration flight often tucks legs up, reinforcing the compact impression. The white and, especially in summer plumage, contrasting rump extends up in a wedge over back. In flight gives diagnostic, very sharp and full whistle, 'chuwit'. Flocks keep contact with short 'kük' calls. At nest site displays around midnight with repetitive series of 'krrrüh-ee-krrrü-ee…', with a weird, buzzing ring not unlike that of Broad-billed Sandpiper. Nests on bogs in extreme north and in Europe winters mainly around Mediterranean but also locally on W European coasts (though bulk in tropical Africa). In winter and on passage usually in shallow marshes, on flooded meadows or lake margins and on estuaries, in south at ponds and saltpans.

Redshank

Spotted Redshank

Redshank

summer

winter

juv

Spotted Redshank

juv

summer

winter

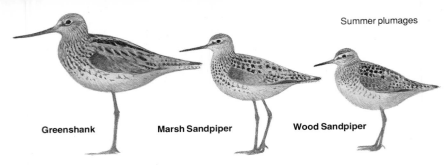

Greenshank   Marsh Sandpiper   Wood Sandpiper

Greenshank *Tringa nebularia*   L 30–35 cm, WS 53–60 cm

Largest of the *Tringa* sandpipers, with tall and powerful carriage and with faintly upcurved bill. In summer plumage grey on back with black markings untidily arranged in longitudinal bands and with black arrowheads and spots on breast and flanks. Juv. much like ad. at distance but has more pointed feathers above which are dark with pale edges, giving slightly streaky, 'wet-combed' pattern; often shows paler 'ridge' extending from breast-side halfway up side of neck which ad. lacks, a small 'mark' visible at surprisingly long distance. In winter plumage paler above, grey with faint patterning and with dark loral stripe incomplete, is pale in front of eye. In flight, white wedge up back unlike Wood Sandpiper and with paler tail than Spotted Redshank. Legs green-grey (occasionally with yellowish tinge). Flight call an indrawn, well-articulated, 3-syllable whistle, 'tchew-tew-tew', when flushed sometimes more shrill and 'cracked' 'kruip-kruip-kruip'. Displays high in air with loud, rhythmic, occasionally almost diver-like 'kluwü-kluwü-kluwü…', alarm a Redshank-like 'kyu kyu kyu…'. Hunts small fish in shallow water with rapid runs. Nests at bogs or other wetlands, sometimes in open woodland. Migrates south end Jun–Aug (ads.) and Aug–Oct (juvs.), returning north Apr–May; increasing numbers winter Britain and Ireland. Passage and winter habitat much as Spotted Redshank.

Wood Sandpiper *Tringa glareola*   L 19–21 cm, WS 36–40 cm

Longer-legged and more delicate than Common and Green Sandpipers, much smaller than Greenshank. Ad. in summer plumage slate-grey with dirty-white spots above, worn individuals often looking brown at distance. Juv. identified by regularly arranged yellow-brown to dirty-white spots on mantle. Legs greenish. In flight told from Green Sandpiper by paler underwings, narrower wings, less contrasting tail markings and different call. In flight utters pleasing whistled 'jiff-jiff' or 'jiff-jiff-jiff', which in alarm can become both piercing and 'jumpy' and excitable. Displays with fast yodelling 'lüllti-lüllti-lüllti…' Nests on bogs and mosses, abundant in far north (rare in N Scotland). On autumn passage end Jun to Aug–Sep (Oct) not uncommon on sea coast and inland, juvs. from mid Jul. Forages on freshwater margins and flooded meadows, rarely on exposed coasts. Migrates north mid Apr–May, at night like all *Tringa* waders.

Greenshank

Wood Sandpiper

juv

summer

winter

Greenshank

juv

Wood Sandpiper

summer

Juveniles

Wood Sandpiper　　　Green Sandpiper　　　Common Sandpiper

Common Sandpiper　*Actitis hypoleucos*　　　*L 19–21 cm, WS 32–35 cm*

A short-legged and long-tailed wader, typically with crouched stance and rocking rear body, often perches on boulders. Looks uniform dark grey-buff above with snow-white abdomen which runs up in a small wedge in front of wing-bend. Juv. (see picture p. 249) slightly scaly above with pale buff fringes. Winter plumage similar to juv. Flight usually low over water, when long tail and prominent white wingbars characteristic. Wingbeats are rapid and vibrating and alternate with short glides on stiff downward-angled wings. On rising, a characteristic repeated and penetrating 'hee-dee-dee'. Song a rapidly repeated series of clear needle-sharp notes, 'pipitiwee'deeh-pipitiwee'deeh...', often heard throughout day and night. Alarm a penetrating urgent 'heeep'. Common and often the only wader at many inland waters. Avoids exposed coast, prefers stony shores or those with some sheltering vegetation. In Britain also common on passage, Apr–May and Jul–Oct; a few winter in south.

Green Sandpiper　*Tringa ochropus*　　　*L 21–24 cm, WS 41–46 cm*

A dark-backed, nervous and very shy wader, often not discovered until flushed. In flight rather distinctive, with blackish, broad wings and conspicuous white rump and belly. Wing action is clipping and a little snipe-like. Most easily confused with Wood Sandpiper, but is more robust, has shorter legs and is darker above. Juv. is darker above and has brownish-ochre spots on mantle and wings. Bobs rear body. Nests in old thrush nests in woodland, but stops off on migration singly or a few together, mainly in ditches and gullies, at small pools and at well-hidden, preferably muddy freshwater margins, though also on seashores on passage. Call a sharp yet mellow 'tuEEt-wit-wit'; on rising, occasionally repeated hard 'pik' notes. Song in the same tone, a stream of yodelling, ringing 'tlUeetiht-tlUeetiht...' alternating with e.g. 'tittu'ee-tittu'ee...'. Alarm at nest 'pik-pik-pik'. Females start to migrate early Jun, males a bit later and juvs. in Jul–Aug; return passage Mar–May. Small numbers winter in Britain, where shows liking for watercress beds.

Solitary Sandpiper　*Tringa solitaria*　　　*L 18–21 cm, WS 38–44 cm*

Very rare vagrant from N America, mostly in autumn. Colour pattern resembles Green Sandpiper's while body shape is more like Wood Sandpiper's. Has dark central band on tail and rump, thus lacks white rump of Wood and Green. Often found in Green Sandpiper habitat, i.e. smaller pools and well-hidden shores. Call a usually high-pitched 'tyeek-tyeek' or 'kleeü-kleeü', not unlike Green's in tone.

Common Sandpiper

Green Sandpiper

summer

Spotted Sandpiper

summer

Common Sandpiper

Green Sandpiper summer

Solitary Sandpiper

juv

juv

Green Sandpiper

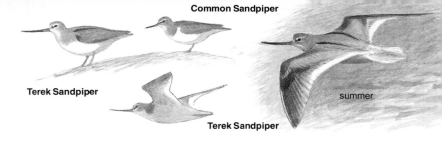

Common Sandpiper

Terek Sandpiper

Terek Sandpiper

summer

Terek Sandpiper *Xenus cinereus* L 22–25 cm, WS 38–42 cm

Size of Green Sandpiper, recalls Common Sandpiper in carriage and flight action, rocks rear body. Recognised by upcurved and long bill, steep forehead, dirty-grey and colourless plumage with black V on back, the partially visible black carpals and the short yellow-grey (in winter plumage yellow) legs. In flight, pale grey panels on trailing edges of wings are striking, impression recalls Redshank. Juv. like ad., but black band on back more indistinct and shaft streaks on scapulars and wing-coverts usually show a diagonal marking towards tip, forming an anchor. Call quite variable, usually a fast 'chü-dü-dü', softer and more melodious than Redshank's, and also on rising a slightly excited, rolling 'trürrrüt' or 'kürr-rürrrüt'. Song a slowly repeated deep-sounding 'klueewu' or 'krrueewu', uttered in display flight with shallow vibrating wingstrokes. Occurs mainly on muddy riversides and lakeshores, nest typically placed among bits of greyed driftwood on riverbanks. Very rare vagrant in Britain, mostly May–Jul, exceedingly rare Aug–Sep, but has twice wintered.

Marsh Sandpiper *Tringa stagnatilis* L 22–25 cm, WS 39–44 cm

Strikingly long-legged and delicate, with straight and thin bill; body size smaller than Redshank's. In summer plumage grey and dark-patterned above, neck and breast distinctly streaked or dark-spotted, and breast and flanks often appear neatly spotted. From late Aug appears in winter plumage, when almost uniformly pale ash-grey above with darker carpal. Juv. has similar pattern to juv. Greenshank, but with browner ground colour; moults early (from Aug) to 1st-winter. In flight legs project far beyond tail. Tail diffusely vermiculated in centre, and rump and wedge up back white like Greenshank. Lacks wingbar but has slightly paler secondaries. Legs green-grey, but during breeding season sometimes more yellow-buff. Flight call a clear fast whistle, 'keeu' or 'kiew', often repeated, and sometimes a rapid 'kiup kiup kiup'. Nests on shallow grass-covered freshwater shores. Common on passage in E Mediterranean at shallow lowland lakes and flooded areas. Usually wades in shallow water. Winters mainly in tropical Africa but seen regularly in S Spain, so some probably migrate to W Africa via W Mediterranean. Returns mainly Apr–May and leaves again Aug–Sep. Breeds Finland and Latvia (recent northward range expansion). Very rare but about annual in Britain, mostly May–Aug (Apr–Oct).

Terek Sandpiper

Marsh Sandpiper

Terek Sandpiper

summer

juv

Marsh Sandpiper

summer

winter

juv

Spotted Sandpiper *Actitis macularia* L 18–20 cm, WS 30–34 cm

Very similar to Common Sandpiper in appearance and behaviour. Characteristic in summer plumage, with prominent dark spots on underparts and ruddy legs. Juv. differs from Common Sandpiper in shorter tail, more yellow-buff legs, less patterned breast-sides, and more prominently stripe-marked wing-coverts contrasting with more uniformly coloured back. Bill often seems a touch shorter and very slightly 'dropping' towards tip. In flight shows less white on secondaries, wingbar is obvious only on primaries. Call on rising like Common Sandpiper's but rather sharper and often disyllabic. Vagrant from N America, mostly May–Jun and Aug–Oct; has overwintered several times in Britain.

Greater Yellowlegs *Tringa melanoleuca* L 29–33 cm, WS 55–63 cm

Size of Greenshank but with yellow legs and dark back, lacking white wedge up back. In summer plumage has elements of black on mantle and heavy dark spots on breast and belly-sides. Slightly upturned bill like Greenshank, longer and heavier than that of Lesser Yellowlegs. Call trisyllabic, very like Greenshank's, but slightly softer in tone. Vagrant from N America, not recorded annually in Europe.

Lesser Yellowlegs *Tringa flavipes* L 23–25 cm, WS 45–51 cm

Smaller and more attenuated than Greater Yellowlegs, with shorter, perfectly straight and fine-tipped bill. Standing, appears tall and long-winged. Juv. has grey-brown tone to mantle, from Sep replaced in 1st-winter plumage by a paler, more neutral grey colour. Head often looks smudgy mouse-grey with prominent eye-ring and white supercilium in front of eye. Call a typical *Tringa* whistle, usually uttered twice; not unlike that of Greater Yellowlegs but higher-pitched and faster, 'kew' or 'kyü-kyü, not unlike Marsh Sandpiper. The more frequent of the two yellowlegs in W Europe, with a few annually, mostly in Aug–Oct.

Long-billed Dowitcher *Limnodromus scolopaceus* L 27–30 cm, WS 42–47 cm

A large, robust wader with long straight bill with which it probes in snipe-like manner. In autumn mostly juvs. or birds moulting to 1st-winter plumage are found, difficult to tell from the extremely rare Short-billed Dowitcher. Main differences are in calls and in markings on tertials, greater secondary coverts and scapulars: on Long-billed these feathers lack or have very slight pale markings except for rusty edges. The winter feathers on mantle are drab grey-brown with narrow dark shaft streak. In summer plumage has something of Curlew Sandpiper's colour pattern: underparts rusty-toned, liberally barred with dark and pale spots/fringes, and more intensely streaked on neck and breast. In flight shows pale wedge or slit on back like juv. Spotted Redshank. Flight call much higher in pitch than Short-billed's, usually a single 'kyip' or loud 'peev' with a squeaky ring, can recall a woodpecker or Oystercatcher. Not uncommonly uttered twice, 'peev-ip', and rarely three times (sounds twittering). Vagrant from N America. A few annually in Britain and Ireland, mostly Sep–Nov; occasionally overwinters.

Short-billed Dowitcher *Limnodromus griseus* L 25–29 cm, WS 41–46 cm

Somewhat shorter-billed (normally) than Long-billed Dowitcher and with different call. On rising utters a usually trisyllabic rattling 'chu-tu-tu' or 'küll-üll-üll', recalling Turnstone's call in pitch and ring. Juv. has distinct pale markings in dark centres to tertials, greater coverts and scapulars (cf Long-billed) and a more pale orange-rusty tone overall than Long-billed. Only one definite record in Europe (in Ireland).

Common Sandpiper
juv

**Spotted
Sandpiper**
juv

juv
Lesser Yellowlegs

juv moulting
to 1st-winter
Greater Yellowlegs

1st-winter
Wilson's Phalarope

juv
Long-billed Dowitcher

juv
Short-billed Dowitcher

Long-billed Dowitcher 1st-winter

Snipe

Pintail Snipe

Pintail Snipe *Gallinago stenura*   *L 25–27 cm, WS 44–47 cm*

Very like Snipe, but appears slightly more squat owing to its shorter bill, blunter wingtips and shorter tail (not reaching beyond wingtips). Most easily told from Snipe by wing pattern, is more uniformly dark on underwing, and above lacks white trailing edge to secondaries and has more contrasting pale panel on secondary coverts. Lower scapulars have a narrower and less distinct outer fringe. Has more barred pattern on upperparts and lacks Snipe's distinct broad striping on back, and secondary coverts are also more vermiculated or barred. Display very peculiar, almost like rolling trill of swift but consists of very high-pitched whining sound. Very rare vagrant from Siberia; migrates through Middle East, where possibly a few overwinter.

Woodcock   *Scolopax rusticola*   *L 33–35 cm, WS 55–65 cm*

The Woodcock is much bigger and more rounded than the snipes, and has a slower wing action and an attractive red-brown plumage. It is best known for its display, 'roding', which can be seen in spring and, in cases of second broods, long into summer. At this time the male flies with fast jerky wingbeats along a particular route at dusk, uttering a series of grunting 'oo-orrt' calls followed by a high explosive squeaking call. In flight also gives a rapid 'etsh-etsh-etsh'. When flushed in woodland, it zigzags away between the trees; wing movements slightly loose and a swishing wing noise is heard just as it rises. Young can already fly away short distances at 10 days old. Nests commonly in woodland containing marshier areas such as small pools, muddy-edged streams or lakeshores. Feeds on worms and insects found by boring with bill in mud and loose leaf-litter. Northern/eastern populations move out in Oct–Nov but hardly ever seen on migration (a markedly nocturnal migrant). Mostly resident in Britain, where also smallish numbers visit from Continent on passage and in winter.

Great Snipe

Jack Snipe

Snipe

Woodcock

Great Snipe   *Gallinago media*   L 27–29 cm, WS 42–46 cm

Slightly bigger than Snipe, plumper-bodied with slightly shorter bill, longer legs, more barred belly and more contrasting wing-coverts. In flight, differs from Snipe in greater bulk and more rounded shape of body and wings (more Woodcock-like), slower flight, belly barring, white outer tail feathers and two clear white bands framing the darker greater coverts. Very slow to take fright and rises at only a few metres' distance, and then quite silently or with a few low, hoarse 'aitch-aitch-aitch' calls. Does not zigzag on rising; flight path generally straight and ending in rather abrupt 'flopping down'. Rare and local breeder on marshy mountain slopes and drier bogs with willow in Scandinavia, in Poland in vast tussocky marshes. Males gather in groups and display on tussocks. Very faithful to its display sites, as well as to its stop-off sites during migration. Calls consist of a rising and falling chirping as if from chinking ice-sticks, followed by a wooden bill-clattering which runs into a whizzing buzz. Migrates southeast Aug–Sep, when found generally in drier terrain than Snipe. Very rare visitor to Britain, mostly in Aug–May.

Snipe   *Gallinago gallinago*   L 25–27 cm, WS 37–43 cm

Easily distinguished as a snipe by its long bill pronounced head markings and feeding action. Probes with long bill in mud which it does with very jerky and mechanical movements. Squats when danger threatens, in water sinking up to two-thirds below surface. On rising, which is explosive at c10–15 m distance, it pitches sideways a few times and utters one or two harsh 'ketsch' calls. Flight is clipping. Performs aerial display with fluttering climbs and dives, air vibrations in outer tail feathers produce a loud humming. Song a loud rhythmic 'tick-a, tick-a, tick-a...', often given from fencepost, treetop. Active dawn and dusk. Common on bogs, wet meadows and shore meadows, on passage also in all kinds of muddy areas. Northern/eastern populations migratory, Jul–Oct and Mar–May. Mainly resident Britain and Ireland, also passage and winter visitor from N Europe Aug–Apr.

Jack Snipe   *Lymnocryptes minimus*   L 17–19 cm, WS 30–36 cm

Visibly smaller and shorter-billed than Snipe. Sits tight until a metre's distance, and seen mostly as it flies up: the short bill, the stiff-necked and upward-angled posture, triangular head and the pointed tail on slightly short rear body can then often be seen. It occasionally pitches on rising and usually drops down again immediately. On the ground, the black-brown, green-glossed back with broad straw-yellow stripes is diagnostic. Breeds fairly sparsely on watery bogs with sedge and cottongrass, usually on forest bogs but in tundra also in the willow region. Gives display flight like Snipe, but call is even more difficult to pinpoint: a very peculiar muffled 'kok-ooa-kok-ooa-kok-ooa ... (kloppala)' like a distant galloping horse. May also perch on telegraph pole or similar site and display. On migration and in winter found in traditional snipe country, but often in drier habitat, always with sheltering vegetation. In Britain occurs as passage and winter visitor from N Europe during Sep–May, often with pronounced peaks in Mar–Apr and Oct.

Great Snipe

Snipe

Jack Snipe

Great Snipe

display

Snipe

Jack Snipe

Wilson's Phalarope   *Phalaropus tricolor*   L 22−24 cm, WS 35−38 cm

Bigger and more elongated than Red-necked Phalarope, with longer bill and yellow legs. When feeding, walks or wades just as much as it swims. Lacks obvious wingbar in flight. In autumn appears mostly in more or less 1st-winter plumage, with uniform grey upperparts and without blackish ear-coverts (see p.249). In summer plumage female is striking, with ash-grey crown and parts of back, rusty-orange breast and chestnut-brown bands on mantle. Male considerably plainer, some mostly grey. Very quiet. Vagrant from N America; in Britain and Ireland recorded in all months May−Nov, but especially Aug−Oct.

Grey Phalarope   *Phalaropus fulicarius*   L 20−22 cm, WS 37−40 cm

A high-arctic wader which lives at sea during non-breeding season. Swims on water and picks invertebrates from surface like Red-necked Phalarope, but in all plumages distinguished by its thicker and less pointed bill. Summer-plumaged female a striking brick-red below and with black-and-white head pattern; male clearly duller in colour, often with some pale spotting in the black on head and with more black at bill-tip. In winter plumage pure unmarked grey on mantle and with black bill. In flight shows broad white wingbar, grey rump and, on ad., paler fore wing-coverts than winter Red-necked. Summer-plumaged female shows marked contrast between dark body and white underwing-coverts. Call a very hard and sharp 'pik' or 'kit'. On breeding grounds females chase a male and utter rather far-carrying rolling 'prrüt'. Scarce and sporadic visitor to Britain, mostly late Sep−Nov, very rare in other months; occasionally hundreds driven inshore by autumn storms. Winters off coast of W Africa.

Red-necked Phalarope   *Phalaropus lobatus*   L 18−19 cm, WS 31−34 cm

Immediately attracts attention by its swimming habits, often spins around on the water to whirl up plankton and mosquito larvae, which it pecks up at incredible speed. Has very thin and pointed bill, which distinguishes it in all plumages from Grey Phalarope. Male less colourful in plumage than female. In full winter plumage, seldom seen in Europe, mantle is ash-grey with broad white bands. Juv. has reddish-ochre bands on dark ground colour above and brownish-pink neck-sides, though colours fade fairly rapidly. Flight is fast and fidgety, body looks rather boat-shaped and wings show a broad white wingbar. Gives short sharp calls in flight, mainly a rather woodpecker-like 'kitt' and a squeaking 'kirrik'. In breeding area long aerial pursuits of a male by 2-3 females constantly uttering 'kitt'. Nests on open tundra from sea level to 1300m in Scandinavian mountains, most abundantly beside bogs and deltas with small stagnant pools. Very rare and declining breeder in Scotland. Scarce on migration, which is in southeastward direction, during Jul−Aug (Oct); winters at sea in Indian Ocean and Persian Gulf, returning during late Apr−Jun.

Grey Phalarope

Red-necked Phalarope

Wilson's Phalarope

1st-winter

♀ summer

winter

winter

Grey Phalarope

juv/1st-winter

♂ summer

♀ summer

juv

juv

♀ summer

Red-necked Phalarope

♂ summer

Great Skua   *Stercorarius skua*   *L 53–66 cm, WS 125–140 cm*

The largest skua and strikingly heavy, short-tailed and broad-winged compared with other skuas, more compact than Herring Gull. Besides the silhouette, the brilliant white primary-base flashes above and below are its foremost field characters. These can, however, be less conspicuous on upperside, especially on juv. Juv. generally darker than ad., usually with pale marks near tips of mantle and wing-covert feathers. Breeds locally in loose colonies on islands in N Atlantic. Very aggressive at the nest. Alarm call short deep 'tuk, tuk'; also has a gruff 'a-ech'. Feeds by parasitising other seabirds but also takes live fish, eggs and birds. Summer visitor to N Scotland Mar–Sep, wintering mostly in Atlantic; passage birds (incl. some Icelandic breeders) seen most coasts, Mar–Apr and especially Aug–Oct, with occasional winter and inland records.

Pomarine Skua   *Stercorarius pomarinus*   *L 65–78 cm, WS 113–125 cm*

In flight larger and bulkier than Arctic Skua, with broader wings, more rounded and fuller belly profile and heavier bill. Summer-plumaged ad. has long broad central tail feathers which are twisted at tip, forming a blob. Occurs in a pale and a rarer dark phase. Pale phase resembles Arctic Skua, but is darker black-brown above and on vent and breast. Breast-band and flanks often with broken barring on female and younger birds, but on older males more uniform black-brown; and often confined to a dark wedge on breast-side. In winter plumage head and breast entirely mixed with brown (sometimes also belly) and with shorter tail (identified as ad. by black unmarked underwing-coverts). Ads. on autumn passage in N Europe (from Jul to Nov) are normally in summer plumage, sometimes having lost tail projections. Juv. very similar to juv. Arctic, varies in markings but majority give a uniformly dark brown impression in the field with slightly paler light-and-dark-barred rump, vent and underwings, faintly paler nape and also a pale panel at primary bases below; at reasonable distance primary coverts can be seen also to have a pale base, so that a double pale patch is formed on underwing. Tar-black individuals (though with pale double patch) occur, as well as paler ones with buff-grey head and broad buff-grey fringes. Bill pale blue-grey at base and dark at tip, is larger and more conspicuous than on Arctic. Blurred faintly vermiculated patterning on nape characteristic, as also lack of pale tips to primaries; a few of the paler examples have pale tips. Tail of juv. looks rounded in the field, central pairs of feathers only just visibly elongated and rounded at tips. Full ad. plumage not reached until 4 years of age. In 2nd summer fairly juv.-like, but with longer central tail feathers, paler nape and paler belly. Breeds on tundra, where feeds to large degree on lemmings, so breeding success varies greatly from year to year. Parasitic like Arctic Skua, more aggressive and even kills e.g. smaller gulls. In Britain, autumn passage Aug–Nov, with peak often later than that of Arctic, in Oct–early Nov; in spring seen late Apr and May. Occasional inland (mostly juvs.) and in winter.

Great Skua

Pomarine Skua

Arctic Skua

256

Arctic Skua   *Stercorarius parasiticus*   L 46–67 cm, WS 97–115 cm

Elegant, with long all-dark wings and long pointed tail projections, fast and rather falcon-like in flight. Harries terns and gulls to rob them of their prey. Occurs in a pale and a dark phase, both with some variation. Pale birds are commoner in the north, with mostly darker ones in south of range. Juv. varies in coloration, palest ones being grey-buff with dark vermiculation and barring below and with cream-coloured head, and darkest being completely tar-black. A rusty-orange or cinnamon-brown tint to nape shawl and feather fringes above is characteristic (cf Long-tailed and Pomarine Skuas). Important specific characters are streaked head and nape and also pale tips to primaries. Some tar-black completely unmarked birds can lack obvious spots at primary tips. In flight flatter-bellied, with narrower wings and longer and more pointed central tail feathers than Pomarine. Axillaries and underwing-coverts usually dark-barred, but ground colour matches body colour so coverts often appear darker and less patterned than on Pomarine. Individuals with dark unmarked underwing-coverts occur. All juvs. have a clear pale patch at base of primaries, but greater primary coverts never show a second pale patch like Pomarine's. On upperparts, rump is generally darker and less regularly patterned; a rule of thumb is that at distance rump never appears paler than nape shawl (reverse is the rule on Pomarine). The palest invididuals often have a buffish patch at base of primaries above, as well as characteristic pale base to spread tail. At breeding site utters drawn-out slightly mewing 'geeah' almost like Kittiwake, also gives short repeated 'kook'. Nests on bird-rich sea coasts, often in loose colonies, in N Scotland on moors near the sea. Parasitises other birds by skilfully harrying them in the air so that they drop or disgorge their prey; gulls, terns and auks are the commonest victims. Migrates mostly in Aug–Sep (Oct), chiefly to S Atlantic, returning in Apr–May; rare in W Europe in winter.   *Map p. 256*

Long-tailed Skua   *Stercorarius longicaudus*   L 35–58 cm, WS 92–105 cm

The smallest skua, narrow-winged and long-tailed, slender-bodied but deep-chested with small head and short but heavy bill. Ad. summer has long tail projections, pale breast which gradually darkens on belly, and brown-grey mantle which contrasts with brown-black flight feathers. Juv. very variable, but generally greyer in tone than juv. Arctic Skua and with longer projecting central tail feathers (blunt at tip); palest ones have wholly creamy-white head and all-white belly (juv. Arctic never has white belly), darkest ones look uniform dark brown-grey but always have some amount of pale fringing above. Characteristic of juv. plumage are narrow uniform-width fringes on mantle, combination of uniformly toned and unpatterned breast and vermiculated flanks plus a paler area on upper belly towards breast. Undertail-coverts and under-wings are often regularly barred dirty-white and dark grey, without Arctic's buff and rusty tones. Primary tips relatively rounded, normally dark but sometimes with narrow pale edging. At all ages, only two or three primary shafts are noticeably pale in the field. Bill short but relatively deep, inner half blue-grey and outer black. Nests above timberline in Scandinavian mountains and on the tundra. Very dependent on supply of rodents, mostly lemmings, for breeding, so numbers vary from year to year; non-breeders wander about the mountain in flocks. Scarce on passage, seen mainly in Aug–Sep (Nov) and in May. Markedly pelagic in wintering areas in S Atlantic.

Great Skua

Pomarine Skua

♀

pale phase
Arctic Skua

Long-tailed Skua

Great Skua

juv

Pomarine Skua

♂

♀

3rd/4th-cal autumn

Arctic Skua pale phase

Long-tailed Skua

dark phase

Arctic Skua

juv

juv

juv

Pomarine Skua

juv

juv

juv

Arctic Skua

juv

juv

juv

Long-tailed Skua

juv

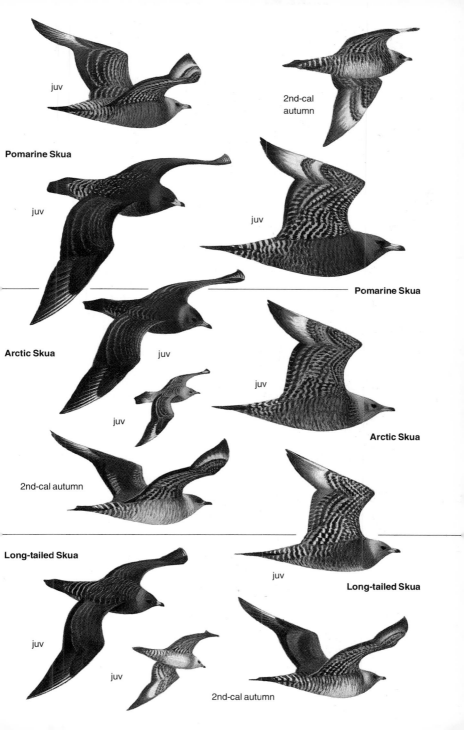

juv

2nd-cal autumn

Pomarine Skua

juv

juv

Pomarine Skua

Arctic Skua

juv

juv

juv

Arctic Skua

2nd-cal autumn

Long-tailed Skua

juv

Long-tailed Skua

juv

juv

2nd-cal autumn

Slender-billed Gull

1st-winter

ad

ad

Mediterranean Gull *Larus melanocephalus*   *L 36–38 cm, WS 98–105 cm*

About size of a Black-headed Gull, but with paler grey mantle and broader wings which are wholly white at tips. In summer has black head, in winter a characteristic dark mask behind eye (ear-coverts). Has proportionately heavy bill which 'droops' towards tip, blood-red with a black band or tip on ad. and dark flesh-coloured with blackish outer part on 1st-cal-year birds. Juv. moults its heavily brown-patterned mantle as early as Aug. In 1st-winter plumage wing pattern like Common Gull in corresponding plumage, but has more contrasting wing markings, paler mantle and broader and shorter wings than latter. In 2nd-winter plumage and subsequent summer has black markings of varying extent at wingtips. Calls shriller and more nasal than Black-headed Gull's and more like Little Gull or Arctic Skua in tone, often 'eu-err' or 'eooe'. Noisy in spring but silent in autumn and winter. Nests on flat shores and islands beside sea or larger lakes, usually in large colonies. Winters largely in W Mediterranean, regular in small numbers along Atlantic coast up to English Channel. Scarce in Britain, but recorded in all months (occasionally breeds).

Slender-billed Gull *Larus genei*   *L 42–44 cm, WS 102–110 cm*

Resembles a Black-headed Gull without hood, but is bigger, has more attenuated body shape and in flight the longer and broader wings are beaten more slowly. Parties often fly in formation like larger gulls. Imms. differ from young Black-headed Gulls in longer bill, which is pale buffy-orange, often with extreme tip dark but sometimes completely unmarked. Eye region and ear-coverts show only faint dusky marking, which makes eye look smaller than on Black-headed, and it appears strikingly 'long-nosed'; wings are also paler and more 'bleached'. In fresh plumage (autumn and spring) ad. has distinct pink tinge below. Calls coarser and deeper than Black-headed's. Occurs fairly sparsely and locally around the Mediterranean at shallow, often saline lakes, lagoons and deltas on coast, more numerous at Black and Caspian Seas. Very rare vagrant to Britain.

Mediterranean Gull

Slender-billed Gull

Mediterranean Gull

summer

2nd-winter

1st-winter

juv moulting to 1st-winter

winter

Black-headed Gull
1st-winter

1st-winter

Slender-billed Gull

1st-winter

Little Gull

Little Gull   *Larus minutus*   L 25–27 cm, WS 70–77 cm

Clearly smaller than Black-headed Gull, with lighter and more vigorous flight. Takes insects from water surface like Black Tern. Underwing strikingly slaty-black and pale grey above without dark tip but with white border making wings look rounded. Entire head is tar-black in summer plumage; in winter plumage (p. 271) has grey skull-cap, dark ear spot and pale grey neck-boa. Juv. has brownish-black mantle, in autumn exchanged for grey (1st-winter plumage); wing markings vary in degree of darkness, some have almost all-dark primaries. 2nd-cal-year birds in May still have juv. wing, but to varying extent dark hood and tail-band. 2nd-winter and 2nd-summer like ad., but some small black markings at wingtips and paler grey underwing (p. 271). Calls characteristic, a repeated, hard tern-like 'kyek', often as 'kiye-kyek-kyek', or nasal 'euw', imms. a rather harsh, rasping 'e-aihk'. Display call a shrill 'ke-veu, ke-veu, ke-veu...' like Black-tailed Godwit. Nests on shallow, vegetated lakes and marshes but winters at sea. Most juvs. migrate end Jul–Sep, peak for ads. is Oct–Nov. In Britain rather local, seen all months (has bred).

Black-headed Gull   *Larus ridibundus*   L 38–44 cm, WS 94–105 cm

In all plumages easy to identify in flight by white leading edge and black rear border to primaries, these being dark grey below with narrower white leading edge. After moult to winter plumage in Aug, head is white with dark mark around eye and on ear-coverts and with two diffuse dusky bands over crown (see pp. 267, 269), together with paler red legs and bill. In 1st-winter plumage has grey mantle and buff-pink bill base and legs. Widespread and abundant, is seen commonly at fresh waters, seashores, on cultivated land, often with Common Gulls on newly ploughed fields, in cities, harbours etc. Breeds colonially, often in large numbers, especially at reedy lakes and on islands and coastal marshes. Calls very characteristic but difficult to transcribe, include a nasal melodious 'auhr', near colonies usually screaming and obtrusive, grating. In Britain mainly resident, with additional passage and winter visitors from N Europe during Aug–Apr.

Little Gull

Black-headed Gull

264

Little Gull

juv

summer

1st-summer

juv

Black-headed Gull

summer

juv

Common Gull 2nd-winter   **Kittiwake** winter

Common Gull   *Larus canus*   L 38–44 cm, WS 106–125 cm

Smaller than Herring Gull, with more rounded head profile, black eye and more slender greenish-yellow bill producing 'amiable' expression. In winter has brown-grey spots on rear head and nape, and less yellow bill and often with dark ring around tip. Juv. dull grey-brown above and with scaly pattern of paler greyish fringes. In 1st-winter plumage has grey mantle without or with odd dark markings. In late spring 2nd-cal-years often look very pale and washed out on wings and with mid-grey mantle. In 2nd-winter plumage like ad., but to variable extent has dark markings along leading edge on primaries and primary coverts. Calls have a particular 'Common Gull ring', frequent ones in the repertoire being a nasal 'keow' and a drawn-out shrill 'glieeoo'; alarm a persistent repeated 'gleeu-gleeu-gleeu'. Feeds on fish and aquatic animals, as well as insects, worms and eggs and young of birds. Breeds on freshwater lakes and along coasts. Often seen with Black-headed Gulls on newly ploughed fields. In Britain mainly resident but with pronounced southward dispersal after breeding, also common passage and winter visitor from NE Europe.

Kittiwake   *Rissa tridactyla*   L 38–40 cm, WS 95–108 cm

A markedly pelagic gull which breeds in large colonies on cliff precipices (locally on coastal buildings) in N Atlantic. Most resembles a Common Gull in flight, but has wholly black, 'dipped-in-ink' wingtips. A good field character is that primaries inside the black tip are noticeably paler than back and secondary coverts. Juv. (p.270) has striking black zigzag marking above. Often look narrow-winged against bright sky. Juv. has grey mantle and distinct black neck-boa, through 1st winter. 2nd-cal-year summer and ad. winter show diffuse grey boa and dark patch over ear-coverts. Juv. can be confused with juv. Little Gull, but is bigger, has proportionately larger head and bill area and broader wing bases and also a steadier, more powerful flight. In light wind has higher wingbeat frequency than Common Gull, while in good winds it careens elegantly in deep arcs like shearwaters. Very noisy at nest sites, with shrill, rather nasal 'kevi-week' which echoes around the cliff faces; also has a gruff 'kek-kek-kek'. Food is small marine animals, fish and offal. Common at sea in North Sea area and Atlantic. Seen from land during passage and in westerly storms, especially in spring and autumn, also occasionally inland.

Common Gull

Kittiwake

summer

winter

Common Gull

Kittiwake

summer

winter

Black-headed Gull

summer

Ring-billed Gull

2nd-winter

winter

Ring-billed Gull   *Larus delawarensis*   L 43–47 cm, WS 118–132 cm

Very like Common Gull, c10% bigger and with heavier bill and proportionately broader wings. On ground often stands more upright, is deeper-breasted or front-heavy and has slightly longer legs than Common Gull. Summer-plumaged ad. has pale iris and yellow bill with black band. In 1st-winter plumage variable; characteristic is the conspicuously pale mantle with rather 'randomly' positioned pale brown arrowhead markings and pale fringes (though can completely lack dark markings on mantle). Tail-band less clearly defined than on juv. Common, typically split into 2–3 bands on outer feathers and above 'main band' there is often a shadow in form of an additional narrow band. Spots on neck and breast-sides often more distinct and become U-shaped on flanks. Secondary coverts always look slightly irregularly patterned, often one or more coverts are new pale grey ones, producing a 'more untidy' impression than Common Gull's neat pattern on folded wing. Tertials normally have narrower pale fringe than on Common. Bill is pink with sharply defined black outer part and pale at very tip; bill size varies, overlaps with Common Gull's. In 2nd-winter plumage has irregular remnant of tail-band and often dingy remnants of dark on individual secondaries. Rare visitor from N America, regular Britain and Ireland (recorded in all months).

Laughing Gull   *Larus atricilla*   L 36–41 cm, WS 102–115 cm

In all plumages a fairly unmistakable gull, markedly slim and long-winged and with characteristically dark grey upperparts. Bill long and drooping, in winter black with blood-red tip. In summer plumage has sooty-black head, white eye-crescents, and dark red bill with black band near tip. In 1st-winter plumage dark, almost sooty; entire underwing is dark grey and has grey on neck, breast and flanks. Vagrant from N America.

Franklin's Gull   *Larus pipixcan*   L 32–36 cm, WS 91–97 cm

Smaller than Black-headed Gull, round-headed, short-legged, fairly broad-winged and with obviously darker grey mantle than Common Gull. In summer plumage jet-black head and blood-red bill. In all other plumages distinctive: entire rear head dark sooty, and has conspicuous white eye-crescents. Vagrant from N America.

Bonaparte's Gull   *Larus philadelphia*   L 28–30 cm, WS 85–90 cm

Small, elegant and rather tern-like, picks food from water surface like Little Gull. Summer-plumaged ad. has brown-black head and bill and white eye-crescents. Differs from Black-headed Gull in all primaries being white and translucent below, with only a narrow dark border. In winter plumage has 'cute' facial expression, like Black-headed but black bill and grey neck-boa. In 1st winter wing markings above 'tidier', with blacker diagonal band, greater primary coverts are unmarked grey on inner edge and more dark-marked towards outer. Vagrant from N America.

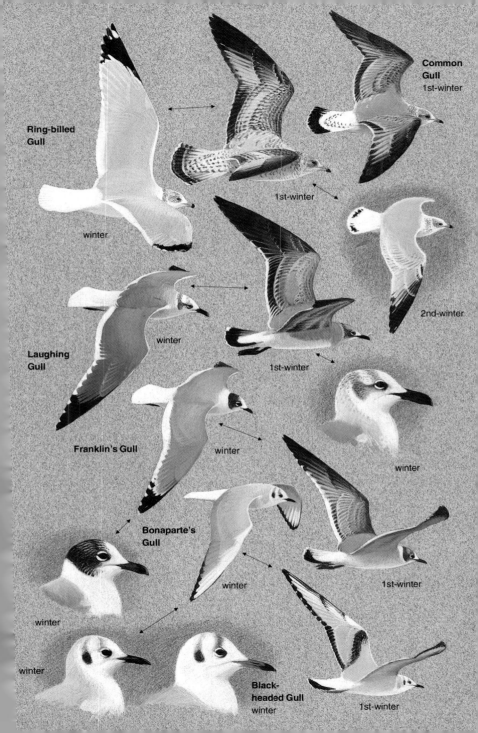

Ring-billed Gull

winter

Common Gull
1st-winter

1st-winter

2nd-winter

Laughing Gull

winter

1st-winter

winter

Franklin's Gull

winter

winter

Bonaparte's Gull

winter

winter

1st-winter

winter

Black-headed Gull
winter

1st-winter

Ivory Gull   *Pagophila eburnea*   L 40–43 cm, WS 106–118 cm

Unmistakable: ad. all white; juv. with variable extent of dark spots above and with an odd blackish-grey area around bill-join. In the air body appears big and cigar-shaped, wings are broad at base but with pointed 'hand'. Forward flight is surprisingly light and elegant, and when gliding the faintly arched wings are held slightly above the horizontal. Feeds on fish and all kinds of small marine animals, as well as excrement, prey remains and carrion left by polar bears and seals. A high-arctic bird in the pack-ice and drift-ice zone. Appears very rarely in NW Europe, majority being juvs. during winter months.

Sabine's Gull   *Larus sabini*   L 27–32 cm, WS 83–92 cm

Long-winged and with small head, graceful actions and elegant flight; shallowly forked tail is often difficult to see. Ad. summer has dark grey hood which is normally retained until mid Oct. In winter plumage has all-white face and dark skull-cap on rear head and down across nape. Grey mantle and wing-coverts clearly darker than on Kittiwake and Little Gull. Juv. has dark grey-brown mantle and black-brown outer primaries with clear border against snow-white rear wing (triangle); the dark markings on head and breast make it appear dark-headed at distance. Underwings have dark shading along arm (fainter on ad.). An arctic N American species with nearest breeders in Greenland. Winters out at sea off coasts of Africa and occurs regularly in Atlantic off W Europe, though seen only infrequently from land, mostly in Sep–Oct during westerly storms.

Ross's Gull   *Rhodostethia rosea*   L 29–31 cm, WS 83–91 cm

A small gull, nearer Little Gull than Kittiwake in size, with long pointed wings, wedge-shaped tail and tern-like flight. In the field the pink underside, broad white trailing edge and grey underwing are the most striking characters. Head is small, round and delicate and with markedly short bill. In summer plumage has diagnostic black neck-ring, in winter a grey neck-boa and dark oblong spot on ear-coverts. Central tail feathers are elongated, project like a 'peg', and on imm. are black-tipped, giving impression of an odd black patch at stern rather than a tail-band. Intensity of pink varies individually (often present on 1st-summers). Nests on arctic tundra, chiefly in E Siberia, locally in Greenland and N Canada; rest of year in arctic/subarctic waters, usually pack-ice zone, strongly pelagic. Very rare in Europe.

1st-winter   juv   Kittiwake   winter

Ivory Gull

1st-winter

Sabine's Gull

summer

juv

Sabine's Gull

juv

juv

Little Gull

winter

Ross's Gull

summer

1st-winter

winter

summer   2nd-winter   **Great Black-headed Gull**

summer

1st-winter

1st-winter

Great Black-headed Gull *Larus ichthyaetus*   L 57–61 cm, WS 155–170 cm

Size of Great Black-backed Gull but more closely related to Mediterranean Gull and with same plumage development as latter. Most easily confused with subad. Herring Gull, but has more rectangular head with markedly flat forehead and long bill. In flight, attenuated and rather disproportionate owing to the prominent head. Summer-plumaged ad. has black head and bright white eye-crescents, which in all plumages are bolder than on Herring Gull. In 1st-winter plumage has wholly grey mantle, when upperparts as 1st-winter Common Gull's. Subad. and ad. winter have dark ear-coverts like Mediterranean Gull. A C Asiatic breeder, migrates to Caspian, Indian and Arabian coasts. Rare E Mediterranean, regular at fish ponds in Israel.

Audouin's Gull *Larus audouinii*   L 48–52 cm, WS 127–138 cm

Smaller, noticeably paler and narrower-winged than Herring Gull, gives elegant impression. Grey legs and dark red bill with black tip. In flight, very little white on black primary tips and without contrasting broad white trailing edge to wing. Juv. most like Lesser Black-backed Gull, i.e. darker than juv. Herring and without obviously paler inner primaries: head, neck and breast with uniform grey ground colour, underparts mixed shades of grey and with darker patch on rear flanks, mantle brownish-black with clearly defined paler buff fringes (like Lesser Black-back), and underwings look regularly dark-barred; tail almost all-dark, contrasting with whitish tail-coverts. In 1st-winter plumage acquires new mantle feathers which are grey-brown in centre with a broad grey border; feathers are sometimes predominantly grey. In 2nd-winter plumage rather like 1st-winter Mediterranean Gull, with sharply defined black tail-band and with large pale panel across median secondary coverts bordered by brown lesser coverts. Bill initially dirty-olive with dark outer third, then greenish-yellow and, at 2–3 years, red. Breeds relatively rarely and locally in colonies, usually on smaller islands. More pelagic than Herring Gull. Many remain around the colonies in winter; some migrate west towards W African coast after breeding, imms. at end Jul–Aug and older birds in Sep–Oct.

Great Black-headed Gull

Audouin's Gull

Audouin's Gull juv

Yellow-legged Gull

Audouin's Gull 2nd-summer

Audouin's Gull
1st-winter

summer

2nd-winter

Audouin's Gull

juv

Herring Gull   *Larus argentatus*   L 55–67 cm, WS 130–158 cm

One of the commonest gulls on our coasts. Bigger than Common Gull, with yellow iris and pink legs. Does not attain full ad. plumage until 4th cal-year. In 1st-winter plumage has wholly brown-mottled mantle, in 2nd-winter with 20–80% grey feathers and iris becomes paler. Subad. in spring/early summer may have very faded wingtips, can be taken for one of the white-winged species. Race *argentatus* in Scandinavia slightly darker than W European *argenteus*. Race *omissus* in inland Finland has even darker grey mantle and pale yellow legs (cf Yellow-legged Gull). Calls short or drawn-out deep-voiced 'aoou', alarm a 'chuckling' 'ag-ag-ag'. Common on coasts and larger lakes, often nests in colonies on islands or cliffs. Takes fish and fish offal, eggs, bird young, carrion and refuse, often seen at refuse tips. Hunts small birds migrating over sea.   *Map p. 276*

Yellow-legged Gull   *Larus cachinnans*   L 55–67 cm, WS 130–158 cm

Possibly a race of Herring Gull and in all respects close to it. Has an obvious darker mantle than Herring Gulls from W Europe, and lacks dark mottling on head and neck in winter plumage. Legs yellow, orbital ring red and bill deeper orange-yellow with more extensive red near tip than Herring. In Mediterranean basin race *michahellis*, in Atlantic islands *atlantis*, and from Black Sea eastwards *cachinnans*. In E Turkey and Armenia closely related form *armenicus* with a dark shadow next to red spot on bill (sometimes missing in breeding plumage) and darker iris. Yellow-legged is a very scarce visitor to Britain Jul–Feb (Mar).   *Ill. p.273, map p. 276*

Glaucous Gull   *Larus hyperboreus*   L 62–68 cm, WS 142–162 cm

Slightly bigger than Herring Gull, more front-heavy and in body shape most like Great Black-backed. In flight shows markedly broad arm and relatively short hand. Ad. has pale grey mantle and all-white wingtips. In 1st-winter plumage delicately mottled grey-buff with dirty-white primaries, at distance looks sandy-coloured; bill pale pink with well-defined black outer third (very characteristic). Plumage often very pale towards spring; in May–Jun dirty-white overall with isolated new pale brown-grey mantle feathers and new brown-grey median secondary coverts (as darker band across wing). In 2nd-winter plumage mantle and scapulars have mixture of pale brown-grey, mixed-brown and white feathers, bill has rather less well-marked dark tip and iris is paler; variable, however, some (probably high-arctic birds) are very pale. Interbreeds with Herring Gull in Iceland, hybrids have dark pigmentation in wingtips. Calls and habits as Herring Gull's, but is in the main an arctic bird. Small numbers winter Britain and Ireland.   *Map p. 276*

Iceland Gull   *Larus glaucoides*   L 52–60 cm, WS 130–145 cm

Generally smaller than Herring Gull and has more rounded head profile, shorter bill and (chiefly juv.) longer, slimmer wings than Glaucous Gull. Ad. in flight at distance difficult to tell from Glaucous, but smaller head and bill usually decisive. At rest, wings extend far behind tail. In 1st-winter plumage rather like Glaucous, but bill brown-grey or brownish-pink at base and border with darker tip diffuse (bill usually looks all-dark at distance), though towards late winter can have buff-pink base and contrasting dark tip like Glaucous's. Plumage varies in degree of paleness, a few have almost greyish primaries and strong pigmentation while others look entirely dirty-white at distance. Plumage development as Herring Gull's; in 2nd-winter plumage with scattering of pale grey feathers on mantle, iris becoming paler, and blue-grey to yellow-grey bill base with dark outer third but extreme tip pale. Canadian race *kumlieni*, with dark grey mark on primary tips, is vagrant to NW Europe. More pelagic than Glaucous Gull, does not come to land so much as latter; often hangs in wind and snatches prey from water surface. Nearest breeding area Greenland; relatively common in winter in Iceland and in small numbers also in north and west parts of British Isles.   *Map p. 276*

juv

summer

Herring Gull

Glaucous Gull
winter

Iceland Gull
winter

Great Black-backed Gull   *Larus marinus*   L 64–78 cm, WS 150–170 cm

Bigger and broader-winged and darker above than Lesser Black-backed of W Europe and with more white at wingtips, on perched bird large white tips to primaries are always visible. Legs grey-pink and bill remarkably powerful with marked gonys. Juv. and 1st-winter birds very like young Herring Gull; tail is normally paler and more admixed with white, and shows less contrast between outer and inner primaries. Immatures (1st-winter onwards) usually have paler, less patterned head which sets off the dark bill more strongly. In 2nd-winter plumages most birds still patterned brown and grey-brown on mantle and scapulars. Some get slaty-coloured feathers on the mantle, but often the first blackish feathers are acquired during subsequent spring moult to 2nd summer (Jan–Apr). 2nd-winter birds often have a white spot on one or two outermost primaries. Voice deeper than Herring's. Breeds commonly to sparsely on rocky coasts and at some larger inland waters, usually solitarily but locally in colonies. Feeds on fish, eggs and young of birds, carrion etc, also able to kill full-grown ducks. Largely resident.

Lesser Black-backed Gull   *Larus fuscus*   L 52–67 cm, WS 128–148 cm

In flight, slimmer and slighter than Great Black-backed, with smaller bill and yellow to yellow-orange legs. W European race *graellsii* is slate-grey above and can be confused with dark-mantled Herring Gulls; those breeding in Baltic countries, race *fuscus*, are black above and most like Great Black-back, though only with one white spot on first feather of wingtip. Those in S Norway, Denmark and Swedish west coast, race *intermedius*, are intermediate. Young Lesser Black-backs differ from Herring in their 1st year in having uniformly dark flight feathers without Herring's pale 'window' on inner primaries, more dark colour on tail and generally darker overall impression. Dark on bases of greater coverts often forms a dark band along the opened wing, while nape is slightly lighter than on young Herring (see p. 278). Migratory; imms. remain south, so 2nd-cal-year birds are scarce and 3rd-cal-year less common, especially in Baltic. Migrates in Jul to mid Oct, returns from end Feb (*graellsii*) and in Apr (*fuscus*). Western populations now increasingly overwinter in N Atlantic area. Habits as Herring Gull's, but breeds more locally in larger colonies, often forages on fields.

Herring Gull

Great Black-backed Gull

Lesser Black-backed Gull

Yellow-legged Gull

Glaucous Gull

Iceland Gull

Great Black-backed Gull

Lesser Black-
backed Gull

fuscus

graellsii
summer

2nd-winter

Herring Gull

1st-winter

2nd-winter
(−2nd-summer)

Lesser Black-backed Gull

juv (with a few
1st-winter feathers)

2nd-winter

juv

Great Black-backed Gull

Common Gull 1st-winter

1st-winter
Ring-billed Gull

2nd-winter

1st-winter
Iceland Gull

Glaucous Gull
2nd-cal May-Jun

1st-winter
Glaucous Gull

2nd-winter

Herring Gull 1st-winter

Herring Gull 2nd-winter

Iceland Gull

1st-winter

Glaucous Gull

1st-winter

Lesser Black-backed Gull

juv

Great Black-backed Gull

juv

2nd-winter
Great Black-backed Gull

Common Gull

Herring Gull

Lesser Black-backed Gull *graellsii*

Gull-billed Tern juv   **Sandwich Tern** juv

Gull-billed Tern   *Gelochelidon nilotica*   L 35–38 cm, WS 95–110 cm

Like Sandwich Tern but more gull-like in flight, with broader wings, stouter body and with heavier and shorter all-black bill. Tail shorter and rump grey. When perched, shows long legs like gull. Juv. has highly variable dark markings in feathers of mantle, scapulars and coverts, some being heavily marked like young Sandwich and others almost unmarked. Wings usually look uniform pale grey. Head pale with dark shadow through eye and finely streaked hindcrown. Winter-plumaged ad. has juv-like head pattern but with whiter crown and darker ear-coverts. Hunts over fields, pasture and wetlands near coast. Takes various small animals, such as insects, reptiles, crabs and small rodents. Flight call characteristic, a gruff nasal 'chu-vek', also series of croaking 'kway-kway-kway'. Rare but annual on passage in Britain, on coasts, mostly during May–Sep.

Sandwich Tern   *Sterna sandvicensis*   L 36–41 cm, WS 98–105 cm

A large, slim and narrow-winged tern which often flies at a good height and with deep wingbeats. Conspicuously pale, looks almost all-white except for long black cap and has long black bill with extreme tip dipped in yellow. When perched, the substantial cap, bushy at nape, and the short (cf Gull-billed Tern) legs are characteristic. In winter plumage white forehead, which is acquired from as early as end Jul. Juv. has distinct dark subterminal markings on mantle and wing-coverts and brown-streaked crown with dark forehead; from as early as Aug mantle feathers are replaced by completely unmarked grey ones. Often noticed by its characteristic call, a slightly scraping, cracked and rather penetrating or hurriedly drawn-out 'kier-vek', often also just a short 'eerk'; young in autumn have a more feeble voice. Found almost exclusively on sea coasts and feeds mostly on fish. Hovers above water and plunges from high up. Nests colonially on islands, peninsulas or secluded tongues of land. Most move after completing nesting (Jul) to fish-rich sites, where they often congregate. Migration to winter quarters (W African coasts) takes place rather later than with other terns, in Aug–Oct, and it is usually the first tern species seen in spring, in Mar.

Gull-billed Tern

Sandwich Tern

Gull-billed Tern

Sandwich Tern

Common Tern   *Sterna hirundo*   L 31–35 cm, WS 82–95 cm

Very like Arctic Tern, but has paler belly and black tip to red bill. Looks larger-headed, with flatter forehead and bigger bill and shows more white above gape than Arctic. Legs slightly longer and at rest tail and wingtips fall level with each other. In flight looks 'bigger-winged', in particular hand is fuller. The 4–5 outer primaries are slightly darker grey towards tip and contrast with inner ones (more worn since they are grown in earlier). Juv. differs from juv. Arctic in orange-red to buff bill base and leg colour and blacker leading secondary coverts; dark subterminal markings on back and covert feathers vary, on some being very conspicuous and on others barely visible, and in addition has more extensive pale colour on forehead and beneath eyes. In flight, blacker leading edge to wing, darker and more uniformly toned primaries, darker secondaries forming a band along trailing edge (difficult to make out at distance) and head/bill markings are the most important characters. In winter plumage ad. acquires white forehead and mostly black bill (also 1st-winter birds). Noisy at breeding colonies, with drawn-out ringing 'krreeer', rapid 'kye kye kye kye…' or 'kirri-kirri-kirri…'. On migration flight usually short 'kip' calls. Alarm a drawn-out 'krreee-aihr'. Occurs along sea coasts as well as at larger inland lakes and rivers; to lesser extent on outskirts of island groups than Arctic. Feeds on fish. In Britain, summer visitor and passage migrant Apr–Oct.   *Map p. 286*

Arctic Tern   *Sterna paradisaea*   L 33–35 cm, WS 80–95 cm

More tied to coast than Common Tern. Has smaller and darker red bill without clearly marked dark tip, steeper forehead, greyer underparts, shorter legs and longer tail streamers than Common. Juv. has red bill base initially but bill becomes all-dark towards late summer, has more dark around eyes than juv. Common and head is 'prettier-looking'. In flight appears shorter-winged and with narrower hand than latter. Wing is a silvery pale grey gradually darkening towards tip and with diffuse dark grey band on lesser coverts. Dark on secondary coverts varies, on some being hardly discernible and on others blackish, but is always less clearly defined than on juv. Common and is not so close up to leading edge. Noisy at nest colonies, utters series of piteous 'pee-pee' calls and feeble ringing 'krreer', chases off other birds with dry rattling 'kt-kt-kt-kt', and human approach is greeted with drawn-out 'kree-err'. Common breeder in Baltic, regionally common in uplands of N Scandinavia and numerous on arctic coast; catastrophic decline in Shetlands over last decade. Feeds largely on small fish. Undertakes the longest migration of all bird species, spends winter months in pack-ice belt around Antarctic. Returns Apr–May, migrates Jul–Oct.   *Map p. 286*

Roseate Tern   *Sterna dougallii*   L 33–38 cm, WS 75–80 cm

Decidedly paler grey above than Common and Arctic Terns and tinged pink below. At rest shows longer tail streamers, which extend a good way beyond wingtips, and also relatively long legs. Base of bill becomes red towards breeding season and is most extensive in mid-summer when up to half of bill can be red. In flight, short-winged, long-tailed and in degree of paleness more like Sandwich Tern. In Aug–Sep sometimes has shorter tail feathers and outer primaries contrastingly dark. Juv. characteristic, like juv. Sandwich with dark-patterned mantle feathers, dark forehead and dark legs; forehead becomes white towards Sep and mantle feathers are replaced by unmarked pale grey ones while still in N Atlantic. Noisy around breeding site, commonest call a disyllabic 'chu-vee', rather reminiscent of Spotted Redshank but more cracked in tone, juv. often as 'kirr-ip'; alarm a straight 'aaahrk', also characteristic. Local and rare breeder on islands and spits along shallow sheltered coasts. Winters on W African coasts. Seen in Britain end Apr–Oct.   *Map p. 286*

Common Tern juv

summer

Arctic Tern juv

summer

Roseate Tern juv
(moulting – 1st-winter)

summer
May-June

Little Tern   *Sterna albifrons*   L 22–24 cm, WS 48–55 cm

The smallest of our terns, appears rather stunted and has considerably faster and jerkier wing action than other terns. Juv. has dark brown subterminal feather markings above (scaly pattern) and at first with a warm buff tinge; fades and becomes more 'black-and-white', but is always recognised by size and buff-coloured legs and bill. Very loud and noisy. Calls most recall Sandwich Tern, are shrill or raucous in tone. Most often heard are a short 'ay-ihk' and a rolling 'kürree-ik, kürree-ik, kürree-ik'. Juv. has a clearer 'peeip'. Feeds on fish and other small animals. Nests on sandy or shingly shores. Arrives Apr–May, departing Jul–Oct.

Caspian Tern   *Sterna caspia*   L 47–54 cm, WS 130–145 cm

About size of Common Gull, with strikingly big bright red bill, carrot-red on juv. In flight, long pointed wings and deep, markedly slow and elastic wingbeats. The dark underside of primaries is also conspicuous. In winter plumage dark cap is speckled white on lores, forehead and crown. Juv. has speckled brown crown, slightly dark-mottled mantle and indistinct dark marks on tips of flight feathers, wing-coverts and tail feathers. Call unmistakable and bird usually announces its arrival with its very loud rasping 'kakra-rascha' (a sheet of tin-plate being drawn over a rough concrete floor); in family parties, which are often seen in late summer, parents give short rasping 'krehrr' and young respond with squeaky whistle, 'uee-vee, uee-vee'. Prefers to fish in fresh or brackish water; in Baltic birds move from nest sites on more remote islands on outskirts of archipelagos to nearby freshwater lakes or to brackish-water bays in order to fish. Migrates in Aug–Sep and returns in Apr to beginning of May. In Britain a rare but annual vagrant, usually to coast but also inland, mostly in Apr–Oct, especially May–Jul.

Little Tern

Caspian Tern

Lesser Crested Tern

Common Tern

Arctic Tern

Roseate Tern

286

Little Tern

juv

Caspian Tern

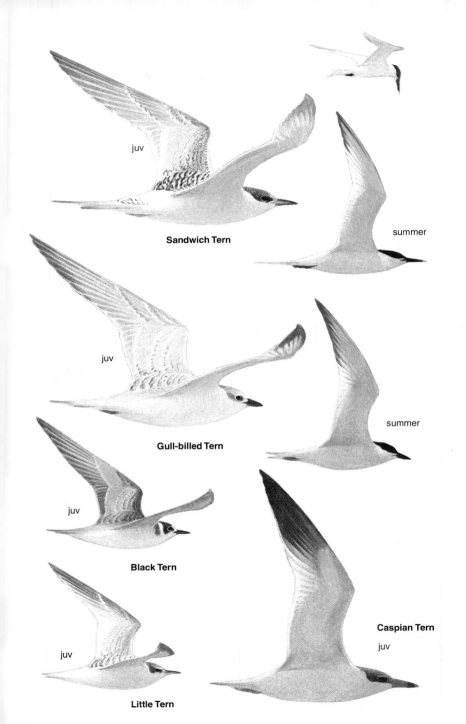

Sandwich Tern

juv

summer

Gull-billed Tern

juv

summer

Black Tern

juv

Little Tern

juv

Caspian Tern

juv

juv

summer

Common Tern

juv

summer

Arctic Tern

juv

juv **Arctic Tern**

summer

2nd-cal (Sep)

Roseate Tern

Royal Tern   *Sterna maxima*   L 45–50 cm, WS 112–120 cm

About 20% smaller than Caspian Tern, with longer and more slender orange bill. In flight, slimmer and narrower-winged and has longer and more forked tail. Most easily confused with Crested Tern, but has more orange bill, paler mantle and whitish rump (both crested terns have grey rump) and has sturdier build. All-black crown only for short period at start of breeding, during rest of year has white forehead which extends far back and often encloses eye. Chiefly an American species but breeds at Banc d'Arguin in Mauretania. Vagrant to W Europe.

Crested Tern   *Sterna bergii*   L 46–49 cm, WS 118–125 cm

Size of Royal Tern but lighter, with slimmer wings and body, and has darker mantle and grey rump. Bill lemon-yellow, often with greenish tint on juv., and has white above bill base even in summer plumage. Belongs to fauna of Indian Ocean and eastward to Pacific Ocean, with nearest breeders in Red Sea.

Lesser Crested Tern   *Sterna bengalensis*   L 35–37 cm, WS 100–107 cm

Like Sandwich Tern but with yellow-orange bill which is heavier at base. Clearly smaller than Royal Tern and with grey rump and tail. Juv. has greyish-yellow to yellow-orange bill and pale forehead and crown to immediately behind eye; juv. less dark-patterned than Crested Tern. Nearest breeders in Red Sea and Libya. Has bred in Ebro (Spain) and Po (Italy) Deltas; solitary birds have held territory in Sandwich Tern colonies on Mediterranean coast of Europe, and a female has interbred with Sandwich in Britain (Northumberland). Calls rather softer than those of Sandwich. Vagrant to W Europe. In Aug–Oct many migrate from Libya along N African coast and out to Atlantic, to winter off tropical W Africa, returning May–Jun.   *Map p. 286*

Elegant Tern   *Sterna elegans*   L 38–41 cm, WS 102–110 cm

Very like Lesser Crested Tern but has slightly longer and slimmer bill which looks more decurved. Rump and tail paler, look white in field. Breeds along Pacific coast in S California and Mexico. Possibly recorded a few times in W Europe.

Forster's Tern   *Sterna forsteri*   L 33–36 cm, WS 86–89 cm

In summer plumage like Common Tern, but with heavier bill which is paler orange with black tip. Upperparts silvery-grey with characteristic paler primaries. In juv. and winter plumages has characteristic black mask around eye, black bill and all-white crown, looks very pale and uniform on back and wings. Vagrant from N America.

Bridled Tern   *Sterna anaethetus*   L 30–32 cm, WS 77–81 cm

Barely size of Common Tern, with dark brown-grey back, narrow white neck-band next to black crown and with white forehead extending as a supercilium above and behind eye. Bill and legs black. A tropical species with nearest breeding sites in Mauretania and in Red Sea. Vagrant to W Europe.

Sooty Tern   *Sterna fuscata*   L 33–36 cm, WS 82–94 cm

Larger than Bridled Tern, with strikingly long pointed wings and Swallow-like long and forked tail. Sooty-black on mantle and crown, with white forehead which does not extend behind eye, black bill and legs. Juv. very dark brown-grey on mantle, head, breast and flanks, with paler fringes above. A tropical species breeding in large colonies on isolated islands. Highly pelagic. Vagrant to Europe, from end of May to Aug.

summer

winter

Royal Tern

winter

Crested Tern

summer

winter

summer

**Lesser
Crested Tern**

Forster's Tern
1st-winter

1st-winter

summer

Bridled Tern

Sooty Tern

Black Tern *Chlidonias niger* L 22−24 cm, WS 63−68 cm

A small dark tern with light, rather jaunty flight. Hunts insects over water surface like a big leisurely swallow, hovers and elegantly snatches prey from surface. The dark plumage is replaced early, from late Jun onwards, by a paler winter plumage, in Jul−Aug usually showing pale on head and patchily on underparts. Juv. differs from juv. White-winged Black in more uniformly grey upperparts incl. rump and also in having a small dark 'peg' on breast-side at wing-join. Calls include nasal and shrill 'kyay' or 'kyek', a cracked 'kerre'; contact call a short 'kik'. Breeds often colonially at shallow well-vegetated lowland lakes and marshes. Migrates end Jun to Aug, ads. first and juvs. later (odd ones into Oct). Towards late summer gathers in large flocks chiefly in Waddenzee area before moving to coasts of tropical Africa. Returns end Apr−May. In Britain variable passage, mostly May and Aug, when behaviour like Little Gull (can be confused at long range over sea).

White-winged Black Tern *Chlidonias leucopterus* L 20−23 cm, WS 63−67 cm

Rather like Black Tern but showing more contrast, with brilliant white rump and leading edge of wing and with black underwing-coverts. In winter plumage generally paler on upperparts than Black Tern; dark head markings are more restricted, and dark area on rear crown sometimes has pale fringes producing a pale grey impression. Juv. has paler wings and tail than Black Tern; 'saddle' contrastingly dark against paler wings, white rump and white outer tail feathers, lacks Black Tern's 'peg' at wing-join, and has shorter tail, rounder head shape and shorter bill and also broader wings. Calls harsh and loud: include 'kwek' and 'krrek', sometimes not unlike Common Tern; also 'kverr-kek', rather like Little Tern but softer. Habitat and feeding as Black Tern, but more tied to shallow seasonal marshes and wetlands. Vagrant to Britain, mostly May−Sep; annual.

Whiskered Tern *Chlidonias hybridus* L 23−25 cm, WS 70−75 cm

Resembles Black Tern in behaviour, but has faster and steadier flight and also plunge-dives. Ad. uniform grey above with silvery wings. Juv. very difficult to separate from White-winged Black, though mantle is browner with buff elements and wings are more uniformly pale and lacking in contrast compared with latter; usually, but not always, has diffuse dusky area at wing-join, and also more streaked crown and thicker bill than White-winged Black. Variations and effects of light, however, make head markings and contrasts in wing pattern difficult to judge in field. Juv. moults into winter plumage (though not wings) from end of Aug; then has black bill and paler crown than other *Chlidonias* terns and at distance appears to have wholly white crown. Call a hoarse cracked 'aihrk' or 'eeirk' with same pitch as Black-winged Stilt. Fairly common at marshes at food-rich lakes in parts of S Europe. Vagrant north to Britain Apr−Oct, especially May−Jun.

Black Tern

White-winged Black Tern

Whiskered Tern

summer

ad moulting (autumn)

summer

Black Tern

juv

White-winged Black Tern

juv

summer

summer

Whiskered Tern

juv

summer

juv

White-winged Black Tern
summer

winter

Black Tern
juv

Black Tern
summer

Whiskered Tern
summer

Guillemot   *Uria aalge*   *L 38–45 cm, WS 64–73 cm*

A pronounced seabird which comes ashore only to breed. Differs from Razorbill in its bill shape and slightly paler grey-black upperparts, head verging on brown. More northerly populations have darker coloration above. A common variant (known as 'bridled') has white eye-ring and white line behind eye. In flight slightly larger than Razorbill, with longer and more pointed fore area and with feet clearly visible at stern. Underwings are darker, with soiled markings on coverts, dark axillaries and with paler flight feathers than Razorbill. In winter plumage has more white on 'temples' intersected by a black line; on some the dark colour at base of neck forms complete neck-band. Winter plumage is worn only during autumn in southern part of breeding range, and as early as Nov−Dec many moult to attain all-dark head (moulting individuals in late autumn can be taken for Brünnich's Guillemot); imms., however, wear winter plumage until well into May. Nests in large dense colonies on cliffs facing the sea. Noisy at breeding sites, giving high growling 'arrr' or 'ooarrr' calls, the young uttering plaintive piping 'pee-vü'. Feeds mainly on fish. Leaves breeding ledges about Aug, returning from Jan.

Brünnich's Guillemot   *Uria lomvia*   *L 39−43 cm, WS 65−70 cm*

Blacker above than Guillemot but a shade paler than Razorbill. Has shorter nape, shorter and stouter bill and in summer a white gape streak and also lacks Guillemot's dark markings on flanks. In Arctic is smaller than the Guillemots breeding there, but perhaps as large as or even bigger than southern-breeding Guillemots. In winter plumage darker on head than the two other large auks and often with irregular black flecking also on throat and cheeks, giving it a more dark-headed appearance. Winter plumage is retained until at least early spring. Juv. occurs in two colour phases, one summer-like with black-brown throat and one with entirely white throat and cheeks. In flight compact, rather hunched and with bill pointing slightly downwards; underwings paler than Guillemot's but not showing Razorbill's contrast between coverts and flight feathers. An arctic auk seen only rarely in North Sea area but which probably winters there in small numbers.

Razorbill   *Alca torda*   *L 37−39 cm, WS 63−67 cm*

Blacker above than Guillemot. In flight shows more white on sides of rump and 'invisible' feet (coincide with the longer tail) and also whiter coverts and blacker flight feathers on underwings. Bill tends slightly upward in flight. In winter plumage has more black on head than Guillemot. Juv. in autumn has smaller bill than ad. and can be confused with Brünnich's Guillemot. Often nests side by side with Guillemots, but usually in fewer numbers on bird cliffs than latter; in Baltic also in small colonies on outer skerries of island groups. Feeds mainly on fish. Leaves breeding sites early, often in Jul, to winter mostly at sea, returning in Feb−Mar.

Guillemot

Brünnich's Guillemot

Razorbill

winter

summer

Guillemot

summer

winter

Brünnich's Guillemot

winter

summer

Razorbill

Black Guillemot   *Cepphus grylle*   *L 30–32 cm, WS 52–58 cm*

Is not like any of the other guillemots but in winter plumage, especially in flight, can be taken for some other pale waterbird. The straight flight path with rapid whirring wingbeats and the conspicuous white wing patches, however, usually make it easy to recognise. Juv. resembles winter-plumaged ad., but is darker on forehead and has dark barring on wing patches. 2nd-cal-year summer becomes black but retains dark-marked secondary coverts, can look all-black. Occurs in smaller concentrations but is more widespread than other guillemots. At nesting sites utters almost irritatingly high, persistent whistles, 'peeeeeeh'. From nest sites behind rocks and under boulders, the incubating bird and later the young utter whistling and cheeping calls that are difficult to locate. Breeds on rocky and stony coasts. Feeds on fish and other small animals which are caught by diving near the bottom. Resident, but partial migrant in Baltic. Considerably less pelagic and more sedentary in winter than other auks.

Puffin   *Fratercula arctica*   *L 26–29 cm, WS 47–63 cm*

In summer unmistakable. After breeding season loses the outer parts of the bill and then has a smaller and predominantly yellow and grey bill. In winter, face and particularly lores also become a darker grey. Juv. has even thinner bill and, especially in flight, can be confused with Little Auk (see below). Has a typical auk flight with straight course and rapid wingbeats, but at nest sites manoeuvres with greater skill than Guillemot and Razorbill. Obviously smaller than Guillemot, with darker greyish underwings. Nests in burrows excavated by itself or by rabbits on grassy slopes and in landslip precipices on coast, often in immense colonies. Feeds on fish. Pelagic in winter, a few in Mediterranean and rare inshore.

Little Auk   *Alle alle*   *L 17–19 cm, WS 40–48 cm*

Despite its small size, about that of a Starling, can be confused with other auks. On the water, the short podgy neck and the head with its almost negligible little bill are striking. In flight, its strangely bobbin-shaped and 'bill-less' profile and the very fast wingbeats are characteristic features. Wings are relatively long, white below and (if one can manage to make it out) with a white stripe in middle of arm. Juv. resembles winter-plumaged ad. but is browner and duller in tone. Nests in enormous colonies in cavities on mountain precipices. An arctic auk breeding in its millions in Spitsbergen and Greenland, with a small colony also in N Iceland. Winters at sea, regularly south to the North Sea, and seen especially in association with westerly storms when it comes closer inshore. In Britain regular winter visitor only in north, in certain years in larger numbers, scarce and irregular elsewhere; occasionally blown inland.

Black Guillemot

Puffin

Little Auk

Black Guillemot

winter

Puffin

juv

winter

winter

Little Auk

winter

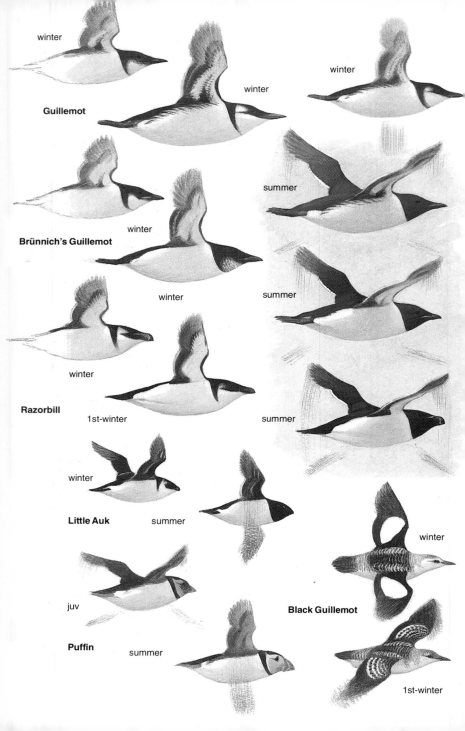

winter

Guillemot

winter

winter

winter

Brünnich's Guillemot

summer

winter

summer

winter

Razorbill

winter

1st-winter

summer

winter

Little Auk

summer

winter

Black Guillemot

juv

Puffin

summer

1st-winter

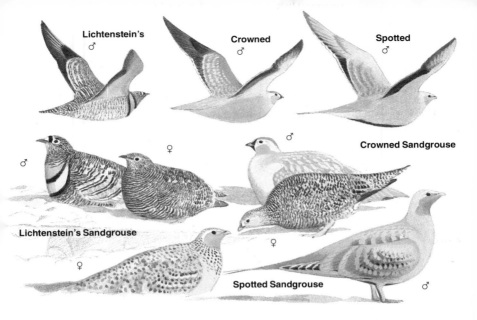

Lichtenstein's ♂

Crowned ♂

Spotted ♂

♂

♀

Crowned Sandgrouse

Lichtenstein's Sandgrouse

♂

♀

♀

Spotted Sandgrouse

♂

Lichtenstein's Sandgrouse   *Pterocles lichtensteinii*   L 24–26 cm, WS 48–52 cm

Smallest sandgrouse, size of Turtle Dove. Male characteristic; female densely vermiculated dark, looks grey at distance with 'gentle' eye and pale eye-ring. Squats when approached and difficult to see in daytime. Most active at night, comes to waterholes at dusk to drink, when calls with a sharp 'quitall'. Other calls a rather purring 'trrrr' and a rather frog-like 'kwark-kwark-kwark'. Breeds in stony semi-desert with some trees and bushes, typically on dried-out riverbeds with acacias. In W Palearctic breeds in the southernmost parts of Sinai Peninsula, Israel and Jordan, SE Algeria and in extreme SE Morocco and adjacent parts of Algeria.

Crowned Sandgrouse   *Pterocles coronatus*   L 27–29 cm, WS 52–63 cm

Smaller than Black-bellied Sandgrouse. Male pale chamois-leather colour at distance, isolated black mask around bill-join characteristic. Female greyer and densely cross-flecked/barred, with unmarked yellow chin and without clear eye-ring. In flight shows contrasting dark flight feathers both above and below (cf Lichtenstein's and Spotted). Call a loud, slightly cackling 'chaga-chagarra'. In winter gathers in flocks and around waterholes, mostly in morning. Breeds relatively commonly in desert or semi-desert, on stony and on sandy substrate. Range extends patchily over N Sahara from S Morocco to Egypt and S Israel.

Spotted Sandgrouse   *Pterocles senegallus*   L 30–35 cm, WS 53–65 cm

Slightly bigger than Crowned Sandgrouse, at distance fairly uniform grey-buff and olive-grey above with darker spots on back and wings, female with dark eye-stripe and streaked crown and breast. In flight shows pale primaries above, but with a dark band along whole rear edge of wing. Dark belly patch easiest to see in flight. Noisy in flight, a bubbling 'queet-too'. Flocks in non-breeding season (seldom 50 together). Occurs on desert steppe or in sand deserts. Range extends through N Sahara from S Morocco to Libya; also breeds E Egypt, N Sinai, S Israel and NE Jordan.

Black-bellied Sandgrouse   **Pin-tailed Sandgrouse**

Black-bellied Sandgrouse   *Pterocles orientalis*   *L 33−35 cm, WS 70−73 cm*

Seen chiefly in mornings when flying to lakes or smaller pools to drink. Flight path is straight and rapid with fast wingbeats; at distance look like Golden Plovers. Black belly and black flight feathers below, buff with blue-grey flight feathers above. Often draws attention to itself in flight by a soft rolling 'churr (choorr) …churr…' (more a rolled 'l' than a rolled 'r'), not unlike half a Turtle Dove song; on take-off a more drawn-out 'aschurrrr'. Occurs on steppes and in semi-desert with or without low scrub, often on high plateaux and poor pasture. In Iberia rare and local, in N Africa and Turkey relatively common. Feeds mainly on seeds.

Pin-tailed Sandgrouse   *Pterocles alchata*   *L 31−39 cm, WS 54−65 cm*

Smaller than Black-bellied Sandgrouse and easy to tell from latter in flight by long tail extension and lack of black belly, on ground by dark eye-stripe. Male looks greenish above. Call louder, 'katarr-katarr', rather like *Aythya* duck. At nest sites performs display flight in pair formation with breathtakingly fast dives in gentle curves, when wings produce whistling sound. Local and fairly scarce in similar terrain to Black-bellied, but more widespread in Europe than latter. In winter gathers in large flocks, occasionally of thousands. Has decreased in Europe during 1900s, mainly through cultivation of suitable nesting habitats. Food mainly seeds.

Pallas's Sandgrouse   *Syrrhaptes paradoxus*   *L 30−41 cm, WS 63−78 cm*

A C Asiatic species, very rare vagrant to W Europe. Slimmer-bodied than Pin-tailed, with similar needle tail and elongated, pointed longest primary (more so on male, represents 6−10 cm of wingspan above). In flight shows entirely white underwings and dark 'Rough-legged Buzzard band' over belly.

Black-bellied Sandgrouse   Pin-tailed Sandgrouse

Pallas's Sandgrouse

Black-bellied Sandgrouse

Pin-tailed Sandgrouse

Stock Dove　　　　　　　　**Woodpigeon**

Woodpigeon　*Columba palumbus*　　　　　*L 40–42 cm, WS 75–80 cm*

Always easy to recognise by white markings on wings and neck, which are conspicuous at long range. In flight, bulkier, deeper-chested and longer-tailed than Stock Dove. Juv. lacks white on neck. On take-off and landing wings make loud clatter. In display flight climbs with fast clattering wingbeats and glides slowly downwards on stiff wings. Call a soft 'blowing' of varied transcription, 'doo-doooh, doo doo-du', with desolate ring and having the character of an owl's call. Has increased in numbers in recent decades and is common in all kinds of woodland, parks and large gardens. Feeds on various berries, seeds and buds; beechmast and acorns are an important food in autumn. Often forages regularly in the morning and evening on fields. Northern and eastern populations migratory, on passage Sep–Oct and Mar–Apr often appear in large flocks.

Stock Dove　*Columba oenas*　　　　　*L 32–34 cm, WS 63–69 cm*

Clearly smaller than Woodpigeon with shorter tail. Flight is steadier and faster and it looks better proportioned. Can be confused with city pigeon but lacks obvious black wingbars. Older birds have paler, slightly silver-glossed median and greater wing-coverts, whereas juvs. look more uniformly grey on wings. Male gives a rapidly repeated disyllabic 'oou-o, oou-o, oou-o…'. Gives display flights like city pigeons on V-held wings. Choice of nesting terrain depends chiefly on presence of suitable nest holes such as Black Woodpecker holes, nestboxes, holes in buildings and stone walls etc. Occurs sparsely but in places commonly in open woodland and cultivated country. Food similar to Woodpigeon's, and the two species often feed together on fields. Northern and eastern populations migrate like Woodpigeon, but slightly later in autumn and earlier in spring than latter.

Woodpigeon

Stock Dove

juv

Woodpigeon

Stock Dove

Long-toed Pigeon   *Columba trocaz*   L 38–40 cm, WS 72–76 cm

Endemic on Madeira. Nests in damp laurel forests at high altitude. Like a Woodpigeon in shape, but much darker grey and with an indistinct glossy silvery patch on neck-side surrounded by purplish and glossy green feathers. Wings short, all-dark. Woodpigeon is now extinct on Madeira. On La Palma, Gomera and Tenerife (Canary Islands) the closely related and rather similar Bolle's Laurel Pigeon *C. bollii* and also the Laurel Pigeon *C. junoniae* breed.

Rock Dove   *Columba livia*   L 31–34 cm, WS 63–70 cm

Ancestor of domestic and feral pigeons. In W Europe occurs naturally on rocky coasts, in Mediterranean countries mostly in rocky mountainous and desert terrain. Differs from Stock Dove and Woodpigeon in its black wingbars and white lower back. In some places (incl. Scotland) feral pigeons also nest on sea cliffs and are then impossible to separate in the field from Rock Doves. These feral pigeons sometimes associate with Rock Doves and interbreeding probably takes place. In display flight glides on raised wings uttering a sombre cooing 'dooo-roo-dooo'.

Collared Dove   *Streptopelia decaocto*   L 31–33 cm, WS 47–55 cm

A small, slim, long-tailed dove, pale buff with a black band on neck. Confusion most likely with Turtle Dove (see also Laughing Dove). In active flight shows longer tail, paler overall impression and paler underwings than Turtle Dove. Tail markings less contrast-

ing, has broader whitish-grey tips to tail feathers and lacks Turtle Dove's black subterminal band. In display flight glides on slightly downward-curved wings and fanned tail and prominently demonstrates undertail markings. Juv. lacks neck-band and is greyer in coloration. Call a rapidly repeated deep 'koo-kooo, koo'. Originates from Asia but has spread northwest during 1900s. Occurs commonly in parks and gardens in built-up areas, also farms, villages. Resident, though odd ones move south.

Rock Dove

Turtle Dove

Laughing Dove

Rock Dove

Collared Dove

Turtle Dove

Rufous Turtle Dove　　　　　　　　　　　　　　　**Turtle Dove** juv

Rufous Turtle Dove　　*Streptopelia orientalis*　　　　　L 33–35 cm, WS 53–60 cm

Like a large Turtle Dove, but with heavier build and generally darker. Ad. like Turtle
Dove on mantle and wing-coverts, but dark feather centres bigger, more diffusely
defined and more rounded towards tip; Rufous Turtle looks dark brown with pale scaly
markings, Turtle pale red-brown with dark brown spots. On juv./1st-winter, wing-
coverts are darker and have distinct pale grey tips forming pale bars across wing;
impression of pale barring on wing-coverts remains on ad. but is less obvious. Has grey
terminal band on tail without a blackish subterminal band like Turtle. Neck patch has
grey-blue tips to the black feathers (whitish on Turtle Dove). Vagrant from C Asia,
mostly late autumn to winter.

Turtle Dove　　*Streptopelia turtur*　　　　　　　　L 26–28 cm, WS 47–53 cm

A small, lightweight dove with slightly rocky and pitching flight. On take-off and landing
tail markings conspicuous. Brown-red upperparts, darker underwings and shorter tail
distinguish it also in active flight from Collared Dove. Juv. has more grey-brown or
grey-buff overall appearance, lacks dark feather centres and neck patch. In western N
Africa east to N Libya and Middle East, paler and more washed-out race *arenicola*
occurs. Common in cultivated country with open deciduous woods, clumps of trees
and gardens, also in oases and scrub with scattered trees. Often retiring at nest site.
Seen perched in pairs or small parties on telephone wires and in middle of fields and
meadows. Makes its presence known mostly, however, by its call, a soft purring 'toorr,
toorr…' or 'turr, turr'. Feeds on plant and grass seeds. In Britain regular summer visitor,
mostly to southern half, Apr–Sep, has decreased in some areas; also passage migrant
from Continent, mainly Apr–May and Aug–Oct.　　　　　　　　　　　*Map p. 304*

Laughing Dove　　*Streptopelia senegalensis*　　　　　L 25–27 cm, WS 40–45 cm

Size of Turtle Dove but with more rounded wings and longer tail. Tail markings as Turtle
Dove's, but white tips grade into blue-grey near centre and are not sharply defined.
Varies markedly in colour, overall impression usually dark with deep brownish-red
upperparts and blue-grey wing-coverts. Lack of dark feather centres above and dark
patterning on breast-sides distinguish it at all times from Turtle. Locally very dirty and
nondescript, especially in big cities e.g. Istanbul. Song somewhat like Collared Dove's
but weaker, more pumping and with more syllables, e.g. 'pooo poo puOO-pOOu-
hoo'. Common in towns and villages, gardens, cultivations and oases.　　*Map p. 304*

Namaqua Dove　　*Oena capensis*　　　　　　　　　L 26–28 cm, WS 28–33 cm

Very small, long-tailed dove. Male has black face and breast. Copper-red on
underwings. An African species. Rare and local in S Israel. Vagrant to N Africa.

Not illustrated

Turtle Dove

Laughing Dove

Cuckoo   *Cuculus canorus*   L 32−34 cm, WS 55−65 cm

Long-tailed and with pointed wings, with rather Kestrel-like silhouette. Often seen in flight, which is fast and straight but with rather placid wingbeats; does not lift wings above body level, and has a rather sway-backed profile owing to shape and attitude of head. Distinguished from Sparrowhawk by its pointed wings. Female resembles male but has a tinge of brown in a band across breast. Juvs. have pale fringes above, below are barred also on breast and throat and have a distinct white patch on nape; usually darker, more slate-grey in ground colour. Occurs in a not uncommon rufous phase in which juv. and female have brownish-red ground colour. In May−Jun gives its familiar 'kuk-kooh' call, usually from top of a tree. When irritated by proximity of a rival, male also utters a hoarse chuckling 'gug-gug-gug-che-che-che'. Female has Whimbrel-like, explosive and bubbling chuckle. Occurs commonly in most types of open country with element of bushes and trees, as well as in open woodland and in N Europe high up in the mountain birch forest. In midsummer leads a secretive existence. Feeds on insects, especially hairy caterpillars (which are avoided by many other bird species). In late summer juvs. are often seen watching out for caterpillars from fenceposts and low bushes. The Cuckoo lays its eggs one by one in other birds' nests; the Cuckoo hatchling ejects other eggs or young from the nest and is then reared by the host parents. Each female specialises on one species whose eggs resemble her own. Over 100 different host species have been recorded in Europe: Meadow Pipit, Dunnock, Reed Warbler, Pied Wagtail and Redstart are the commonest. Migrates to tropical Africa from end Jul to beginning Sep, returning mid Apr−May.

Oriental Cuckoo   *Cuculus saturatus*   L 30−32 cm, WS 51−57 cm

Very like Cuckoo, and all differences in appearance small and partly subject to individual variation. Slightly smaller than Cuckoo, appears slightly shorter-tailed and with firmer (not so 'limp') posture. Head appears bigger and bill stronger. The grey form is slightly darker above on wings and back, below having on average broader bars on belly and with more yellow-buff or creamy ground colour. Markings on undertail-coverts (sometimes missing) more as broad blotches arranged crosswise (narrow uniform bars on Cuckoo). Female varies from grey to rich red-brown, like Cuckoo. Brown form has heavier markings, especially on upperparts where it has uniform broad blackish bars on rump and tail (more broken and irregular patterning on Cuckoo). Call a disyllabic 'poo-poo', quite different from Cuckoo's in that both syllables are similar in pitch and length, have Hoopoe character; repeated 6–8 times and at a faster rate than in Cuckoo, often introduced by a more rapid series 'poo-poo-poo-poo-poo'. Nearest breeding area in easternmost Europe and eastwards in the taiga zone. Prefers more secluded forest than Cuckoo, also dense bushy thickets, often shy and retiring. Long-distance migrant to SE Asia. Recorded a few times in Europe outside Russia.

Cuckoo

Oriental Cuckoo

Cuckoo

♀ grey phase

♀ red phase

juv

Cuckoo ♂

Oriental
Cuckoo ♂

♀

Great Spotted Cuckoo

Clamator glandarius   *L 38–40 cm (juv. 35 cm), WS 58–66 cm*

Unmistakable in flight, with disproportionately long tail and Cuckoo-like flight. Juv. has bronze-coloured primaries and black cap. 1st-summer birds show bronze colour and black ear-coverts. Call a quarrelsome 'krree krree krree', almost like Great Spotted Woodpecker's chatter call. Relatively scarce and to an extent irregular in open or semi-open country. Parasitises crows, mainly Magpie and Azure-winged Magpie. Young (sometimes lays several eggs in same nest) grows up alongside host's young. Food mostly larger insects. Arrives from end Mar, departs Aug–Sep. Very rare vagrant to Britain.

Yellow-billed Cuckoo

Cuckoo

Ring-necked Parakeet

1st-cal
autumn

1st-cal autumn
Black-billed Cuckoo

Yellow-billed Cuckoo *Coccyzus americanus* L 28–32 cm, WS 40–48 cm
Smaller than Cuckoo, but with similar slim profile with long wings and tail. Brown above with rusty-toned primaries. Tail black below with conspicuous whitish tips and outer web to outer feathers, on juv. dark grey with dirty-white tips, but always more sharply marked than on Black-billed Cuckoo. Clear pale eye-ring and yellowish bill base. Often perches out of sight on inner branches. Very rare vagrant from N America. Most records Britain and Ireland, mid Sep to mid Nov.

Black-billed Cuckoo *Coccyzus erythrophthalmus* L 27–31 cm, WS 38–42 cm
Like Yellow-billed Cuckoo but slightly smaller. Primaries are never obviously rusty, but juv. often has a warmer brown tone on outer webs of primaries. Tail less contrastingly marked, grey below with slightly paler tips. Ad. has black bill and red orbital ring. On juv. (more likely in Europe) eye-ring is buff and less conspicuous and bill usually grey at base. Behaviour and status as Yellow-billed, but is even rarer.

Ring-necked Parakeet *Psittacula krameri* L 38–42 cm, WS 42–48 cm
The only species of parrot in the region. All-green, with long tail and black and pink neck-band (lacking on juv.). Formerly bred in Iraq. Introduced into Egypt, Israel, England, Holland and Belgium.

311

Barn Owl   *Tyto alba*   L 33–39 cm, WS 85–93 cm

Best known for male's distinctive shrieking call. Size of Long-eared Owl, pale with characteristic heart-shaped face and black eyes. Nominate race *alba* in British Isles and in France, Spain and Italy very pale, white to yellowish-white below. Male may or may not have a few dark spots below, female has spots at least on flanks. Intergrades in N/E Europe into *guttata*, which is darker above and a deep rusty-yellow with dark spots below. In flight the wings, which are beaten jerkily and stiffly, are proportionately shorter and the head larger than on Short-eared Owl, and general appearance is paler and more uniform in colour. Male's territorial call, given also in flight, is a clear vibrant shriek c2 seconds long. Alarm call in flight a straight shrill shriek, and attacks intruders with a short extremely sharp shriek. Young beg with a drawn-out hissing. Nests in lofts and in hollow spaces in barns, outhouses, hollow trees etc. Hunts over open cultivated country with fields, ditches, scrub and low plantations. Daily rhythm varies individually, hunts actively at dawn and dusk but calls are heard only during dark. Feeds mostly on smaller rodents, also occasional small birds. Chiefly resident and sedentary, imms. wander during their first year.

Short-eared Owl   *Asio flammeus*   L 34–42 cm, WS 90–105 cm

When perched, characteristic in its heavily blotched plumage and deep black eye surrounds which give it a rather fiendish expression. Its small 'mouse ears' are raised only when the bird is on its guard. In flight, long wings are beaten jerkily and rather stiffly, but glides and circles speedily and elegantly and with great manoeuvring skill. Distinguished in flight from Long-eared Owl by longer wings, paler and more variegated overall impression, though varies individually in colour tone and contrast. Primaries have conspicuous rusty-yellow patch at base and fewer and more distinct dark bars towards tip. More diurnal than other owls, hunts mostly in late evening and early morning and therefore fairly easy to see. Male's call is a soft pumping 'doo-doo-doo-doo-doo', female's a hoarse 'cheeee-op'. Breeds in large open areas such as moors/heaths, swamps and marshes, tussocky meadows and fields. Feeds chiefly on small rodents, and its presence is in many respects dependent on their availability, but also takes birds and their young and some smaller animals in poor rodent years. In Britain partial migrant, with additional large winter immigration from Scandinavia Sep–May.

Marsh Owl   *Asio capensis*   L 35–37 cm, WS 82–99 cm

An African owl with an isolated presence in NW Morocco. Like Short-eared Owl, but dark brown and when perched almost unmarked above and with dark iris. In flight shows rusty-buff primary bases like Short-eared. Commonest call, uttered also in flight, a deep frog- or Rook-like 'kaa', given singly or several in succession. Occurs on tussocky swamplands.

Barn Owl

Short-eared Owl

Marsh Owl

alba

guttata

Barn Owl

Short-eared Owl

Long-eared Owl   *Asio otus*   L 35−37 cm, WS 84−95 cm

Differs from Tawny Owl in orange-red eyes and long ear-tufts; at rest tufts are lowered and not visible. In flight, wings are beaten in mechanical jerks and stiffly as if in splints, then most easily confused with Short-eared Owl. Body more uniformly streaked below, whereas Short-eared has pale abdomen and darker breast/neck. Long-eared also has shorter wings, and wingtip barring is more blurred and less contrasting. Nocturnal but hunts mostly at dusk and dawn, on rare occasions in middle of day. Male's territorial call, repeated at c3-second intervals, is a pumping, hollow 'HOOO', like a short blow into an empty bottle. Female has a clearer and more drawn-out 'hoouuu', but more common is for her to answer with a feeble 'keee-e', oddly nasal and slightly mechanical. Alarm 'kvik-kvik' and bill-clicks. Young that have left the nest give themselves away by clear whistled begging calls, 'peee-e'. Breeds relatively commonly in old nests of crows or birds of prey in light woodland or clumps of trees. Requires open meadows, moors or marshland for hunting and is associated most with hilly cultivated country. Food mainly voles, but mice and small birds are important prey regionally or periodically. Resident in large parts of Europe, but migrant in N Scandinavia and Finland, often leaving late in Oct−Nov and returning Mar−Apr (May); some winter in Britain.

Eagle Owl   *Bubo bubo*   L 60−75 cm, WS 160−188 cm

Europe's biggest owl, ten times heavier than Long-eared Owl, weighs c2−4 kg. Can kill a Goshawk. Has conspicuous ear-tufts. In flight, the short tail, broad wings and the rather pointed face are striking features; wingbeats are shallow, stiff and surprisingly fast. Represented across whole Palearctic by about 20 races, which vary in size and in colour tone. Generally smaller and paler in the south, *hispanus* in Iberia is smallest in Europe. In N Africa and Middle East race *ascalaphus*, which is clearly smaller and paler and which in extreme desert regions can be pale sandy-coloured with pale brown patterning. In Siberia from Urals eastwards race *sibiricus*, which is bigger and paler with greyish-white ground colour. Variation within one region can be appreciable, however, some Scandinavian birds being almost uniformly dark brown above and others heavily mottled rusty-buff and brown. Male calls most intensively in Feb−Mar and during the day from sunset and for an hour or so thereafter: a far-carrying 'HOO-o' (audible at up to 5km), repeated at intervals of c8 seconds. Female replies with a similar call but about an octave higher, often slightly hoarse and with less emphasis; she also has a hoarse yapping 'VAYew'. The young beg intensely with hoarse strained 'chooEEsh'. Alarm a shrill sharp 'ke-ke-keKAYu' and bill-clicking. Breeds in widely differing habitats, from large forests to desert tracts, but resorts to rocks, precipices and ravines providing sheltered ledges for the nest. In N Europe mostly in woodland and at cliffs near coast. Feeds on smaller mammals and medium-sized birds, along coast often gulls and ducks. Often hunts rats at refuse tips. Highly sedentary, but imms. roam about in their first year in search of their own territory.

Long-eared Owl

Eagle Owl

Long-eared Owl

Eagle Owl

Snowy Owl

♂ displaying

♀

Snowy Owl *Nyctea scandiaca* L 55–65 cm, WS 142–166 cm

Almost as big as Eagle Owl, but tied to upland moor and tundra. Male is smaller than female and lacks or has only a few dark spots. Juv. is intensely spotted dark and often amazingly hard to find when resting during the day. Flight powerful and wings markedly pointed. Territorial call a short, soft, slightly moaning 'gawh', repeated at intervals of a few seconds. Male's alarm call is a coarse 'kraik-kraik-kraik', like agitated female Mallard; female has similar alarm but higher and more cracked. Female also has shrill whistled shriek, 'seeeuue', and young off nest beg with similar call. Dependent on y lemming or other rodents; breeding and presence within area indicated vary greatly between different years, almost totally absent from Scandinavian mountains in poor rodent years. May move long distances south in some winters, to moors and open farmland of e.g. N Britain, when hunts mainly at dusk. Bred N Britain 1967–75, regularly present since; otherwise very rare, irregular vagrant to Britain.

Hawk Owl

Hawk Owl   *Surnia ulula*

L 36–41 cm, WS 74–81 cm

More diurnal than other owls, often perches like a big stout Great Grey Shrike on top of e.g. telegraph pole. In flight, like a large Sparrowhawk with long tail and small pointed wings, and with fast and shallow wingbeats. Often seen in clearings, along power-line lanes or similar open places in the boreal forest, as well as more commonly in thin open woodland around the tree line. Nests in hollow trees, rarely in old crow nests. Feeds mainly on voles and lemmings; number of breeding pairs within an area fluctuates greatly from year to year. Territorial call a drawn-out (4–6 seconds) fast shivering or bubbling trill, 'prullullullu...', heard mostly during darker hours of day, sometimes in daytime. Female replies with drawn-out hoarse, slightly hissing call which ends abruptly, 'kshuu-lip'; this call and variants are used when agitated and also by young as begging call. Alarm at nest a jerky series of hard loud 'ki-ki-ki-ki...' or 'kew-kew...' calls, not unlike Kestrel. Normally sedentary, but in some years irruptions occur south to S Sweden and in extreme years even farther south.

Tawny Owl *Strix aluco*   L 37–39 cm, WS 94–104 cm

A crow-sized, plump owl with all-black eyes. Ground colour varies from greyish to red-brown, but grey individuals very uncommon in Britain. In flight, wings seem comparatively short, and when gliding they are held slightly curved downwards. Breeds commonly in open mixed or deciduous woodland, often near human habitations. Such places as oak woods, large gardens and parks, avenues of trees etc are favoured as they often offer a good supply of nesting holes. Owing to its strictly nocturnal habits, it is usually at dusk that it is seen. Occasionally it is discovered at its daytime roost on a branch, pressed tight against a tree trunk, usually given away by alarm calls of tits. Male's territorial call consists of two mellow whistled hoots, slightly desolate but clear and woodwind in tone: 'pooOOH', after 1–4 seconds followed by 'poo, poo-ho-ho, HOOO'O'O'O'O'O', the latter part drawn-out and tremulous; sometimes the first or second part is omitted. Female has a feebler cracked version of the same call; she also replies with a sharp 'klee-VIT' or 'kew-VIK' (also heard from male). Alarm is similar. Male also has a more uncommon drawn-out bubbling trill. Young beg with a hissing 'sheee-ep'. Feeds mainly on small rodents but has comparatively varied diet: hedgehogs, birds, frogs, worms, etc.

Hume's Tawny Owl *Strix butleri*   L 37–38 cm, WS 95–98 cm

A desert species with a local distribution around Arabian Peninsula, nearest breeding sites being in Israel and Egypt. Like Tawny Owl in proportions but smaller and paler. Underparts pale with ochre vermiculations, upperparts greyer with more contrasting dark/light barring on flight and tail feathers. Face dirty-white with characteristic reddish-yellow iris and dark band in centre of forehead. Territorial call a 5-syllable 'vooooo, hoohoo hoohoo' with first syllable drawn-out and lacking Tawny's wavering quality in final syllables. Nests in cavities in rock faces or buildings along ravines and dried-out riverbeds, typically with proximity to a water source and acacias or palm groves.

Tawny Owl

Hume's Tawny Owl

Tawny Owl

Hume's Tawny Owl

Tawny Owl

grey phase

red phase

Hume's Tawny Owl

Ural Owl   *Strix uralensis*   L 58–62 cm, WS 124–134 cm

Like a very big washed-out Tawny Owl with long tail. Male's territorial call is a muffled hooting, 'VOOhoo…(c4-second pause)…voohoo-oVOOho'. Call is heard at up to 2 km distance. During courtship period also utters a series of gruff hoots which rise very slightly in pitch and drop at the very end, 'voovoovoovoovoovoovoovo'. Female has a variant of same call but harsher and hoarser in tone. Male uses territorial call to announce his arrival with food and female then replies with a hoarse disyllabic 'ku VEU'. Alarm call is a short bark, very like a dog's, 'vraff' or 'vraff-aff' from female and lower and softer from male. During mating female gives a hoarse twitter. Young have a hissing begging call, 'psheee-ep', very like Tawny Owl's. Breeds sparsely, locally more commonly, in coniferous and mixed forest, in C Europe also in alpine beech forest. Food consists mainly of small rodents, which are captured in clearings, glades, on bogs and other open terrain. Numbers fluctuate to a lesser extent than with other small-rodent specialists, which suggests that various birds, e.g. Hazel Grouse, Black Grouse and Jay, constitute an important alternative food source during poor rodent years. Nests in hollow tree stumps, in nestboxes or rarely in stick nests. Very aggressive at nest site and often drives off other owl species in its territory. Strikes with great force at the face of any human being who approaches the young.

Great Grey Owl   *Strix nebulosa*   L 64–70 cm, WS 134–158 cm

An unmistakable, large grey owl with characteristic 'annual rings' on the face. Sits and listens or watches for voles from a bush, tree or pole of hay-drying rack, usually 1–4m above the ground. In summer seen hunting throughout entire day. Flight is composed and well balanced, glides long distances. A broad dark band on the long tail, two pale panels on the broad wings and the large head are distinctive in flight. Male's territorial call is audible at a maximum of 400 m distance, calls only during darkest hours of night. The call is muffled and difficult to locate, its strength sounds constant irrespective of distance, and it somewhat recalls Bittern's voice in tone. It consists of usually 10–12 hoots slowly pumped forth, and accelerating and dropping slightly towards the end (the series takes 6–7 seconds). When agitated, a call roughly twice as fast but weaker. Female answers male with a high and surprisingly feeble 'kyiep-kyiep-kyiep'. During courtship-feeding and mating she has a high, cracked trilling call (young have similar begging call) and a weak whining 'kyo' or more energetic 'koeeyo' combined with a low cooing. If a human approaches the nest, both sexes react by bill-snapping and give a muffled and harsh 'hoch-hoch-hoch' alarm; when greatly threatened, female also gives a piercingly high shriek. Occurs in coniferous and mixed forest with fields, bogs or similar open areas. Presence is dependent on availability of small rodents, and species is locally fairly common in some years while in others it partially emigrates or becomes very unobtrusive. Breeds in large stick nest.

Ural Owl

Great Grey Owl

Ural Owl

Great Grey Owl

Pygmy Owl

Pygmy Owl *Glaucidium passerinum* L 16–18 cm, WS 34–36 cm

Easy to identify from its diminutive size. Makes its presence known by a rhythmically repeated, rather Bullfinch-like straight whistle, 'pyuh' (at close range 'pyuk'), when excited sometimes with a rapidly vibrating 'pyuuuu' inserted. Often sits in top of a spruce and whistles, most intensively at dusk and dawn. Female has a thin 'seeee', not unlike a Hazel Grouse, and young have similar begging calls, occasionally given twice, 'tseee-tseee'. Also heard in autumn is a rapid, slightly disjointed series of clear whistles which rise towards the end, 'chet, cheet, cheet, chit, chit'. Active by day. Waves tail sideways. Flight over open ground is woodpecker-like, with rapid series of wingbeats followed by glide in a deep arc. Food is rodents but also small birds, which give intense alarm in its presence. Breeds fairly commonly in coniferous and mixed forest and is often encountered at edge of bogs and glades. In winter also in open and more cultivated terrain, in deciduous woods and around farmyards where there is a good supply of small birds. Stores prey in nestboxes. Nests in woodpecker holes.

Tengmalm's Owl *Aegolius funereus* L 24–26 cm, WS 52–58 cm

A small large-headed owl. Distribution/habitat and behaviour make confusion with Little Owl rather unlikely. Tengmalm's is decidedly nocturnal and difficult to see. During the day it hides within a dense spruce but is then not at all shy of man. Male advertises himself most intensively in winter and spring but also in autumn, though always at night. Advertising or territorial call is a fast, slightly vibrating series of hollow barking hoots, 'po po po po po', varying in length and tone between different males; it is uttered frequently (at intervals of a few seconds) over long periods. When agitated, it may change into a long uninterrupted vibrating series. Also has a nasal 'kuweuk' and a warning hard 'kip', 'kep' or similar calls. Fledged young have a chocolate-coloured plumage and beg with hoarse whistles, 'ksreee'. Is dependent on availability of small rodents and nests commonly in some years and very sparsely in others. Nests in holes in trees, mainly in old Black Woodpecker holes, also in nestboxes, most commonly in old tall coniferous forest with slight mixture of deciduous trees, but also up in mountain birch forest. On rare occasions takes birds up to size of a thrush. In some years emigrates in large numbers and then appears relatively far outside its actual breeding range, even very rarely in N Britain.

Pygmy Owl

Tengmalm's Owl

Pygmy Owl

juv

Tengmalm's Owl

Scops Owl   *Otus scops*   *L 19–20 cm, WS 50–54 cm*

In S Europe is easiest to confuse with Little Owl because of its small size, but has ear-tufts and delicately vermiculated plumage. Ear-tufts are often lowered and it then acquires a rounded head shape. Ground colour varies from warm brown to almost grey. Markedly nocturnal. Very difficult to detect at daytime roost. If flushed, it flies away a shortish distance. Is thrush-sized with relatively long wings. Flight path straight, with series of wingbeats alternating with glides on slightly downward-held or flat wings and somewhat reminiscent of a nightjar. Territorial call a clear whistle like Pygmy Owl's, 'ku(a)', at closer range sounding like 'tuok', rhythmically repeated at intervals of 2–3 seconds, at times in duet with female, whose call is then slightly higher and more nervously squeezed out; can be confused with midwife toad's call (though shorter, like Greenwich time signal). Alarm a high shrill 'pieeee'. Occurs commonly in cultivated country with plantations, gardens and groves, often in parks and avenues of trees in towns and villages. Mostly migratory, leaving for tropical Africa in Sep–Oct and returning in Feb–Apr; overwintering birds can be heard calling from Jan. Feeds mainly on insects. Very rare vagrant to Britain.

Striated Scops Owl   *Otus brucei*   *L 20–21 cm, WS 54–57 cm*

Very like grey phase of Scops Owl but paler and more uniform in colour lacking rusty-brown tones. More distinctly and more neatly streaked, lacks obvious white spots on scapulars and the light blotches between darker vermiculation seen on underside of Scops Owl. Ground colour varies somewhat geographically, warmer buff-grey to almost wholly grey. Advertising call a monotonously repeated or pumping 'baup-baup-baup-baup...'. Behaviour and habits as Scops Owl. Occurs in arid cultivated country, in parks, gardens, oases etc. Has a patchy distribution from Uzbekistan south to Pakistan and in southeast corner of Arabian Peninsula, west to Iran. Local and rare in S Israel and adjoining parts of Sinai Peninsula and in Euphrates area in SE Turkey. Migrant in C Asia but mostly sedentary in Middle East.

Little Owl   *Athene noctua*   *L 21–23 cm, WS 50–56 cm*

Within large parts of Europe the only owl in its size-class, more diurnal than Scops Owl and is seldom difficult to identify. Most often encountered towards close of day as a brown-grey, thickset and broad-headed lump on a telegraph pole, rock, barn roof or fence. If surprised at its daytime roost, usually low in a tree, it usually flies only a short distance away. Flies in deep undulations with folded wings in glide. Moves quite easily on ground, incl. hopping. Also hovers. If agitated, adopts more upright posture and bobs and curtsies like a Robin. Territorial call is a drawn-out, faintly rising 'koooah'. Has a similar but shorter and more piercing call, 'kiU', when alarmed an excited 'kip-kip-kip...' almost like Common Tern. Young beg with a characteristic drawn-out, steady hissing 'hssss'. Occurs in open, usually cultivated areas and semi-desert, often near gardens, avenues of trees and various buildings which provide cavities for nesting. Feeds on rodents, small birds, insects, worms, snails etc.

Scops Owl

Little Owl

Striated Scops Owl

Scops Owl brown phase grey phase

Little Owl

juv

Great Grey Owl

Hawk Owl

Ural Owl

Short-eared
Owl

Snowy Owl

Tengmalm's Owl

Pygmy Owl

young just out of nest

Hawk Owl

Ural Owl

Great Grey Owl

Red-necked Nightjar

Nightjar *Caprimulgus europaeus*

L 26–28 cm, WS 54–60 cm

A nocturnal bird. If flushed from its daytime roost, it often flies only a short distance and alights again along a thick tree branch. Flight is soft and owl-like, with long glides on stiff wings. Silhouette is rather cuckoo-like. Male has white patches on the three longest primaries and the two outer pairs of tail feathers; female is somewhat darker and lacks white markings in flight. Is noticed mostly by male's dry purring night-time song, which consists of a churring 'rrrrrrrrrr...' alternating between two pitches and which can go on for hours with only short pauses. Flight call is a nasal 'kru-ik'. During courtship period has a display flight: male claps his wings and flies with slow wingbeats alternating with glides on raised wings, when the white patches are demonstrated. Feeds on insects captured in flight, when the extremely large 'gape' is used as a net. Prefers open wooded areas, glades, clearings or heathland, most of all dry sparse pine forest. Migrates in Aug–Sep, returning in May.

Red-necked Nightjar *Caprimulgus ruficollis*

L 30–32 cm, WS 58–64 cm

Slightly bigger than Nightjar, differs from latter in paler buff-grey colour and in rusty tint on neck and parts of head. Both sexes have distinct white patches on the three longest primaries and on the two outermost tail feathers, smaller and rather more diffuse on female. Most active at dusk. Catches insects in the air, often glides on V-held wings. Active during the night, from about one hour after sunset. Song is loud and penetrating, a hollow and monotonously repeated 'kuTOK-kuTOK', like a double strike on a dead tree trunk. In parts of N Africa race *desertorum*, with paler and greyer plumage, can be confused with Egyptian Nightjar; latter has pale wing spots only on outer web of primaries and they are barely discernible in flight. Red-necked Nightjar is relatively common in dry bushy terrain with scattered trees or groves, in light woodland or plantations with open sandy or stony patches. Migrates in Oct (Nov) and returns in latter part of Apr.

Nightjar

Red-necked Nightjar

328

Common Nighthawk

Nightjar

♂

♀

♀

Red-necked Nightjar

Nubian Nightjar

Nubian Nightjar *Caprimulgus nubicus* *L 21–22 cm, WS 46–53 cm*

Clearly smaller than Nightjar, with shorter tail and more rounded wings. In flight shows conspicuous white patches on outer primaries and tail feathers (less extensive on female) and rusty colour on inner primaries and outer secondaries. Song a hollow 'kiwa-kiwa' repeated rather irregularly at intervals of 1–4 seconds, recalls a distant barking dog. Breeds in northern E Africa and southern Arabian Peninsula; in W Palearctic occurs only in Arava Valley in S Israel and adjoining parts of Jordan (northernmost point of Rift Valley). Nests in desert or semi-desert, usually with bushy or dense low vegetation.

Egyptian Nightjar *Caprimulgus aegyptius* *L 24–26 cm, WS 58–68 cm*

Size of Nightjar but considerably paler, grey-buff or sandy-coloured with no very obvious markings. In flight shows contrasting darker brown primaries above, and whole underwing looks pale and washed-out. At certain angles a paler band is visible on the outer primaries formed by whitish patches on inner webs, though lacks bright white spots of male Nightjar and both sexes of Red-necked Nightjar. Song a series of fast 'korr' notes, slowing somewhat towards end of each series. Breeds in desert or semi-desert with sparse scrub or other vegetation, usually near water. Occurs in C Asia, Iraq, parts of Iran and in N Africa; long-distance migrant to tropical Africa. Very rare vagrant to Europe.

Common Nighthawk *Chordeiles minor* *L 23–25 cm, WS 59–68 cm*

Highly distinctive with markedly long and pointed wings and shallowly forked tail. On ground, slightly smaller, colder in plumage tone and more evenly patterned than Nightjar, with unbarred dark flight feathers and on male white throat band. Both sexes have conspicuous white oval patches across primaries, visible also on perched bird. Very rare vagrant to W Europe from N America, Sep–Oct. *Ill.p.329*

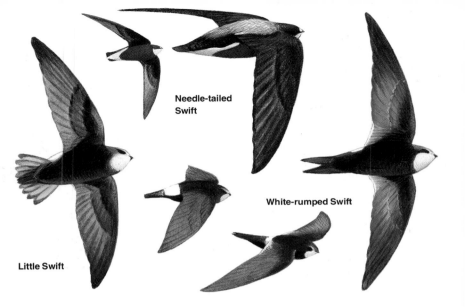

Needle-tailed Swift

White-rumped Swift

Little Swift

Little Swift   *Apus affinis*   L 12 cm, WS 34–35 cm

Has white rump like House Martin. Much smaller than Swift, with slower, bat-like flight, fast series of wingbeats alternating with short glides. Wings relatively short, with fairly pale undersides. Tail short, with outer feathers grey. White throat patch, often large but occasionally smaller and dirtier (imms.?). Calls variable and not unlike Swift's, but usually faster, slightly coarse and less drawn-out and screaming, e.g. repeated 'veep' and a clear almost insect-like 'stip sti sti sti sti sti sti…'. Nests in holes in buildings and in House Martin nests among other sites. Partly resident though majority migrate south of the Sahara, returning Feb–Mar. Extremely rare vagrant to Britain.

White-rumped Swift   *Apus caffer*   L 14 cm, WS 34–36 cm

Like Little Swift and easy to overlook among flocks of latter. However, has Swift-like forked tail, more pointed wings, narrower white rump patch and white trailing edge to secondaries. Breeds in Atlas Mountains and locally in southernmost Spain (provinces of Cadiz, Córdoba and Almería, where numbers are increasing), mainly in old nests of Red-rumped Swallow. In Spain chiefly migratory, leaving in Sep–Oct and returning often late in May.

Needle-tailed Swift   *Hirundapus caudacutus*   L 19–20 cm, WS 50–53 cm

Clearly bigger than Swift, with very powerful and rapid flight, markedly spool-shaped body and short tail which is square-ended, though rear end looks rounded in the field. Tail feathers terminate in thin spines or needle-like projections. Colour pattern unique: body brown with white vent and throat, light band along back and wings green-glossed black with white markings on tertials. Vagrant from Asia, mostly May–Jun.

Little Swift

White-rumped Swift

Alpine Swift *Apus melba* L 20–22 cm, WS 54–60 cm

Larger and with noticeably slower wingbeats than Swift, can even give impression of Hobby; has white underparts with brown breast-band. Calls like Swift's but less high and piercing, with alternating slow rolling trills, often an initially accelerating and then drawn-out 'chit rit rit rit it it itititit chet et et et…'. Common, usually in mountainous districts and also in alpine regions. Nests in rock crevices and taller buildings. Gathers in screaming parties over towns, catches insects over wetlands. Returns mostly in Apr and departs in Sep. Annual vagrant to Britain.

Pallid Swift *Apus pallidus* L 16–17 cm, WS 42–46 cm

Often overlooked within its range owing to its similarity to Swift, which also breeds in the Mediterranean countries. Largely replaces latter in those areas nearest Mediterranean Sea. Against a dark background, identified by its lighter and more brownish colour. Often difficult to identify against the sky, but has paler flight feathers and greater coverts contrasting with dark leading edge of wing (particularly marked in good lighting from below). Larger pale throat patch and faint scaly markings on flanks are often impossible to see in the field. Beware: ad. Swifts in autumn are faded and look brown in comparison with sooty-black juvs. Calls resemble Swift's. Breeds commonly, mainly in buildings. Arrives earlier, in N Africa (where a few may winter) from end Feb, and departs later, Sep–Oct (Nov), than Swift. Very rare vagrant to Britain.

Swift *Apus apus* L 16–17 cm, WS 42–48 cm

Throughout N Europe the only regular species of swift. Differs from swallows and martins in its all-dark plumage and narrower, scythe-shaped wings, which unlike swallows' are never folded in during wingstroke. Totally adapted for a life in the air and therefore occurs over most habitats. Often seen feeding in large numbers together with swallows and martins over lowland lakes and other wetlands. Usually breeds colonially beneath roof tiles and in holes and apertures in buildings and walls, occasionally also in hollow trees and nestboxes. Feeds on aerial insects and spiders, which it catches by 'raking' them in in its large gape. During its often wide-ranging feeding excursions the food is stored in the crop in the form of a thumbnail-sized ball. Is totally dependent on weather suitable for flying insects and may undertake long flights out of adverse weather zones. Young (and to some extent also ads.) are uniquely adapted for this: after several days of food shortage they fall into an energy-sparing torpor, and by this means can survive up to 10–15 days' starvation (when growth ceases). Around breeding sites, often above roofs of houses, groups of Swifts perform 'formation flights' at dizzy speed giving rolling, piercing screams, often in chorus with the ones beneath the roof tiles. Migrates during Jul–Sep, sometimes later in cases of late nesting, and does not return until late Apr–May.

Alpine Swift

Pallid Swift

Swift

Alpine Swift

Pallid Swift

Swift

juv

Kingfisher

♀

Kingfisher   *Alcedo atthis*   L 16–17 cm, WS 24–26 cm

Despite, or perhaps because of, its colours the Kingfisher is not that easy to get sight of. It is usually through its call, a penetrating and very characteristic loud 'zeeeee' or 'sreeee', that it is noticed. Often it is just seen speeding by, when the back flashes pale turquoise-blue. Flight is fast and consists of whirring wingbeats interrupted by brief glides. It sits for long periods on a branch in the shade of an alder or osier branch stretching out over the water, and the green-blue back is then transformed into camouflage. Occurs on clear flowing rivers and streams, preferably with branches hanging out over the water, also at times at ponds and small ditches. During dispersal/migration and in winter can be seen at a variety of wetlands where there are fish, e.g. harbours, canals and reedy lakes. Nests in sand or earth banks, excavating a nest tunnel up to a metre long. Food fish, aquatic insects and other smaller animals. In Britain many move to coasts for winter.

White-breasted Kingfisher   *Halcyon smyrnensis*   L 26–28 cm, WS 40–43 cm

Thrush-sized, with long tail and long wings, in flight with relatively slow wing action. Striking pale blue patch at base of primaries. Juv. duller in colour. Has very startling calls, commonest being a loud, rather explosive chatter recalling Green Woodpecker's flight call; song a clearer trill like a whistle being blown, 'kil-kil-kil-kil-kil'. Uncommon on wooded shores of lakes, rivers and streams, also in plantations and palm groves and not always in direct association with water. Feeds on insects, lizards etc in addition to fish.

Pied Kingfisher   *Ceryle rudis*   L 24–26 cm, WS 45–47 cm

Unmistakable; female has only single breast-band. Often perches in open, frequently hovers and dives from high up. Has piercing high vibrating calls and high whistles. Relatively common locally on ponds, river deltas and coastal lagoons.

Belted Kingfisher   *Ceryle alcyon*   L 28–35 cm, WS 47–52 cm

Almost size of Jackdaw, dark greyish blue-green on back and head. Both sexes have dark breastband, female also with rufous band below it. Tied to water, also fishes on sea coasts. Startling laughing or harsh rattling call on take-off. Rare vagrant from N America.

Kingfisher

White-breasted Kingfisher

Pied Kingfisher

Kingfisher
♂

Pied Kingfisher
♂

Belted Kingfisher
♂

White-breasted Kingfisher

Little Green Bee-eater

Blue-cheeked Bee-eater

Little Green Bee-eater   *Merops orientalis*   L 22–25 cm, WS 29–30 cm

Much smaller than Blue-cheeked Bee-eater and lacks latter's rusty throat, but has black band dividing throat from breast. Call a clear sharp 'tree-tree-tree…', 'tree-it' or similar. A tropical species, in W Palearctic confined to S Israel and Nile basin.

Blue-cheeked Bee-eater   *Merops superciliosus*   L 27–31 cm, WS 46–49 cm

Has entirely emerald-green upperparts and belly with rusty-red underwing-coverts and throat and also longer tail projections than Bee-eater. Call very like latter's but slightly higher-pitched. Occurs in open semi-desert type of country, often beside watercourses like Bee-eater. Very rare vagrant to Europe.

Bee-eater   *Merops apiaster*   L 27–29 cm, WS 44–49 cm

An unmistakable bird. Often perches on telephone wires. Hunts insects in flight, often over hillsides, in very graceful and elastic soaring flight interspersed with series of rapid wingbeats of almost maximum amplitude (270°). Juv. somewhat variable, but almost entirely green above (though crown brownish-red) and lacks or has only suggestion of tail projections; at distance can be mistaken for Blue-cheeked. Migrates in flocks which often pass high overhead, when revealed by their calls. Have a rolling 'schrrruk' or 'schrrü' with a penetrating bell-like ring which carries for several hundred metres. Relatively common in open or semi-open country, usually breeds colonially in excavated holes in sandbanks, steep eroded faces or occasionally directly in the ground. Feeds mostly on larger insects such as bumblebees, hymenopterans, hoverflies etc. Returns to S Europe Apr–May, departs end Aug–Sep. Rare but annual vagrant to Britain, eruptive and occasionally seen in flocks far outside breeding range; has even nested in Britain.

Little Green Bee-eater

Blue-cheeked Bee-eater

Bee-eater

Blue-cheeked Bee-eater

juv

Bee-eater

Roller *Coracias garrulus*   *L 30–32 cm, WS 66–73 cm*

At closer range unmistakable, but at longer distances, especially in flight, can be mistaken for a pigeon or crow. In its straight flight it most resembles a Stock Dove, but is slimmer-bodied, has bigger, more rounded and somewhat Lapwing-like wings and also a longer, markedly thin tail. Juv. has pale and more turquoise plumage. Often seen perched on an elevated lookout, from where it makes Redstart-like sorties towards larger insects on the ground and sometimes in the air. Generally quite active and moves frequently between different perches. Telephone and power lines are favourite lookout posts, and the Roller is a characteristic roadside bird in places where it occurs more commonly. At breeding site male performs an aerial dance, at times followed by female: with jerky wingbeats it spirals up high above the trees and then, with acrobatic half-rolls, plunges towards the ground, all the while giving croaking calls. Often heard at other times is a harsh and sonorous 'rak' or 'rak-ak', like rolling two dried walnuts between the palms of the hands. Nests in tree holes but needs open sunny areas where it can hunt food, so is seen in lightly wooded terrain or around groups and avenues of trees out on open ground. Feeds on beetles, grasshoppers and other insects, worms, small frogs etc. Rare vagrant to Britain, mostly in May–Jul.

Hoopoe *Upupa epops*   *L 26–28 cm, WS 42–46 cm*

Despite its contrasting plumage pattern, the Hoopoe is difficult to detect on the ground. In flight, however, it is a revelation of 'firework-display' proportions, recalling if anything a gigantic butterfly. It is an amazing experience to follow a Hoopoe as it flaps and bounces on rounded wings over a couple of allotments and a few stone walls only to flop down on the ground and disappear as if by magic. When alarmed it freezes, and does not rise until one is almost upon it. Crest is normally lowered and when bird is pecking in the ground it looks narrow and delicate. Territorial call is a far-carrying hollow 'poo-poo-poo', resembling most a brief phrase from a Tengmalm's Owl. Also has a low, hoarse hissing 'ah-ah-ah-ah'. Common in cultivated country with a mixture of open woods, parks, gardens and olive plantations combined with arable and pasture, also in oases. Feeds on insects and larvae extricated with the long bill from recesses and soft earth, incl. beetle larvae living in cattle dung. Very scarce but regular visitor to Britain in spring, with a peak in late Apr–May (has stayed to nest), also regular but even scarcer in autumn in Aug–Oct.

Roller

Hoopoe

Roller

Hoopoe

cryptic
posture

Wryneck *Jynx torquilla*

L 16–17 cm, WS 25–27 cm

Very distinctive owing to its elongated body shape, its rather sluggish actions and its unobtrusive behaviour combined with its nightjar-like coloration. At a cursory glance most likely to be mistaken for a large warbler, first and foremost an imm. Barred Warbler. In flight, which is shallowly undulating, it glides long distances on closed wings. After arriving at the breeding site, it is mostly through its call that it attracts attention; this is a monotonous plaintive or piping 'tü-tü-tü-tü-tü-tü-tü', which can be confused with Lesser Spotted Woodpecker's call. Breeds in open deciduous or mixed wood, in parks and gardens; nest sited in natural tree hole or nestbox. Feeds chiefly on ants at various stages of development, taken both on ground and from trees. Main arrival Europe Apr–May, migrating to tropical Africa Aug–Oct; overwinters rarely in Mediterranean countries. In Britain extremely rare breeder (formerly common); also regular on passage, especially from Scandinavia Aug–Oct.

Grey-headed Woodpecker

Green Woodpecker

Levaillant's Green Woodpecker

Black Woodpecker

♂

♀

Black Woodpecker   *Dryocopus martius*   L 45–47 cm, WS 64–68 cm

Size of a Jackdaw and all-black; male has red crown, on female reduced to a red 'postage stamp' on nape. In flight can perhaps be mistaken for a species of crow. Over longer distances flight path is relatively straight and wing action fluttery and irregular, as if the bird were 'treading water' and trying to stay afloat, compensating for each dip with a few extra powerful wingbeats. The undulating flight otherwise so typical of woodpeckers is seen mainly just before landing. In flight utters series of piercing abrupt screams, 'prree, prree, prree, prree, prree', or a somewhat softer 'krük, krük, krük…'. In spring gives a 'klee, klee, klee, klee, klee', like Green Woodpecker but higher and more metallic. Also utters a drawn-out metallic 'kleeee-e' when perched. As a drumming post usually selects the biggest pine or dead aspen in the neighbourhood, also telegraph poles. Drumburst is of almost unbelievable power and very far-carrying: it varies in length (typically, *c*20 strikes per 2 seconds), but is always even in rhythm and

intensity and drawn-out; female also drums infrequently. Occurs sparsely to fairly commonly in old forest, both pure pine and deciduous, but is most numerous in older mixed forest. Often excavates its nest hole in a large aspen or pine. Feeds on various tree-dwelling insects, especially *Camponotus* ants. Migratory tendencies in some autumns, can then be seen at passage sites and outside its true habitat.

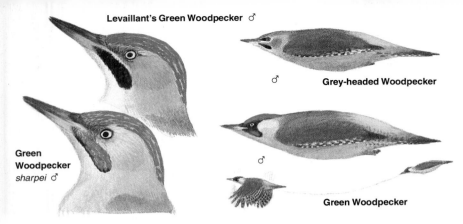

Levaillant's Green Woodpecker ♂

♂

Grey-headed Woodpecker

Green
Woodpecker
sharpei ♂

♂

Green Woodpecker

Grey-headed Woodpecker   *Picus canus*   L 25–26 cm, WS 38–40 cm

Like Green Woodpecker but slightly smaller and slimmer, has less well-marked 'highwayman's mask' and a dark eye, with little or no red on crown and greyer overall impression. Fairly shy and retiring in spring and makes its presence known mostly through its call. Often difficult to catch sight of and is usually not seen until it flies. Flight profile shows less heavy head and bill area, more slender bobbin-shaped body and longer tail than Green Woodpecker. Spring call more melancholy and whistling than Green's, 'pü, pü, pü, pü, pü, pü, pü, pü…pü…pü…pü'; tone is feeble and plaintive and units are hesitant towards end as if exhausted. Flight call a short 'kvik', recalling Great Spotted Woodpecker's. Drums more often than Green; bursts weak and feeble but increase in strength towards end. Breeds in C Europe in thick-stemmed deciduous forest, groves, parks and larger gardens, often beside streams, in Scandinavia in mixed coniferous forest with nearby older stands of aspen. Nest usually in a large aspen. In winter in Scandinavia often comes to fat put out for tits and woodpeckers. Feeds on insects and their larvae. Shows great site fidelity and little tendency to migrate.

Map p. 340

Green Woodpecker   *Picus viridis*   L 31–33 cm, WS 40–42 cm

Bigger than Grey-headed Woodpecker, and at closer range its characteristic head markings are unmistakable. In Iberia race *sharpei* occurs, which lacks black in face and in which male has more red in moustachial stripe. Male in particular has bright yellow rump, conspicuous in flight. In flight usually gives a rather shrill 'kü-kü-kük'. Territorial call a powerful, slightly descending 'klü-klü-klü-klü-klü-klü-klü', more rounded and mellower in ring than Grey-headed's; calls most at dawn. Female has a thinner 'pü-pü-pü-pü-pü-pü-pü', more like Grey-headed's but less squeaky. Drums rarely, and then as Grey-headed weakly and with trembling quality lacking power or thrust. Occurs in deciduous or mixed wood, around avenues of trees or isolated clumps in cultivated country. It forages not only on trees but also on ground, specialises in plundering anthills. Highly sedentary.

Map p. 340

Levaillant's Green Woodpecker   *Picus vaillantii*   L 30–32 cm, WS 41–43 cm

Very like Spanish race of Green Woodpecker, but has black moustachial stripe and above this a pale 'gape-line' bordering the dark grey lores. Female has grey- or black-speckled crown with red only on nape. Calls resemble Green Woodpecker's. Occurs only in Atlas Mountains in N Africa, mostly in woodland or on slopes with scattered trees.

Map p. 340

♀
**Grey-headed
Woodpecker**

♂

♀

juv

Green Woodpecker

♂

1st-cal
♂ autumn

Yellow-bellied Sapsucker

Yellow-bellied Sapsucker
Sphyrapicus varius
L 18−20.5 cm, WS 32−34 cm

Most like Three-toed Woodpecker, with striped head and barred mantle/back. Male has dark throat (deep red) and upper breast and red crown, female red throat and dark breast. In 1st winter dark parts of head and body are dirty brown-speckled, not black. Extremely rare vagrant from N America.

Middle Spotted Woodpecker
Dendrocopos medius   L 20−22 cm, WS 33−34 cm

Often mistaken for Great Spotted Woodpecker, but separated by its smaller size, all-red crown, incomplete cheek-bar and underpart markings. More restless than its larger relative; often gleans caterpillars from far out on branches in treetops and often perches diagonally like a passerine. Call quite like Great Spotted's in tone but softer and lower in pitch, 'güg', regularly repeated in a series; often gives rattling 'gig gegegeg'. In spring drums very seldom, but instead has a mewing call more reminiscent of *Picus* woodpeckers: it is repeated rather irregularly with marked pauses, 'kwäh, kwäh, kwäh, kwäh…kwäh, kwäh…kwäh'. Is closely associated with deciduous woodland containing oaks. Feeds on insects, only to minor extent extracted from trees (weaker bill). Has declined in much of Europe.

Syrian Woodpecker *Dendrocopos syriacus*   L 22−23 cm, WS 34−38 cm

Differs from Great Spotted Woodpecker mainly in lack of black joining nape with moustachial stripe, but also has less white on tail feathers and duller red vent. In the field sides of head and neck look more white and plainer-patterned, and on male red nape patch is slightly bigger. Calls resemble Great Spotted's but softer and more rounded, 'chük', also given in drawn-out chattering series. Drumburst begins like Great Spotted's but is longer and dies away at end. Common in woodland, parks, gardens and around clumps of trees. Great Spotted is tied more to uplands in S Europe, with Syrian in low-lying cultivated country.

Middle Spotted Woodpecker

Syrian Woodpecker

**Middle Spotted
Woodpecker**

**Great Spotted
Woodpecker**
pinetorum ♂

♂

♀

Syrian Woodpecker

White-backed Woodpecker
lilfordi ♂

numidus ♂ **Great Spotted Woodpecker**

Great Spotted Woodpecker *Dendrocopos major* *L 22–23 cm, WS 34–39 cm*

The commonest of the 'pied' woodpeckers. Female lacks red on nape. Juv. has red crown and paler pink vent. Belly often becomes slightly drab buff through contact with tree trunks. Races in S and C Europe (mainly *pinetorum*) generally have pale areas of plumage more grey-buff than white; inN Africa *numidus* has more red on belly and breast. Commonest call is a metallic 'kük' or 'kik' ('chik'); when irritated it is repeated as a rapid chatter and occasionally accelerates and changes into a dry excited rattle. Its drumming is by far the fastest of all the woodpeckers and consists of c10−15 strikes per second; occasional individuals may give a longer drumburst. Drums on dead branches and trunks, also telegraph poles, metal chimneys etc. Common in woodland, gardens and parks. Feeds on insects and their larvae, eggs and young of birds, and on seeds of trees, especially conifers. Shortage of spruce and pine cones can cause northern populations to erupt in some years.

White-backed Woodpecker
Dendrocopos leucotos *L 24−26 cm, WS 38−40 cm*

The largest of the 'pied' woodpeckers. Appears bigger and heavier than Great Spotted. Amount of white barring above varies. The white-backed impression also varies depending on extent to which underlying white back feathers are ruffled up. Juvs. have red crown. In Balkans and Turkey race *lilfordi*, which has dark-barred lower back, narrower white barring on upper back and more heavily streaked flanks. Call, 'kuk', is deeper and softer in tone and not so loud as Great Spotted's, is occasionally repeated in a chattering series; when excited, gives a rolling, grating 'prrrrrrrr'. Drumburst is markedly longer than Great Spotted's, usually c2 seconds long, rather sluggish at start but accelerating towards end, most like that of Three-toed Woodpecker. Is tied to older forests with decayed and fallen deciduous trees, often beside banks of lakes or streams. Lack of rotten trees in modern commercial forests has caused a serious decline in this species' numbers in 1900s, the healthiest Scandinavian population remaining in W Norway. In e.g. Balkans found also in pure spruce forest. Highly sedentary.

Great Spotted Woodpecker

White-backed Woodpecker

**Great
Spotted
Woodpecker**

♀

♂

juv
**Great
Spotted
Woodpecker**

♂

♀

White-backed Woodpecker

Three-toed
Woodpecker

Lesser
Spotted Woodpecker

♂

Lesser Spotted Woodpecker   *Dendrocopos minor*   *L 14–15 cm, WS 25–27 cm*

Small size immediately distinguishes it from all other woodpeckers. Lack of red on vent
gives female especially a strikingly black-and-white appearance. Often hops far out on
small branches, but prefers to retain the typical woodpecker posture with body in line
with branch. Makes its presence known with a 'kik' call, like Great Spotted Woodpecker's but more feeble, and a rather Wryneck-like 'kee-kee-kee-kee-kee-kee-kee-kee'.
Drumburst is longer, more constant and weaker compared with Great Spotted's, just
over a second long and given rapidly twice with a brief lull in the middle. Both sexes
drum. Breeds in deciduous or mixed woodland, often near lake and stream banks with
swampy deciduous corridors of e.g. alder, in upland birch forest as well as parks and
large gardens. Excavates nest hole in soft decayed trunks or thicker branches. Is often
unobtrusive and easy to overlook. Often joins roving tit flocks in autumn. In winter visits
reedbeds. Resident; in N Europe may in some years erupt on a relatively large scale.

Three-toed Woodpecker   *Picoides tridactylus*   *L 21–22 cm, WS 32–35 cm*

An unmistakable woodpecker, male with yellow crown and both sexes with bold stripe
markings. In C Europe race *alpinus*, obviously darker with dark-vermiculated mantle/
back and dirtier flanks. Has 'kik' call like Great Spotted Woodpecker, but it is more
liquid and softer in tone, more like 'kjück', though it varies and fledged young have a
rolling vowel-less call reminiscent of agitated Fieldfare. Both sexes drum frequently in
late winter to spring. Drumburst begins tentatively, increases in strength and continues
uniformly and with good 'articulation', length c1.3 seconds; most resembles Black
Woodpecker's but is weaker and not so uniform and straight. Fairly common in spruce
or mixed forest with spruce but also in mountain birch forest. Often found in rather
swampy spruce forest beside bogs or in damp strips in the forest. Feeds mostly on lower
part of dead and dying spruces. Punctures bark to abstract sap, leaving a ring or zigzag
pattern of small pecks on spruce trunks. Often quiet and unobtrusive but fairly fearless.
Resident, but northern populations show migratory tendencies in certain autumns.

Lesser Spotted Woodpecker

Three-toed Woodpecker

Lesser Spotted
Woodpecker

♀

♂

Three-toed
Woodpecker

♂

♀

Skylark   *Alauda arvensis*   L 18–19 cm

One of our commonest birds. Robust and pot-bellied, often raises crown feathers into a
small crest, though never so long and pointed as on Crested Lark. Bill relatively short
and fairly stout. Plumage tones vary, usually looks warm buff-brown in N Europe,
though some individuals are paler grey-buff while others, mainly freshly moulted in
autumn, have a rich brownish-red tone above. In S Europe and to even greater degree
in Middle East and S Russia overall impression is greyer. Juv. peculiarly dark-spotted
and with scaly ochre markings. Juv. feathers of larks are often of 'poor' quality, are often
remarkably faded towards Jul (ill. p.18). Both ad. and juv. have a complete moult (i.e.
incl. tail and flight feathers) in late summer. In flight shows whitish band along trailing
edge of wing, a distinction from Crested and Woodlark. Noisy in flight, with pleasing
but variable 'chrriup', 'trruwee' or similar. Song unmistakable, a continuous stream of
trilling and babbling series, often with interwoven mimicry, given mostly in fluttering
stationary flight high up in air. Sings from first light and during all daylight hours. Feeds
on insects and other invertebrates, plant matter and seeds. Flocks in autumn and
winter, often on stubble and ploughed land. In Britain mainly resident; also passage and
winter visitor Sep/Oct–Mar/Apr, mostly from N Europe.

Oriental Skylark   *Alauda gulgula*   L 16 cm

C Asiatic species, rare but regular in winter in S Israel and probably other parts of
Middle East. Slightly smaller than Skylark, longer-legged and with proportionately rather
longer and more pointed bill, shorter tail and primary projection, has features of
Woodlark in flight but not so short-tailed. Has more rusty-toned fringes to wing feathers
and ear-coverts compared with Skylarks in the region in question, and dull rusty-buff
outer tail feathers and trailing edge to wing. Behaviour unlike Skylark's, feeds in cover of
taller plants and low bushes in open cultivated and steppe country and like Woodlark
sits tight, rising only at a few metres. Call a dry, slightly buzzing 'bazz bazz' or 'bazz
trrr'.

Woodlark   *Lullula arborea*   L 15 cm

Like Skylark, but fairly distinctive in behaviour and overall impression. Has short tail,
more contrastingly marked head with broad whitish supercilia almost meeting on nape
and rusty-brown unstreaked ear-coverts. Alula and primary coverts broadly pale-tipped
above, producing a diagnostic small mark on leading edge of wing. In flight the
peculiarly short tail is noticeable, as are the broad wings and deep undulating flight in
which rapid fluttering series of beats alternate with 'body glides' on entirely closed
wings. Its flight call is a yodelling or fluting 'deedlui' or 'tütlee-ueet' lacking Skylark's 'r'
sound. The soft, melancholy song consists of series of repeated yodelling phrases, one
moment accelerating and the next dropping in pitch or abruptly ceasing. Sings at night and
in morning. Occurs in woodland glades, undulating country with scattered trees, young
plantations, also on alpine meadows and sparsely timbered heathland. Feeds mostly on
insects and seeds. It is now fairly rare and local in S Britain.

Skylark

Woodlark

autumn

Skylark

spring

Skylark

Oriental Skylark

Oriental Skylark

Woodlark

Crested Lark

Woodlark

Crested Lark   *Galerida cristata*   L 16–18 cm

Has long pointed crest, powerful bill, and compared with Skylark is greyer and less boldly marked on mantle/back. Ground colour varies and is often correlated with the local soil colour: some N African birds are e.g. sandy-coloured and plainer, while others are warmer and more rusty-toned. Bill length also varies. Has a short tail with rusty-red or cinnamon-coloured sides and short wings which produce soft and flapping beats in flight. On rising usually gives a 'du-ee', and in various situations a varied but very characteristic soft fluting 'tuee-tuu-teeooo' not unlike Woodlark's. Song slower and usually with clearer notes than Skylark's and unlike latter does not repeat phrases in long series; different variants of call and imitations of other bird species are included in repertoire. Sings from exposed perch or in song flight high in air. Very common and a characteristic bird in much of the low-lying cultivated country around Mediterranean; in N Europe something of a 'backyard bird', breeding along road embankments, railway tracks, around industrial sites and warehouses and silos. Often forages on dry sandy ground. Food as Skylark's. Very rare vagrant to Britain.

Thekla Lark   *Galerida theklae*   L 16 cm

Very difficult to separate from Crested Lark, especially in parts of N Africa. In Europe distinguished by shorter crest, shorter and stubbier bill and also more clearly defined spots on breast. Thekla has grey to sandy-coloured axillaries (rusty-tinted on Crested), but this is difficult to see in the field. Rump is distinctly cinnamon-coloured and contrasts with back (something not shown by Crested). In N Africa some types have longer bill, thinner breast streaking and more sandy-coloured upperparts. Calls very like Crested Lark's. Song generally more intense with faster trills and more finch-like. Occurs in more stony and more bushy areas, often higher up on mountainsides and in more undisturbed, less cultivated terrain. Readily perches on bushes, unlike Crested Lark. Resident.

Dupont's Lark   *Chersophilus duponti*   L 18 cm

Size of Skylark, with thickset body and short tail but with long and slightly curved bill. Colour pattern like Skylark's, in fresh plumage with pale fringes giving a peculiar scaly impression as on juv. larks or Quail. In C Algeria and in Libya race *margaritae*, which is paler and predominantly rusty-red compared with nominate *duponti* from Spain. Has very unobtrusive habits and is reluctant to fly (wings markedly rounded in flight). Runs quickly among cover of tussocks and plants; occasionally stands erect, when neck appears markedly long. Song a rather Linnet-like twitter with interspersed 2−4-syllable fluting notes. Call a distinctive, slightly tinny 'choo-chee'. Occurs on scrub and grass steppe, in winter also on cultivated land in company of other larks. Relatively common locally in C Spain. Feeds on insects and seeds, often pecks in soft earth and sand as well as in animal droppings.

Crested Lark

Thekla Lark

Dupont's Lark

N Africa

N Africa

Crested Lark

Thekla Lark

Spain

Spain

margaritae

duponti

Dupont's Lark

Lesser Short-toed Lark *heinei* spring

Short-toed Lark *longipennis* spring

Short-toed Lark   *Calandrella brachydactyla*   L 14 cm

Size of Linnet and clearly smaller than Skylark. Rather variable in plumage, but always gives a pale impression with relatively pointed and finch-like bill. Face has broad pale supercilium and a dark eye-stripe behind eye. Most have a rusty- or cinnamon-coloured crown. Breast pale and with little streaking, markings usually restricted to breast-sides; in spring has a usually distinct dark neck patch, a feature used as a signal and which may be regulated according to mood. Lesser coverts (carpal) often unmarked. Tertials very long and cover almost entire length of primaries. C Asiatic race *longipennis* is generally greyer, with narrower streaks on mantle/back and smaller bill than nominate *brachydactyla* in S Europe. In N Africa *rubiginosa*, paler, more sandy-coloured and always with rusty crown. In bouncing 'yo-yo' song flight gives a characteristic short series of well-spaced notes, 'püt, chül ül ül ül ül', occasionally with small trills and mimicry inserted. Flight calls finch-like, often given twice, 'chilp chelp', 'chüp chülüp', 'peeyup' or 'chip' like Tawny Pipit's; occasionally with 'r' sound (mainly on take-off) and then more like Skylark, e.g. 'chrrüt'. Common on dry steppe, semi-desert and poor arable land. Annual vagrant to Britain, with most in May and Sep—Oct.

Lesser Short-toed Lark   *Calandrella rufescens*   L 13—14 cm

Varies geographically and sometimes difficult to separate from Short-toed Lark. Spanish race *apetzii* is darker, more grey-brown and more heavily marked than Short-toed, with obvious streaking on breast and body-sides, is like a small Skylark. Lacks conspicuous supercilium and eye-stripe and has more rounded head shape. Bill on average shorter and more uniformly thick, not so conical as Short-toed's. Has marked primary projection (c12 mm). Nominate *rufescens* from Canary Islands has more brownish-red plumage. In N Africa race *minor*, which is paler and more warm sandy-coloured than Spanish race and with narrower streaking. C Asiatic birds, chiefly race *heinei*, have in general finer streaks on breast and upperparts but have greyer ground tone. In C Turkey *aharonii* (depicted), very grey with narrow distinct breast markings. Flight call character-istic, wader-like buzzing 'tchrrr(ü)' or double 'trr chrrr', sometimes almost vowel-less, or harder 'chirr', 'drrrit' or 'dyurrrup', though not always different from Short-toed's. Song continuous and varied and contains much mimicry. Occurs in usually flat steppe-like terrain, typically on salt steppe and dried-out lakeshores. Mostly resident in S Spain, migratory in C Asia. Extremely rare vagrant to Britain.

Short-toed Lark

Lesser Short-toed Lark

♀

Short-toed Lark

♂

fresh (autumn)

aharonii fresh

apetzii

Lesser Short-toed Lark

Skylark

Calandra Lark

Bimaculated Lark

Bimaculated Lark   *Melanocorypha bimaculata*   *L 17 cm*

Smaller and shorter-tailed than Calandra Lark and with more distinct facial markings. In spring and summer normally paler and more warm buff-toned than Calandra. In autumn face usually more contrasting, with purer white supercilium, more rusty-toned cheeks, darker culmen, and thinner dark streaks on mantle/back. Most easily distinguished from Calandra in flight: the markedly more pointed wings are paler, more uniform in colour and lack white trailing edge, and tail has white spots at tip like Rock Sparrow. Appears slightly Quail-like on rising. Flight calls often more like Skylark's, 'krrüit', 'churrup', also a 'pchi-pcherp' or 'tyip'. Song like Calandra's. Occurs on steppe and in semi-desert, often on stony mountain slopes and plains, partly replaces Calandra Lark above 1500 m. Chiefly migratory. Very rare vagrant to W Europe in late autumn.

Calandra Lark   *Melanocorypha calandra*   *L 18–19 cm*

A big, heavily built lark with large head, stout Greenfinch-like bill and with a black patch on neck-side. Neck patch is smaller on female and barely visible on some individuals in autumn. Characteristic in flight, with dark wings (all-black below) with broad white trailing edge. Sings in circling song flight, often very high up; the long black wings and the closed tail combined with a stiff wing action give impression of a much larger bird. Song consists of a stream of short phrases or individual 'words', often imitations of other species, and characteristic fast jingling or vibrating calls, e.g. 'peechur ir ir ir' or 'klitra a'a'a'a', which recall Corn Bunting's song and are probably a mixture of mimicry and the lark's own voice. Flight calls often harsh and coarse, e.g. 'kcheerreek', sometimes jingling. Common on steppe and in open cultivated country, mainly on arable land. Resident in Europe, in winter locally in large flocks. Food seeds, shoots and insects. Very rare vagrant to Britain.

Bimaculated Lark

Calandra Lark

Shore Lark

autumn

Bimaculated Lark

spring

♂ spring
displaying

Calandra Lark

autumn

Shore Lark *penicillata* ♂

Shore Lark *Eremophila alpestris* L 15–17 cm

Characteristic with its black and sulphur-yellow markings. In winter plumage less contrasting and lacks black 'horns'. Mantle/back strikingly grey or sandy-coloured and less streaked than on Skylark; male is the least streaked and from distance looks very uniform in colour. In Balkans race *balkanica* and in Asia Minor race *penicillata*, both of which belong to a more southerly group of races in which the black on cheeks is joined with the black breast-band. Compared with the *penicillata* depicted on p. 359, those from Balkans are warmer pink on nape and have pale yellow facial markings. In Atlas Mountains in Morocco race *atlas*, which resembles the northern group and is attributed to it. At breeding site is unobtrusive, slips behind rocks and small mounds; is often therefore noticed only by its alarm call, a varied 'peeeh', sometimes 'peeu' very like Snow Bunting and sometimes combined with a Yellowhammer-like 'tyu', also a sharp 'tsiepp' (*penicillata*). Flight call a di- or trisyllabic short, high and penetrating 'tsee-tuee-tseea' or 'tsee-tseea'. Song is like Snow Bunting's in tone, a slightly uneven verse which is sometimes repeated to become a more prolonged lark-type twitter. Breeds sparsely and locally on treeless upland or alpine moor, preferring dry stony plateaux or gravelly ridges. In winter on open heath-type terrain, in N Europe especially on shore meadows and sandy shores. Feeds mostly on insects, seeds and plant matter. Has decreased in parts of Scandinavia in recent decades (and observations of migrants along S Baltic coast now rare), this being reflected in steep decline in numbers wintering in Britain (mainly Oct–Apr, east coast). Has bred in Scotland. Map p. 356

White-winged Lark

Temminck's Horned Lark

♂

♀
autumn

♀

Temminck's Horned Lark

Black Lark

♂ spring

Temminck's Horned Lark *Eremophila bilopha* L 13–14 cm

Smaller than Shore Lark, entirely unstreaked sandy-coloured above and with white and black head-and-breast pattern. Calls as Shore Lark's. Occurs locally and relatively rarely in low-lying desert and semi-desert.

White-winged Lark *Melanocorypha leucoptera* L 19 cm

Size of Calandra Lark, with conspicuous wing pattern with broad white rear border. Most males have unstreaked rust-red crown, ear-coverts and lesser coverts; female more subdued in coloration and more streaked. Breeds on steppe in Kazakhstan. Vagrant to Europe.

Black Lark *Melanocorypha yeltoniensis* L male 21 cm, female 19 cm

Summer-plumaged male black with grey bill. In fresh winter plumage has long pale buff fringes concealing much of the black. Female smaller than male and similar to Calandra Lark, but differs in having dark legs and lacking white trailing edge to wing. Breeds on steppe in Kazakhstan, often beside wetlands. Recorded only a few times in Europe.

Desert Lark   *Ammomanes deserti*   *L 16–17 cm*

Size of Skylark, rather dumpy but long-tailed and with relatively heavy bill which is orange-yellow at base. Colour varies geographically in accordance with local rock types, normally dull grey-buff above and slightly streaked on breast. Tail rusty, with broad, diffuse dark terminal band. Call a quiet 'chu' or 'chee-lu', a little like Crested Lark in tone. Sings from perch or in flight; song more varied than that of Bar-tailed Desert Lark, melodic, slightly melancholy and chattering, often in phrases of 2 or 3 syllables, 'chur-rur-rir', 'churruweea' or similar. Relatively common in mainly undulating semi-desert or desert with stony areas, on mountain slopes, eroded surfaces etc.; not shy, often patrols roadside-stops and oases. Breeds in large parts of N Africa and Middle East, nearest sites in SE Turkey.

Bar-tailed Desert Lark   *Ammomanes cincturus*   *L 15 cm*

Somewhat smaller than Desert Lark, generally paler and warmer sandy-buff above, whiter on belly and without streaking on breast. Appears larger-headed, with rounded crown and shorter bill. Very active and makes jerky runs, looks long-legged. Has rusty tint to tertials and other flight feathers, in flight shows sharply demarcated black terminal band to tail and darker primary tips. Song simple, characteristic, 'deer-dool-DÜÜ', with rather desolate ring, final syllable drawn-out and more far-carrying. Flight call a short purring 'prreet' and 'see-wü'. Scarce to common in large parts of Sahara and in Middle East. Prefers open plains or slightly undulating desert or semi-desert; thrives on sandy or gravelly ground.

Dunn's Lark   *Eremalauda dunni*   *L 14.5 cm*

Like Bar-tailed Desert Lark, but has heavier and usually more swollen bill and bolder facial markings, especially moustachial stripe and the dark line beneath eye. Has streaked crown, mantle and breast-sides, crown and mantle/back normally with rusty-toned ground colour in contrast to greyer nape, though rusty tone fades in worn plumage. Tail has black outer feathers, unlike on the two desert larks, and tertials reach almost to tips of primaries. Occurs in flat or slightly undulating desert. Has a patchy distribution in southern part of the Sahara and S Arabian Peninsula. Occurs irregularly north to Israel and Jordan.

Thick-billed Lark   *Rhamphocoris clotbey*   *L 17 cm*

Unmistakable. Female has more restricted dark markings on head and breast and juv. is uniform sandy-coloured. In flight, long-winged with large head and black flight feathers with broad white trailing edge. Calls in flight rather variable, often short 'dripping' notes e.g. 'prit', 'blit-blit' or 'ku-ip'. Song clear, slightly jingling sequences of notes, chattering. Sings from perch or in song flight. Occurs mainly in stony deserts in N Africa from Morocco to Tunisia south of Middle Atlas and also in Saudi Arabia and Jordan. Distribution in Middle East poorly known.

Hoopoe Lark   *Alaemon alaudipes*   *L 18–20 cm*

A large, elongated and pale lark with long curved bill. Back colour varies, usually warm sandy-buff, sometimes more grey. Black spots on breast vary individually. In flight shows contrasting white wingbar and trailing edge. Moves very quickly, runs away rather than flying. Song mournful and desolate in the morning, a series c10–15 seconds long of flute-like 'düü' notes, first accelerating and then dropping and slowing, drawn out and ringing in middle. Has distinctive song flight in which male flips over in a half-roll at top of flight path and then drops towards ground again. Occurs in flat or slightly undulating desert or semi-desert with some soft sand or earth, relatively common throughout N Africa and Middle East.

Dunn's Lark

Desert Lark

Bar-tailed Desert
Lark

Dunn's Lark

♂ fresh

Thick-billed
Lark

Hoopoe Lark

Crag Martin   *Ptyonoprogne rupestris*   *L 14.5 cm*

Bigger than Sand Martin, with more vigorous flight, often makes incredibly fast dives.
Cold brown-grey above but with darker flight feathers. Pale sandy-coloured below,
with contrasting dark underwing-coverts, dirty throat and brown-tinted ventral area.
Has white spots near tail-tip, visible only when tail spread. Quiet, especially during
non-breeding season. Calls recall a distant finch or Short-toed Lark, e.g. 'chip', 'chup'
or 'chirr'. Nests on cliff faces or buildings in mountain districts and deep ravines. Nest is
a half-cup of mud. Breeds from sea level up to c2500 m but also feeds at even higher
altitudes. In winter found at lower levels, often patrols back and forth along sheltered
mountainsides and hills, often next to rivers and large lakes.

Rock Martin   *Ptyonoprogne fuligula*   *L 12.5 cm*

Smaller and paler than Crag Martin, but very like latter in appearance and actions. Has
pale unstreaked throat and less contrasting dark underwing-coverts. A mainly African
species which replaces Crag Martin in the Sahara and the tropics. Call a clear 'seep' or
'seep-seep' and a dryer 'ptrrr'. Occurs in ravines and fault faces in desert regions, in
Egypt often around ancient monuments. Resident.

Brown-throated Sand Martin   *Riparia paludicola*   *L 12 cm*

Very small, with weak and fluttering flight. Looks dingy and insignificant, with no
prominent features. Juv. (appears from Jan) has pale scaly patterning above like juv.
Sand Martin. Call a low rasp like Sand Martin's, but softer, less dry: 'chrrr', also a harsh
'steeh'. Usually found at rivers and other watercourses. Nests in tunnels excavated in
sandbanks. Resident.

Sand Martin   *Riparia riparia*   *L 12 cm*

The only brown-backed martin in northern Europe. Has dull brown upperparts and
clear breast-band, and also dark underwing-coverts. Juv. has pale buff fringes above,
looks scaly. Call characteristic, a dry vowel-less rasp. Breeds colonially in excavated
burrows in sand-pits or steep banks, which makes its occurrence rather local. Often
forages by rivers, ponds and lowland lakes, and like other swallow species takes aerial
insects and spiders. Often double-brooded, but more northerly populations single-
brooded. From mid Jun onwards (first-brood juvs.) large concentrations of Sand Martins
can be seen, especially at roost sites in reedbeds. Migrates to tropical Africa in
Aug−Oct, returning in Mar−May.

Crag Martin

Rock Martin

Brown-throated Sand Martin

Sand Martin

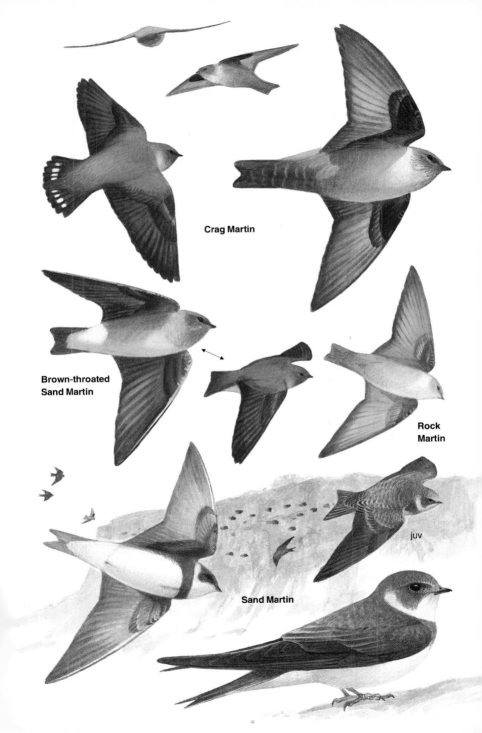

Crag Martin

Brown-throated Sand Martin

Rock Martin

juv

Sand Martin

Red-rumped Swallow   *Hirundo daurica*   L 16–18 cm

Appears leisurely in flight, glides frequently and for long periods. Tail streamers are shorter but somewhat thicker than Swallow's and are often closed up. Juv. has shorter streamers than ad. Often sails lazily back and forth along a slope catching insects in the air. Quiet, but in flight gives short, rather sharp, usually nasal and rasping calls, e.g. 'uweeht', 'kchwaiht' or 'tchrreet', occasionally House Sparrow-like chirps. Song is like an uninspired Swallow's song but with a more nasal and rasping tone. Locally common in areas with mountains and cliffs which provide protective cavities and caves for nesting. Also nests in ruins, under bridges and in other buildings. Builds a mud nest like House Martin's but with a tunnel-like entrance at the top. Migrant, arriving in Mar–Apr, some as early as Feb. Vagrant to Britain, mostly in Apr–May and Sep–Nov, more frequent in recent years; has oversummered once (Dorset).

Swallow   *Hirundo rustica*   L 19–22 cm

With its long tail streamers can be confused only with Red-rumped Swallow. Upperparts all-dark without paler rump, but with pale 'windows' on tail feathers. Underparts vary, in N Europe (incl. Britain) white or creamy-coloured, in Asia Minor more rusty-tinted and in Egypt a strong brownish-red. Juv. in autumn has tail streamers only c1 cm long and a paler, more rusty-buff tone to forehead and throat, as well as grey-brown breast-band. Call a jingling and cheerful 'vit' or 'vit vit'. Song is often striking, a prolonged crystal-clear twitter with interwoven mimicry and now and then rounded off with a typical creaking as from an unoiled hinge. Common in cultivated country with villages and farms. During migration periods often gathers in large flocks together with other swallows and martins over marshes and reedbeds where there is a good supply of airborne insects; at these times roosts in reeds. Builds its nest, a half-cup of mud, on rafters and in recesses inside barns, outhouses, under bridges and on other buildings. Migrates to Africa in Aug–Oct, returning end Mar–May; a few winter in southernmost Spain and Portugal and they arrive around Mediterranean as early as end Feb. Race *savignii* resident along Nile. In Britain occasional stragglers can be seen up to Dec.

House Martin   *Delichon urbica*   L 12.5 cm

Identified at all times by its white rump. Juv. in autumn has a dark wash on breast-sides and at certain angles can give impression of having a breast-band. Call a clear but scratchy 'prrit'. Song, usually delivered from a telephone wire, is a babbling twitter on the same theme. Nests colonially on buildings and cliff faces. Occurs in a wide variety of open or semi-open terrain, often beside water but not necessarily near habitations. Food as Swallow's but often hunts at higher level. Migrates to tropical Africa in Aug–Oct, returning Apr–May; in Britain stragglers seen up to Dec (and very occasionally even in Jan–Feb).

Red-rumped Swallow

Swallow

House Martin

Red-rumped Swallow

Swallow

juv

Swallow

juv

House Martin

Rock Pipit *Anthus petrosus* *L 17 cm*

A large dark pipit with long bill and black or dark brownish-violet legs. Varies in appearance. In Britain and W Europe, mainly race *petrosus*, generally darker and with heavier breast streaking than Baltic birds, race *littoralis*, which can be confused with Water Pipit. Some *littoralis* are more neutral grey on crown, nape and mantle and have breast with reduced markings and pink tint. In winter plumage very dull grey-brown with olive-green tone above and large obscure breast spots; often lack prominent supercilium but have distinct pale eye-ring. Outer tail feathers grey. Call a slightly drawn-out 'peeest', most like Tree Pipit's but less buzzing, straighter and more vocal. Song very like Meadow Pipit's, performed in descending song flight on stiff wings. Relatively common but often unobtrusive, breeds only on stony or rocky shores. Takes insects, crustaceans and snails among seaweed and rocks. In Britain resident, with some autumn/winter dispersal; *littoralis* is a winter visitor.

Water Pipit *Anthus spinoletta* *L 17 cm*

In summer plumage has pink underparts with streaking reduced to breast-sides and flanks; neutral grey crown and brown-grey mantle. In winter plumage breast more streaked, but has paler brown-grey upperparts than Rock Pipit, with more distinct supercilium and whiter wingbar. Outer tail feathers white. Relatively common above tree line on alpine meadows. In winter at lakeshores and wetlands down to sea level. C Asiatic race *coutelli* is found in winter in Middle East; winter plumage browner and with pale areas dingier than on nominate race. Call like Rock Pipit's, a sharp slightly drawn-out 'peeht', often harsh in tone, also as 'hueez' or 'hueez tyüt'; song like Rock's. Nominate race is a winter visitor to S Britain, Oct−Apr.

Buff-bellied Pipit *Anthus rubescens* *L 17 cm*

A N American and E Asiatic species, one record in Europe. In winter plumage more yellow-buff below and with narrower and more distinct breast and flank streaking than winter-plumaged Water Pipit. Siberian race *japonicus* regular in winter in S Israel and probably other parts of Middle East: has darker and heavier streaking than Water Pipit, somewhat recalls Meadow Pipit. Call remarkably like Meadow Pipit's.

Rock Pipit

Water Pipit

Tree Pipit

Meadow Pipit

Red-throated Pipit

Water Pipit
spinoletta
summer

Rock Pipit
littoralis
summer

Rock Pipit
summer

Rock Pipit
winter

Buff-bellied Pipit
rubescens

winter

Water Pipit
winter

Tree Pipit   *Anthus trivialis*   L 15 cm

Very like Meadow Pipit and most easily separated by voice. Is more a bird of wooded areas, however, and when disturbed is more likely to fly up to a branch. On the ground it often moves a little stealthily with measured steps and slightly crouched posture, often pumps tail slowly. More robust in build than Meadow Pipit, has plainer mantle, and coarse breast streaking changes into thin streaks on flanks (on Meadow more equal in strength). On head, eye-ring is broken in front of eye by short loral stripe and yellow submoustachial stripe is more distinct compared with Meadow's. Flight call characteristic: a harsh or discordant buzzing 'bizzt' or 'büzzt', at times a thinner 'zeeit' is heard. In song flight rises fairly vertically with rapid wingbeats and then slowly parachutes down to its starting point or a perch nearby, usually the top of a tree. Song consists of series of trills which first accelerate but then slow down as the bird drops. It is more powerful and varied than Meadow Pipit's: introduction is rather Chaffinch-like and the end usually consists of a few whistles which become more and more drawn-out, 'seea, seea, seeea, seeea, seeeeh'. Alarm a rhythmically repeated 'tzüt'. Common in widely differing types of forest which provide open areas for foraging, also breeds around upper tree line in mountains. Migrants also occur on meadows and freshwater margins, but avoids being too exposed on ground. Arrives Apr–May, departs Aug–Sep; passage through Britain to Oct.   *Map p. 366*

Meadow Pipit   *Anthus pratensis*   L 14.5 cm

Slightly smaller than Tree Pipit, with more distinctly streaked mantle and rump and with breast and flank streaks more uniform in width. Head shows narrower and less prominent submoustachial stripe, less well-marked lores and often pale around eye, has 'quizzical' expression. Characteristic call on rising a sharp 'pseet, pseet…pseet'; in flight also a thin chirping 'tyüt' or 'tyit', a clear ringing Dunnock-like 'teeseetsee' and a coarse 'chüt üt üt üt…'. Alarm a persistent 'stit-it'. Song simpler and more mechanical than Tree Pipit's, usually divided into 3–4 sections: rapid accelerating 'tseep' notes, more spaced and more drawn-out 'tsüht' notes, and a rapid trill (sometimes almost vowel-less), usually in that order; performed in a first rising then slowly descending song flight, but also from top of a bush or post. Often raises tail slightly. Breeds sparsely to commonly in open meadowland, shore meadows, bogs and heaths, often found on water meadows and marsh edges; characteristic bird of upland moor. In winter also in fields, marshes and on coasts. In Britain partial migrant, also common passage and winter visitor from N Europe Aug–May.   *Map p. 366*

Red-throated Pipit   *Anthus cervinus*   L 15 cm

Differs from Meadow Pipit in rusty-red throat, but is also more contrastingly marked on mantle and flanks and has heavily streaked rump and uppertail-coverts. Amount of red on throat and breast varies, in 1st-winter plumage merely dirty-white to warm buff on throat. 1st-winters differ from Meadow in more contrasting impression, have more distinct whitish wingbar and dark and light streaks on mantle; streaks on breast and flanks are also broader and more distinct. Flight call characteristic: a long drawn-out and very high 'speeeeeh' which normally drops slightly in pitch, at times, especially from a group of birds, a shorter and lower-pitched 'spüüh' or just 'stüh' is heard. Song like Meadow Pipit's, but more vehement and with more but shorter components and interwoven 'speeeeh'. Also has a disyllabic rolling 'churrup'; alarm a monotonously repeated 'tyü' or 'tyüt'. Breeds sparsely in N Scandinavian mountains but more commonly towards arctic coast on open grassy or boggy terrain with willow scrub. On passage occurs in similar habitats to Meadow Pipit but often difficult to see on ground. Vagrant to Britain and W Europe, Apr–Jun and Aug–Nov.   *Map p. 366*

Tree Pipit

1st-winter

ad autumn

Meadow Pipit

summer

Red-throated Pipit

1st-winter

♂ summer

Olive-backed Pipit *Anthus hodgsoni* $\frac{2}{\cdot}\left(\text{see } 369\right)$ L 14.5 cm

Resembles Tree Pipit, but slightly smaller and mantle/back more olive-green in tone and almost unstreaked. Head distinctively marked, with a broad supercilium (buff-yellow in front of and whitish above and behind eye) accentuated by a dark border to crown. Has distinct dark and light spot on rear ear-coverts, more marked than on Tree. In worn plumage has a colder grey-brown tone above, closer to Tree Pipit. Call a somewhat drawn-out 'tseep', in tone closer to Tree but more vocal, less buzzing. Behaviour and habitat as Tree Pipit. Annual vagrant to NW Europe from Siberia, mostly Sep–Oct.

Pechora Pipit *Anthus gustavi* L 14 cm

Very like Red-throated Pipit in 1st-winter plumage, but shorter-tailed, rocks tail and walks or sneaks more like Tree Pipit. Upperparts even more clearly marked, with black and distinct white to yellowish-white lines on mantle and more prominent whitish wingbars. Has distinct primary projection (cf Red-throated). Head usually looks rather plain, contrasting with very well-marked black spot on neck-sides. Often shows short dark eye-stripe on lores breaking eye-ring at front (Red-throated usually has unbroken eye-ring). Unobtrusive and extremely skulking, very hard to flush from ground vegetation. Quiet, but has diagnostic hard 'tsep'. E Siberian species; very rare vagrant to Europe, mostly end Sep to beginning Oct.

Richard's Pipit *Anthus novaeseelandiae* L 18 cm

Skylark-sized and visibly larger than Tawny Pipit, longer-legged and longer-tailed and with heavier bill and very long hindclaw. Has dark-streaked breast and more streaked mantle. Is less well marked on lores, eye-stripe is more prominent behind than in front of eye (reverse applies in Tawny). In fresh plumage has warm ochre or rusty-orange tone to breast and flanks and relatively thin streaks on breast. Autumn observations in W Europe are normally of 1st-cal-year birds with much juv. plumate remaining: they often show coarser streaking on breast and a sprinkling of feathers with broad dark centres on mantle and also have a more subdued buff ground colour. Call in flight a characteristic loud 'pchrreep' or 'prrreep', like House Sparrow and with a particular coarse, slightly nasal quality. Song simple, consisting of a few chirping or trilling phrases repeated 2–4 times. Occurs very rarely but regularly in Europe, mostly end Sep to beginning Nov, usually on long-grass fields and shore meadows.

Blyth's Pipit *Anthus godlewskii* L 17 cm

Very like Richard's Pipit in plumage, but has shorter and more pointed bill and shorter tail, is shorter-legged and has shorter hindclaw, and is more like Tawny Pipit in body form and actions. On the median coverts the dark centres have a more oblong shape, are more squarely and sharply cut off against the pale fringe compared with Richard's; this applies only to ads., birds in their 1st autumn usually having unmoulted juv. coverts (identical to those on Richard's). Has short and fairly hard 'chep' like Tawny Pipit's, also a more drawn-out call resembling Richard's but softer and slightly higher in tone. Vagrant from C Asia, a few records in Europe.

Long-billed Pipit *Anthus similis* L 19 cm

Closely resembles Tawny Pipit, but is darker grey above with longer bill and shorter hindclaw, longer and darker tail. Song more varied than Tawny's, with 2–4 notes slowly repeated in straight song flight or from perch. Fairly rare on dry slopes in Lebanon, W Syria, N Israel and westernmost Jordan.

Tree Pipit

Olive-backed Pipit

Pechora Pipit

fresh
(spring)

Richard's Pipit

juv – 1st-winter

Long-billed Pipit

Blyth's Pipit

1st-winter

Tawny Pipit   *Anthus campestris*   L 16.5 cm

Body size as Yellow Wagtail and almost unstreaked sandy-coloured, though a few dark streaks on breast-sides are usual. 1st-cal-year birds in Sep and even Oct often have some juv. feathers, i.e. are more spotted on breast and more streaked on mantle (*cf* Blyth's and Richard's Pipits). Calls fairly variable, incl. a drawn-out 'tseeep', a 'tschilp' resembling House Sparrow's, short 'chup' etc. Song a slowly repeated 'zeerüh' or 'tzeerlüh', slightly melancholy and metallic in tone. Sings in undulating song flight, with a verse in descent phase of each undulation, or from exposed perch. Breeds uncommonly in dry heath-type terrain with sparse vegetation and bare areas, in S Europe also in mountainous regions and on alpine meadows. On passage also on dry farmland, often in same habitats as Short-toed Lark. Feeds mostly on insects. Migrates Aug–Sep (Oct), returns Apr–May. In Britain a very scarce migrant, mainly Aug–Oct with a few Apr–Jun.

Pied Wagtail   *Motacilla alba*   L 18 cm

In Europe two races, *yarrellii* in Britain and Ireland and locally on adjacent Continental coasts, and *alba* in rest of Europe. In *alba* male has black crown and nape contrasting sharply with grey mantle, female has grey nape shading into black crown (2nd-cal-year female can also have grey crown). In *yarrellii* male is all-black above and has sooty-grey flanks, female is dark grey on mantle/back but has black crown, rump and uppertail-coverts. Moult Aug–Sep to winter plumage, when less black on head and the pale parts of head initially have a faint lemon-yellow tinge. Black breast-band distinguishes it at all times from other wagtails. Juv. looks plainer grey but with darker grey triangular patch in centre of breast. In 1st-winter plumage difficult to identify racially in the field. In Morocco race *subpersonata*, with much more black on head. Call a melodious and 'cheery' 'pe-vit' (*yarrellii* more 'tchizzik') or 'tslee-vit'. Song lively and twittering with call-like notes. Common in most habitats with open sunlit areas with insects. Often nests on buildings and near water, e.g. on bridges, riverbanks etc. Icelandic/Scandinavian birds pass through Britain Mar–May, Aug–Oct. British breeders chiefly resident.

Tawny Pipit

Pied Wagtail

juv   *yarrellii* ♀ winter

♂ summer   ♂ winter

subpersonata

juv

Tawny Pipit

Pied Wagtail

alba ♂

yarrellii
♂ winter

1st-winter

Grey Wagtail   **Yellow Wagtail**

Grey Wagtail   *Motacilla cinerea*   *L 18–19 cm*

Differs from Yellow Wagtail in noticeably longer tail, entirely grey mantle and back, and darker contrasting brownish-black wings. Summer-plumaged male has black throat and entire underside bright yellow, female with whiter sides to belly and white throat with variable degree of darker elements. 1st-winter female has bright yellow only on vent and rump (tail-join), breast is more ochre-tinted. In flight the long tail and on many the white wingbar are conspicuous. Call like Pied Wagtail's but sharper, more clearly articulated and higher-pitched, 'stit' or 'ztee-tit'. Song consists of series of call-like notes. Tied to running water when breeding, in winter also at lakes, watercress beds and on coast. Elegant and lively in movements, catches insects among rocks and in runnels. Wags tail and stern up and down. Resident in large parts of Europe, but in winter moves from uplands to lower areas.

Yellow Wagtail   *Motacilla flava*   *L 17 cm*

Represented in W Palearctic by several races with quite different head patterns, though all have yellow belly and green-toned mantle and back. In S Scandinavia and Continental Europe nominate *flava* breeds, in Britain *flavissima* (female like male but considerably paler), and in N Fennoscandia *thunbergi* (dark grey crown, dull black ear-coverts and lacks prominent supercilium). In S Europe represented by three races: *iberiae* in Iberian Peninsula and parts of S France, *cinereocapilla* in Italy and adjacent parts of Balkans, and *feldegg* in Balkans and around Black Sea; further east, towards steppes of C Asia *beema* (see p. 376). Juv. has yellow-buff underparts (lacks bright yellow tone) and broad supercilium accentuated by dark border, olive-brown upperparts, conspicuous dark brown malar stripe and has a band of dark spots across breast; underparts fade rapidly and juv. in Aug, like 1st-winter females, can be confused with Tawny Pipit as well as with Citrine Wagtail. In winter plumage often very variable. Calls pleasing, typical is an agreeable 'tsee-e' or 'tsree-e', in *feldegg* a slightly rolling 'tsrreei'; also has a clear ringing Dunnock-like 'zee-see-see' and short 'pseet'. Song is a rather chirping sequence of call notes usually delivered in a display posture with breast puffed out (see illustration). Breeds fairly commonly on lush damp meadowland or in marsh fringes; in autumn often on pastureland, where cattle etc are exploited as 'beaters' to flush out insects. Migrates Aug–Oct, returns Apr; also passage through Britain Mar–Jun and Aug–Oct (incl. 2–3 races).

Grey Wagtail

Yellow Wagtail

Citrine Wagtail

Grey Wagtail

flava ♂ summer

flavissima
♂ summer

flava ♀ winter **Yellow Wagtail**

flava
♀ 1st-winter

thunbergi ♂

cinereocapilla ♂

iberiae ♂

feldegg ♂

feldegg ♀

Yellow Wagtail

beema ♂

beema ♀ 1st-wir

flava ♀ 1st-winter

juv

Citrine Wagtail   *Motacilla citreola*   L 18 cm

Most like Pied Wagtail in body shape and tail length. Spring male unmistakable. On female extent and intensity of yellow on underparts vary, typically shows broad yellow supercilium which continues in a border around ear-coverts. In 1st-winter plumage most like a pale Yellow Wagtail (head pattern best distinguishing mark). Has broad supercilium, often tinted brownish-buff in front of eye towards forehead, broad and usually pure white behind and continuing down and framing the darker ear-coverts; the pale border around ear-coverts varies in width and is sometimes less conspicuous. In addition has grey mantle, two broad white wingbars, and pale, whitish belly and ventral area (vent normally yellow on Yellow Wagtail except on unmoulted juv.); breast often has grey or brown-grey tinge and on some a gorget of spots towards throat. Overall impression is usually of grey-and-white pattern similar to Pied Wagtail (race *alba*), but some have warm yellowish-buff tint to head and breast (though never bright yellow like ad.). Flight call diagnostic, a straight sharp 'srreep', higher and more drawn-out than in race *feldegg* of Yellow; some populations/races of Citrine, however, call more like Yellow Wagtail. Breeds on boggy areas and meadowland, often found beside water. Vagrant to W Europe, mostly juvs./1st-winters in Sep−Oct, but occasional summer-plumaged birds are seen in May−Jun.   *Map p. 374*

♂

♂ 1st-summer

♀

1st-winter

Citrine Wagtail

Waxwing   *Bombycilla garrulus*   *L 18 cm*

Unmistakable. Wing markings often reveal age. Juv. wing shows pale only on outer web of primaries (forming white line along the feathers); on ads. this is yellower and broader and they also have white edging around tip. The small red plastic-like projections on secondaries are absent or are fewest in number on young females, and longest and most numerous on ad. males. In flight very reminiscent of a Starling, but has faster, more graceful flight and slimmer profile. Call a characteristic silvery 'sirr', which from flock in flight sounds like a surging ring. Song unassuming, with simple call-like phrases. Breeds sparsely or uncommonly in northernmost coniferous belt, usually in older forests with berry-rich shrub layer. In winter months feeds chiefly on berries of e.g. rowan, Swedish whitebeam, rose hips etc and then visits parks, gardens and other areas with plentiful berries. Food supply and other factors mean that it appears in greatly fluctuating numbers from year to year within wintering range indicated. In Britain usually not seen until end Oct, typically in Nov, and scarce, but during periodic invasions widespread in larger numbers. In spring and summer also takes insects, caught smartly in flight almost like Bee-eater.

Dipper   *Cinclus cinclus*   *L 18 cm*

A peculiar, short-tailed and pot-bellied passerine, sooty-black and coffee-brown with dazzling white bib. Varies somewhat in darkness and in belly colour; British birds (race *gularis*) have distinct reddish-brown tone below bib. Occurs on fast-running waters, especially stony torrents and streams, but in winter also on slower-flowing rivers. In boulders, foam and gloomy water spray its shape often melts in and its appearance is often sudden, often typically preceded by a sharp and penetrating, somewhat rasping 'strits'; at the same moment a chubby black bird comes dashing past close above the water on whirring wings, following the line of the stream. Sits on a rock and at regular intervals descends and disappears down to bed of stream. Seeks out various insect larvae, snails, fish eggs etc; having succeeded, it pops up to surface and, as if to recover its breath, often floats downstream a bit on half-spread wings before getting out. Song quiet, somewhat disjointed, of grating and twittering sequences and phrases. Resident so long as open water remains in rivers and streams, but many northern birds migrate Oct−Nov (vagrants from Scandinavia occasionally reach E Britain).

Waxwing

Dipper

Waxwing

♂

Dipper

juv

Wren   *Troglodytes troglodytes*   L 9.5 cm

After Goldcrest/Firecrest Britain's smallest bird, rusty-brown with a short cocked tail. Abundant in woodland, but also found in gardens, parks and open scrubby areas, on farmland and in reedbeds; has also colonised Scottish islands, where often lives on bird cliffs. Frequently found low down in dense shrubbery, in piles of brushwood, dry-stone walls etc. In general, however, it is the song that draws attention to it: a prolonged, excited and rapid verse high up on the scale and with a vibrant quality. Call a dry 'chek' or more rolling 'cherrr', often drawn out into a hard rattle; also has a mechanically repeated 'chet...chet...'. In Britain mainly sedentary or dispersive, with some migrants from Continent (e.g. Scandinavia) Oct−Apr.

Dunnock   *Prunella modularis*   L 14.5 cm

An unobtrusive, thicket-loving bird with strikingly dark overall appearance. Movements slow and bunting-like, but thin bill recalls a warbler. 1st-winters in autumn often show more brown-grey tone to head and look very insignificant. From top of a low bush, especially at dawn, male gives its squeaky but pleasing warble, like Wren's in tone but slower rate of delivery. Call a strong and emphatic 'seeh' or 'steei'. A very high, ringing 'sissississ' is heard from migrants in flight. Breeds in tangled woodland, in clearings, in spruce plantations, and from Britain southwards also in gardens, parks, scrub and hedgerow bushes in farmland. Feeds mostly on various seeds, but largely on insects during breeding season. In Britain and Ireland sedentary, with additional visitors from N Europe mainly in Sep−Mar/Apr.

Alpine Accentor   *Prunella collaris*   L 18 cm

Somewhat like an outsized Dunnock. Most prominent characters are contrasting dark greater wing-coverts, one or two pale 'dotted' wingbars, pale wing panel, pinebark-red streaking on sides and yellow base to lower mandible. Flight undulating and finch-like. Quite often its call is heard without the bird being seen or the source of the call being located. Usually a rolling mono- to trisyllabic 'chürrupp' rather similar to a low-pitch penny whistle is heard, or a slightly Linnet-like 'chu-chu-chu', also a shorter and sharper 'tchü' or 'pürrt', sometimes combined 'tchü...tchürr'. Song varies in length, is melodious and with clear ring, with trilling whistles and squeaky sounds, has similarities to both Northern Wheatear and Black Redstart songs. Occurs sparsely to relatively commonly in mountainous districts, normally on high-alpine plateaux and slopes without taller vegetation. In winter at lower levels, often beside resting-spots or buildings (e.g. chalets). Prefers south-facing positions and frequently forages in snow-melt zones. Very rare vagrant to Britain.

Wren

Dunnock

Alpine Accentor

Wren

Dunnock

juv

Alpine Accentor

Siberian Accentor   *Prunella montanella*   L 14.5 cm

Like a Dunnock in build and actions, but has broad intense ochre-yellow supercilium
and ochre-yellow on throat and breast. Ear-coverts blackish, crown grey-brown in
centre with black sides bordering supercilia. Neck-sides grey. Streaks on mantle and
sides of body have a rusty-brown or chestnut-brown tint. Call a trisyllabic 'seereesee'.
Song recalls Dunnock's. Breeds in a narrow belt in N Siberia from Ural Mountains
eastward to Pacific coast and locally in mountain regions in C Siberia. Long-distance
migrant to E China and Korea. Very rare vagrant to NW Europe, mostly in Oct.

Black-throated Accentor   *Prunella atrogularis*   L 15 cm

Identified by black throat and by fact that mantle/back is less rusty-brown and has
coarser and blacker streaks (more like Dunnock). Most easily confused with Siberian
Accentor, especially in autumn when pale fringes on some individuals (mainly
1st-winter females) partly conceal the black throat. However, has less intensely yellow
supercilium, and fringes to throat and submoustachial stripe are dirty-white in contrast
to ochre breast. In addition, ear-coverts are often less intensely black. Neck-side grey.
Occurs in tangled vegetation in wood or scrub. Breeds in two separate regions, nearest
being in Ural Mountains with a further area around Tien-Shan Mountains in C Asia.
Winters within the southern breeding range and south to N Pakistan. Extremely rare
vagrant to Europe, recorded only twice outside USSR (in Finland in Oct and in Sweden
in Jun).

Radde's Accentor   *Prunella ocularis*   L 15.5 cm

Somewhat bigger than Dunnock, with black ear-coverts, black crown and contrasting
broad white supercilium. Mantle/back olive-brown in fresh plumage and streaked, in
worn plumage acquires a paler grey-buff tone. Underparts warm grey-buff, with darker
streaking on flanks and with unmarked pale 'curry-coloured' breast and buffish-white
throat. Often has suggestion of dark malar stripe and in worn plumage a necklace of
dark spots. Female has less contrasting head pattern than male. The purer white
supercilium should distinguish Radde's from autumn Black-throated Accentors which
lack obvious black throat. Song like Dunnock's, but with more pronounced jingling
sound. Occurs in mountain regions at 2000–3000 m on rocky slopes with wood or
bushes of e.g. cedars and juniper shrubs. In winter down to 1000 m.

Siberian Accentor

Black-throated Accentor

Radde's Accentor

Siberian Accentor

summer

Black-throated
Accentor

1 st -winter

Radde's Accentor

Robin   *Erithacus rubecula*   L 14 cm

Fairly unmistakable with its upright posture, plump body and red breast. Usually hops on ground; often not shy, but unobtrusive during breeding period. Song unmistakable, a rippling stream of crystal-clear notes with arbitrary changes of tempo; in autumn markedly melancholy and quieter. Characteristic is a sharp ticking 'tic', often repeated 'tic-ic-ic...' like winding up a clockwork toy, often heard from within shrubbery at migration watchpoints during passage periods. Also has a thin indrawn 'seeeh', and night-flying migrants give a thin 'seei' or 'seeseei'. Breeds commonly in various types of woodland, in Britain also frequently in gardens and parks (elsewhere often in damp spruce forest). Feeds on ground-dwelling insects and various berries and fruits. Mostiy resident in Britain, with additional winter visitors from Continent Sep–Apr.

Thrush Nightingale   *Luscinia luscinia*   L 16.5 cm

Very like Nightingale, but a shade darker above, more Song Thrush brown, and has darker, slightly brown-grey breast and flanks which are seen as diffusely mottled. Tail distinctly rusty-red, especially when spread, but duller in tone than on Nightingale. Song very characteristic and far-carrying, often audible at 1 km: contains clear indrawn whistles, 'tinny' fluted 'jook' notes and rattling sequences, each theme repeated mechanically several times; is slower in tempo and more monotonous than Nightingale's, but individual variation can be appreciable. Sings mostly at night and in morning. When nervous gives loud indrawn 'heeet', also has a short sharp 'tsit' and 'tsitterr'. Alarm near nest a dry creaking call. Occurs in terrain with dense shady shrubbery, and is relatively common in cultivated country around groups of deciduous trees, along rivers and lakeshores and in rank gardens. Feeds on insects, worms, snails, berries and fruits. Migrates to E Africa in Aug, returning in May. Very rare but annual vagrant to Britain during May–Oct.

Nightingale   *Luscinia megarhynchos*   L 16.5 cm

Plumage differences from Thrush Nightingale subtle: above, warmer, more brownish-buff, and with paler and brighter rusty-red tail like a female Redstart; breast less mottled; neck-sides and indistinct supercilium have a velvety-grey tint, ventral area is yellowish-buff, and legs pale yellowish-pink. In autumn plumage upperparts darker, as is breast, which can then look spotted. Song like Thrush Nightingale's but more varied and with faster tempo and with features recalling a *Sylvia* warbler, remarkably like song of eastern Orphean Warbler. Calls include 'hueet' or 'huee' (like Thrush Nightingale) and a creaking 'errk'. Locally common in terrain similar to Thrush Nightingale, but also in dryer habitats such as maquis and cultivations around Mediterranean. Migrates end Jul to beginning Oct, returning end Mar to early May. In Britain, breeding restricted more or less to southern half.

Robin

Thrush Nightingale

Nightingale

Robin

juv

Thrush Nightingale

Nightingale

♂ autumn

♀ autumn

Siberian Rubythroat

Siberian Rubythroat   *Luscinia calliope*   L 16.5 cm

Male unmistakable, with ruby-red throat, white supercilium and moustachial stripe and black lores. Female like Thrush Nightingale, but with bolder facial markings. Tail uniform brown. Call a loud whistle, 'ee-lü', and a coarse 'chak'. Song sustained, chatty, with thrush-like whistles and masterful mimicry. Behaviour and habits as Nightingale or Thrush Nightingale. Vagrant to Europe from Siberia.

Rufous Bush Robin   *Cercotrichas galactotes*   L 15.5 cm

Two races: in Iberian Peninsula, N Africa and Israel *galactotes*, which is paler and more rusty-toned above; in Balkans and Turkey *syriacus*, with more grey-brown upperparts. The characteristically marked tail is often raised and spread in rhythmic pumping movements. Sings from top of bush or tree or in song flight (butterfly-like, bird parachutes on raised wings and fanned tail). Song in short, well-spaced phrases, musical and thrush-like with trills and mimicry; a 'tewee-u' like Song Thrush is often heard. Other calls quite variable, often slightly hoarse and strained, e.g. 'dyük', 'tcheeip' or harder 'teeut' and a low rolling 'schrrr'. Relatively uncommon in Europe in semi-open dry terrain with scrub, e.g. gardens, fruit-tree plantations and olive groves and also stands of prickly pear. Not shy, but on passage very unobtrusive. Arrives in May, earlier in Middle East and N Africa. Extremely rare vagrant to Britain.

White-throated Robin   *Irania gutturalis*   L 16.5 cm

Like small thrush with a long and all-black tail, often cocked like Blackbird. Unobtrusive but not shy. Sings from exposed perch or in song flight, gliding on stiff spread wings and tail. Song of chattering well-spaced verses, sometimes sustained: grating notes and wooden 'chrrr r'r'r'r'r' mixed with more fluting whistles, recalling Rüppell's Warbler and parts of the song of Black Redstart. Call a loud 'tsee-chüt'. Breeds in scrub, mostly on upland slopes and ravines with Kermes oak and juniper. Leaves Aug–Sep, returning mid Apr–early May. Vagrant to Europe, mainly in May.

Rufous Bush Robin

White-throated Robin

Rufous Bush Robin

galactotes

syriacus

♀

White-throated Robin

♂

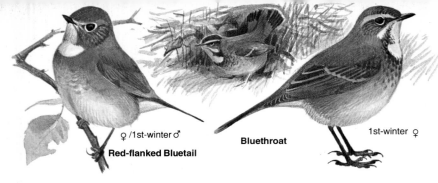

♀/1st-winter ♂

Bluethroat

1st-winter ♀

Red-flanked Bluetail

Red-flanked Bluetail *Tarsiger cyanurus* *L 14 cm*

Male unmistakable. 1st-summer male (sings and holds territory) and female alike in coloration, olive-brown with rusty-coloured flanks and distinctive facial expression: angular (peaked) head, a peculiar 'cheeky' bill, a distinct pale eye-ring and pale bib. The blue tail sometimes appears dark. Sings mostly from midnight to sunrise, usually from treetop, a relatively short verse, like Redstart's in tone, usually with a rolling or trembling final flourish, e.g. 'tsiuseelee-tsiuseelee-chutirrrr'. When agitated, a weak short 'hueet' and a dry 'keck-keck'. Breeds in deep undisturbed coniferous forests, often in hilly terrain. Wide distribution in Asia, rare and local in Finland and NE Europe. Leads a secluded life and is mostly very shy, especially when singing. Very rare vagrant to NW Europe, in Britain in Sep–Oct (one May–Jun).

Bluethroat *Luscinia svecica* *L 14 cm*

Apart from throat/breast pattern, the rusty-red tail base plus the broad pale supercilium are important species criteria in the field. Occurs in Scandinavian mountains as race *svecica* (with red throat patch) as well as on Continent as race *cyanecula* (white throat patch). In central parts of European Soviet races *volgae* and *pallidogularis*, normally with red throat patch; in Turkey *magna*, with wholly blue throat. Throat markings vary, and 2nd-cal-year male can have reduced amount of blue and red while older females sometimes have traces of blue. In autumn when plumage fresh, the blue and red on throat are partly or wholly concealed by pale fringes. Unobtrusive, hops on ground next to shrubbery and scrub, typically with cocked tail. Male's song very varied: in full version an endless gushing of clear, fine ringing notes, rapidly tripping and tumbling, often accelerating bell-like notes such as 'tree tree tree tree tree…' or 'ting, ting, ting…'; mimicry and call notes are also interwoven. Call 'tchak', often 'tsee-tchak-tchak', like a halyard striking against a flagstaff. In Scandinavian mountains breeds commonly in luxuriant birch forest and willow terrain, often beside running water; on Continent along swampy lakeshores and ditch banks with bushes. Arrives Mar–May, departing from Aug. In Britain scarce passage migrant (has bred), mostly Aug–Oct, with fewer in Mar–May.

Red-flanked Bluetail

Bluethroat

Red-flanked Bluetail

♂

♀

svecica ♂

♀

juv

Bluethroat

Redstart   *Phoenicurus phoenicurus*   *L 14 cm*

Characteristic with its upright posture and rusty-red tail, which is rapidly quivered at regular intervals. Male conspicuous, with black throat and brilliant white forehead. Female most easily confused with female Black Redstart, though never looks drab grey below but is often warm buff or faintly rusty-tinted on belly and always has pale throat; rather plainly marked but typically has pale eye-ring and rusty wash to breast and flanks. Males in autumn have the black throat and white forehead partly obscured by pale fringes. In Greece and Asia Minor race *samamisicus* (ill. p. 393), which has darker grey upperparts, little white on forehead and prominent white wing panel (even female shows light panel). Sings energetically from as early as first light, often from a high perch (e.g. treetop). Song consists of a clear and slightly melancholy verse, almost always introduced by a 'hüit' and a subsequent rolling 'tuee-tuee-tuee-tuee', most like Pied Flycatcher's. Race *samamisicus* has a somewhat different song, slower and more grating. Call like Willow Warbler's, but often combined with alarm call into a diagnostic 'hueet-tic-tic'. Breeds in open woodland, often on sandy heaths with pines, in parks and large gardens. Nest placed in natural holes or nestboxes. Food consists of insects and their larvae, more rarely berries and fruits. Arrives Apr—May, departs from mid Aug, with autumn passage through Britain peaking in Sep and lower numbers through Oct.

Black Redstart   *Phoenicurus ochruros*   *L 14 cm*

Male dark grey with variably sooty-black throat and breast (sometimes also mantle) and with white wing panel. Female like a sooty or dingy female Redstart and always with darker throat and belly. 1st-summer male variable: some just like female; others with black on throat and, rarely, as ad. male, though lacking wing panel. In Iberian Peninsula and Morocco race *aterrimus*, which is jet-black with grey skull-cap (ill. p. 392). In southern Turkey and Middle East race *semirufus* (ill. p. 393), which has rusty-red belly and little or no white in wing and can be confused with Redstart. In north and east Turkey *ochruros*. Song is more or less split into 3—4 forcedly delivered sections: these vary, but often heard is a sharp Wren-like introduction, 'svee-svee-svee-svee-svee', followed by a characteristic vowel-less crackling noise as from crunching gravel or small metal balls. Sings from an elevated perch, e.g. a rock, chimney, TV aerial, church tower or similar spot; often surprisingly difficult to locate. Call 'tseep', when agitated 'tseep-tseep-tseep', often followed by a 'tak-tak-tak'. In S Europe tied to mountainous regions; elsewhere often breeds in towns where residential and industrial buildings have had to replace species' original habitat, in Britain sporadically and rarely up to N England. Food as Redstart's, but more often catches insects in the air and is sometimes seen hovering and fluttering along walls, underneath roofs etc. In Britain, rare summer visitor Apr—Sep, with passage migrants from Continent Mar—May and Sep--Nov; a few winter, often at traditional localities.

Redstart   Black Redstart   Moussier's Redstart

♂

♂ 1st-winter

Redstart

♀

♀

♂

♂ 1st-winter

Black Redstart

Moussier's Redstart ♀

♂

Redstart
samamisicus ♂

Black Redstart
aterrimus ♂

Moussier's Redstart   *Phoenicurus moussieri*   L 13 cm

Endemic in NW Africa. Common in mountain districts with open woodland up to 3000 m, in winter at lower elevations. Male unmistakable. Female smaller, shorter-tailed with more rosehip-red underparts than female Redstart, also shows tendency towards pale wing panel. Song a relatively long verse moving between rasping 'eer' sounds (like Serin) and more vocal 'svee-svee' sounds. Call a thin 'heeh' like Thrush Nightingale, alarm a gravelly 'trrrrr' and variants.   *Map p. 390*

Güldenstädt's Redstart   *Phoenicurus erythrogaster*   L 18 cm

Large as Rock Thrush and clearly bigger than Redstart. Breeds in high mountains in C Asia (4000-5500 m), with isolated population in Caucasus. In winter in valleys down to 1000 m.

Blackstart   *Cercomela melanura*   L 14 cm

Entirely grey with black tail. Song consists of short, well-phrased, rather melancholy rolling whistles, with deep fluty quality. Characteristic bird of rocky desert areas with scattered acacias and bushes in S and E Israel, adjacent parts of Jordan, Sinai Peninsula and further south, incl. in Sahel zone in Africa south of Sahara.

Güldenstädt's Redstart

♀

♂

Black Redstart
semirufus ♂

Blackstart ♂

Males 1st-winter

Whinchat

Stonechat

Siberian
(Eastern)

Whinchat   *Saxicola rubetra*   *L 12.5 cm*

A short-tailed, variegated bird which perches upright on bushtops. In all plumages broad white or buff supercilium prominent. Summer-plumaged male has blackish ear-coverts and white patches on scapulars and on primaries. In autumn sexes alike, buff to rich reddish-ochre in colour, and all birds are typically spotted above. Has white patches at tail base, difficult to see except when landing. Song very variable, often disjointed and whimsical; basic theme a rapidly delivered rasping twitter mixed with mimicry. Easily mistaken or overlooked when perched and 'chattering' with mimicry and its own 'squeaks'; often sings at night. Gives persistent alarm with sporadic 'yu tek-tek' calls. Breeds on open or bushy meadowland, often beside wetlands but also on dryer heath. Arrives Apr−May, departs Aug−Sep, with passage through Britain (from Scandinavia) up to Oct.

Stonechat   *Saxicola torquata*   *L 12.5 cm*

Rounder-headed and longer-tailed than Whinchat, with wholly black or black-brown tail which is constantly flicked. Male has black throat, on female brown to grey-buff. In Continental Europe and in N Africa race *rubicola*, in which male very contrasting with blackish mantle (fringed brown in autumn and in 1st summer) and rusty-orange on breast. In Britain and Ireland and along coast of Portugal race *hibernans*, darker and more brownish-red below and has broader brown fringes above. In fresh autumn plumage females not uncommonly have pale throat, but they lack Whinchat's supercilium. Song more monotonous than Whinchat's, of short twittering phrases, can recall Whitethroat's; sometimes sings in song flight. Often nervous and often utters a pebble-clinking 'trak' or 'trak-trak' and a clear 'weet', often 'weet-trak-trak'. Breeds in open bushy country, typically in mountain tracts and hilly terrain. In Britain favours heaths and commons with gorse, especially near coast; mainly resident, but disperses in autumn and winter.

Siberian (Eastern) Stonechat   *Saxicola (torquata) maura*   *L 12.5 cm*

Traditionally regarded as a race of Stonechat but may be a full species; replaces latter in Siberia and C Asia, breeds mainly on bogs and wetlands. Has white or pale ochre rump and female lacks dark throat in all plumages. On summer male white collar extends farther back onto nape and at least male in 1st-summer often has purer white belly-sides. In winter plumage paler, females and 1st-cal-years with pale throat, supercilium, pale greater-covert fringes forming wingbar and a pale secondary panel. Races with variably prominent white at tail base, mainly *variegata* and *armenica* from C Asia, migrate through parts of Middle East to E Africa. Vagrant to Europe, in Britain mostly Oct−Nov but also other months (incl. spring).

Whinchat

Stonechat

Whinchat

winter

♂

♀

Stonechat

♂

♀

♀
winter

Siberian (Eastern) Stonechat

♂ 1st-summer

♂ 1st-winter *variegata*

♀ winter

2nd-cal ♂

ad ♂

2nd-cal ♀

ad ♀

ad ♀

2nd-cal ♂

2nd-cal ♂

2nd-cal ♂

2nd-cal ♂

Black-eared Wheatear
melanoleuca

♂ 1st-winter

♂ 1st-winter

ad ♀ winter

♀ winter

♀ winter

♂ 1st-winter

♀

♂ winter

2nd-cal ♀

♂

ad ♂

Black-eared Wheatear
hispanica

juv

♀

♂

Northern Wheatear   *Oenanthe oenanthe*   L 15−16 cm

The only wheatear in N Europe. Conspicuous black-and-white tail markings. Male has black mask and yellow-ochre breast. Moults to winter plumage in Jul−Aug, when sexes become more difficult to separate, though ad. male shows black lores; 1st-summer male has brown (not black) flight feathers. In Greenland and Iceland race *leucorhoa*, which is slightly bigger, in autumn usually more intensely rusty-toned below and with generally broader black terminal band on tail. In N Africa race *seebohmi*, in which male has black throat; female sometimes resembles male or has black lores and darker brown ear-coverts. Song a rapid series of rasping and creaking notes mixed with mimicry. Call

a loud but yet slightly indrawn 'heeht'. Sings in song flight. Alarm 'chak'. Common in open country, e.g. enclosed pasture, heaths/moors, shore meadows and upland moors with exposed areas and some rocky parts or walls offering cavities for the nest. Feeds on insects. One of earliest of tropical migrants in spring, arriving Britain early Mar though with most in Apr; departs Sep, with passage migrants to Oct/Nov.

eastern
♀ ad winter

western
♀ 1st-winter

eastern
♀ 1st-winter

Black-eared Wheatear

♂ 1st-winter
(female looking)

♀ 1st-winter

Pied Wheatear

♀ ad winter

Isabelline Wheatear *Oenanthe isabellina* L 16 cm

Like female Northern Wheatear in fresh winter plumage, but is bigger, longer-legged and also paler and more uniformly grey-buff. Wing paler owing to broader buff feather edges. Tail has a broader dark terminal band (dark brown). Sexes alike but male generally has darker lores. In autumn difficult to distinguish from pale female Northern Wheatears, but has paler wings (tertials with broader edges) and paler, less rusty-toned ear-coverts. Often gives a tricoloured and less variegated impression than Northern. Song often delivered in hovering flight and is quite distinct from that of other wheatears,

in part very loud, liquid and rich in expert mimicry; often introduced by disjointed, surprisingly high 'wolf-whistles' and 'peeep' calls. Call a clear 'cheep' like domestic chick, when alarmed also a varied clicking 'chick' or 'tshk'. Relatively common on treeless steppes, high plateaux and on grassy slopes up to 3500 m above sea level, often on sheep-grazed terrain. Returns Mar–mid Apr, departs Aug–Sep. Feeds on insects, often takes beetles and ants. Extremely rare vagrant to Britain, in Sep–Nov and May.

Isabelline Northern Finsch's Pied Black-eared Desert

seebohmi ♂

Northern Wheatear

♀/1st-cal ♂
♀ winter

ad ♂ winter

Isabelline Wheatear

♂ summer

winter

Black-eared Wheatear ♂

Pied Wheatear ♂

Finsch's Wheatear ♂

Desert Wheatear   *Oenanthe deserti*   L 14–15 cm

Has all-black tail (white only at very base). Male warm sandy-coloured, with jet-black throat and wing connected on side of neck and buffish-white fringes to innermost secondary coverts and tertials. 1st-summer male less contrasty, grey-buff above and with brown wings. Female pale sandy-buff and with brown-toned ear-coverts, indistinct pale supercilium and variable throat markings (usually pale but occasionally patterned dark). Both sexes often have a pale strip along wing bordering scapulars. Race *atrogularis* in C Asia is more brown-grey above and more ochre on breast compared with *homochroa* in western N Africa; *deserti* in Middle East is intermediate. In winter plumage black throat is partly hidden by pale fringes and upperparts generally darker and greyer. Song a short, slightly melancholy whistle monotonously repeated, e.g. 'deeyerruu', sometimes with short, dry crackling 'knestrr' slipped in. Call 'chee-ü'; alarm a sharp 'tek' or a dry rattle like rapidly tapping a piece of dry wood. Occurs on dry sandy or gravelly steppes and in semi-desert, preferably with some low scrub, in Asia up to 4000 m. Vagrant from C Asia, mainly end Oct to Nov.

Black-eared Wheatear   *Oenanthe hispanica*   L 14.5 cm

Somewhat slimmer and longer-tailed than Northern Wheatear, less inclined to move about on ground and perches more horizontally. On majority, tail shows more white towards tips on 2nd–4th pairs of feathers and more black on outer feathers. Dimorphic, both sexes having either dark or pale throat. Two races: in west *hispanica*, and from S Italy eastwards *melanoleuca*. Race *hispanica* has on average less black on head and a purer and more intense ochre tone on mantle and crown. Race *melanoleuca* often has entirely black-and-white pattern in late spring. 1st-summer male has brown flight feathers and scapulars and is often more tinted and grey-mottled on crown and mantle. Female *melanoleuca* in spring is chocolate-brown to hazel on crown/mantle merging into dark brown on scapulars, with ear-coverts and throat to varying degree dark-patterned, breast often rusty-tinted (darkest at wing-bend) and belly dirty-white or buff. In autumn grey-brown on upperparts and normally lacks pale supercilium or obvious pale scaly markings, breast with rusty-brown tone which contrasts with pale throat (cf Pied Wheatear). Female *hispanica* is generally paler and warmer rusty-buff on upperparts and more frequently shows a paler supercilium. Sings from exposed perch or in song flight. Song is of fairly monotonously repeated and well-spaced phrases, not so urgent and lively as in Northern Wheatear; phrases vary, can be a vocal trilling like flight call of Skylark, scratchy like Serin, or a hard rolling-pebble sound like Black Wheatear. Subsong chattering and slightly Linnet-like with various mimicry. Other calls a low rasping 'gsch', sometimes more drawn-out 'kscheup', and a hoarse grating 'shrrr'. Relatively common on usually maquis-covered slopes with outcropping rocks, also steep eroded surfaces, large gardens, beside ruins etc, but never in areas totally lacking trees or bushes. Migrates Aug–Sep (Oct), returning Mar–Apr. Rare vagrant to Britain.

Desert Wheatear

Black-eared Wheatear

Desert Wheatear 1st-winter ♂   ad ♂

2nd-cal ♂

♀ summer

Black-eared Wheatear

♀ eastern

♂ eastern

♂ western

st-winter ♀ astern

♀ western

Pied Wheatear *Oenanthe pleschanka* L 14.5 cm

Very like Black-eared Wheatear in shape and behaviour, tail pattern identical. Male in summer has black back and wing which meet black throat and is white on crown and nape-shawl. In autumn the black throat is partly concealed by pale fringes, densest towards breast where sometimes form a paler border against ochre breast; mantle and crown grey-brown with buff fringes concealing dark areas, producing scaly or chequered impression, and a distinct pale supercilium is characteristic; wing with creamy or rusty fringes. 1st-winter male varies, usually darker on mantle than ad. and with narrower and dingier fringes to wing and also darker breast, though variation appreciable. Female very like eastern race of Black-eared: in spring/summer generally darker and more grey-brown above, with faint pale supercilium (mostly behind eye); throat varies, is normally dark-toned and in worn plumage often with black markings; often pale towards chin whereas lower throat and breast dirty-brown and slightly spotted, often shows faint rusty tone towards breast-sides contrasting clearly with dirty-white belly. Darkest-throated females are paler grey on nape and parts of head. Autumn female drab grey-brown with rustier tone to breast, flanks and ear-coverts, majority with more tinted throat than Black-eared and seldom showing latter's contrast between pale throat and darker breast; shows pale fringes above (gives scaly impression) and more pronounced pale supercilium. Song like Black-eared Wheatear's, phrases are often somewhat shorter and more forced, can recall Black Redstart. Other calls include a varied dry 'tzek', occasionally a grating and twice-repeated 'trret-trret' like Wren, also drawn-out rattle, and a vocal 'psyEEIp' like Yellow Wagtail. Nests on cliff faces, ravines and slopes. Often perches horizontally, catches insects in air or on ground. Migrates Sep–Oct, returning Mar–Apr. Very rare vagrant to Britain.

Finsch's Wheatear *Oenanthe finschii* L 14.5 cm

Robust and large-headed. Male has broad black band joining wing and throat with pale mantle/back (pale grey-buff in autumn, creamy-white in summer). Female grey above with brown-toned ear-coverts, ad. usually with dark markings on throat. Black tail markings anchor-shaped with narrow white terminal band. Male has pale tips to flight feathers and primary coverts. Often sings in flight short phrases like Black-eared Wheatear but more varied; from perch gives chattering, tuneful song with both vocal and hard rasping and rattling notes. Fairly uncommon, usually found on steep rocky cliffs or ravines. Partial migrant (short-distance).

Black Wheatear *Oenanthe leucura* L 18 cm

The only all-dark wheatear in Europe. Male sooty-black, female dark brown. Bigger than other wheatears, with slower and heavier flight. Song comprises phrases resembling those of Blue Rock Thrush with sprinkling of hard scratchy notes but often with coarse rolling sounds, e.g. 'schrl rl rl rl', and thin 'shee' or 'stee', sometimes more chattering. Occurs sparsely, mainly in mountainous regions on dry, stony and rocky slopes, often with scattered trees and bushes which are habitually used as lookout posts. Extremely rare vagrant to Britain.

Pied Wheatear

Finsch's Wheatear

Black Wheatear

Pied Wheatear

♀ summer

♀ winter

♂ summer

♂ 1st-winter

Finsch's Wheatear

♀ winter

♂

♀

♂

Black Wheatear

Cyprus Pied Wheatear   *Oenanthe cypriaca*   L 13.5 cm

Possibly race of Pied Wheatear. Resembles latter in behaviour and general appearance but is slightly smaller with shorter primary projection and white on tail rarely reaching tip of feathers. Male almost identical with Pied, while female differs in having more black and gives a very dark overall impression. In fresh plumage female resembles winter-plumaged male, but becomes gradually darker on crown/nape, then becomes paler again during early summer (when some females can be difficult to distinguish from males). 1st-summer males have shed some tertials which contrast with rest of secondaries (unlike Pied in 1st summer). In fresh plumage in autumn both sexes are rich pinkish-ochre on breast and belly, darker than Pied. Song very different from Pied Wheatear's, consists of a monotonously repeated series of rather cicada-like electric sounds, 'bizz bizz bizz bizz bizz'. Breeds only on Cyprus at various levels up to c3000 m. Prefers open undulating terrain with rocks or stony areas and some scattered bushes or low trees. Arrives from beginning of Mar and migrates end Sep–Oct (Nov). Rare on passage in Egypt and Israel.

Mourning Wheatear   *Oenanthe lugens*   L 14.5 cm

Smaller than Hooded and White-crowned Black Wheatears, more slim and well proportioned and most easily confused with Pied, though has smaller or shallower black bib and pale of nape-shawl does not extend onto mantle. Male has whitish inner webs to primaries and outer secondaries, producing a paler panel over primaries in flight; this is most marked on race *lugens* in Egypt north to Syria, but visible also on *halophila* in western N Africa. Underwing shows strong contrast between pale flight feathers and blackish coverts and axillaries. Vent is rusty-toned, less obvious in faded plumage. Ad. female of *lugens* resembles male, while female *halophila* is pale brown-grey on back and crown with varying degree of dark on ear-coverts and chin. Relatively common in desert or semi-desert, usually on stony or gravelly slopes or plateaux with isolated trees or taller bushes; often perches on wires or in top of a tree.

Hooded Wheatear   *Oenanthe monacha*   L 17.5 cm

A big, elongated, large-winged and very long-billed wheatear. Characteristically hunts larger insects in the air; expert flyer, assiduously pursuing butterflies high up. Male can be taken for a White-crowned Black Wheatear as the black of breast extends well down towards belly and the often large wings conceal the white belly. In fresh winter plumage the black areas are somewhat obscured by pale fringes, more so on 1st-winter male, which has ochre tone to crown, belly and to fringes on the areas of black and also to tail. Female greyish sandy-coloured above with paler, warm dirty-white belly; in fresh plumage darker above, more rusty-buff below, and slightly orange-pink on rump. Tail of female is slightly washed-out reddish-ochre with brown central feathers and brown tips to remaining feathers (extend c2 cm up outer web of outermost pair). Song is short phrases of varied clear thrush-like notes mixed with pebble-clinking sounds. A pronounced desert species, found in barren vegetation-impoverished ravines and on rocky mountainsides. Resident, but some dispersal away from breeding areas takes place.

Cyprus Pied Wheatear

Mourning Wheatear

Hooded Wheatear

1st-summer ♂

♀ summer

Cyprus Pied Wheatear

♀

♀

Mourning Wheatear

♂

♂

♀ winter

Hooded Wheatear

Red-rumped Wheatear   *Oenanthe moesta*   L 16 cm

Rather bigger than Northern Wheatear, fairly distinctive, obviously robust and large-headed. Has red rump and almost all-black tail, though latter is rusty-red at base. Male has grey crown merging gradually into dull sooty-black mantle; dirty-white below, with black throat. Younger males in their first non-juv. plumage (from Jul of 1st cal-year) have more brownish-grey mantle and a touch of rusty colour to crown. Female pale, sandy-coloured with variably rusty-toned head and rump; tail is rusty with diffuse brown terminal band and central feathers. Birds in Middle East, *brooksbanki*, have generally more grey mantle and less rusty rump. Song varied, chattering with rolling phrases of both clear whistling notes and coarse rough notes. Relatively common in N Africa, preferring open flat terrain of semi-desert type, usually in areas with open ground combined with small bushes which are often used as perches. Nests in hollows in ground or among rocks.

Red-tailed Wheatear   *Oenanthe xanthoprymna*   L 14.5 cm

Size as Northern Wheatear and similarly rather front-heavy, with short tail and slightly heavier bill. Two races, of which western *xanthoprymna* breeds in E Turkey and westernmost Iran and winters sparingly in Egypt, Sinai Peninsula and Arabian Peninsula. It has a rusty-red rump with contrasting white tail base (a few with faint rusty tail base). Male looks dingy grey above, with contrasting black throat and pronounced whitish supercilium; wings are sooty-black with broad pale fringes to greater coverts and flight feathers, showing no appreciable contrast with scapulars, though in worn plumage wings become darker and blackish towards carpal. In fresh plumage breast and belly have a distinctive brownish-pink hue, though this fades and becomes more dirty-white towards summer. Females of this race are sometimes like males, while others are dingy grey on throat and have a faint rusty tone to ear-coverts and normally less intense rusty colour on rump. In eastern race *chrysopygia* of C Asia, both sexes have paler throat and rusty base to tail like Bluethroat. Song varying, typical wheatear song with short phrases of alternating melodious whistles and more coarse sounds. Occurs in mountain districts, mainly on barren mountain slopes with boulders and landslip precipices up to 4000 m. In winter in lower regions and also on cultivated ground.

White-crowned Black Wheatear   *Oenanthe leucopyga*   L 17 cm

A big, glossey jet-black wheatear with white crown when adult and the only one with virtually all-white outer tail feathers. In juv. and 1st-winter plumages has all-black head and then resembles Black Wheatear, though lacks prominent black terminal tail band but younger birds in particular have darker spots towards tips of outer five pairs of tail feathers. Song varied, often composed and well phrased, consists of a few clear mellow notes but various mimicry and gravelly elements are also often heard. Very much a desert species, extending into central Sahara, prefers stony ravines and wadis with scattered acacias, also near human settlements and oases.

Red-rumped Wheatear

Red-tailed Wheatear

White-crowned Black Wheatear

Red-rumped Wheatear

♀

♂ fresh Middle East

♂ worn N Africa

eastern

western ♀

Red-tailed Wheatear

western ♂

western ♀/1st-cal ♂ winter

western ♂ winter

White-crowned Black Wheatear

ad

ad

1st–2nd-cal

♂ winter

Rock Thrush   Blue Rock Thrush

Rock Thrush   *Monticola saxatilis*   L 19 cm

A small short-tailed thrush with long bill. Male very striking, grey-blue and rosehip-red with brilliant white panel on back (used as a signal and thus varies in extent). Female paler than female Blue Rock Thrush, pale-spotted above and with rusty-red tail. Has characteristic song flight: rises with lark-like fluttering wingbeats and then parachutes down to perch, all the while with fanned tail glowing rusty-red. Song like that of Blue Rock Thrush, but with softer, more flowing phrases, tone resembling Redwing's. Other calls include a clear 'diu', a 'chak', and a drawn-out soft rattling 'kschrrrr' like Woodchat Shrike. Occurs in mountain regions, often higher up than Blue Rock Thrush and typically on stony alpine meadows and sparsely vegetated slopes, but locally also in lowland areas. Feeds on insects, worms, lizards and other small animals and on berries. Migrates to tropical Africa at end Aug to Sep, returning Mar to early May. Very rare vagrant to Britain, mostly in May–Jun.

Blue Rock Thrush   *Monticola solitarius*   L 20.5 cm

Male an unmistakable sloe-blue in colour, in fresh winter plumage with fine buff-grey fringes. 1st-summer male has some female-like markings, mainly on throat, belly and vent. Female variable, some with distinct bluish tinge to upperparts, darker and longer-billed than female Rock Thrush and also has longer and dark brown (not rusty-red) tail; in autumn has warmer buff fringes. Song Blackbird-like in tone, short fluting phrases, e.g. 'chu sree, churr teetee…', often repeated with relatively long pauses. Subsong quiet, an unbroken stream of similar sounds and often containing Starling-like creaking notes. Otherwise relatively silent, but has a 'chak', a Nuthatch-like 'veeht veeht' and high 'tsee' calls. Occurs in mountains, often at sun-warmed ravines and rock faces, down to sea level, and in winter often at coastal cliffs and by ruins and buildings. Shy and unobtrusive, often disappears around a ridge in smooth flight with soft elastic wingbeats. Not infrequently perches on rock summits and makes sorties after insects like Spotted Flycatcher. Food as Rock Thrush's. Partly resident but at lower levels in winter, though many European birds, especially females, migrate to N Africa.

Rock Thrush

Blue Rock Thrush

♂ winter

♂

Rock Thrush

♀

♂

♀

Blue Rock Thrush

Grey-cheeked Thrush *Catharus minimus* L 18 cm

An American vagrant. Clearly smaller than Song Thrush in size, with more rounded head shape and proportionately shorter bill. Grey-brown above with diffusely greyish flanks with not much spotting, which is characteristic of the genus. Face shows grey ear-coverts and diffuse eye-ring (mainly as dirty-white, slightly pointed 'bracket' behind eye). Breast is buff (in spring often only faintly) with distinct black spots which merge gradually into the grey flanks. Bill black with pale yellowish-pink inner half to lower mandible. Underwing shows two pale buffish-pink or whitish bands, a feature typical of *Catharus* thrushes and well visible in flight. Call a somewhat drawn-out high, slightly nasal 'veeüh(r)', normally higher-pitched than Veery's. Very unobtrusive, keeps low in dense bushy vegetation. Very rare vagrant mainly from arctic Canada; most records are from England, and almost exclusively in the last three weeks of Oct.

Swainson's Thrush *Catharus ustulatus* L 18 cm

Warmer, more olive-toned above than Grey-cheeked Thrush, with a bold pale buff or rusty-yellow eye-ring. Normally rich buff on breast and sometimes faintly rusty-yellow on neck-sides with dark spots which become gradually paler and merge into pale grey of flanks. The regular thick eye-ring, often continuing into a supercilium above lores, is the main distinguishing character compared with other *Catharus* thrushes. Underwing shows striking pale buffish band. Call a short quiet 'kük' or 'vünk', like a large drop falling on a clear water surface. Very rare vagrant from N America at end Sep−Oct.

Hermit Thrush *Catharus guttatus* L 17 cm

Differs from above two species in cinnamon-coloured rump and slightly rusty-coloured tail (like Thrust Nightingale). Tail is somewhat darker towards tip and slightly forked. Tail colour not always easy to see; often cocks tail and then slowly lowers it. Fringes to primaries and coverts also have a warmer brown tone contrasting slightly with rest of upperparts, and in addition flanks have a buff tone unlike on the other species. Head markings most resemble those of Grey-cheeked Thrush; eye-ring is complete but thin and more dirty-white and bill is not so contrasty or so obviously bicoloured as that of Grey-cheeked. Underwing has ochre band. Call a fairly deep 'kwuk'. Recorded a few times in Europe, mostly in Oct.

Veery *Catharus fuscescens* L 17 cm

The warmest-toned of the four *Catharus* thrushes, soft rusty-brown above, most intensely on rump. Diagnostic is the much reduced spotting on the breast, with only obscure brown-grey spots. Sides of body grey. Flicks wings and raises and lowers tail when nervous. Call a characteristic but varied 'veeair' or 'wheew', slightly mewing and drawn out. Behaviour and habits as Hermit Thrush; recorded a few times in Europe.

Wood Thrush *Hylocichla mustelina* L 19 cm

Clearly bigger than all above-mentioned species. Conspicuously rich brownish-red above and with very sharply defined black spots on breast and belly, incl. belly-sides. Recorded twice in Europe (Isles of Scilly and Iceland). *Not illustrated*

American Robin *Turdus migratorius* L 25 cm

Size of Blackbird, with uniformly dark grey or brown-grey upperparts and rusty-red underparts. Head greyish-black with striking white markings around eye and above lores, throat dark-streaked. Call 'chut' or 'chut-chut-chut', and in flight on migration a somewhat Redwing-like lisping 'see-lee'. Vagrant from N America, mainly autumn−spring. *Not illustrated*

Gray-cheeked Thrush

1st-winter

Swainson's Thrush

1st-winter

Hermit Thrush

1st-winter

Veery

1st-winter

White's Thrush

Siberian Thrush

1st-winter
♂

♀

♂

♂

1st-winter

Eye-browed Thrush

Dusky Thrush

eunomus
ad ♂ winter

1st-winter
naumanni

1st-winter
intermediate

**Black-throated
Thrush**

atrogularis
ad ♂ winter

1st-winter ♀
atrogularis

White's Thrush   *Zoothera dauma*   L 28 cm

Slightly bigger than Mistle Thrush but somewhat shorter-tailed. Unmistakable, bestrewn with black crescent-shaped marks. In flight shows black and white bands on under-wing. Very shy and skulking, normally keeps on the ground in cover of vegetation. Has undulating flight. Quiet but has a drawn-out 'zeeea'. Song distinctive: a straight drawn-out whistle, desolate and dying away, which is repeated at intervals of 2—5 seconds; usually two pitches are audible, probably from two individuals (female and male?). Breeds in Siberia, with nearest population in S Ural Mountains. Very rare vagrant to N Europe, mainly autumn—winter.

Siberian Thrush   *Zoothera sibirica*   L 22 cm

Size of Song Thrush, long-billed. Male wholly blue-grey with striking white supercilium and with distinct white bands on underwing. 1st-winter and summer male with varying amount of buff speckling on ear-coverts and throat, also show buff spots on unmoulted outer greater coverts. Female warm brown, has broad white supercilium and spotted underparts. Flight call 'zit', like Song Thrush but softer. Very rare vagrant from Siberia east of Yenisei River, mainly in late autumn.

Eye-browed Thrush   *Turdus obscurus*   L 22 cm

Slightly smaller than Song Thrush; rather featureless, with unspotted pale rusty-tinted underparts and white supercilium with dark lores the most striking characters. Ad. male grey on head and neck as well as throat. Female and 1st-winter male rather pale, olive-brown above with greyer ear-coverts and breast-sides and with pale throat; in autumn has pale drop-shaped spots forming narrow bar on greater coverts. Flight call a drawn-out, slightly strained 'seeeh' reminiscent of Redwing. Very rare vagrant from Siberia, mostly in Oct.

Dusky Thrush   *Turdus naumanni*   L 24 cm

Two races, both occurring very rarely in Europe and Middle East. Race *eunomus* breeds in a broad belt across N Siberia and is the most frequent in N Europe: looks dark in the field in fresh plumage has blackish mantle and scapulars and head markings and black arrowhead spots below; wing looks rusty-red. Nominate race *naumanni* has a more southerly distribution: it is less contrasty, has rusty-red spots below and rusty tail, but frequently shows greyish-white fringes to wing like a Redwing. Flight call a slightly strained 'geeh', often given twice, like Fieldfare, also a 'chak-chak'. Records in Europe are mostly in the winter months, from end of Sep onwards.

Black-throated Thrush   *Turdus ruficollis*   L 24 cm

Size of a Blackbird but slightly shorter-tailed. Neutral grey above with paler grey fringes to wings, and dirty-white almost unspotted belly; underwing-coverts rusty-red. Two races. Race *atrogularis* has black throat and breast, obscured by pale fringes in fresh plumage; female and 1st-winter male less striking, but recognised by neutral grey mantle and by almost unspotted belly contrasting with dark-spotted breast. Race *ruficollis* (Red-throated Thrush) has rusty-brown breast and tail; female and 1st-winter male have rusty supercilium and throat-sides, breast spotted rusty-red and also dark malar stripe. Flight call a quiet 'sip', on rising and when agitated a single, double or triple 'chak' ('chak-chak-chak'). Nearest breeders in Ural Mountains and with an isolated population in Caucasus. Winters west to Iran and vagrant to Europe, Israel and Egypt. Most records in NW Europe are of males during the winter months.

Ring Ouzel

♂

♂ torquatus

♂ 1st-winter
alpestris

♀ 1st-winter

Ring Ouzel *Turdus torquatus* L 24 cm

Male is sooty black with white breast-band and pale fringes to wing and also an often striking bill pattern, buffish-yellow with black tip. Female brown with dark scaly markings on breast-band. In fresh plumage in autumn both sexes have more pronounced pale fringes creating scaly pattern, and on 1st-winter female no paler breast-band is apparent. In all plumages conspicuous pale fringes to wing which are also visible in flight, looks paler and wing appears more translucent against light. Tail also appears longer in flight than Blackbird. In the Alps race *alpestris*, with broader and more conspicuous pale fringes, some males with more dark brown-grey (as opposed to black) ground colour. Song varies considerably: chattering, with basic theme 2−4 fluting whistles, e.g. 'tiulee, tiulee' or 'tchrreet tchrreet', sometimes followed by a twittering sequence as in Redwing. On take-off or when alarmed a scolding 'tuk uk uk uk', sometimes merely 'tchep', and a clearer rolling 'chuirr'. Fairly shy, but more inclined than Blackbird to settle in open on a bush or tree (Blackbird usually flees into bushes). In N Europe breeds relatively sparsely on steep rocky banks and slopes, scree slopes, locally (Norway) at sea level; in Britain a moorland bird. Common in mountains of C and S Europe, often in alpine coniferous forest. Both races winter in Mediterranean region. Summer visitor to Britain Apr−Sep, also passage migrant (e.g. in lowland fields) Mar−May and Aug−Nov. *Map p. 416*

Fieldfare Mistle Thrush

Blackbird   *Turdus merula*   L 24–25 cm

Male entirely black with orange-yellow bill and eye-ring, female dark brown with slightly paler brown throat and breast. Juv. dark brown with ochre mottling and shaft streaks. 1st-summer male has brown flight feathers and partly dark bill. Lives to great extent on ground and often escapes under a bush, protesting with a series of tongue-clicking 'chak' calls which change into a shrill metallic screeching. Also makes presence known with a piercing high 'sree' and a thin indrawn 'tseeh'. Song can be heard from resident males as early as Jan/Feb and continues through to Jul. Song consists of a few well-articulated meandering or yodelling flute-like notes followed by a more chuckling second section. Breeds commonly in all types of woodland with rich undergrowth, in parks and in gardens, also in more open scrub. Food consists of worms, snails and insects together with various berries and fruits. Partial migrant in Britain, where also very common passage and winter visitor from N and E Europe late Sep–Mar (May).

Fieldfare   *Turdus pilaris*   L 25.5 cm

Common in N Europe, and the most frequently observed of the spotted thrushes in Scandinavia. Fairly unmistakable with its grey head, cold reddish-brown back and arrowhead spots below. In flight shows white underwings and wedge at leading edge of wing. Voice is, like Magpie's, croaking, impossible to describe but nevertheless characteristic. Most often heard is a croaking 'chak-chak-chak (-chacharrr)' like the sound from a large pair of garden shears; in migration flight a thin 'seee'. Song, delivered in flight or from top of a tree, is a virtually tuneless squeaky babble with interspersed chatters. Often associates with other thrushes on short-grass fields, first locating worms by hearing and then extracting them; also eats a lot of fruits and berries. Often nests in loose colonies, preferring tall park-like birch or pine wood and often in town parks; also in mountain birch forest and even on treeless tundra, where nests on buildings or man-made constructions. Migrates late, often in flocks in Oct–Nov. Often seen in large flocks in association with influxes of cold air from north (in Sweden also called 'snow magpie', heralding the first snows). A few pairs breed in Britain, where mainly a common passage and winter visitor late Sep–Apr, chiefly Nov–Mar.

Ring Ouzel

Blackbird

Fieldfare

416

♂

Blackbird

♀

Fieldfare

Redwing   *Turdus iliacus*   *(Rannoch) A loud, evenly descending + soft warbling series of shaken notes*   *L 21 cm*

Easily recognised by its distinctive facial markings and rusty-red flanks. At a distance the white to rusty-buff supercilium is its most conspicuous feature. In flight, distinguished from Song Thrush by its thin indrawn 'tsüeep' call. Song is in two parts: first a few loud flute-like notes and then a low, usually prolonged and vehemently delivered twitter. The fluted notes vary greatly, but, as the birds imitate one another, usually only one type is heard within any one area. A common variant is a rolling 'chirre, cherre, churre', dropping in pitch, like accidentally slowing down a gramophone record by touching it. Quite often just a rapid 'teecheu-teecheu' is heard. Also utters a muffled 'kuk' and has a hard rattling alarm. Breeds in lower and bushier terrain than Fieldfare, a characteristic bird of Scandinavian mountain birch forest. In winter on fields and in open woods. Migrates at night, end Sep to Oct, returning Apr—early May. In Britain a scarce breeder in Scotland, but common and widespread winter visitor.

Song Thrush   *Turdus philomelos*   *L 23 cm*

Rather like Mistle Thrush in markings, but smaller, shorter-tailed and lacks latter's pale edges to wing feathers. In flight shows rusty-buff underwings, easily told from Redwing by its flight call, a short ticking 'zip' or 'tik'. Song varied, with soft fluted notes and mimicry, consists of abrupt phrases which are spoken rather than sung; each phrase is repeated 3—4 times and then, after a short pause, a new one takes over. Habitually sings at dusk. In Britain and Ireland is common in parks and gardens and in woodland, often feeds on lawns; in Scandinavia and eastwards relatively shy, breeds in most types of woodland, most abundantly in rather damp and mossy coniferous or mixed forest with rich undergrowth. Feeds on worms, snails, insects and various fruits and berries; smashed snail shells on stones are often the work of a Song Thrush. Mainly resident in Britain, where also passage and winter visitor from N and C Europe during Sep—Apr (May).

Mistle Thrush   *Turdus viscivorus*   *L 27 cm*

A big, heavy and rather long-tailed thrush. Like Song Thrush in markings, but has pronounced pale grey fringes to wings and dark spots on sides of breast often merge in a dark band. Flight is markedly undulating, with wings closed pigeon fashion during gliding phase. Rump slightly paler, more buff than rest of upperparts, and characteristic white tips to outer tail feathers often visible on alighting (see p. 416). In most cases it is the flight call, a dry rattling 'rrrrr', that reveals that a Mistle Thrush 'is in the air'. Song recalls Blackbird's in tone and a sluggish Song Thrush's in form, consists of short fluting phrases with well-marked pauses. Often sings when other thrushes are silent and not infrequently in poor weather, e.g. light rain. Breeds in larger gardens and parks, woods, orchards, shows liking for conifers; in winter often in fields. Feeds on worms, snails, insects, fruit and berries. Mostly resident in Britain, with some from Continent Sep—Apr.

Redwing

Song Thrush

Mistle Thrush

418

Redwing

winter

Song Thrush

juv

Mistle Thrush

Savi's Warbler　　*Locustella luscinioides*　　　　　　　　　　　*L 14 cm*

Most closely resembles River Warbler, but warmer brown above and with plainer breast. Differs from Reed Warbler in its darker brown colour above and a distinct olive-brown tone across breast, often showing as obscure blotches, and also has longer undertail-coverts which are pale-tipped. Its rather jerky movements, tail-bobbing and tendency when alarmed to 'tumble' down into vegetation also distinguish it as a *Locustella* species. Creeps or walks on ground (base of reeds) with rather measured steps, like a Tree Pipit. Occurs relatively commonly mainly in reedbeds and indeed usually sings from a reed stem. Song is like Grasshopper Warbler's, but is faster and lower in pitch, if anything a dull buzzing. Call an abrupt 'pitch', when excited a hard chatter. Very rare summer visitor to SE Britain, Apr—Aug.

River Warbler　　*Locustella fluviatilis*　　　　　　　　　　　*L 13.5 cm*

Distinguished from Grasshopper and Savi's Warblers by combination of unstreaked grey-brown upperparts and indistinctly streaked or spotted breast. Also has unusually long pale-tipped undertail-coverts. Secretive and difficult to detect other than by song, which is prolonged and mechanical in character and reminiscent of a sewing-machine, 'tze tze tze tze...'; tone is electrical and very hypnotic, recalls a wart-biter bush-cricket. Chooses a more elevated songpost than Grasshopper Warbler, usually 2—5 m up in a bush or tree. Found in wooded swamps, rows of alders, willow scrub or similar terrain along rivers, streams, ponds or other waters, also in interior of damp woodland. Very rare vagrant to Britain, May—Sep, incl. in song in summer.

Grasshopper Warbler　　*Locustella naevia*　　　　　　　　　　　*L 13 cm*

Unobtrusive and when not singing difficult to detect, usually creeps around among weeds and grass. Not over-shy, however, and occasionally clambers up inquisitively among the plant stems, energetically bobbing tail (characteristic of *Locustella* species). If flushed, it flies off a short way, rather jerkily, and the obviously rounded tail is often seen. Gives a dark and diffusely streaked impression, olive-brown above and with dirty-white or yellowish underparts. Breast often has a tinted band and a tendency to streaking towards throat, some showing clearly streaked breast. All have dark streaks on rear flanks and on undertail-coverts. Has faint supercilium. Song consists of a monotonous insect-like reeling at high frequency, which can carry on for hours with only short pauses. Sings from a low bush or tall weed, most intensively at dusk and dawn. Call a hard, slightly explosive 'stit'. Occurs in rank meadowland and marsh fringes, often on canal banks and along ditches. Feeds on insects. Arrives Apr—May and departs Aug—Oct. Rather uncommon and local in Britain.

Savi's Warbler

River Warbler

Grasshopper Warbler

420

Savi's Warbler

River Warbler

Grasshopper Warbler

Lanceolated Warbler   *Locustella lanceolata*   L 12 cm

Very difficult to separate from Grasshopper Warbler. Is smaller and shorter-tailed and normally has more clearly and more distinctly streaked breast, especially on lower part and on breast-sides. Crown and mantle are more streaked (on Grasshopper more like 'spots'). Tertials have narrower and more distinctly defined pale edges and wing is slightly shorter. The dark shaft streaks on undertail-coverts are narrow and of uniform width, on the most heavily marked individuals club-shaped or oval; on Grasshopper they are arrowhead-shaped, i.e. broadest at base and narrowing towards tip. Ground colour of undertail-coverts dirty-buff to rusty-buff, with relatively distinct pale tips to longest pair. In spring usually buff to grey-buff below with very distinctly defined breast and flank markings (on Grasshopper spots are more diffuse). 1st-winter usually has a tobacco-brown colour, lacking olive-green elements. Song very like Grasshopper Warbler's. Skulking and difficult to flush, keeps well concealed low in vegetation. Breeds in scrub or woodland, preferring damper areas with dense undergrowth. Vagrant to W Europe from Siberia, mainly Sep and first half Oct, but also a few in Jun.

Pallas's Grasshopper Warbler   *Locustella certhiola*   L 13.5 cm

Somewhat bigger than Lanceolated Warbler and with some features of Sedge Warbler owing to its prominent supercilium, its dark crown, virtually unmarked underparts and reddish-brown rump. Tail is characteristically patterned: underside looks dark grey-black with pale greyish tips except on central pair of feathers, above is red-brown with dark bars. Tertials have a pronounced pale tip or a spot on inner web towards tip. Some individuals are like Sedge Warbler in tone, while others are rich rusty-brown above like Moustached Warbler. Seems to migrate in partial juv. plumage: birds trapped in W Europe in Sep show juv. features, with paler crown, less prominent pale supercilium and yellowish underparts. Song like beginning of Sedge Warbler's song: e.g. 'tik-tik-tik-tik svaya-svaya-svaya kurrekurre swee-swee-swee-swee'. Frequents rank grassy or weed vegetation with some bushes, normally beside ditches, streams, marsh and other wetlands. Extremely rare vagrant to W Europe from Asia, majority on Fair Isle, Shetland, in Sep.

Graceful Warbler   *Prinia gracilis*   L 10 cm

Often difficult to catch sight of but very noisy. Nondescript pale grey-buff, delicately dark-streaked above, and with long tail which points in various directions. Tail feathers are black and white at tips. Male has a faint cinnamon tone to crown, a peering eye with pale nut-brown iris, and a strangely black mouth interior. Bill and mouth are black during breeding season on male, brown on female. Song varies somewhat in pitch, consists of a monotonously repeated 'zerr-vit', 'zoorr-lüt' or the like, usually with a characteristic hypnotic ring, sometimes a more Linnet-like 'steer-lit'. Characteristic penny-whistle trill often follows a song phrase. Also has a short mechanical ticking call, 'plit plit'. Locally common in areas with scrubby ground vegetation, often at marsh edges with rushes and tamarisks. Often keeps in small groups; flight like Bearded Tit's.

Scrub Warbler   *Scotocerca inquieta*   L 10 cm

In the field rather different from Graceful Warbler; has slightly elongated body with large flat-crowned head, and legs appear to be placed far back. In Middle East race *inquieta*, with pronounced dark eye-stripe, grey or greyish-white supercilium, black-streaked crown and faintly streaked mantle/back. In western N Africa race *saharae*, paler, looks faded and has unstreaked mantle/back. In semi-desert with bushes; secretive but often hops about in open on ground beside bushes.

1st-cal autumn
Grasshopper Warbler

Lanceolated Warbler

1st-cal autumn
Lanceolated Warbler

Pallas's Grasshopper Warbler

♀

♂ summer
Graceful Warbler

Scrub Warbler

Lanceolated Warbler

Graceful Warbler

Scrub Warbler

Fan-tailed Warbler   *Cisticola juncidis*   L 10 cm

Distinctive by its small size, tail markings and contrastingly patterned mantle. Difficult to see but active and noisy. In bouncing flight or from cover of grass gives a single or repeated, mechanical hard 'plit' (alternatively 'kwit' or 'chet') like a diminutive Redshank. The song proper is a rhythmically repeated hypnotic 'tzet' delivered in a bouncing flight in wide circles: rapid series of wingbeats to reach top of an undulation, the 'tzet' is uttered, bird drops a little, then rises again and so on. With each series of wingbeats the tail is fanned, which in low morning sun produces a regular twinkling from up in the sky. Common to sparse in occurrence on open grasslands, e.g. in stands of sedge and rush, in fields and grassy banks, but not tied to water. Feeds on insects. Resident.

Cetti's Warbler   *Cettia cetti*   L 14 cm

Looks relatively large and robust, with dull plumage of grey and chestnut-brown and with broad rounded tail which is often cocked. In Middle East race *orientalis*, which is less reddish-brown above and paler below than nominate *cetti* in southern Europe. Is always 'jittery', extremely retiring and difficult to observe, but has very loud voice. Song is an explosive outburst of abrupt and bubbling notes, e.g. 'plüt...püt, plütiplüt plit plüti plüti plüti', often provoked by disturbance. Also has a drawn-out rolling 'pling', like clockwork toy being wound up, and a loud abrupt 'pitch', also a Reed Bunting-like 'teeh'. Common in swamp vegetation and among dense thicket along all types of watercourses, typical habitat is overgrown ditches. Feeds on insects and berries. Resident.

Moustached Warbler   *Acrocephalus melanopogon*   L 12.5 cm

Resembles Sedge Warbler but is considerably more brownish-red, in fresh plumage almost chestnut-coloured above and with warm rusty-brown flanks and breast-sides, often with a rusty-tinted faintly streaked band across breast. In eastern part of range is less reddish-brown and more like Sedge Warbler. Head contrastingly patterned, with blackish-brown crown, dark grey-brown ear-coverts and a broad greyish-white supercilium. Sedge Warbler has buff-white supercilium, paler central crown and paler ear-coverts. Is unobtrusive, moves about low in reeds and often hops on ground. Often holds tail raised, and when alarmed it flicks and bobs it nervously. When foraging, it gives a loud harsh double-churr, 'trr-trr', when tail-flicking a hard very short 'tcht', and when irritated (by e.g. a conspecific or the like) a drawn-out 'tr-trrrrrr'. Song is like Reed Warbler's but less harsh, and contains clear, mellow notes and trills, characteristic being subdued high 'lü lü lü lü'. Occurs in dense shore vegetation, especially reedbeds and bulrush stands. Resident in southernmost Europe, and in winter the only representative there of the *Acrocephalus* warblers.

Fan-tailed Warbler

Cetti's Warbler

Moustached Warbler

424

Fan-tailed Warbler

Cetti's Warbler

fresh

worn

Moustached Warbler

Great Reed Warbler *Acrocephalus arundinaceus* L 19 cm

Size of a small Song Thrush. Like Reed Warbler in coloration, but has more prominent supercilium, rather grey-tinted face, and bill is obviously heavier. Song like Reed Warbler's but considerably coarser in tone and very loud, consisting of themes repeated 1−3 times, both hard creaking sounds and high falsetto notes and squeaks; phrases usually introduced with two hard creaky 'k' notes, e.g. 'Krr-Krr, tsep, kerretsiep, tsee-e, tsee-e, kerre-kerre, kreek-kreek-kreek, chee, chee...' like an unoiled stone-crusher. Call a hard 'krek' almost like Moorhen; fledged young beg with frog-like 'kvaik'. Occurs in reedbeds, on smaller ponds and canals as well as in extensive stands of reed. Migrates in Aug−Sep, returning Apr−May. Vagrant to Britain (mostly in south), mainly May−Jun, often in song.

Sedge Warbler *Acrocephalus schoenobaenus* L 13 cm

Has conspicuous buff or greyish-white supercilium, dark stripe through eye and an 'angry gape-line'. In addition has dark crown, dull grey-buff and lightly streaked mantle, pale wing panel, rusty-buff flanks and cinnamon-coloured rump. Imms. in autumn often have a distinct brownish-buff central crown-stripe and faintly spotted or speckled breast. Song resembles Reed Warbler's, but is more lively and varied with long voiced trills and sequences, often introduced with accelerating creaking 'trr' notes, and includes mimicry. Sings from a branch or reed stem, often performs short fluttering song flight in middle of singing. Call a hard 'chek' like Lesser Whitethroat and a dry, straight and fast churring 'trrr', on rare occasions given twice. Occurs in rank shore vegetation, usually in reeds or sedge swamp with bushes as well as along overgrown ditches and ponds. Food mostly insects. Migrates in Aug−Sep (Oct), returning in Apr−May.

Aquatic Warbler *Acrocephalus paludicola* L 12.5 cm

Secretive and rather *Locustella*-like in actions and behaviour. Snipe-like stripes on head, with broad yellow-buff supercilium and crown-stripe. Mantle has distinct black-brown stripes centrally bordering two broad yellowish-white stripes. Back, rump and uppertail-coverts are streaked, which is exceptional on Sedge Warbler. Tail is rounded but feathers more pointed. On ad., breast is streaked at sides (often also in centre) and down onto flanks. 1st-winter individuals are bright straw-coloured, breast lacking or with very little streaking, have strikingly pale, slightly greyish primaries and very pale, almost pearly-pink legs. Song more monotonous than Sedge Warbler's, composed on the whole of two notes, e.g. 'errr-dididi', without tempo changes. Call a tongue-clicking 'chak' or 'chek' and a dry churr. Occurs uncommonly on waterlogged tussocky meadows, in marshland and around watercourses with unbroken stands of mainly sedge. Migrates west and southwest in Aug−Sep and then found rarely in W Europe (mostly imms.); returns end of Apr to mid May.

Great Reed Warbler

Sedge Warbler

Aquatic Warbler

Great Reed Warbler

Sedge Warbler

1st-winter

1st-winter

Aquatic Warbler

Blyth's Reed Warbler   *Acrocephalus dumetorum*   L 12 cm

Markedly 'colourless', greyish-buff above with a touch of olive-green on rump, wing lacking contrast. 1st-winter slightly warmer in tone. 'Sullen' face, with flatter forehead and longer bill than Marsh Warbler. Supercilium most pronounced above lores, is more prominent than eye-ring. Wing shorter and more rounded than on Marsh (6 primary tips visible), with emargination on 3rd and 4th primaries (counted from outermost, 1st being tiny), the 3rd discernible in the field, falling short of longest secondary (see also p. 11). Legs darker than on Marsh. Song delightful and varied, usually composed and with well-spaced phrases as in Song Thrush. Repeats themes 5−8 (2−10) times, typical theme has two sections: 1−2 hard or tongue-clicking sounds followed by musical whistling or yodelling (often expert mimicry), e.g. 'trek-trek CHUEE' or 'chrak-chrak CHU-EE-LOO'. Sings at night, often from 3−7 m up in tree or bush. Call a fairly soft 'chek', when excited 'chek-tchr'; alarm 'trrrr'. Occurs in bushy terrain, e.g. at forest and marsh edges, in dense regenerating growth, etc. Very rare vagrant to Britain, mainly late Sep−Oct.

Marsh Warbler   *Acrocephalus palustris*   L 12.5 cm

Difficult to separate from Reed and Blyth's Reed Warblers other than by song. Brownish-buff above with faint olive tone and warmer buff rump; whitish lemon-buff below, sometimes with buff flanks. Has a gentle expression, with more rounded head shape than Blyth's Reed, and pale eye-ring predominates over supercilium. Best distinction is its more contrasting wing: tertials dark with well-defined pale fringes, primary tips (8 visible) have pale border, usually visible in field. Emargination on outer web of 3rd primary falls outside longest secondary. Song very lively, full of mimicry, flowing and liquid with trills and warbles like Bluethroat; interweaves diagnostic nasal 'tzay-beee'. Both sexes sing. Call a short, somewhat variable 'chek' or 'tret', and a slightly rattling 'terrrrr' as from a dry seed-case. Scarce to locally common in rank herbaceous vegetation, e.g. in nettles and cow parsley, typically along ditches and in marsh. Migrates Aug−Sep, returning from mid May. In Britain rare local breeder and rare on passage.

Reed Warbler   *Acrocephalus scirpaceus*   L 12.5 cm

Warmer buff above than Marsh Warbler, with rusty-toned rump and darker legs. Head elongated, with long flat forehead/crown and with pale eye-ring predominating over short supercilium. Ad. often has 'angrier' expression than Marsh, partly owing to pale iris. Song monotonous and grumpy: a stream of hard, short, grating and nasal notes, always with rolling 'r', repeated 2−4 times, with interwoven mimicry; most like Sedge Warbler's, but slower and lacks latter's tempo changes and high vocal trills. Call a low 'kresh' or 'kek-kshe' or shorter 'kche'; alarm a drawn-out rattle, coarser than Marsh Warbler's, 'krrrrr'. Tied to reedbeds, but on passage also in bushes. Migrates Aug−Oct, returns from mid Apr.

Blyth's Reed Warbler

Marsh Warbler

Reed Warbler

Blyth's Reed Warbler

1st-winter

Marsh Warbler

1st-winter

Reed Warbler

Clamorous Reed Warbler   *Acrocephalus stentoreus*   *L 18 cm*

Slightly smaller than Great Reed Warbler, with which most easily confused, but has proportionately longer and more rounded tail, shorter primary projection and more elongated bill. Coloration varies: in Palestine often darker brown with all dark bill and less pronounced supercilium. Song much like Great Reed's though sharper in temp, with fewer high cracked notes, repeats themes 3−4 times; a characteristic phrase sounds like 'rod-o-petch iss'. Occurs locally in reeds or other tall marsh vegetation.

Thick-billed Warbler   *Acrocephalus aedon*   *L 18 cm*

Size of Great Reed Warbler, with strikingly long tail, short wings, rounded head and broad and thick bill. Reed Warbler coloration, with obvious eye-ring. Occurs in Blyth's Reed Warbler habitat, not tied to water, sometimes perches in open on top of a bush. Song melodious and varied with high clear whistles. Call a loud 'chok-chok'. A C Asiatic species a few autumn records in W Europe.   *Not illustrated*

Paddyfield Warbler   *Acrocephalus agricola*   *L 12 cm*

Like a cross between Reed and Sedge Warblers. Short-bodied and with short wings and long tail. Warm brown above, darker than Reed Warbler, though 1st-winter is more pale grey-buff (sometimes with faint olive tone), with distinct rusty tone to rump and tail base. Underparts strikingly pale, throat whitish with a pale wedge on neck-side, and faintly rusty-buff flanks. Has broad whitish supercilium, accentuated by narrow dark border above. Bill relatively short, looks rather thrush-like in that it is dark with yellowish base to lower mandible. Actions lively, often raises and flicks tail. Song has fast tempo and high pitch, most like Marsh Warbler's but lacks latter's tempo changes and long running trills, is more monotonously chattering and has fewer rasping or clicking calls, includes mimicry; lacks Reed Warbler's thick grating elements. Call a soft or relaxed tongue-clicking 'dzak'. Breeds at lowland wetlands with reeds, mainly in the dryer parts with some bushes and herbaceous plants. Very rare vagrant to NW Europe, mostly Jun−Oct.

Booted Warbler   *Hippolais caligata*   *L 11.5 cm*

Phylloscopus-like owing to its small size and rounded head shape. Relatively short-winged and long-tailed. Sandy-buff or pale brownish-buff above. Has pale supercilium accentuated above by a barely discernible darkish border. Lores are pale as on all *Hippolais*; sometimes a faint eye-stripe is apparent. Flight and tail feathers often look faded on outer web, tail feathers have dirty-white tips and outer ones a narrow whitish edge. Legs pale buff-pink (*cf* Olivaceous Warbler). Song like a speeded-up Garden Warbler's, a hurried chatter reminiscent of the twitter at the end of Redwing's song. Call 'tsek', short and terse like two pebbles being struck together, often repeated 3−4 times; alarm 'trek-k', not unlike Stonechat. Occurs in shrubbery and osiers, usually in open country and beside wetlands, also gardens, wood edges, etc. Rare vagrant to NW Europe from Asia, mostly Sep–Oct.

Clamorous Reed Warbler

Paddyfield Warbler

Booted Warbler

Clamorous Reed Warbler

Great Reed Warbler

Paddyfield Warbler

1st-winter

summer

Booted Warbler

Olivaceous Warbler

Olive-tree Warbler *Hippolais olivetorum* L 15.5 cm

Noticeably bigger than Icterine Warbler, looks dingy grey above with pale wing panel over tertials and greater secondary coverts. Dirty-white below, occasionally with faint sulphur-yellow tinge to breast and throat. Has long straight forehead (males defending territory often raise crown feathers, producing steep forehead and angular head), long and powerful yellow-orange bill and pale supercilium in front of eye. Rare, but locally fairly common in open, often bushy deciduous wood, often in oak forest and olive groves. Relatively shy and keeps concealed within foliage. Song harsh and raucous (Great Reed Warbler quality), usually long repetitive sequences of regularly repeated phrases, e.g. abrupt 'kuchok' and 'kerre'. Call a hard sharp 'tuc' or 'tzek'. Migrates in Aug, returning early May.

Olivaceous Warbler *Hippolais pallida* L 13 cm

Most easily confused with Marsh and Reed Warblers, especially in autumn when many have a warmer buff tone, also very like Booted and Upcher's Warblers. Strikingly pale and insipid, and also slender and attenuated in shape. Coloration varies from sandy-buff to pale brown-grey or greyish with faint olive tinge above; dirty-white below, in fresh plumage often with warm buff tone to flanks. Has bland facial pattern, with faint but clearly discernible supercilium, often a noticeable 'angry' gape-line, and a broad bill base (though narrower on race *elaeica* in E Mediterranean region) which from below is bright pale yellow (orange on Reed Warbler). Song is surprisingly like Reed Warbler's but is faster and more liquid. Calls include in particular a varied 'chek' or 'tch', sometimes as 'chr' or drawn-out 'che-ch-ch', which is given frequently and is coupled with a downward dip of the tail; also has a 'trrrrr', like Sedge Warbler's but more drawn-out. Breeds mainly in semi-open bushy or scrubby terrain with scattered low trees, such as olive plantations, gardens and willow and tamarisk bushes along banks and ditches. Very common in E Mediterranean region and in parts of N Africa, fairly rare in Spain and probably partly replaced by Melodious Warbler. Migrates in Aug–Sep, returning mid Apr to early May. Extremely rare vagrant to Britain, Aug–Oct.

Upcher's Warbler *Hippolais languida* L 14 cm

Between Olivaceous and Olive-tree Warblers in size. Short-bodied with long tail, which it swings sideways like an excited shrike. Warm grey above, with contrasting darker grey-brown flight and tail feathers. Has pale supercilium, most prominent above eye and continuing a short distance behind it. Song not unlike Olivaceous Warbler's but repeats short phrases which have quality of a Whitethroat, perhaps most reminiscent of a magnified subsong of latter species. Call a hard 'chuk'. Sparse and local breeder in dry scrubland or plantations. Arrives late, not until May, and departs early.

Olive-tree Warbler

Olivaceous Warbler

Upcher's Warbler

Olive-tree Warbler

'fresh

Olivaceous Warbler

Upcher's Warbler

Melodious Warbler   *Hippolais polyglotta*   L 13 cm

Very like Icterine Warbler, but lacks or has not very prominent pale wing panel, more rounded head shape, and warmer, more brownish-green tone above. Below, usually distinct pale yellow (lemon-mousse), often with more intense yellow patch on breast, though underparts vary, can be whitish yellow-buff. Wings are shorter, so primary projection is only just half length of tertials (equal on Icterine). Legs brown (more grey on Icterine). Song is a prolonged, rapid and *Sylvia*-like babble; some individuals are masterly mimics, recall Marsh Warbler. Also has short song flight in which relatively rounded wing shape detectable. Call a varied chattering 'tchret-tret', usually given twice, and a short, soft and low 'chet' or 'tch'. Habitat as Olivaceous Warbler, often in willows and shrubs by water. Returns mid Apr to early May. In Britain, scarce migrant Aug–Oct, fewer May–Jul.

Icterine Warbler   *Hippolais icterina*   L 13 cm

Only slightly bigger than Willow Warbler, but with its upright posture and peaked crown and straight forehead looks quite big. Normally has obvious pale-yellow wash to underside and a pale wing panel with pale lores (i.e. no eye-stripe), pale yellow eye-ring and grey legs. Odd birds dingy buff-white below and sometimes, chiefly in autumn, lack conspicuous wing panel (ads. moult in winter quarters). Juvs. on autumn passage have less obvious wing panel than spring ad. Differs from *Phylloscopus* warblers in head shape and pale lores, from Melodious in pale wing panel, longer primary projection (equal to longest tertial) and grey (not brown) legs. Song is masterly, varied and rich in mimicry: each sequence is repeated 2–5 times, and often begins with Starling-like 'shrr, shrr, shrr…'; a characteristic high, slightly creaky violin-like note, e.g. gently meandering 'shoo leeu', is heard throughout. Call, a soft yet explosive 'tett e'eüt' or 'hippolüeet', is also interwoven in song, which gives away slow or atypical individuals; also has a nasal 'chep' or 'che', when excited often combined as 'che che che te-lü', the short staccato notes like House Sparrow chatter. Common to scarce in woodland edge, parks and gardens with plenty of undergrowth, sometimes in open forest dominated by conifers. Migrates Aug–Sep, returning Apr–May. In Britain, scarce migrant Aug–Oct, fewer Apr–Jul.

Melodious Warbler

Icterine Warbler

Dartford Warbler

Marmora's Warbler

Tristram's Warbler

434

Melodious Warbler

Icterine Warbler

1st-cal autumn

Dartford Warbler   *Sylvia undata*   L 13 cm

A small dark bird with long tail and short wings giving characteristic silhouette. Male looks all dark grey from behind, but has dull wine-red colour on throat, breast and belly-sides; throat feathers have small white tips, often forming indistinct pale moustachial stripe. Females duller, imms. especially being paler and more rusty-buff below. Belly often clearly demarcated white. Buff or warm ochre bill base and sometimes reddish gape. Nine times out of ten shows pale patch at alula, lacking on Marmora's Warbler. Often fearless but mostly keeps well hidden, reveals itself by a slightly varied drawn-out 'tchrairr' or 'tr-tchiairr'. Best seen when male sings from bushtop or in brief song flight: a short verse of scratchy and; compared with e.g. Subalpine Warbler, quite deep notes in same tone as call, e.g. 'tchuirr-trr-uirr-trr-uirr-tchirr', sometimes more sustained and vacillating; a few very sombre, slightly rattling 'ter ter ter-ter' notes may be inserted. Relatively common in low maquis and garrigue. Resident or partial migrant. In Britain confined to gorse heathlands in extreme S England.   *Map p. 434*

Marmora's Warbler   *Sylvia sarda*   L 13 cm

Usually looks rather uniform grey with paler belly. Has long tail and markedly long bill with conspicuous pale base, pink to raspberry-red on race *balearica* in Mallorca and more yellowish on nominate *sarda*. On ad. male the red eye and orbital ring stand out against the dark grey head. Legs straw-yellow to pink. Mainly younger females have more dark brown upperparts, white eye-ring, dirty-buff legs and dark brown iris. Calls: when feeding usually a somewhat variable low 'drrrt' or 'kchurr', sometimes not unlike House Sparrow's 'chirrp'; alarm (when excited) a short 'sleet'. Song pattern like Dartford Warbler's but higher and less harsh, often with a short clearer trill popped in or as a terminal flourish. Sings from top of bush or in song flight. Locally common in Mallorca, mainly in dry maquis near coast, in Corsica and Sardinia, mainly on mountain slopes up to *c*900 m. Behaviour and habits as Dartford Warbler's. Nominate race a partial migrant to N Africa; *balearica* mostly resident. Feeds on insects, spiders and berries, incl. *Ephedra*. Recorded once in Britain, in May–Jul 1982.   *Map p. 434*

Tristram's Warbler   *Sylvia deserticola*   L 12 cm

Like a Spectacled Warbler in behaviour and shape, but longer-tailed. Ad. male more obvious, whereas younger males and females are close to Spectacled in coloration, though throat usually shows more rusty tone setting off a whitish moustachial stripe. Calls frequently, a short muted 'trck' or 'trick-it'. Endemic in Atlas Mountains in scrub or open forest in mountains or hills. Partial migrant, some moving south in winter to low-lying semi-desert areas.   *Map p. 434*

Tristram's Warbler

Dartford Warbler

♂

juv

♀

juv

♂ Mallorca

Marmora's Warbler

♀

Subalpine Warbler *Sylvia cantillans* L 12 cm

Smaller than Lesser Whitethroat. Male ash-grey above, dingy orange to dark reddish-ochre below on throat and breast, with red orbital ring and white drooping moustache. Females vary: full adult like 1st-cal-year male, with faint rusty tone to throat and tendency towards white moustache and usually with orange orbital ring and yellowish-white eye-ring; other females (2nd-cal-year) pale grey-buff, some with completely dirty-white underparts. In autumn very like Lesser Whitethroat, but with paler ear-coverts, colder grey rump and pale legs (buff to flesh-coloured). Male sings from a bush, low down in tree or in song flight: a continuous *Sylvia* chatter (varying in length), fast and scratchy but with clear and sometimes yodelling passages. Subsong slow and hesitant, can recall Sedge Warbler, also includes mimicry. Call like Lesser Whitethroat's but lower and softer, 'che' or 'che-rr'. Relatively common in maquis and open wood with scattered bushes, found commonly in mountain regions up to 1500 m. Migrates end Aug—Sep, returning mid Mar—Apr. Vagrant to Britain, mostly May—Jun.

Spectacled Warbler *Sylvia conspicillata* L 12 cm

Resembles a very small short-tailed Whitethroat. The rusty-red wing/shoulder is conspicuous at long range and normally the blackish tertial centres are well defined. Male dark greyish-pink below with sharply demarcated white throat; grey head with dark grey-black lores (sometimes also forehead) and pale eye-ring. Female overall markedly pale, spring ad. pale grey-brown above; 1st-winter of both sexes warmer buff, with contrast between upper- and underparts fairly small. Legs pale ochre or almost orange. Ad. has ochre to reddish-ochre iris, on 1st- and 2nd-cal-year female iris appears dark in the field. Call a very typical rattle, 'trrrrrrr', rattlesnake-like and fairly prolonged, also a short 'tek'. Usually sings in song flight, a series of sharp rolling and squeaky notes, e.g. 'tsee-u kyirrerirr etrirr chirr', most like Stonechat. Subsong includes melodious variations on the call. Occurs in areas with low scrub and taller herbaceous vegetation, typically in garrigue and shrub steppe of semi-desert type. Moves restlessly between low bushes, hops around on ground and now and then shows itself on top of a bush or plant. Partially resident; European birds migrate to northern Sahara, returning Mar—Apr.

Desert Warbler *Sylvia nana* L 11.5 cm

Has ochre to orange iris, pale eye-ring and pale yellowish legs. In Asia race *nana*, pale grey-brown above with slightly rusty-toned wings and obviously rusty tail and rump. In Sahara *deserti*, which is paler and more yellow-buff in colour. Call a short harsh sound followed by a rattle, 'kasch-chur-ur-ur-ur-ur-ur' (Israel). Very much a desert species, often around lower bushes, hops on ground. Often associates very closely with Desert Wheatears. Very rare vagrant to N Europe from C Asia, mostly late autumn (the five British records being in Oct—Dec).

Subalpine Warbler

Spectacled Warbler

Desert Warbler

2nd-cal ♀

Subalpine Warbler

♂

ad ♀

Spectacled Warbler

♂

♀

nana
Desert Warbler

1st-winter ♀
Spectacled Warbler

Garden Warbler   *Sylvia borin*   L 14 cm

Uniformly grey-buff without contrasting features. Has gentle facial expression with rounded crown, clear eye-ring. At close range slight nuances in plumage noticeable: mouse-grey neck-sides and a warmer tone to belly-sides. Tertials and primaries have pale tips, well visible in field. Skulks in vegetation in luxuriant mixed woods and scrub with dense undergrowth. Hides in foliage and makes presence known mostly by its song, a rather monotonous babbling of soft clear notes, most like Blackcap's but lacking latter's high flute-like notes. Otherwise fairly silent, but has tongue-clicking alarm, 'chek', rhythmically repeated; rarely, gives low 'vachr'. Feeds on insects and berries. Arrives normally later than Blackcap and Lesser Whitethroat, from mid Apr but mostly May; migrates Aug–Sep, with passage to late Oct/Nov.

Lesser Whitethroat   *Sylvia curruca*   L 13.5 cm

Generally grey-brown above with browner wings, grey crown and nape and darker grey ear-coverts. Varies somewhat: some are paler, more grey-buff above and with darker ear-coverts barely noticeable, others dull brown and with contrasting slate-grey ear-coverts. Differs from Whitethroat in dark legs, brown wings without rusty fringes and lack of or only faint eye-ring (usually beneath eye). In autumn sometimes more patterned on face, with eye-ring (though always broken at front and rear) and an indistinct supercilium. Siberian race *blythi* has been recorded as a vagrant in Europe: in fresh winter plumage has paler and warmer brown tone above, especially on tertial fringes, and whiter underparts lacking contrast between dirty-tinted breast and white throat typical of nominate *curruca* in Europe. Song a short rattle on one note (wooden rattle); also has a *Sylvia*-type chatter, often as subsong or as introduction to the rattle, and this on its own is difficult to distinguish from Whitethroat's corresponding song. Call a tongue-clicking 'chek', becoming harder and louder if agitated. Occurs in semi-open terrain with bushy vegetation, e.g. sloe, juniper and young spruces. Feeds on insects and berries. Migrates Aug–Oct to E Africa, returning Apr–May.

Whitethroat   *Sylvia communis*   L 14 cm

Differs from Lesser Whitethroat in paler iris and clear white eye-ring, pale legs, longer tail and brownish-red fringes to secondaries. Male in spring often has pink tinge to breast contrasting with white throat and a touch of grey on crown. 1st-winters (and females also in 2nd cal-year) have brown iris. Song is a sprightly but chiefly blustering little verse, easily committed to memory; at beginning of breeding season in particular, a continuous chatter more like Garden Warbler's song is also heard. Call when alarmed or excited characteristic, a nasal 'ved, ved, ved', sometimes interwoven in song; also a drawn-out 'dchaer' and a harder 'chek'. Breeds in sun-exposed sites with bushes and weedy thickets, wooded pasture, ditch banks and field and wood edges. Arrives Apr–May, departing Aug–Sep, with passage migrants to Oct.

Garden Warbler

Lesser Whitethroat

Whitethroat

Garden Warbler

Lesser Whitethroa

1st-winter

♂

Whitethroat

1st-winter

Blackcap   *Sylvia atricapilla*   *L 14 cm*

A large, uniformly grey-toned warbler with a distinctive jet-black cap, female more grey-brown with rusty-red cap. Often difficult to see once trees are in leaf; noticed chiefly by song, an attractive rippling melody in which introduction is squeaky, fumbling for the right notes, only to change suddenly into a fluting display of soft well-articulated notes. Song is usually shorter than Garden Warbler's, but interwoven mimicry of latter and other species and sometimes more prolonged chattering can make it difficult to separate the two. Call and alarm a hard 'tek', harder and more vigorous than Garden Warbler's; also a 'cherr' and, when really alarmed, 'tek-tek-tek-tyekcherrr'. Requires dense yet airy woodland, from mixed deciduous wood to town parks. Arrives in Britain from late Mar (a couple of weeks earlier than Garden Warbler), though most in Apr−May, departing Aug−Sep; passage migrants also mid Aug−Oct (Nov) and small numbers overwinter Britain. British and W European Blackcaps migrate southwest and are common in winter around W Mediterranean (some reach tropical W Africa), while birds breeding east of a line cutting through Scandinavia migrate southeast.

Barred Warbler   *Sylvia nisoria*   *L 15 cm*

A large warbler. Ad. in spring appears dark at distance, grey with a tinge of brown above and pale below with dark wavy barring. Yellow iris characteristic, orange-yellow on ad. male, dirty-yellow on female and 1st-summer male, and sepia or brownish-buff on 1st-summer female. 1st-winters in Aug−Sep are generally sandy-coloured and not very barred, have dark iris and can be confused with Garden Warbler; however, have paler fringes to median and greater coverts (slight suggestion of wingbars), paler fringes to tertials and rump, and also usually have faint dark markings on undertail/vent. Also Barred is bigger, longer-tailed and heavier-billed, and its movements slower, almost Wryneck-like. Often shy. Sings from bushtop or in butterfly-like song flight; song like a slow Garden Warbler's in pattern, like a deep-voiced Whitethroat in tone with interwoven harsh 'arrr' sounds, is most often noticed by its rattling (moped-like) drawn-out call, 'arrrt-at-at-at-at'. Prefers open sun-dried bushy areas with hawthorn, sloe and juniper. Migrates Aug−Sep to E Africa, returning latter half May. In Britain a scarce passage migrant, mostly east coast, Aug−Oct (mostly 1st-winters), rare in spring.

Arabian Warbler   *Sylvia leucomelaena*   *L 14.5 cm*

Most easily confused with Orphean Warbler, but slightly smaller, longer-tailed and has shorter primary projection; bill smaller, and eye always looks dark in field. Head recalls Sardinian Warbler: entirely black without contrastingly darker ear-coverts and with white throat; often has broken whitish eye-ring which Orphean lacks in spring. Females and 1st-summer male have more slate-grey or brownish-black hood. Long tail strikingly dark, contrasts with grey upperparts, is swung downwards unlike in other *Sylvia* species. Song a sequence of varying length, not unlike Upcher's Warbler, sometimes recalling Blackcap's meandering sections but with coarser, more raucous voice, does not have Orphean's repetitions. Call 'chack-chack', not unlike Red-backed Shrike's alarm. Breeds in areas with acacias, along Red Sea north to Arava valley in S Israel.

Blackcap

Barred Warbler

♂

♀

Blackcap

1st-winter

♂

Barred Warbler

Rüppell's Warbler *Sylvia rueppelli*   *L 13.5 cm*
Male unmistakable. Ad. female occasionally almost like male; most have dark-mottled throat and forehead, with pronounced submoustachial stripe. 1st-winter and 1st-summer females have pale throat; differ from Sardinian Warbler in greyer mantle/back and paler fringes to secondaries and greater coverts. Call when foraging a flat 'chrr', on take-off occasionally 'chirr', when alarmed a Barred Warbler rattle in miniature, 'cherr r'r'r'r'r'; also a 'plüt' or 'plit' like dripping water, which is often drawn out into a staccato almost like Cetti's Warbler. Song is gravelly, often prolonged and monotonous, 'trr trr chit tit chrr trr...', occasionally more squeaky and vocal with Serin-like features. Relatively common in maquis, often among juniper and Kermes oak, also in oak forest with dense undergrowth. Returns from end Mar, departs Aug−Sep. Extremely rare vagrant to Britain.

Sardinian Warbler *Sylvia melanocephala*   *L 13 cm*
A typical Mediterranean bird. Size of Lesser Whitethroat, fairly robust with short wings, energetic movements and often cocked tail. Male distinctive, with velvety-black head, greyish-white throat, grey body, red orbital ring and dirty-red iris. Ad. female has grey head (occasionally almost black) and red orbital and eye-rings. Juv. has warm brown tertial fringes and white eye-ring. Male acquires red orbital and eye-rings as early as 1st-winter plumage (Aug−Sep); post-juv. moult normally includes inner secondaries, some moult completely in summer of 1st cal-year. Iris cinnamon-brown on 1st-cal-year male, brown on 1st-cal-year female. Female relatively dark, with clear contrast between throat and breast. Race *momus* in Middle East has whiter throat and paler fringes to tertials as on Rüppell's and Cyprus Warblers. Most characteristic call is a sudden, startlingly loud burst like a stuttering engine, pitch varying with mood; usually of 4−6 syllables, 'chret-tret-tret-tret-tret', or 'tetwee-tik-tik-tik-tik'. Alarm a prolonged stutter; also utters solitary 'chett' or 'tche' and softer 'ju'. Song is a persistent verse of creaking and squeaky notes, sometimes forming a prolonged chatter. Occurs in maquis and in bushes. Resident, but many move south in autumn. Rare vagrant to Britain.

Orphean Warbler *Sylvia hortensis*   *L 15 cm*
Clearly bigger than e.g. Sardinian Warbler, and iris yellow on ad. Juv. has dark iris, gradually becoming paler, 1st-summer females normally have grey-brown iris. 1st-winters are like 1st-winter Barred Warbler, but with darker ear-coverts and lacking latter's scaly pattern. Western populations have very simple song, 2−4 syllables, fairly coarse and deep, e.g. 'tchrrüe, tchrrüe, tchrrüe, chrrrree-ü' or 'trr chüt pyu-pyu-pyu chrüt-chrüt-chrüt'. Eastern birds (Balkans) have a fuller song, sometimes not unlike Nightingale's. Call a Blackcap-like but deeper 'tchak' and a rattling 'trrrrr', which when irritated can become staccato. Fairly common in taller maquis, plantations, wooded hillsides. Shy. Extremely rare vagrant to Britain.

Rüppell's Warbler

Sardinian Warbler

Orphean Warbler

Rüppell's Warbler ♀

♂

Sardinian Warbler

♂

♀

Orphean Warbler

♀

♂

♂
Cyprus Warbler

♀ 1st-winter

♂

Ménétries's Warbler

Cyprus Warbler   *Sylvia melanothorax*   L 13 cm

Most like Rüppell's Warbler in build and general impression, and with similar silvery-grey fringes to tertials and greater coverts (though brown on juv. and grey-brown on 2nd-cal-year female). Tertials and 1−2 inner secondaries are replaced in 1st autumn. Male has black hood and dark-mottled throat and breast, always with obvious white moustachial stripe, eye reddish-brown and with flesh-coloured to reddish orbital ring and to varying degree white eye-ring. Ad. female similar to male in the field, but has graphite-grey hood and slightly more brown-toned mantle. 1st-summer female has darker iris, grey-brown head with or without odd darker blotches but always with characteristic spots on throat and breast. 1st-winter female often lacks visible spots below. Gives staccato 'tchurr tchurr tchurr', softer and weaker than Sardinian Warbler's, and on take-off a 'tchit' or 'tchüt'. Song a *Sylvia* chatter, less coarse than Sardinian's. Breeds only in Cyprus, common in most areas with dense scrub. Partly resident, but many migrate south to southeast, to Sinai, Arabian Peninsula and Egypt.

Ménétries's Warbler   *Sylvia mystacea*   L 12.5 cm

Somewhat smaller and shorter-tailed than Sardinian Warbler. Active, and tail frequently in motion. Male has black ear-coverts and forehead, merging gradually into grey-brown mantle; usually pink or faintly reddish-ochre on breast and throat, outlining pale submoustachial stripe. Female also paler below, more buff, without Sardinian Warbler's dirty-brown breast-sides. Wings have paler sandy-coloured fringes. Eye often with pale eye-ring, chiefly in 1st−2nd cal-years and on female and thus more like Subalpine Warbler. Iris brown in 1st−2nd cal-years, reddish-brown on ad. male. Occurs in thickets and scrubland, e.g. next to plantations and along water-courses. Song softer and more musical than Sardinian's. Call a 'chak' or buzzing 'chrrr', and a staccato 'cha-cha-cha-cha' like Rüppell's Warbler.

Cyprus Warbler
♂ juv–1st-winter

Rüppell's Warbler
♀ winter

Cyprus Warbler
♀ winter

momus 1st-winter ♀
Sardinian Warbler

Subalpine Warbler
♀ winter/1st-winter ♂

1st-winter
Lesser Whitethroat

1st-winter
Barred Warbler

1st-winter
Orphean Warbler

bonelli

Bonelli's Warbler

orientalis

Chiffchaff
collybita winter

Bonelli's Warbler   *Phylloscopus bonelli*   L 11 cm

Small and pale. Greyish above with bland washed-out face, especially at lores, and often with complete thin pale eye-ring, whitish underparts; has contrasting green edgings to wing and tail feathers and green rump. Western race *bonelli* somewhat paler and more grey-green and has darker tertials with paler fringes; eastern *orientalis* more dirty-grey above and with less conspicuous green wing edgings, is easier to confuse with Chiffchaff. Behaviour like Willow Warbler's. Song an insignificant short trill, 'chee chi chi chi chi', not unlike a very clear Greenfinch trill or Cirl Bunting's song. Call of *bonelli* 'tuee-e', longer and more piercing than Willow Warbler's, of *orientalis* a characteristic short 'chip', like distant Crossbill or newly fledged House Sparrow. Relatively common in woodland in mountain districts, mainly in open or low oak forest or oak-mixed forest. Departs Aug–Oct, returning Apr. Rare vagrant to Britain.

Willow Warbler
yellow-green individual

Wood Warbler

duller individual

Wood Warbler *Phylloscopus sibilatrix* *L 12.5 cm*

Bigger than Willow Warbler, long-winged and broad-shouldered and with short and broad tail which from below give it an elliptical triangular shape. Usually brightly coloured, with moss-green upperparts, pale yellow face/breast and striking pure white underparts. Tertials have contrasting yellowish-white fringes. Less full-coloured individuals, with almost grey upperparts and with only a faint dirty-yellow tinge to face, occur rarely. Song silvery, a series of ringing 'zip' notes which accelerate and merge into a metallic shivering trill. Call a distinctive, slightly plaintive 'tiuh', also repeated as a song, 'tiuh-tiuh-tiuh-tiuh-tiuh' like Wryneck. Often moves about high up in foliage, typically in crouched horizontal posture hopping like a Garden Warbler. Locally common in tall-stemmed, airy deciduous or mixed woodland. Migrates early, in Aug, returning from mid Apr.

Wood Warbler

Willow Warbler

Chiffchaff

Willow Warbler *Phylloscopus trochilus*   *L 11.5 cm*

Abundant in N Europe. Very like Chiffchaff, but has longer primary projection, paler legs, is usually paler above and yellower on throat, breast and supercilium; north-ernmost populations are more washed-out, more brownish-grey and often lack yellow in plumage. Young on autumn passage in 1st-winter plumage often entirely yellow below, northern ones more yellow-buff or pale buff. Autumn ads. show contrast between yellow breast and white belly. Song a melancholy languorous verse which descends and falls away in clear notes, the beginning being sometimes Chaffinch-like and ending in a short flourish. Call a soft 'hueet', Common in all types of woodland and scrub with deciduous element. Migrates Aug—Sep (passage through Britain to end Oct), returning from Apr.   *Map p. 449*

Chiffchaff *Phylloscopus collybita*   *L 11 cm*

Slightly smaller than Willow Warbler, often drabber grey-green, has dark legs and generally less yellow in plumage. Primary projection shorter than on Willow Warbler, especially on British and W European race *collybita*. Latter is smaller, shorter-winged and darker greenish-brown above than Scandinavian race *abietinus*, and supercilium is often poorly marked, especially behind eye; *abietinus* in autumn are never bright yellow below like imm. Willow. Race *tristis* from Siberia turns up very rarely in NW Europe, mainly in Oct—Nov: lacks visible yellow in plumage, often has darker cheeks (tobacco-brown or slightly sooty), has jet-black legs and darker bill. Eastern Chiffchaffs in autumn often show a diffuse greyish wingbar. Song is a jolting series of notes irregularly put together, 'silt, salt, salt. silt, silt, salt...'. Call very like Willow Warbler's, but more monosyllabic, 'hweet'. Race *tristis* has a distinct 'tee-U', with accentuated but lower final vowel than European Chiffchaffs (resembles call of Hume's Yellow-browed Warbler). Other eastern Chiffchaffs with *tristis* characters utter uninflected 'heet' rather like Thrush Nightingale. Breeds in deciduous and mixed woodland, in north of range also in pure coniferous. Arrives earlier than Willow Warbler, from mid Mar, and departs Aug—Oct, passage continuing through Nov; winters commonly in S Europe. Small numbers also winter Britain, where also numerous on passage.   *Map p. 449*

Radde's Warbler *Phylloscopus schwarzi*   *L 12 cm*

Rather more robust and large-headed than Willow Warbler, with relatively thick and short bill, heavy supercilium and pale yellowish- or greyish-pink legs. Conspicuous supercilium is reinforced by a broad dark eye-stripe and dark-mottled ear-coverts. Supercilium often ochre-tinted in front of eye. Upperparts dark olive-green with warmer green tone to primary fringes. Underparts dirty-white to sulphur-yellow on 1st-winters, with to varying extent darker breast-sides and rusty-yellow vent. Call is tongue-clicking in character but lower in pitch than Dusky Warbler's, with a muted or restrained ring, 'tuk' or 'tuk-tch', does not recall Lesser Whitethroat and in particular the double call is diagnostic. Very skulking, keeps low down in vegetation. Vagrant from Siberia, mainly in Oct.

Dusky Warbler *Phylloscopus fuscatus*   *L 11 cm*

Long and distinct supercilium and pale flesh-coloured legs distinguish this species from Chiffchaff. Has browner upperparts, more neutral grey-white underparts, thinner bill and more neat head shape than Radde's Warbler. Supercilium is dirty-white to faintly rusty-tinted; if any difference in tone is visible in front of or behind eye, it is always whitest in front (reverse applies on Radde's). Call short, always simple and like Lesser Whitethroat, 'chek', fairly loud in the field. Habits as Radde's, but less tied to low vegetation. Vagrant from Siberia, mainly in Oct.

Willow Warbler

summer

1st-winter

abietinus
winter

abietinus
summer

collybita
summer

Chiffchaff

tristis
winter

Radde's Warbler
1st-winter

Dusky Warbler
1st-winter

Arctic Warbler   *Phylloscopus borealis*   L 12 cm

Slightly larger and stouter than Willow Warbler, appears larger-headed and has strikingly long and heavy supercilium accentuated by a broad dark eye-stripe and dark-mottled ear-coverts. Has short whitish wingbar (autumn birds often have suggestion of second wingbar on median coverts). Tertials remarkably lacking in contrast. Compared with Greenish Warbler, has heavier bill, more patterned ear-coverts and tinted flanks. Song a monotonous stutter on one note (sometimes shifting between two or three pitches), somewhat similar to Bonelli's Warbler's but longer (2.5–3 seconds) and straggling slightly towards end. Call a sharp Dipper-like 'tzri' or 'tziet', harder and more piercing when alarmed. Very rare and irregular breeder in Scandinavia, usually on luxuriant brookside gullies and slopes with mountain birch. Mainly a Siberian species. Winters in SE Asia and does not return to Scandinavia until mid Jun. Autumn vagrant to W Europe.

Greenish Warbler   *Phylloscopus trochiloides*   L 11 cm

Smaller than Willow Warbler, often with more peaked crown and straighter forehead, looks large-headed and 'short-naped'. Very active, moves nervously. Plumage generally colder and greyer, with long pale yellow to greyish-white supercilium, short dirty-white wingbar (rarely, may be worn off in spring) and darker legs. Tertials plain. Belly often uniform greyish-white, occasionally with faint buff tinge but never obviously yellow. Song bustling, impulsive, begins with the 'zlee-vit' call (very like Pied Wagtail) and continues with a short jerky phrase, accelerating towards end, of very clear and piercing notes, often ending abruptly, like Wren song. Occurs in woodland, often in spruce or mixed forest and typically close to ravines or slopes. Spends much time high up in branches. Migrates southeast in Aug, returning latter half of May. Vagrant to Britain in autumn (mostly Aug), with fewer in spring (mostly Jun, often in song).

Two-barred Greenish Warbler
Phylloscopus (trochiloides) plumbeitarsus   L 11 cm

Possibly a race of Greenish Warbler; replaces latter in easternmost Siberia and in China. Behaviour and calls as Greenish, but has an obvious second wingbar on median coverts and the greater-covert bar is broader and runs along the whole row of coverts. Is also somewhat darker above, has more contrast on tertials and also in head markings, with darker crown and more pronounced eye-stripe behind eye. Recorded once in Europe, in Isles of Scilly, England, in Oct 1987.

Green Warbler   *Phylloscopus (trochiloides) nitidus*   L 11 cm

Very like Greenish Warbler, is identical in behaviour and song, but greener above, more like a Wood Warbler, and has sulphur-yellow tone to breast, throat and supercilium. Call often trisyllabic. Breeds in woodland and bushy areas.

Arctic Warbler

Greenish Warbler

Green Warbler

Willow Warbler
northern

1st-winter

Arctic Warbler

1st-winter

Greenish Warbler

1st-winter
**Two-barred Greenish
Warbler**

Green Warbler

Yellow-browed Warbler   *Phylloscopus inornatus*   L 10 cm

Smaller than Chiffchaff, strikingly contrasty with long yellowish supercilium and double wingbar. Tertials usually have broad whitish fringes towards tip and other wing feathers are white-tipped. Indistinct central crown-stripe. Ground colour varies somewhat, often warm moss-green above and dirty-white below but can be more grey-green above. Overall impression in spring/summer sometimes more grey-green and with worn wing feathers lacking pale fringes. Calls often, a longish indrawn 'tsueeht' often with peculiar lisping tone. Song a short verse of call-like notes, e.g. 'tseeuh cheweeht cheweeht'. Nervous, moves jerkily, often up in treetops. Annual vagrant from Siberian taiga, mainly mid Sep−Oct.

Hume's Yellow-browed Warbler   *Phylloscopus (inornatus) humei*   L 10 cm

Very like Yellow-browed Warbler, of which it is perhaps a race. Is paler and greyer above, with less contrasting markings on wing feathers, and lacks or has only poorly marked upper wingbar. Whole wing looks more uniform in colour with only one broad pronounced wingbar. Can be confused with Greenish Warbler, but differs in broader and more distinct wingbar and paler tips to tertials and suggestion of central crown-stripe. Legs blackish and bill darker than on *inornatus*. Call a clearly double-note 'tze-veet' or 'slee-wee', can be likened to a slowed-down version of Greenish Warbler's. Song consists of a drawn-out, descending, slightly Redwing-like note. Very rare vagrant from mountain regions of C Asia.

Pallas's Warbler   *Phylloscopus proregulus*   L 9.5 cm

Barely size of Goldcrest, looks large-headed, has broadly striped head and overall is contrastingly patterned in green, yellow and white. Can be taken for a Goldcrest but most likely to be confused with Yellow-browed Warbler, though has distinct yellow crown-stripe and yellowish rump. Call a high 'heeht' or slightly inflected 'hueeht', sharper and straighter than Chiffchaff's but can approach latter's. Vagrant from Siberia, annual in Britain mainly in Oct−Nov.

Goldcrest   *Regulus regulus*   L 9 cm

Goldcrest

Europe's smallest bird (with Firecrest). Male has bright orange base to feathers of crown-stripe, yellow on female. Reveals its presence in wood by a high trisyllabic 'see-see-see', more sibilant in tone than Coal Tit's call. Song a high, rising and falling 'seeh sissisyu-see sissisyu-see siss-seeitueet' (*cf* Treecreeper). Juv. lacks crown-stripe. Prefers coniferous or mixed wood, especially with spruce. Often accompanies tits in autumn/winter. Large influxes to Britain from Continent, Sep−Apr.

Firecrest   *Regulus ignicapillus*   L 9 cm

Firecrest

Differs from Goldcrest in its broad white supercilium, dark eye-stripe and heavy 'cheek-pouches'. Male has orange crown-stripe and both sexes have faint bronzy tinge to shoulders. Song simpler, increasing in strength towards end, 'sissisisisitt'. Call like Goldcrest's, also a more tit-like piping 'peep' rhythmically repeated. Found in all types of wood in C and S Europe. In Britain, rare breeder in south and scarce passage and winter visitor from Continent Sep−Apr (often in bushes).

Yellow-browed Warbler
1st-winter (Oct)

Hume's Yellow-browed Warbler
1st-winter (Oct)

Pallas's Warbler
1st-winter (Oct)

Goldcrest

♀

♂

Firecrest

♀

♂

Pied Flycatcher   *Ficedula hypoleuca*   L 13 cm

A pot-bellied, short-tailed passerine which makes sallies after insects in the air. Male normally sooty-black or slate-grey above in summer plumage, but some individuals brownish-grey like females (white forehead patch distinguishes them from females). Birds from W Europe generally more black than birds further east; Siberian race *sibirica* predominantly grey. Birds from N Africa *speciguiera* with large white spot on forehead as well as bases of primaries also have all black tail and sometimes white half-collar. After moult in Jul–Aug both sexes are brownish above and virtually inseparable in the field, though males have blacker uppertail-coverts and tail. 1st-winters in Aug–Sep often have a few median coverts with faint pale tips. 1st- and 2nd-cal-years often lack any visible white at base of primaries. Song consists of a clear ringing but slightly melancholy verse, composed of 3–6 different themes delivered in varying sequences, e.g. 'tseelü tseelü tseelü weecha weecha tsekewee tsekewee tsekewee shrüü', sometimes with interwoven mimicry of e.g. Tree Pipit, Great Tit or Blackcap. Song can be confused with Redstart's. Call a sharp clear 'pwit' or 'huit', often combined with tongue-clicking 'tett' which is sometimes extended into a brief rattle. Breeds commonly in most woodlands and areas with old gardens which offer cavities for nesting; readily accepts nestboxes. Very retiring during moult in Jul–Aug, starts to migrate from mid Aug, returning Apr–May. Local breeder in Britain (in north and west) but more widespread on passage from N and E Europe, especially Aug–Oct (fewer in Apr–Jun).

Map p. 458

Collared Flycatcher   *Ficedula albicollis*   L 13 cm

Male markedly more contrasty than Pied Flycatcher, with white neck-band, pale grey rump and large white forehead patch. Females in spring often difficult to separate from female Pied, are normally more grey in tone, have paler rump and tendency towards pale neck-boa. On all Collared in female-type plumage, the best feature compared with Pied is call and the white patch at base of primaries, latter being broader and more distinct and thickening slightly towards bottom. Winter plumage very like Pied's, though ad. male has large white patch at base of primaries and black wings; 1st-winter normally has more obvious pale spots on row of median coverts forming a second wingbar (cf Semi-collared). Hybridises with Pied Flycatcher on Gotland in S Baltic; male hybrids have incomplete neck-band or with elements of grey in the band in nape area and also have less white at primary bases. Song consists of a slow squeaking and scraping, often with brief final flourish; occasionally a few clear 'zeetlü, zeetlü, zeetlü...' or similar Pied-like passages are also interwoven. At all times gives itself away by its frequently used and distinctive call, an indrawn 'heep' not unlike alarm call of Thrush Nightingale. Alarm a hard 'pik', often combined with call 'heep-pik, pik-...pik...'. When foraging, also has a dry rattle. Occurs most numerously in older deciduous woods and shady gardens. Mainly a C and SE European species; isolated outpost in S Baltic on Gotland (common) and on Öland (local), where returns first half May and departs latter half of Aug. Very rare vagrant to Britain, mostly May–Jun.

Map p. 458

Semi-collared Flycatcher   *Ficedula semitorquata*   L 12.5 cm

Summer-plumaged male has half neck-ring which varies in extent and wing markings most like those of Collared Flycatcher; however, has white tips to inner median coverts producing a second wingbar, but sometimes this merges with the white on greater coverts, producing one big wing patch. Black tail usually shows extensive white on three outermost feathers, separating males from hybrids between Collared and Pied as well as Pied from N Africa. In the brown-grey winter plumage, however, these tips (now pale grey) form an obvious second wingbar. This diagnostic wingbar is also possessed by summer-plumaged females, which are otherwise like female Collared. 1st-winter also has a striking cream-coloured second wingbar. (1st-winter Collared also often show a fairly obvious second wingbar.) Song most like Pied's. Call a high 'tseep', unlike Collared's, more lisping or impure-vowelled; also a tongue-clicking 'tsep' and a 'sree' like Spotted Flycatcher. Local in occurrence.   *Map p. 458*

1st-winter

♂ grey

♀

Pied Flycatcher

♂

1st-winter

Collared Flycatcher

♀

♂

1st-winter

♀

♂

Semi-collared Flycatcher

Spotted Flycatcher   *Muscicapa striata*   L 14 cm

This species' flycatcher mannerisms combined with grey-brown plumage, streaked crown and breast make it easy to identify. Its long flat forehead and peaked crown produce a characteristic profile. Moves elegantly and seriously in its pursuit of flying insects; makes clicking sound in air as it snatches with its broad mandibles at some insect. From its usually exposed perch it utters thin scratchy 'ptsirr' or 'tseeht' calls, often also 'tseet...chüp, chüp'. Song is very insignificant and consists of a few call-like drawn-out squeaks, well separated and drawn back and forth 3−4 times. Juv. pale-spotted above and mottled dark below. Common in open woodland and woodland edge, a characteristic bird of dry open pine forest, also in parks and gardens. Nest is placed on sheltered ledges or niches on broken trees, root piles, on buildings in roof recesses etc, often in very odd sites. Migrates Sep, passage Britain to mid Oct; returns rather late, end Apr−May.

Brown Flycatcher   *Muscicapa dauurica*   L 12 cm

Vagrant from Siberia. Small, compact, bold eye-ring, unstreaked forehead and diffusely streaked breast. Bill broad at base and with yellow base to lower mandible. Call a thin 'see'.   *Not illustrated*

Red-breasted Flycatcher   *Ficedula parva*   L 11.5 cm

Black-and-white tail pattern distinguishes this from other flycatchers (tail is frequently cocked). Always appears small, with alert posture and energetic movements. Eyes look big and the broad bill base often glistens yellow against the light. Male acquires red bib only at 2 or possibly 3 years of age. 1st-winter has variably sized rusty-yellow wedge-shaped spots at tips of tertials and greater coverts. On breeding ground often difficult to find spending its time up in the crowns of trees, where it moves about restlessly. Song is high and melancholy, easily overlooked; it is divided into two parts, an introduction resembling Wood Warbler's or Tree Pipit's song and a second half that dies away like Willow Warbler's. Commonest call a Wren-like dry rattle. Call used intraspecifically is a soft and melancholy 'tülee', also a slightly hissing 'shrrr'. Feeds on insects caught in the air and from branches and leaves in canopy. Breeds relatively commonly in E Europe in tall deciduous or mixed forest. Scarce migrant in Britain, mainly on east coast (in scrub, trees), mid Aug−Oct/Nov, with very few in Apr−Jul.

Spotted Flycatcher

Red-breasted Flycatcher

Pied Flycatcher

Collared Flycatcher

Semi-collared Flycatcher

Spotted Flycatcher

Red-breasted Flycatcher

1st-winter

♂

♀

Bearded Tit

juv ♀

Bearded Tit   *Panurus biarmicus*   *L 16.5 cm*

A tit-like long-tailed bird that lives in reedbeds. Often difficult to see. Male, with black drooping moustache, unmistakable. Ad. female pale buff (like last year's reeds) with contrasty wing markings like male, occasionally with dark lores and, rarely, also with dark markings on crown, often with dark streaks on mantle. Juv. straw-coloured, male with black lores and back stripe, female more uniform on body and head but with greyish lores. Juv. moults to ad. plumage in Jul–Sep. Often noticed by its characteristic twanging 'tying' and 'ping' calls, often rapidly and nervously repeated, sometimes followed by a drawn-out rolling 'chirrr'. Song low, a trisyllabic squeaking. Flight, usually low over the reeds, is slow and weak with whirring wingbeats. Highly productive, 3–4 broods per year; young hatched early may breed in same year. Population size fluctuates considerably; should it become too large, some birds move out to surrounding lakes in autumn, when they fly high up in flocks and move away in unexpectedly steady and fast flight. Feeds on insects, spiders, and for great part of year on reed seeds.

Penduline Tit   *Remiz pendulinus*   *L 11 cm*

A small tit-like passerine tied to marshy areas. Overall impression pale and with characteristic black mask. Female has smaller mask not extending up on forehead, is paler, more buffish-brown, on mantle and has less red-brown blotching on breast. Juv. pale grey-buff and without dark face markings. In most instances is noticed by call, a thin indrawn 'tsee' or 'tseeüh', sometimes a triple 'tsee-tee-tee'. Song is unobtrusive, almost like Coal Tit's, consisting of slow variations on the call (incl. mimicry?). Builds a large, skilfully constructed, pouch-shaped nest which is attached to the outer end of a twig usually suspended out over the water. One of the main materials in the nest is bulrush down; the species is also found at overgrown ponds, marsh fringes, along rivers and similar sites where bulrush occurs. Also requires stands of willows, poplars or other trees. Feeds mostly on insects. Vagrant to Britain, increasingly in recent years (population spread).

Bearded Tit

Penduline Tit

Penduline Tit
nest

♂   ♂   **Bearded Tit**   ♀

Bearded Tit
juv ♂

♂

Penduline Tit   juv

Willow Tit N Scandinavia

Willow Tit British Isles

Marsh Tit Scandinavia

Siberian Tit

Marsh Tit British Isles

Sombre Tit Balkans

Sombre Tit · *Parus lugubris* — L 13.5 cm

Big and long-tailed with a heavy bill. Grey-brown above, with a large dull brown hood and bib delimiting the relatively narrow white cheek. In Turkey race *anatoliae*, which is more neutral grey above and has black crown and chin. Relatively common in woodland and maquis, mainly in mountain districts. Resembles Great Tit in behaviour. In autumn and winter gathers in loose groups, sometimes with other tits. Voice very variable, many call like Great Tit; song is composed of a whistle, repeated rapidly 3−5 times, which is often coarser and more buzzing than Great Tit's, e.g. 'chewu-chewu-chewu-chewu', or based on 'dutewee-dutewee...' or 'pee-chüp'. Other calls include rather Blue Tit-like 'tsee tee cherrerrerrerr', 'tsitchewee cherwee cherwee', 'chee-ep', 'tseechup', a clear piercing 'tzeeh teeh teeh' etc. Resident.

Siberian Tit · *Parus cinctus* ~~ringing~~ — L 13 cm

A large-headed 'fluffy' tit with long tail, dark cocoa-coloured crown and rusty-tinged flanks (not very prominent in worn plumage). At all times is warmer and browner in tone than northern Willow Tits, the black bib also extends further down on breast and is more frayed at the edge; bill is also longer. Has a broad vocal repertoire, many calls are like Willow Tit's, such as e.g. a harsh 'chair-chair-chair' (often preceded by a short 'tsee' or 'tsitsee') and a short 'pseet'; also has Crossbill-like 'chüt chüt', a buzzing 'chee-err' and when excited a distinct 'peev peev'. Song a slightly hoarse 'chip chiep chiep chiep chiep' or a short series of soft chirpy syllables, e.g. 'ptsee-duy, ptsee-duy...' or 'ptsiti-duee, ptsiti-duee...'. Breeds sparsely to relatively commonly in woodland, both in deep coniferous forest and in montane birch forest. Resident and feeds on insects, spiders and seeds. During summer months food is hoarded in bark crevices, lichen clusters etc; in winter readily comes to food put out for birds and is quite fearless of man. Shows very slight tendency to autumn movements.

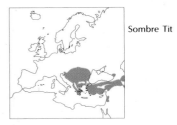

Sombre Tit

Siberian Tit

Turkey

Sombre Tit

Balkans

winter

Siberian Tit

summer

Willow Tit Scandinavia

Marsh Tit   *Parus palustris*   *L 11.5 cm*

Lacks Willow Tit's pale wing panel; in addition has smaller bib, gives impression of
having a smaller head and also has a glossier black cap. Juv. has a duller cap and Marsh
Tits in fresh plumage can show tendency towards pale wing panel. The two species are
most easily separated by call: Marsh has an explosive 'pitchou', a repeated sprightly
whistle, 'chiu-chiu-chiu', and a rapid grating 'psiche-che-che-che-che-che', also a
'tseet' very like that of other tits. Song is a series of monotonously repeated notes such
as 'chip-chip-chip-chip' or 'pichee-pichee…'. Frequents deciduous or mixed wood,
often near streams or lakeshores, and parks and large gardens. Feeds on insects and
seeds, incl. those of grasses and herbaceous plants. Highly sedentary.

Willow Tit   *Parus montanus*   *L 11.5 cm*

The pale wing panel, large head, more dull black crown and looser plumage distinguish
Willow Tit from Marsh Tit. Scandinavian race *borealis* is also paler. More southerly
races are browner on mantle and more dirty-buff below, and British race *kleinschmidti*
is even browner and has rusty-buff flanks. Differences within Europe and Scandinavia
are clinal, so that e.g. Lapland Willow Tits are purer white below than those in S
Sweden. Willow and Marsh Tits differ from each other in voice. Most characteristic of
Willow is its drawn-out harsh and nasal 'CHAY-CHAY-CHAY' or 'tsi-ti CHAY-CHAY';
short squeaking 'ti-ti' or 'sti-ti' calls are also given as contact call. Song is a
'siu-siu-siu-siu-siu' similar to Wood Warbler's, more rarely a buzzing 'zi-ze-zerrrl'. In
Britain and C Europe prefers swampy deciduous woodland areas along streams and
lakeshores; in Scandinavia Willow, in contrast to Marsh Tit, is associated most with
coniferous or mixed forest, but ascends to the birch forest in the mountains. Feeds on
insects, seeds and berries. Resident, but southward movements do occur, especially
from northern parts of breeding range. Race *borealis* is a rare vagrant to Britain.

Crested Tit   *Parus cristatus*   *L 11.5 cm*

Often makes its presence known first by its call. Well visible, unmistakable with its
characteristic head markings and uniform, drab grey-brown upperparts. Call is a rolling
or trilling 'prrululull' or 'prrulululee't'. Song, of same trilling character as call, alternates
between two pitches, 'TSEE'i'i-prrululull-TSEE'i'i-prrululull…'. Very much a bird of
coniferous forest, and in Britain confined to Caledonian forest of Scotland. Typically
encountered around stands of mature pine trees and seldom seen outside extensively
forested regions. Feeds on spiders, insects and various seeds, especially spruce and
pine seeds. Highly sedentary.

Marsh Tit

Willow Tit

Crested Tit

Marsh Tit

Willow Tit

Continental

Scandinavian

Crested Tit

Blue Tit   *Parus caeruleus*   *L 11.5 cm*

Smaller, paler and with more clear blue tones than Great Tit. Juv. has pale yellow also on head. In N Africa race *ultramarinus*, which has blue-grey mantle and dark blue crown. Song is delightfully clear, a continuous ringing 'pseet-see-sirrrrrrr'. In addition, often utters a jittery, rather 'cheeky' 'cherr err err err', a bouncing, silvery 'chee-dee-dee-dee' or 'ptsee-tsee-dee-dee-dee', a 'peezeetzay' and a thin 'psee'. As breeding habitat it prefers open deciduous or mixed woodland as in parks and gardens. In autumn and winter commonly found in reedbeds, where it feeds on insect larvae and pupae overwintering in the reed stems. Food mainly insects and their larvae and, to lesser extent than Great Tit, seeds and berries. Resident, but many move south from northern and eastern parts of breeding range during Sep−Oct, extensive migratory movements being noted more in some years than in others.

Great Tit   *Parus major*   *L 14 cm*

One of the commonest birds in woodland and gardens. Female has narrower band on underparts than male and often less intense colours; juvs. have slaty crown, more restricted dark throat and yellowish cheeks. Its richly varied vocal repertoire not infrequently gives rise to identification problems. Typically heard is a cheery 'tse weeda weet' or 'pink tche-che-che'. A ring particular to the species can nearly always be detected in the various calls, but at regular intervals one can be deceived by some odd vocal manifestation. Song is usually a pleasant seesawing sequence of repeated di- or trisyllabic whistles, e.g. 'tee-tee-tü' or 'twee-teet'. As early as Jan the first Great Tits can be heard singing on sunny days. Breeds in all types of woodland and garden habitats except pure coniferous forest. Food consists largely of oil-rich seeds and fruits, but in breeding season chiefly of insect larvae and other small animals. Resident, but like Blue Tit it erupts from N and E Europe on a large scale in some years.

Coal Tit   *Parus ater*   *L 11.5 cm*

Smaller and more large-headed than Great Tit, with greyish back, dirty-buff underparts and with white nape patch. Moves quickly and restlessly in tops of trees and among outer parts of branches. When foraging, utters a fairly insignificant 'pseet', occasionally 'psitseetsee'; other common calls are a clear, fluting and rather melancholy 'püht', a bright 'p-heet' and a Goldcrest-like 'si-si-si'. The several song variants can be likened to a diminutive Great Tit's, with a weaker and simpler structure. Alarm 'tsee see see see see' like Blue Tit. Prefers coniferous woods (often associates with Goldcrests), but also found in deciduous woods and gardens with at least a few confierss in proximity. Northern populations are at certain times of year dependent on spruce-cone seeds, and when food is short may undertake eruptive-type movements in autumn. Young are fed mostly on insects.

Blue Tit

Great Tit

Coal Tit

N Africa

juv

Blue Tit

juv

Great Tit

♂

♀

♂

♀

Azure Tit *Parus cyanus* L 13 cm

A tit with a long tail, recalls Blue Tit in markings but has fluffier plumage, is completely white below and has blue and blue-grey pattern. Has broad white wingbar and broad white tips to secondary and tail feathers. Occurs in deciduous and mixed wood, often beside wetlands. Behaviour and habits as Blue Tit, like latter often resorts to reedbeds during winter months. Hybrids with Blue Tit occur very rarely and can be difficult to tell from Azure Tit. Calls include a 'tsirr' and a 'tsee-tsee-dze-dze'. A C Asiatic species, only a vagrant to Europe outside Soviet Union. Recorded a number of times in Finland in recent years; several records from Poland during 1900s.

Long-tailed Tit *Aegithalos caudatus* L 12–14 cm

Represents a family of its own, Aegithalidae, and is, in several respects, unique. One of Europe's smallest birds in body volume, recalls a fluffy ball of wool with long tail attached. Northern/eastern race *caudatus* has the head all-white, British *rosaceus* and Continental *europaeus* have a broad dark band from forehead running over eye to nape; intermediate forms occur, and the border line is around S Denmark. Juv. has dark area through eye and over cheeks (narrower on *caudatus*), accentuating a pale eye-ring. In S Spain represented by race *ibericus*, which is generally darker and with stripy cheeks; in Asia Minor by *tephronotus*, with grey back, black bib and rather shorter tail than European birds. In mixed tit flocks Long-tailed immediately distinguish themselves by their short rippling 'tserrr' calls mingled with clicking 'tek' notes. In autumn and winter keep together in families in small tightly knit parties. When, on their roaming excursions, they have to pass over an open area, they gather together making urgent piercing trisyllabic 'tsee-tsee-tsee' calls, and then one after the other in succession they 'cross over', eagerly calling. Song is a thin trill similar to Blue Tit's. Occurs in bushy deciduous or mixed woods, often in swampy terrain near lakeshores and streams, also often in more open terrain with bushes and hedges. Feeds mostly on small insects and spiders. Builds a large elaborate nest decorated with lichens, ovoid with side entrance. Mainly sedentary, but roams in winter.

Azure Tit

Long-tailed Tit

Corsican Nuthatch

Algerian Nuthatch

Krüper's Nuthatch

Rock Nuthatch

Great Rock Nuthatch

Azure Tit

Long-tailed Tit
nest

Long-tailed Tit

Conti-
nental

Scandinavian

British Isles

juv
Continental

S Spain

Asia
Minor

Corsican Nuthatch   *Sitta whiteheadi*   L 12 cm

Endemic in Corsica and the only nuthatch breeding on the island. Breeds at 800—1200 m in forests of Corsican pine. Behaviour resembles that of Krüper's Nuthatch. Song a fast 'tutututututu', varied in tempo, reminiscent of a referee's whistle played at slow speed; also has a Jay-like call and other calls resembling those of Krüper's Nuthatch. Feeds on pine seeds and insects.   *Map p. 468*

Algerian Nuthatch   *Sitta ledanti*   L 12.5 cm

Endemic in coniferous and deciduous forest on two mountains in NE Algeria, discovered in 1975. Like Corsican Nuthatch, but slightly bigger and longer-billed; male has black crown (but not nape) and eye-stripe, female grey.   *Map p. 468*

Krüper's Nuthatch   *Sitta krueperi*   L 12 cm

A small, restless nuthatch which is often found high up in the tops of pines, where it works cones, though moves about at all levels in trees and even in bushes and on the ground. Eye-stripe strikingly narrow, black forehead-cap smaller on female. Character-istic rusty-red breast patch, which is expanded in threat/display posture. Most easily located by voice. Has Nuthatch-like 'veete-veete-veete-veete-veete' (like Black-tailed Godwit display), a peculiar nasal horn-like 'ue-ue-ue-ue', a low 'ksch', a varied 'kyehp' like a Jay in miniature, a more vocal 'kuay' or 'kueet' like a nasal Willow Warbler, and a woodpecker-like 'kup'. Relatively common, mainly in pine forests, from sea level up to the tree line; common also among spruce and cedars in the uppermost coniferous zone.   *Map p. 468*

Rock Nuthatch   *Sitta neumayer*   L 15 cm

Like a large, pale Nuthatch but with longer legs and bill. Usually hops about among rocks. Alert and active but 'coy', and often hides behind a rock or boulder. Has very striking voice. Song is varied, is very clear and penetrating: rather explosive start with an accelerating trill like Wood Warbler's, then changing into a sequence resembling introduction to Willow Warbler's song, and finally going into a rolling trill which turns into Tree Pipit-like '…chuwee…chuwee…chuwee' passages. Other calls also loud, e.g. 'kiu…kiu…', hard 'peet peet peet', sibilant 'pchay'. Occurs among rocks and ruins, also on maquis-covered slopes with scattered bare rocks, up to 2000 m above sea level.   *Map p. 468*

Great Rock Nuthatch   *Sitta tephronota*   L 20 cm

Bigger and larger-headed than Rock Nuthatch, with longer and more powerful bill. Eye-stripe longer and broader, especially towards nape. Noisy, calls like Rock Nuthatch's but lower in tone and slower in tempo.   *Map p. 468*

Algerian Nuthatch   **Great Rock Nuthatch**

Corsican Nuthatch

♂

♀

♀

Krüper's Nuthatch

♂

♀

Rock Nuthatch

Nuthatch   *Sitta europaea*   L 14 cm

Alert and chirpy, is constantly on the move and climbs in all directions on tree trunks and thicker branches. In British Isles and W Europe race *caesia*, which is rusty-buff on breast and belly. In Scandinavia *europaea*, which is white below. In both races the male is chestnut on vent (each feather white-tipped) and flanks, with sharp contrast against lighter belly; female is more rusty-buff, merging into rest of underparts. In Siberia *asiatica*, with shorter bill and tail, snow-white underparts with little or no chestnut on flanks and with typically white supercilium (short supercilium above eye may be seen on *europaea*). In most cases it is the call that reveals its presence among the old oaks, its preferred habitat. Song is a penetrating, almost falcon-like 'peeu, peeu, peeu...' or faster 'wiwiwiwiwiwi...'. Throughout the year, most intensively in autumn and spring, it also gives clear 'hwit', 'chut', nasal and voiceless 'gut', sharp 'sit, sit, sit' or 'pseet, pseet, pseet' notes. Young beg from nest hole with thin 'sree, sree...'. Common in open deciduous or mixed woods, parks and gardens, preferably with element of older oaks. Feeds on spiders, insects, nuts and seeds; often visits birdtables in winter. Plasters mud around opening to its nest hole so that entrance has the right dimensions. Resident. In some years *asiatica* emigrates and can reach N Fennoscandia (has bred there).

Short-toed Treecreeper   *Certhia brachydactyla*   L 12. 5 cm

Very difficult to separate from Treecreeper except by voice. Has longer and more curved bill and shorter hindclaw. Generally more buffish-brown above and dingier below, usually buff on flanks. Supercilium often less contrasting and dirty-buff in front of eye. Also shows small differences in wing pattern (see plate). Song, compared with Treecreeper's, is shorter, considerably more penetrating and also vehement and jolting in delivery, 'sit, sit, sittere-uitt'. Also a high piercing 'zrrieh' and a clear 'zeet'. Inhabits old deciduous woods, parks and avenues of trees, in Mediterranean countries also coniferous forest.

Treecreeper   *Certhia familiaris*   L 12.5 cm

Compared with Short-toed Treecreeper is normally more contrastingly marked, colder brown above, cleaner white below (especially in fresh plumage), and supercilium is purer white in front on forehead. Bill shorter and straighter. A nimble and delicate little bird which climbs spirally up trees in irregular spurts; once it has checked out a rough and insect-rich part of a trunk, it flits down to the lower part of the next tree to continue. It signifies its presence from time to time with loud, thin, piercing 'zrreeht' or 'zeeit' calls. Song has tone of a Wren and consists of a few call-like 'scraping' notes terminating in a thin trill. Often accompanies roving tit flocks. Inhabits woods and parks, in S Europe usually with conifers. Feeds on insects and spiders. Predominantly resident, but some migration takes place, particularly among eastern populations.

Nuthatch

Short-toed Treecreeper

Treecreeper

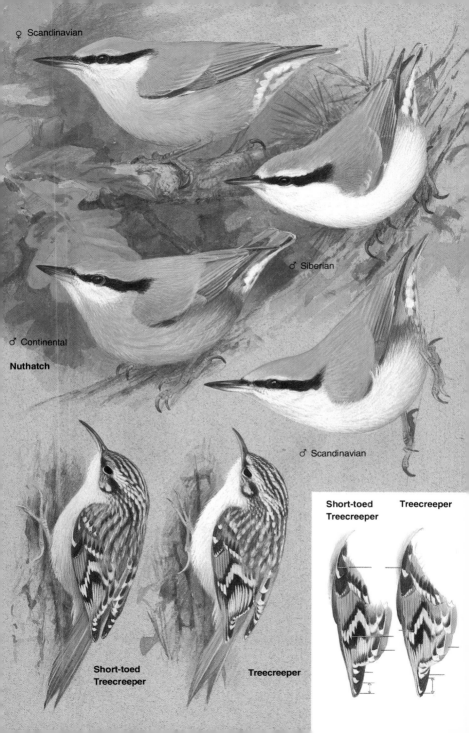

♀ Scandinavian

♂ Siberian

♂ Continental

Nuthatch

♂ Scandinavian

Short-toed Treecreeper

Treecreeper

Short-toed Treecreeper

Treecreeper

Wallcreeper

Wallcreeper *Tichodroma muraria* L 16 cm

Unmistakable. Both sexes have pale throat in winter; in breeding season female has pale throat and sometimes dark patch in region of crop. Creeps around on rocks and

cliffs and constantly flicks wings, producing flashes of the red wing patches. Call a thin piping and high whistles, e.g. 'tuee' or 'tuweeht'. Song variable, consists of repeated high whistles, e.g. 'ti tiu treeh...' increasing in strength and speed. Occurs locally and uncommonly on rocky precipices and in ravines, usually above tree line. In winter moves to lower regions, when also on buildings and ruins. Feeds on insects and spiders which it deftly extracts from deep clefts and crevices with its long slender bill. Extremely rare vagrant to Britain Sep–Jun (has wintered).

Fulvous Babbler

Arabian
Babbler

♂
summer

♀

Palestine Sunbird

Fulvous Babbler   *Turdoides fulvus*   L 25 cm

Body size that of a thrush, with Magpie-like long tail. Warm sandy-buff with rusty tone
on flanks. Typically seen in small parties gliding stiff-winged between low bushes. Often
not shy, but unobtrusive, appears suddenly. Occurs in desert tracts, in Morocco,
Tunisia and Algeria, mainly on sandy plains with low shrubs. Song is of 6 drawn-out,
slightly plaintive whistles dropping in pitch towards end. When flock moves, short,
slightly mechanical trills and short 'peep' calls are also heard.

Arabian Babbler   *Turdoides squamiceps*   L 26 cm

Wholly sandy-coloured with grey tone to head. Typically appears in small parties. Very
vocal, typically soft but piercing 'piu' or 'pi-chük', often in long series. Tied to arid
semi-desert areas with acacias, bushes or palm groves. Occurs around Arabian
Peninsula up to S Israel, where the sole representative of the genus.

475

Common Bulbul

Black-headed Bush Shrike

Palestine Sunbird   *Nectarinia osea*   *L 11 cm*

A very small bird with energetic actions; takes nectar, often found around flowering trees or bushes. Male looks black at distance but is glossy blue and purple; in Jul—Nov/Feb has a more female-like winter plumage, sometimes with scattered blackish feathers. Female and juv. are unassuming grey with faint brownish-green tone over back. Vocal repertoire varied, has several sharp and strikingly loud calls, normal call 'dju-wee' (recalls Scarlet Rosefinch); song a rapid series of high notes, e.g. 'chewi-chi-chi-chi-chi-chi'. Occurs in Middle East from S Lebanon and southward in a belt along coast of Arabian Peninsula.   *Ill. p. 475*

Common Bulbul   *Pycnonotus barbatus*   *L 19 cm*

A Blackbird-sized brown-grey bird, common in cultivated areas and a characteristic bird of gardens, orchards, palm-tree oases etc. Rather retiring, but makes presence known by its loud, obtrusive calls. Most often heard is a stumbling explosive series of bubbling sounds, 'pchuk uk uk pchuk uk uk...uk...uk', most like the that given by a startled Blackbird. Also has a number of short calls which can be bewildering coming from inside shrubbery, e.g. chattering, Fieldfare-like 'chak-ak' or 'pche-rr', but usually recognised by its bubbling, slightly stumbling tone. Sociable, often seen in twos or threes 'chattering' energetically (bubbling). Feeds largely on fruits and berries and is attracted to fruit trees, berry bushes and the like. Young are fed mostly on insects.

Yellow-vented Bulbul   *Pycnonotus xanthopygos*   *L 19 cm*

Similar to Common Bulbul but has white eye-ring and yellow vent. Behaviour, habitat and voice very similar to those of Common Bulbul. A common and obvious bird in much of its range.

Black-headed Bush Shrike   *Tchagra senegala*   *L 22 cm*

A rather odd bird, belongs to shrike family (Laniidae). Occurs relatively commonly in scrubland. Not shy but is unobtrusive and stays mostly on ground or low down in scrub. Hops on ground like a thrush. Undulating flight like that of Great Grey Shrike, usually low over ground. Has characteristic white spots on tail-tip. Usually silent but occasionally utters a grating call. Song startling, consists of clear fluting notes. Displays in circles high up in air with alternating glides and fluttering wingbeats.

Common Bulbul

Yellow-vented Bulbul

Black-headed Bush Shrike

Yellow-vented Bulbul

Common Bulbul

Black-headed Bush Shrike

Isabelline Shrike   *Lanius isabellinus*   L 18 cm

Fundamentally similar to Red-backed Shrike, but has longer tail, is paler and generally more sandy-coloured. Ad. has entirely grey-buff upperparts, black mask and rusty-coloured tail. 1st-cal-year autumn very like Red-backed, but paler, more grey-buff and less scaly above, has a pale buff patch at base of primaries, broader pale fringes to greater coverts and also rusty tail. Very rare vagrant to NW Europe from C Asia, mostly mid Aug to mid Nov.

Red-backed Shrike   *Lanius collurio*   L 17 cm

Male unmistakable, with combination of reddish-brown and black 'highwayman's mask'. Females vary somewhat in colour and rarely may have almost male-like features. Juv. is warm brown and scaly above, can be confused with juv. Woodchat Shrike. Song varied and rich in mimicry; sometimes it is flowing, almost as Marsh Warbler's, but just as often a restrained chattering. Call a slightly explosive and strained 'chev'; when alarmed near nest, utters a harder wheatear-like 'schak-schak-schak'. Breeds in open cultivated country, woodland clearings and bushy heaths, especially in thorny areas (sloe and hawthorn). Feeds chiefly on larger insects such as grasshoppers, beetles, bumblebees etc, but also takes small rodents and small birds. When food is in good supply it spears the surplus on thorns or branch ends and in this way the bird lays up reserves for days of bad weather and inferior supply of sun-loving insects. Arrives May in northern parts of breeding range, migrates to tropical Africa Aug—Sep. Virtually extinct as breeder in Britain, but seen on passage from Continent in May—Jun and Aug—Oct.

Lesser Grey Shrike   *Lanius minor*   L 20 cm

Like a small Great Grey Shrike but has proportionately longer wings and shorter tail. Besides black forehead, distinguishing features are also upright posture, contrast between white throat and pink breast, lack of white supercilium and only faintly white-edged shoulders. Juv. lacks dark forehead and has fine scaly pattern on upperparts. This plumage is gradually replaced in autumn by a winter plumage resembling that of ads. but still without dark forehead. Possibly ad. female also acquires pale forehead in winter plumage. Song chattering and varied, often with rather thrush-like whistles, trills and mimicry. In quarrels with e.g. others of same species gives a forced 'kschvee'. Common in open country with some element of tree clumps and bushes. A characteristic bird in E Mediterranean during migration periods in Aug—Sep and May, when often perches on telegraph wires beside fields and pastures. Feeds mostly on insects, especially larger ones such as grasshoppers and beetles, but also lizards, small frogs and other small animals. Very rare vagrant to Britain, May—Nov.

Ill. p. 480

Red-backed Shrike

Lesser Grey Shrike

Great Grey Shrike

Isabelline Shrike

phoenicuroides
1st-winter

♂

♂

1st-winter

Red-backed Shrike

♂

♀

Great Grey Shrike   *Lanius excubitor*   *L 24 cm*

A conspicuous bird which perches in open on top of a bush or tree or on a telephone wire. Has longer tail and more horizontal posture than Lesser Grey Shrike. Distinguishing features are its lack of black forehead, its white supercilium, white on the shoulders and strikingly short primaries. The white wingbar varies from a small patch at base of primaries to a substantial band across whole wing. In the swinging, undulating flight, series of rapid wingbeats alternate with glides on fully drawn-in wings. Well distributed in various races throughout W Palearctic, in Europe chiefly nominate *excubitor*. In Iberia and on French Mediterranean coast race *meridionalis*: darker above with less white on scapulars and supercilium and has greyish-pink underparts. Common in N Africa is race *algeriensis*: dark slate-grey above, lacks white supercilium and has grey underparts without pink tinge. In Sahara this grades into *elegans*, which is paler, has more white on shoulders and wings and whose range extends to the Sinai Peninsula, where it is replaced in remaining parts of Arabian Peninsula and along Red Sea coast by *aucheri*. Latter resembles *elegans*, but is darker above, has less white on wing and the black mask extends in a narrow band above bill. Song more primitive than other shrikes', chattering mostly with shrill and mouse-like vibrating trills and squeaking sounds mixed with harsh 'vaik' notes. Characteristic is a double note repeated monotonously at lengthy intervals, a short metallic 'schrük' or a nasal 'sheehk-sheehk'. Other calls are a clear ringing 'schrreea' and a drawn-out nasal 'eeh'. Feeds on all kinds of smaller animals, small rodents, smaller birds and insects. Stores up prey; passerines and rodents spiked on thorns give away its presence. Breeds in various open country in association with heath, clear-felled areas, bog or pasture. In Britain a winter visitor in small numbers Oct–Apr, in bushy areas and heathlands (often at traditional sites).

Map p. 478

Great Grey Shrike

Lesser Grey

Great Grey

juv

♂

1st-winter

Lesser Grey Shrike

meridionalis

algeriensis

Great Grey Shrike

badius juv   **Woodchat Shrike**   juv   **Masked Shrike** juv

Woodchat Shrike   *Lanius senator*   L 19 cm

Size of Red-backed Shrike, has characteristic red crown and nape. Female is somewhat duller in colour than male and has white markings at bill base. Contrast between the black and white areas of plumage gives it, not least in flight, a very variegated appearance. Juv. differs from juv. Red-backed in its paler creamy-white markings on shoulders, coverts, base of primaries and rump. Breeding on islands in W Mediterranean is race *badius*, which in all plumages has little or no white on primaries, less white on shoulders and a stouter bill. Juv. of latter race is very like juv. Red-backed, but has paler scapulars and less patterned head. Song very varied, with clear whistles, trills and mimicry, and is not unlike Linnet's. Commonest call a varied grating, usually dry and slightly coarse rattle, 'schrrrrret', sometimes more like 'kschaiiir'. Alarm call resembles Red-backed Shrike's. Occurs in open wood, maquis, gardens and cultivations. In W Mediterranean region is the commonest shrike and on most Mediterranean islands the sole representative of the genus. Feeds mostly on larger insects. Migrates Aug−Sep, returning Mar−Apr. Annual vagrant to Britain, Apr−Oct (especially May).

Masked Shrike   *Lanius nubicus*   L 18 cm

Ad. unmistakable and very parti-coloured in flight. Juv. very like juv. Woodchat Shrike, but is slightly slimmer, longer-tailed and has narrower bill; ground colour grey, not brown. Gradually acquires a 1st-winter plumage which resembles ad. female, but with paler grey mantle/back and crown and without ochre sides to body. In pure juv. plumage forehead is grey with dark vermiculations, but white feathers soon break through and most birds of the year on autumn passage can be identified by white forehead. Flight comparatively weak and unsteady. Song most like that of Olive-tree or Reed Warbler: a continuous repetition of coarse and stuttering, sometimes creaking notes. Commonest call otherwise (usually on take-off) an unvoiced scolding 'krrrrr', very like Woodchat Shrike's, also a slightly vibrating 'shreek'. Locally fairly common in open or semi-open country. Leads a more secluded life than other shrikes, is often rather elusive and frequently conceals itself in thick trees and bushes. Prefers to perch low in trees but also sits in exposed position on e.g. telephone wires. Arrives May and departs Aug to early Sep. Feeds on insects.

Woodchat Shrike

Masked Shrike

482

♀

♂

Woodchat Shrike

juv

♀

juv

Masked Shrike

♂

Starling   *Sturnus vulgaris*   L 21 cm

The Starling can hardly be confused with any other bird in N Europe, though in flight is rather like Waxwing. In spring males can often be distinguished by fact that they have smaller/fewer pale spots, stronger lilac and green gloss to the black and by their bluish bill base. Female has paler iris. Juv. differs from other grey-brown birds in, among other things, its short tail and its waddling and upright gait. Gathers in large flocks from early Jun, when young have left nest. Song varied, with mimicry, creaky chirps and twitters, clicks and drawn-out clear whistles. A specialist in probing grass lawns and mats of seaweed with its long conical bill; to find worms and insects it sticks it in and then opens its mouth, whereby it is able, with its oddly positioned eyes, to inspect the hole. Well-perforated ground bears witness to its ravages. Also feeds on berries, fruits and seeds. Breeds commonly in holes in trees, walls or buildings, often in nestboxes. Roosts in enormous flocks in reeds, tree clumps or on city buildings. Migratory in N and NE Europe, from where huge numbers winter in Britain Oct−Apr.

Spotless Starling   *Sturnus unicolor*   L 21 cm

Replaces Starling south of Pyrenees. Is 'oilier' and more uniform in colour than Starling, has more lilac and blue tinges and lacks Starling's green tone to back. In winter plumage dotted with greyish-white spots (often worn off by New Year), looks slightly grey at distance. Starling appears in Spain in winter (compared with Spotless looks paler owing to its larger pale spots). Song as Starling's but simpler; unlike Starling, seems unable to produce several sounds at same time. Behaviour and food otherwise as Starling's.

Rose-coloured Starling   *Sturnus roseus*   L 21 cm

Summer-plumaged ad. unmistakable, but can be confused with partial albino or leucistic Starlings (have similar markings but with white or buffy-white on the pale areas and they lack crest). Female has shorter nape feathers, less gloss and less black at bill base. Juv. resembles a washed-out juv. Starling, but has contrastingly pale rump, orange-buff bill which is slightly curved, and no dark on lores. In late summer to late autumn this plumage is replaced by a 1st-winter plumage: grey-brown mantle with paler rump, buffy-pink underparts, and dark brown head and wings, latter with paler fringes. Ad. winter has grey-brown fringes obscuring pink areas and pale fringes in the black areas; fringes abrade or are worn off during spring. Flight is light and slightly loose and flappy. Occurs irregularly in fluctuating numbers in open country, mainly grass steppes. From wintering sites mostly in N India it moves north and northwest in spring, stopping to breed only in areas with a good supply of grasshoppers. Has very short breeding cycle (c 1 month) in Jun−Jul, then moves southeast in Jul−Aug. Highly gregarious, breeding colonially in rock crevices, beneath boulders or in holes in buildings. Call in flight a loud clear 'ki-ki-ki', a rather Starling-like 'shrrr', and when squabbling a rattling 'chik-ik-ik-ik...'. In some years appears in larger numbers in SE Europe and is observed sporadically up to NW Europe (mainly males); in Britain mostly imms. and in Jun−Oct.

Starling

Spotless Starling

Rose-coloured Starling

Starling

2nd-cal ♀

♂

juv

Starling
winter

Spotless Starling

Spotless Starling
winter

winter

juv

♂

Rose-coloured Starling

Golden Oriole

Golden Oriole *Oriolus oriolus* L 24 cm

A slender thrush-sized bird with fast, gently undulating, rather woodpecker-like flight. Lives mostly up in the treetops, where amazingly well camouflaged. 1st-year males resemble females, but somewhat yellower on breast and belly and have more contrasting tail pattern. Very shy, is noticed mainly through its characteristic song, a rather melancholy but fast and clear fluting whistle, 'choo-klee-klooee'. Also has a harsh and rather Jay-like call. Breeds in older deciduous woods, larger parks and wooded patches in cultivated country. Breeds in very small numbers locally in Britain, in SE England; also rare on passage, mainly on south and east coasts in Apr–Jul (few in autumn).

Tristram's Grackle *Onychognathus tristramii* L 25 cm

A black thrush-sized bird with rusty primaries which are translucent and very conspicuous in flight. Male gleaming Raven-black whereas female and juv. are duller and brown-tinged and have grey-brown head. Very vocal, has characteristic meandering whistles recalling tuning in short-wave radio, e.g. 'wioowiooweet'. Often in flocks around ravines, riverbeds and cultivations in desert areas. Occurs in S Israel, Jordan, S Sinai and south along coastal Arabian Peninsula.

486

Siberian Jay

Siberian Jay *Perisoreus infaustus* L 28 cm

A characteristic bird of the dense, black-lichen spruce forests of northernmost Europe. Is often come across in family groups; young fledge in Jun. Inquisitive of man: one by one they come gliding down in deep undulations and then all of a sudden land quite close. They often disappear again just as quickly, but their characteristic appearance makes confusion with other species unlikely. Seems to be silent, but many of the northern forest's 'strange' sounds not infrequently come from the Siberian Jay, such as a buzzard-like mewing and a Jay-like scream. Also has a number of other, incl. imitative calls, but all are relatively soft and low-voiced in character. Feeds on insects and diverse small animals, berries, seeds etc, which in autumn it often hides away and stores in bark crevices and lichen clusters; also takes eggs and young from nests of small birds. Resident.

Golden Oriole

Siberian Jay

487

Jay *Garrulus glandarius*   L 34 cm

Unmistakable: strikingly variegated, especially in flight when the white and the pale
blue wing patches and the white rump are conspicuous. Varies somewhat in tone
geographically, in N Africa and Middle East more obviously owing to heavily
black-streaked or all-black crown. A fairly shy but common woodland bird seen in
highest numbers in autumn; Jays then shuttle between the 'home wood' and the
district's oak trees to gather in supplies of acorns for the winter. In longer flights the
wingbeats are fluttering and the flight course slow and unsteady. Flying along a
woodland edge it glides in gentle, deep undulations. Call a noisy and far-carrying
'kraih'; also has a 'peeay' identical with Buzzard's. Breeds in both deciduous and
coniferous woods favouring coppice and stands of young spruce or pine trees, has also
colonised parks and suburban areas. Feeds on insects, tree fruits, eggs and young of
passerines etc. Visits birdtables but rarely seen far from sheltering trees and shrubbery.
In some years northern populations make extensive eruptive movements, some from
N/E Europe even crossing North Sea to Britain.

Nutcracker *Nucifraga caryocatactes*   L 32 cm

At distance looks grey, with grey-black wings and mid-brown crown. Flight silhouette
like Jay's, but has shorter tail, rather more stable flight and appears more front-heavy.
Commonest call is a repeated croak, higher and louder than Carrion Crow's, and a
quiet rumbling or buzzing 'arrrrr', used also when alarmed. A bird of coniferous forest,
in Scandinavia preferring dense spruce forest with nearby hazel stands. Leads a
secluded life in spring–summer, though often perches in tops of spruces. Slender-billed
Siberian race *macrothynchus* feeds on seeds of arolla pine, when these are in short
supply may undertake invasion-type movements westward. Larger-scale eruptions also
occur in some years among Scandinavian birds, but on the whole they are residents.
Feeds on nuts, conifer seeds, insects, worms, and eggs and young of other birds.

Magpie *Pica pica*   L 44–48 cm

Common and well known. Occurs in widely differing environments but usually in
association with man. Male averages slightly larger and longer-tailed than female. Birds
with shorter tail lowest in rank. NW African race *mauretanica* is noticeably smaller, has
a patch of bare blue skin behind eye, black back and uniformly glossy green tail. Is
watchful of humans and gives energetic alarm against birds of prey, cats and other
enemies. As well as the hoarse croaking call, it sometimes gives a low-voiced babbling
song consisting of whining and twittering sounds. Pairs for life. Builds large round or
oval nest of sticks with side entrance, built afresh or repaired from foundation each
year. In particular imms. and birds lacking a territory often gather in flocks towards
evening to roost communally, especially in winter. Omnivorous, food includes eggs
and young from other birds' nests.

Jay

Nutcracker

Magpie

Jay

Nutcracker

slender-
billed

Magpie

Azure-winged Magpie

Azure-winged Magpie   *Cyanopica cyana*   L 35 cm

Smaller than Magpie. Often appears in noisy flocks which pass by in 'follow-my-leader' parties, gliding from tree to tree. Call usually a drawn-out hoarse trilling or screaming 'kschrrreea', occasionally a dry rattle, sometimes followed by a short 'kweet'; a coarser 'krrre' in alarm. Locally fairly common, mainly in unbroken and undisturbed woods and plantations. Rather secretive and shy.

Alpine Chough   *Pyrrhocorax graculus*   L 38 cm

Jackdaw-sized, long-tailed with small head and yellow bill. Has a more Jackdaw-like silhouette than Chough, with narrower wings and narrower, longer and more rounded tail. Highly acrobatic in the air and an expert at soaring: flocks often float like dead leaves on upwinds around mountain tops and precipices. Alpine Chough and Chough have a broad vocal repertoire and in practice are quite difficult to tell apart. Alpine Chough's calls are in general higher in tone and have a more cutting ring: commonest are a fast rolling 'pr'r'r'r'r' or 'prrrrree' (penny-whistle trill) or sharper 'peerrl', sometimes with deeper vowel, a very cutting whining whistle,'tzeeih'. Found only in high mountains with steep precipices, regularly to 4000 m. Sociable, in breeding season almost solely in flocks; often bold around villages and tourist sites.

Chough   *Pyrrhocorax pyrrhocorax*   L 40 cm

Flight silhouette angular, with broad, deeply fingered wings and broad, short and square-ended tail. Imms. have shorter and more orange-buff bill. Occurs locally commonly around rock faces in mountain regions but also in lower areas, and in W Europe along rocky coasts. Behaviour and habits similar to Alpine Chough's, but seldom comes to refuse sites. In winter often in large flocks which patrol upland fields and pastures in Rook fashion. Calls have a more rounded and clearer vowel sound than Alpine Chough's and are more Jackdaw-like: commonest are a fast rolling 'schrrr' or 'kchrau' and through intermediate 'krau' to a more Jackdaw-like 'kyah' or higher, more melodious 'kiao' or 'tsia' to a piercing 'pcheu'.

Azure-winged Magpie   Alpine Chough   Chough

Chough

Alpine Chough

juv

Chough

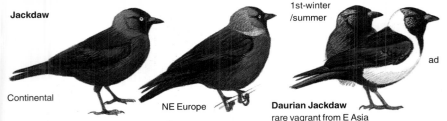

Jackdaw

Continental

NE Europe

1st-winter /summer

Daurian Jackdaw
rare vagrant from E Asia

ad

Jackdaw *Corvus monedula* L 33 cm

Differs from Carrion Crow in its small size, quicker movements, grey nape and pale eye. A skilful flyer and often soars. Flocks carry out acrobatic flight manoeuvres, making effective use of winds and air currents, especially towards evening when they gather for communal roosting. Call is sonorous and more musical than Carrion Crow's: it varies a bit but most often heard is a cutting and metallic 'kya' or 'chak'. The pair maintains a lifelong bond, and even when foraging birds often keep together in pairs. Breeds colonially in towns and villages and also in old woodland and rows of trees offering suitable nest holes, in towns and cities often in older parks and around church towers and other larger buildings; often found around cliffs. Feeds mainly on fields and farmland. Partial migrant, northern and eastern populations migrate via Scandinavia to W Europe.

Raven *Corvus corax* L 65 cm

Our largest passerine, considerably bigger than Carrion Crow and Rook. Often seen in flight, when its silhouette characterised by wedge-shaped tail, heavy head-and-bill area and narrow wingtips. Often soars, when wings held flat and can then easily be taken for a bird of prey. Has far-carrying calls, commonly a deep and metallic, slightly jarring 'krrooap, krrooap', a more Rook-like 'krrahk', and a strangely hollow 'klong' when the bird displays by executing a roll or tumbling vertically towards ground; alarm a persistent, rugged 'arrk-arrk-arrk'. Occurs especially in mountain districts but also other habitats if suitable rock faces or solitary wooded areas available for nesting. Avoids larger built-up areas, is often shy and vigilant. Takes carrion, eggs and young of birds, rodents etc. Resident.

Brown-necked Raven *Corvus ruficollis* L 50 cm

Entirely black with a brownish gloss over nape (though this hard to see in the field). Very like Raven in appearance and behaviour, but smaller, slightly slimmer and has more pointed tail; central tail feathers often protrude a short distance beyond rest. Replaces Raven in desert and semi-desert in Sahara and Arabian Peninsula.

Fan-tailed Raven *Corvus rhipidurus* L 47 cm

Smaller than Raven, in flight has unmistakably short tail and broad wings. In semi-desert terrain from sea level to above 3000 m; often near habitations, refuse-tips.

Jackdaw

Raven

Brown-necked Raven

Fan-tailed Raven

Jackdaw

Raven

Raven   **Brown-necked Raven**   **Fan-tailed Raven**

Hooded Crow
Rook

Carrion Crow   *Corvus corone*   *L 47 cm*

Hooded (*cornix*) and Carrion (*corone*) Crows are races of same species; in the boundary areas intermediate forms occur, e.g. NW Scotland and S Jutland. Hooded Crow is easy to distinguish from other crows by its particular combination of grey and black. Carrion Crows are very like young Rooks and separating them often requires close observation. Carrion Crow has a heavier, more uniformly thick bill with culmen more curved towards tip; the bristles at bill base usually merge with the bill so that culmen profile is not interrupted by a 'bump', and cutting edge towards gape is straighter whereas on young Rooks it often curves up slightly. Also, bill base and gape are blacker on Carrion Crow; on Rooks, especially 1st-years in spring, bill base is often slightly paler. Crow's call is a hoarse croaking with certain variations. Carrion Crow is sociable but to lesser degree a flocking bird than Rook and Jackdaw. It inhabits most open cultivated terrain and is very adaptable to differing food supplies; also steals eggs and young. Partial migrant, N European populations migrate south in Oct−Nov; large-scale passage of Finnish and probably Russian Hooded Crows southwestwards in autumn.

Rook   *Corvus frugilegus*   *L 47 cm*

Has an odd waddling gait and bushy 'trousers', peaked crown and long bill (looks long because of bare grey bill base. Imms., however, often amazingly hard to distinguish from Carrion Crow as they have dark bristly feathers on upper mandible until *c* 1 year of age. These bristles, though, give a rather different impression from those on Carrion Crow (see above), and further Rook has more peaked crown, wings (as well as its entire plumage and structure) are rather 'loose' in construction, alula and primary coverts often e.g. somewhat drooping. Call more nasal and 'straighter' or more evenly articulated than Crow's. Is associated with open, cultivated country to greater extent than Carrion Crow. Often seen foraging on short-grass fields and grassy areas. Feeds more on vegetable matter than Crow but also takes insects, worms and eggs and young of birds. Partial migrant in N and E Europe, incl. considerable passage of Russian birds through S Baltic mid Oct to early Nov; many Continental migrants visit Britain Sep−Apr.

Carrion Crow

Hooded Crow

Rook

hybrid

Hooded Crow

Carrion Crow

rookery

Rook

1st-winter

ad

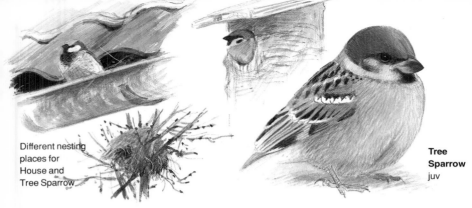

Different nesting places for House and Tree Sparrow

Tree Sparrow juv

Tree Sparrow   *Passer montanus*   *L 14 cm*

Easily distinguished from House Sparrow by its wholly red-brown crown, black cheek patch and white band across nape. Sexes alike. Juv. has greyish centre to crown merging into rusty-brown on sides and lacks or has only suggestion of cheek spot. Like House Sparrow breeds around villages and towns, but is not such a pronounced city bird as that species. It also occurs in open farmland, where may nest in nestboxes and tree holes at woodland edges or in clumps of trees. More mobile than House Sparrow and sometimes consorts with finches and buntings on fields and arable land. Flight call a fast sonorous 'tek, tek, tek…'; also has a nasal 'choovit', and gives House Sparrow-like chirping 'tret' or 'tretret'. More of a seed-eater than House Sparrow, but insects and all kinds of 'birdtable food' also included in diet. Mainly a resident but N European populations migrate, some wintering in Britain Sep−Apr.

House Sparrow   *Passer domesticus*   *L 15 cm*

Tied to built-up areas and farmyards. Male has black bib, lead-grey crown and liver-brown band from eye backwards across nape. Female nondescript grey-buff. When the birds moult in Aug−Oct, males acquire a more brownish-buff plumage in which the black bib is obscured by pale fringes and the grey and liver-brown of head are tinged buff; these fringes gradually wear away and towards early summer the birds show their brightest coloration. In Italy race *italiae*, which approaches Spanish Sparrow in appearance. Call a chatty but monotonous 'chip', 'chap' or 'cheerp', which from large flocks can produce a deafening noise; in flight also gives a shorter 'tveet'. Food consists mostly of seeds and insects. Nests in holes, usually beneath roof tiles, but rarely may also place nest in open in a tree or bush and nest is then skilfully constructed, large, roofed and with side entrance; these nests in open sites are quite common in S Europe. See also next spread.

Tree Sparrow

House Sparrow

Tree Sparrow

♂

♀

House Sparrow

♂

Spanish Sparrows
breeding in a
Stork's nest

Spanish Sparrow *Passer hispaniolensis* L 15 cm

Males easily recognised in spring/summer by chestnut-brown crown and heavy black markings on body; in fresh winter plumage pale fringes conceal much of this diagnostic pattern. Females often impossible to identify, but have faint streaking on underparts. In areas where they overlap, Spanish Sparrow occurs mainly in rural areas and is replaced in built-up areas by House Sparrow. Hybridisation occurs. Breeds colonially, often in large numbers, in gardens and often in orchards or olive groves. Builds open-sited round nest of grass with entrance hole, also in cavities in buildings and in stork nests. Calls resemble House Sparrow's. To some extent migratory and gathers in large concentrations like Starlings at particular roost sites, e.g. small woods or reedbeds, locally in hundreds of thousands. Food as House Sparrow's; causes much crop damage in some places. In Spain four.d only beside Guadiana River in Extremadura.

Rock Sparrow *Petronia petronia* L 14.5 cm

Like a female House Sparrow, but stockier and has a broad pale supercilium and a dark lateral crown-stripe and clearly streaked breast. In flight appears large-headed and short-tailed; flight undulating. Has pale spots on tail-tip which are conspicuous on landing. Yellow patch in crop area seems to be visible only when displaying to partner, in male accompanied by uttering of call/song, a drawn-out sibilant 'vee-viep' or 'viep'. Has quite a number of calls, most of them like House Sparrow's, in flight e.g. nasal 'waip' or 'uee', a stifled and slightly chattering 'schrrüe' or 'kriep', also a species-specific metallic 'zveeh-vü'. Occurs in rocky regions up to at least 2500 m, usually at lower levels and also at smaller eroded precipices, ruins and in villages, in winter also on flat cultivated plains, often together with House Sparrow.

Spanish Sparrow

Rock Sparrow

House Sparrow
italiae

♂ winter
(fresh)

♀

♂

Spanish Sparrow

Rock Sparrow

♂

Dead Sea Sparrow *Passer moabiticus* L 12 cm

Very small. Male has black bib and eye-stripe which are pale-bordered; in summer plumage a yellow spot is visible on neck-side. Female is a replica of female House Sparrow. Call like House Sparrow's but higher and more pleasing, incl. a high 'trreep'. Song a monotonously repeated phrase, e.g. 'tser veep' or 'tser veep eveep'. Tied to watercourses or cultivated areas, often in river basins with tamarisk and reeds. Bred Cyprus during 1980s, now extinct.

Desert Sparrow *Passer simplex* L 13 cm

Very much a desert bird. Both sexes very pale, male pale grey with conspicuous black bill, eye-mask and bib. Wings are variegated in flight, pale with black on primary coverts and in a band along base of greater secondary coverts. Female very uniform, pale sandy-buff with pale bill, wing markings as on male but less contrasting. Juv. resembles female. Song a drawn-out trill recalling Greenfinch. Also has chirping calls like House Sparrow. Occurs rather locally, and is partly nomadic depending on effects of precipitation on availability of grass. Often beside oases, cultivations and settlements.

Pale Rock Sparrow *Petronia brachydactyla* L 14 cm

Slightly smaller than Rock Sparrow, with shorter tail and longer wings. Nondescript sandy grey-brown, without Rock Sparrow's streaking on crop. Wings are darker brown with two paler wingbars and a dingy-white panel on secondaries. Tail as Rock Sparrow's. Has narrow whitish supercilium, white throat, diffuse moustachial stripe and a stout pale bill with more rounded culmen than on Rock Sparrow. Song a monotonous buzzing and rather insect-like 'tzz tzz tzz-tzeeeeeeeei'; flight call recalls that of a distant Bee-eater. Occurs in mountain regions of semi-desert character or stony areas with bushes, in winter also on plains and cultivated ground. Arrives late, often into early May.

Yellow-throated Sparrow *Petronia xanthocollis* L 13 cm

Finch-like, with longer tail and straighter culmen than Pale Rock Sparrow, overall impression darker and lacks white on tail-tip. Male has black bill in summer plumage, in winter and on female horn-coloured. Female without yellow on breast, but clear dirty-white wingbar on median coverts characteristic. Song chirruping, but more melodic and softer than House Sparrow's. Occurs in dry terrain with element of trees, in gardens, date-palm cultivations etc; nests in tree holes.

Dead Sea Sparrow

Pale Rock Sparrow

Desert Sparrow

Yellow-throated Sparrow

Dead Sea Sparrow

Desert Sparrow

**Pale Rock
Sparrow**

**Yellow-throated
Sparrow**

Snow Finches

Snow Finch   *Montifringilla nivalis*   L 18 cm

Very much an alpine bird, bears resemblance to Snow Bunting but the two have very different ranges. Conspicuous in flight owing to its white wing markings. In winter has yellow bill, paler head, mantle and back and lacks black bib. In Turkey and Caucasus race *alpicola*, with paler mantle and brownish crown of same colour as back. Very sociable and large flocks with their 'dancing' flight give impression of snowflakes. On rising, gives a sharp nasal 'pscheeu' or short 'pschie', which varies and sometimes sounds like 'kaihk' or 'keehk'; when alarmed 'pchrrrt'. Locally common on stony and rocky alpine slopes and plateaux above tree line, usually at 2000−3000 m but in summer reaches the highest peaks in the Alps, in winter at lower levels; often appears quite confiding at chalets and villages. Feeds on insects and various seeds.

Avadavat   *Amandava amandava*   L 9 cm

A very small spool-shaped finch, male carmine-red with white pearly spots below and on wings, female and winter-plumaged male grey-brown above and paler grey-buff below, always with characteristic red bill and rump. Can be confused with closely related Red-billed Firefinch *Lagonosticta senegala* breeding in Sahel zone south of Sahara and north to at least Ahaggar in S Algeria (vagrant to Morocco), but latter long-tailed, male carmine-red but with brown wings and white spots restricted to breast, both sexes with pale eye-ring and bluish base to red bill. Song a sustained pleasant high twitter; in flight high-pitched chirping calls. Often in tall grass and reeds at wetlands and in cultivations, locally common in SW Spain and Portugal. Native to India; wild populations in W Palearctic stem from escaped cagebirds.

Common Waxbill   *Estrilda astrild*   L 10 cm

Introduced in E Portugal from S Africa. Brownish with dark vermiculation, red bill and facial mask and belly area.

Indian Silverbill   *Euodice malabarica*   L 11 cm

Native to India west to Persian Gulf; occasional in Israel, possibly introduced. Small, attenuated finch-like bird. Pale grey-brown with whitish rump, creamy-white underparts and strikingly pointed blackish tail. Has an odd bill, pale grey-blue and deep at base with slightly arched culmen. An African twin species, African Silverbill *E. cantans*,

Snow Finch

has expanded northwards and breeds in S Egypt and S Arabian Peninsula: very similar in appearance, but has black rump and delicate barring on wing-coverts. Occurs around cultivations, oases and on grassland with bushes.

winter

♂ spring

Snow Finch

♂

♂ winter / ♀

Avadavat

Common Waxbill ♂

Indian Silverbill

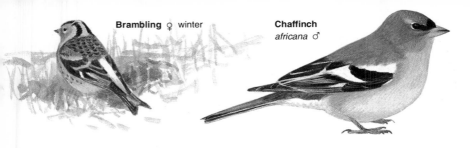

Brambling ♀ winter   Chaffinch *africana* ♂

Chaffinch *Fringilla coelebs* L 15.5 cm

Male is easily identified, while female is less striking but is always told from Brambling by grey or greenish rump. White shoulder, wingbar and outer tail feathers are characteristic features on both sexes (median and lesser coverts). In fresh plumage in autumn, male's markings are partly hidden by brown-buff fringes, but these are progressively shed during late winter. 2nd-cal-year male often retains the brown-grey 'winter bands' on nape until well into spring. In N Africa race *africana* breeds, which is differently coloured: mantle dark moss-green, whole cheek blue-grey and breast pale pink. On Atlantic islands there are a number of races with greenish to blue back and pale pink to buffish-pink breast. Song an accelerating trill with terminal flourish; varies somewhat regionally but is always ringing and far-carrying. Call a high and sonorous 'fink', flight call a softer 'yup' and alarm call a monotonously repeated 'huit'; also has a rolling and slightly metallic ringing 'schrreet', a call which is commoner in C and S Europe. Very common in woodland, parks, gardens or around solitary trees in cultivated country, one of Britain's commonest birds. In winter largely on farmland and often with other finches. During breeding season feeds largely on insects, and for rest of year. N European populations migrate in flocks, often with Bramblings, end Sep−Oct, returning Mar−Apr; many of these winter in Britain.

Brambling *Fringilla montifringilla* L 15.5 cm

Distinguished from Chaffinch in all plumages by its rusty-buff to orangey colour on breast, shoulder and wingbar and in flight by its characteristic white rump. Winter-plumaged male more like female, but has brighter colours and conspicuous pale bill with dark tip. Towards late winter and spring male's head becomes progressively darker as the pale feather fringes are abraded. Flight call like Chaffinch's 'yup' but also has distinctive, uniform wheezing 'eeehp'. Song a Greenfinch-like drawn-out wheeze. At nest site several other, often bewildering calls are heard, such as a regular but well-spaced ticking 'stit' and a harsh 'ayehp' in alarm. In association with song male has a rolling 'schrree' like a fledgling thrush, also a rare song variant with a rattling trill 'chechechechecheche' like an overplayed recording of Redpoll's flight call. Breeds in northern taiga, in many areas mingling with Chaffinch, but replaces latter in alpine birch forest, where abundant. In winter and on passage in flocks on farm fields and in wooded areas (especially beech). Beech mast and hornbeam nuts are important winter food. Passage and winter visitor to Britain Sep/Oct−May; exceptionally rare breeder in north.

Chaffinch

Brambling

♂ 1st-winter

♂

Chaffinch

♀

♀

♀

♂

Brambling

♂ 1st-winter

♀ winter

♂ summer

Hawfinch *Coccothraustes coccothraustes* L 18 cm

Unmistakable, clearly bigger and heavier than e.g. Greenfinch. Bill is dark lead-grey in spring/summer and pale buff in winter. Female duller than male and has grey secondaries and outer edge to primaries. Juv. has buffy and cross-mottled breast and less pronounced face-mask and throat patch. Despite its gaudy markings and immense bill it often goes undetected during summer months. It is shy and unobtrusive and makes itself known mostly by an explosive 'zik' or a sibilant 'srree'. If seen it is a stout, large-headed, compact finch usually passing over in undulating flight at treetop height in a woodland glade, when broad wingbars the most prominent feature, or rising suddenly from an open area of garden or a wooded spot, when white tail markings also

conspicuous. Occurs relatively uncommonly in deciduous and mixed wood and in parks and gardens. With its powerful bill it can crack open kernels of stone-fruits, e.g. cherries; fruits from beech, maples and wych elm, buds and insects, however, form the main food. In winter small groups or flocks roam about and not infrequently visit birdtables, where prefers sunflower seeds and peanuts. Many Scandinavian and E European birds migrate south in Oct–Nov (visit Britain?), returning mainly in Apr.

♂

Canary

Tristram's Serin

Tristram's Serin

♀

Canary *Serinus canaria* L 13 cm

Endemic in Madeira, Azores and Canary Islands but common as a cagebird (mainly the specially bred predominantly yellow variety). Larger and longer-tailed than Serin, with grey back and streaked greenish-yellow rump. Common in Madeira around plantations, gardens and woodland edges. Song as that of cagebird Canaries.

Tristram's Serin *Serinus syriacus* L 12 cm

More elongated and noticeably longer-tailed compared with Serin, and colour pattern different, most like Citril Finch. Grey on head with pronounced yellow forehead and throat, yellow lores and area (ring) around eye. Female more drab, lacking yellow around eye and on throat. Wing looks uniformly yellow-green in fresh plumage, tail has yellow outer edge to feathers. Breast greyish and belly faintly yellow or yellow-green. Has only faint streaking on back and on rear flanks (cf Serin). In flight gives weak but characteristic 'ter-let', lacking Serin's ringing quality. Song twittering, rather Linnet-like. Breeds in mountain regions mostly with cedar and juniper bushes, also in gardens and around plantations; in winter also in more treeless mountain of semi-desert type, south to Sinai Peninsula. Wintering population in northernmost Jordan probably originates from some unknown breeding area.

507

Citril Finch   *Serinus citrinella*   L 12 cm

A small finch with unstreaked or faintly streaked back; in flight does not show pale panels on wing or tail like Greenfinch and Siskin. In juv. plumage drab grey-brown with dark streaking, and without yellow or green traces possessed by other European *Serinus* species in juv. plumage. Younger females have little or no yellow-green on breast or face and look uniform olive-grey. Race *corsicana* breeding commonly in Corsica and Sardinia has browner mantle/back. Flight call a high, harsh 'cheeht', sometimes rapidly repeated and then sounds bouncing, e.g. 'chit it it' rather like Linnet. Call a rather Siskin-like 'tee-e'. Song consists of relatively short phrases with features of both Serin's and Goldfinch's song. Occurs sparsely in high-level coniferous forests and on alpine meadows. Food mainly seeds from conifer trees and various plants.

Serin   *Serinus serinus*   L 11 cm

Often occurs in pairs or small parties, when male easily recognised by its canary-yellow markings. On rising, the yellow rump, the unmarked tail plus lack of conspicuous wing markings are good identification characters. Small size and short stubby bill are also striking. Often difficult to catch sight of and call is therefore very useful in identification. In flight often gives a jingling 'tirrillillit' or 'zr'r'reelit', but also a less easily identifiable Greenfinch-like 'juwee'. Song very characteristic, a prolonged and fast chirping or jingle as from glass splinters. Sings from perch or in song flight with slow sculling wingbeats like Greenfinch. Occurs in parks, gardens and cultivated country with scattered clumps and avenues of trees, preferably with some conifers. Characteristic bird of S Europe. Feeds on tree, grass and plant seeds. In Britain breeds locally and irregularly in S England, otherwise seen occasionally, mainly in Feb–Jun and Oct–Nov.

Red-fronted Serin   *Serinus pusillus*   L 11 cm

Quite variable in plumage, ads. most resemble Redpolls with sooty fore parts and red forehead. Juv. has buff-brown head and is not unlike Twites of race *brevirostris* breeding in Caucasus and adjacent parts of Turkey, which have black patches on breast-sides. Outside breeding season occurs in small flocks which, like Redpoll and Goldfinch, wander about and search through thistles and other plants for seeds. Call a rapid, thin ringing 'titihihihihihi', faster in flight. Song fairly Linnet-like, with frequent croaking 'kveeh' sounds. Occurs commonly within its range in high mountain regions up to c4000 m.

Citril Finch

Serin

Red-fronted Serin

Citril Finch

corsicana ♂

♂

Serin

♂

♀

Red-fronted Serin

juv/1st-winter

Siskin ♂

♂

Serin

Greenfinch ♂

Siskin   *Carduelis spinus*   L 12 cm

Male contrastingly marked in yellow, green and black. Female a drabber grey, but always has green and yellow elements which distinguish it from Redpoll. During breeding season strongly attached to spruce or pine forest, and then feeds largely on conifer seeds which it extracts from between the half-open cone scales with its pointed bill. Sings from top of a spruce or in ecstatic butterfly-like flight over the forest. Has a rolling song with varying pitch changes; can recall Icterine Warbler's but is faster, more twittering, with creaking elements, and sections of song often terminate with a drawn-out rasping 'krreeea'. During winter months in flocks in more open country and main food is then seeds, mostly from alder. Moves between trees on an uneven, restlessly flitting flight path, and gravelly twitter and loud 'tseelü' calls are heard from the tightly knit flock. Winter distribution varies with food supply. Local breeder in Britain, but has adapted to plantations of introduced conifers, and numbers augmented by visitors from N and E Europe in Sep–May; often in gardens in winter, favouring peanuts.

Greenfinch   *Carduelis chloris*   L 15 cm

Our largest yellow-green finch, equipped with powerful bill and 'muscular' build. In autumn ground colour quite dull and not very conspicuous; it is mostly the yellow markings on wings that catch the eye, and tail markings become striking only in flight. Juv. has lightly streaked underparts and back. In flight gives a fast bouncing 'djururrup', and call is a soft 'dvooeet'. Towards breeding season male advertises himself mostly from an elevated songpost with a drawn-out hissing wheeze, 'dchweeeesh', and with sequences of rolling whistles and twitters. The full-scale song can be very mellow and rich and recall that of a Canary. During the most intensive periods male also performs a song flight with slow sculling wingbeats, and by this time (Mar onwards) wear on the plumage has made the green areas brighter. Occurs commonly in more open habitats, from city parks and large gardens to farmland with hedgerows. Feeds on various seeds and in winter readily comes to birdtables where e.g. hemp and sunflower seeds are offered. Mainly resident in Britain, with winter visitors from Continent Oct–Apr.

Siskin

Greenfinch

Siskin

♀

♂

juv

Greenfinch

♂

juv

♀

Bullfinch ♀

Goldfinch

Hawfinch ♂

Goldfinch   *Carduelis carduelis*   L 14 cm

Unmistakable, both in voice and in appearance. Often before the approaching birds are seen they have announced themselves by their characteristic soft but rather piercing 'stikelitt' or monosyllabic 'stik' calls. Juv. differs from other finches in its wholly black tail and typical wing markings, which resemble those of ads.; can be seen with 'juvenile' head until well into Oct. Male's song, a typical finch twitter, is most easily recognised by the interwoven calls. With its relatively short tarsus and its long pointed bill, the Goldfinch specialises on the deep-seated seeds of thistles and teasels and burdocks. It is in fact where these and other winter-standing plants flourish that the flocks are often encountered flying around in autumn and winter. The young, by contrast, are fed largely on insects. In spring and summer inhabits open cultivated country with copses, wooded areas and woodland edge and gardens. Many British breeders move south to Belgium, western France and W Mediterranean in Sep−Oct, returning Mar−Apr; N European populations also pass through during Oct−Nov and Mar−Apr.

Bullfinch   *Pyrrhula pyrrhula*   L 16 cm

A distinctive and easily identified bird. Juv. as female but lacks black cap and has a dingy wingbar. Nominate Scandinavian and N Eurasian races is slightly larger and brighter than Continental *europaea* and British Isles *pileata*. Song is a very quiet warbling chatter with creaky notes and interwoven soft whistles. Call very characteristic, a slightly melancholy and soft whistle, 'dyuh'; contact call among flocks a more finch-like 'chet, chet...chet'. A fairly common bird at forest edges, in scrub, forest plantations, gardens and orchards; in north of range a rather secretive bird of dense forest, typically intermixed with younger stands of spruce. In winter and spring it often visits gardens, orchards and similar places, where it consumes buds; it selects flowerbuds and can cause damage locally to commercial fruit crops. Fresh berries and various seeds, e.g. from mugwort, nettles, maple and ash, are important in autumn/winter. Prefers to take food directly from branches and plant stems. To a great extent resident, but northernmost populations move south through Scandinavia mainly end Oct−Nov and northwards end Mar−Apr; a very few may winter N Britain.

Goldfinch

Bullfinch

Goldfinch

juv

Bullfinch

juv

♂

♀

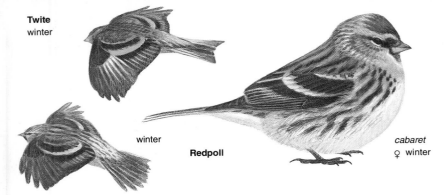

Twite winter

winter
Redpoll

cabaret
♀ winter

Redpoll *Carduelis flammea* *L 12–13 cm*

A small finch with grey and brown tones, slightly 'fluffy' plumage and a gentle, rather Mongolian expression. Has a short and pointed straw-coloured bill, small black bib and red patch on forehead. Variable in plumage, not infrequently lacks red on forehead in 1st-winter plumage. Male often has beautiful pink tinge to breast and sides, with forehead and breast deep carmine-red in summer plumage. In Fennoscandia race *flammea*, which is normally markedly pale in winter plumage and mostly with a greyish tone. W European *cabaret* has a noticeably more brownish-buff tone to the plumage, obvious on mantle and in spring/summer on breast-sides, where it contrasts markedly with white breast. In Greenland race *rostrata*, slightly bigger, more heavily streaked, with a brown and buff tone, and also has a stouter bill (with slightly convex culmen; straight on other races). Northern Redpolls are most easily confused with Arctic Redpoll. Siskin always has some green in plumage, which Redpoll lacks. Flight call an energetically repeated 'dyek-dyek-dyek', normal call a soft rising 'dyuee'. Sings in flight or from perch; song consists of the flight call repeated at different speed and pitch with interwoven rolling 'tee ree ree ree...' and high whirring trills. In W Europe breeds in open and semi-open bushy areas, N Europe breeds mainly in upland birch forest but also in coniferous belt, as well as on bare mountain above tree line. Birch seeds are staple food over much of year; seeds from various plants and, in breeding season, insects and caterpillars are also included in diet. Partial migrant in Britain; also winter visitor in annually fluctuating numbers from N Europe, arriving mainly Oct–Nov and leaving Mar–May.

Arctic Redpoll *Carduelis hornemanni* *L 13 cm*

Very closely related to Redpoll and in all ways similar. Ad. normally identified by unstreaked white rump, little or no streaking on flanks and generally whiter, floury, plumage. Imms. (up to 1 year) more like Redpoll, more brownish-buff with streaked sides and lightly streaked (spotted) rump. Generally more white on forehead than Redpoll. Breeds more on open mountain moors and tundra than Redpoll, but also in upland birch forest. Voice as Redpoll, but flight call slower; call 'dyeeeu'. Very rare winter visitor to N Britain.

Redpoll   Arctic Redpoll

♀ winter

Redpoll

♀ summer

♂ summer

1st-winter

Arctic Redpoll

♂

buff

♂ summer

Twite

winter

Twite *Carduelis flavirostris*   L 14 cm

In summer appears as a dark, highly terrestrial finch. In winter very like Linnet, but has variably intense distinctive 'curry colour' on head and breast and bill is pale yellowish. Pale wingbar is often the most contrasting feature. Male's pinkish-red rump is evident on take-off. Flight call a bouncing Linnet-like 'chut chululut'; call a diagnostic nasal and harsh 'chweet' or 'veeiht', heard also from flock in flight. Moves in mouse-like jerky manner on ground, when utters short 'chee'. Song rugged, chattering, consisting partly of variations on the call and not unlike a Budgerigar's chatter. Breeds relatively commonly on coastal, open, moors, more sparsely on higher mountain moors. In non-breeding season in flocks on coastal meadows, fields and stubble, often on open ground with weed seeds such as excavation areas, refuse tips etc. In Britain mainly resident, with some southward dispersal to coasts in winter, when a few visit from Norway.   *Ill. p. 515*

Linnet *Carduelis cannabina*   L 14 cm

Male easily identified in breeding season. In winter sexes are extremely similar, though male has more intense pinkish-buff tone to breast. The concealing buff-coloured fringes wear or are shed so that the carmine-red markings appear by spring. 2nd-cal-year male can be less bright red, while ad. in Jun is quite magnificent. In flight the brown back and the pale wing flashes are striking characters. In juv. plumage pale buff-toned and conspicuously dark-streaked. Flight call recalls Greenfinch's, an irregular bouncing 'tet-tet-ter-et'. The full-scale song is very melodious, with indrawn twittering, whirring sequences and fluted notes woven together. Sometimes, however, male and also female perch and virtually chatter with call notes, pleasing 'plee-yu' and lively twittering. Associated mainly with open ground with bushes, especially thorn and gorse, young plantations etc, wintering on fields, marshes and rough ground. Partial migrant in Britain; also winter visitor from N Europe, arriving Sep–Oct and leaving Mar–Apr.

Scarlet Rosefinch *Carpodacus erythrinus*   L 14 cm

Ad. male characteristic; the red varies in extent with age. Female and most 1st-summer males dull olive-brown above, recognised by the hefty bill and lack of strongly contrasting colour markings on wings and tail, though show two narrow paler wingbars. Juv. like ad. female, but with richer olive-brown tone above and bolder rusty-buff wingbars and tertial-tips. Migrates in juv. plumage. Call a soft 'djuee' recalling Greenfinch, but has a distinctive harsh tone. Song very characteristic, a clear and sprightly whistle, usually in three parts e.g. 'weedye-weedye-vyu' or 'ste-weedye-vyu', some males also give twitter between phrases. Locally common in open bushy terrain, often in willows beside damp meadows and shores. Feeds on seeds, buds, berries and insects. In Britain a scarce passage migrant, mostly in north, mainly Aug–Oct, with fewer May–Jun; has bred.

Twite

Linnet

Scarlet Rosefinch

Linnet

♂

♀

♂ winter

Scarlet Rosefinch

ad ♂

juv

♀

Great Rosefinch

♀ ♂

Great Rosefinch *Carpodacus rubicilla* L 20 cm

C Asiatic species with an isolated population in Caucasus. Breeds above tree line on alpine meadows above 2000 m; in winter found lower down in valleys. Call a soft 'pyeeu-een, pyeeu-een', recalling Bullfinch.

Sinai Rosefinch *Carpodacus synoicus* L 13 cm

Smaller than Scarlet Rosefinch, ad. male beautiful pink with silky-white cast on crown and ear-coverts. Female nondescript, pale buff-toned; can be mistaken for Trumpeter Finch but has longer tail and darker bill. Noisy, gives variable, slightly squeaky 'tcheeep', 'tcheup' or more drawn-out 'pseeeh'. Occurs sparsely and locally in desert mountain regions in Sinai Peninsula, S Israel and Jordan. In winter in flocks, which invade areas with dried-out plants.

Desert Finch *Rhodospiza obsoleta* L 15 cm

Barely Greenfinch size; unmistakable, with uniform grey-buff body and contrasting black bill and loral mask, and pale pink and white-fringed black wings. Female lacks black lores while juvs and 1st-winters often have light bill. Call a rather Skylark-like 'trreeüt' or 'trrük', in flight also a 'veeip' recalling Twite. Breeds in open dry terrain with trees, bushes or cultivations; in winter in flocks on fields and in cultivations.

Crimson-winged Finch *Rhodopechys sanguinea* L 15 cm

Greenfinch-sized, heavily built finch with pink wing panel conspicuous in flight (less so on female). Easy to distinguish from Desert Finch by dark-streaked brown mantle/back, darker crown and at all times pale bill. Occurs sparsely in dry mountain regions, normally above 2000 m, in winter at lower levels and often near gardens and cultivations. Flight call a soft fluting 'dü-leet, dü-leet' with quality of Woodlark.

Trumpeter Finch *Bucanetes githagineus* L 12.5 cm

A small dumpy finch occurring mainly in stony desert and semi-desert. Male is more grey in winter and has buff bill. Most often noticed by its call (song), which is very distinctive and consists of a drawn-out uninflected note with a metallic buzzing ring, like a toy trumpet. The call is not particularly loud and is difficult to pinpoint. Usually quite cryptically coloured and very fearless, so can be difficult to flush. On rising, utters a weak nasal 'eaip' or 'veechp'. Has recently established itself in the heavily eroded and semi-desert type regions of SE Spain.

Desert Finch

Crimson-winged Finch

Trumpeter Finch

Sinai Rosefinch

♂

♀

♂

Desert Finch

1st-winter
♀

♂

♂

♂ winter **Crimson-winged Finch**

Trumpeter Finch

♀

♂

♀

♂

Pine Grosbeak   *Pinicola enucleator*   *L 20 cm*

An odd finch, large and rounded with a distinctive pale carmine-red tone, female yellow-brown or hairmoss-green in colour, both with a wonderful grey 'padded' rear body. Long-tailed and heavy in flight, which is undulating. Often fearless, hops on

ground or clambers in trees. Call flute-like and 'meandering', 'chuleewü' or just 'puee'. Song of 3−4 call-like fluting meandering notes but at faster pace, e.g. 'chulee chulee chrruee chuee'. Breeds sparsely in northern taiga belt, often in rather mixed, mossy and gloomy spruce forest with bilberry and an underlayer rich in cowberry. In winter in flocks. Normally resident but in some years moves southward in large numbers. Feeds on shoots, buds and berries (often rowanberries in autumn and winter), in summer also insects. Very rare vagrant to Britain.

Crossbill   *Loxia curvirostra*   L 17 cm

A large and hefty finch, large-headed and with mandibles crossed at tip. Male's red rump and female's greenish-yellow rump are striking in flight. Juv. has brown and streaky grey-buff plumage and double pale buff wingbar of varying prominence and can be confused with Two-barred Crossbill. Amount of red on male varies, can have predominantly greenish-yellow plumage with only a few orange-red feathers. Contact or flight call is a characteristic metallic 'kip-kip' or 'glip-glip'. The rather Greenfinch-like song is irregular and fast, with twitters, piercing notes and admixed calls. Alarm a deep 'chük-chük'. Very much a bird of coniferous forest, dependent on seeds mainly of spruce. In some years performs invasion-type movements. Breeding season tied to ripening of cones, so often falls in Feb. As early as late spring gathers in flocks, and then wanders about in search of food.

Scottish Crossbill   *Loxia scotica*   L 17.5 cm

Like Parrot Crossbill but with slightly smaller bill. Variation is such, however, that many cannot be separated from large-billed Crossbills. Sedentary breeder in Caledonian pine forest of Scotland.

Parrot Crossbill   *Loxia pytyopsittacus*   L 18 cm

Compared with Crossbill, has larger, more rectangular head and heavier and more uniformly thick bill, with tip of lower mandible normally not visible in profile. Breeds relatively sparsely in coniferous forest and in annually fluctuating numbers. Feeds chiefly on seeds of pine, which distinguishes it from Crossbill. Flight call a repeated metallic 'küp' or 'kop', normally lower-pitched than Crossbill's, though pitch and timbre vary. Song, heard most often in winter, has a chattering character of call-like 'pchee-PCHÜRR' notes and slightly harsh rolling and rather Greenfinch-like trills. Alarm a loud harsh 'cherk-cherk'. Erupts to a lesser extent than Crossbill and seldom encountered outside coniferous forest regions. Often remarkably confiding, sometimes found on forest roads/paths quietly gathering fallen pine seeds and/or grit. Rare vagrant to Britain (has bred).

Two-barred Crossbill   *Loxia leucoptera*   L 15 cm

Smaller than Crossbill, with more slender bill, and in flight looks slimmer and longer-tailed. Male also has colder, more carmine-red colour. Diagnostic are the double, broad white wingbars and white tips to tertials; on juv. and 1st-winter to 1st-summer, bars are narrower and tertial-tips may be completely worn off. Three calls given in flight: a Crossbill-like but softer and more liquid 'plitt plitt', a Redpoll-like 'chet chet chet', and a typical nasal fluted 'ehp' (toy trumpet). Belongs to Siberian taiga, where staple food larch seeds; also eats spruce, pine and cedar seeds, as well as e.g. rowanberries. In some years erupts, after which may nest in N Scandinavia if spruce seeds plentiful. Rare vagrant to Britain.

Crossbill

Parrot Crossbill

Two-barred Crossbill

Crossbill juv   **Two-barred Crossbill** juv

♂   **Crossbill**

Parrot Crossbill

♂

♀

Parrot Crossbill

♂

♀

♀

Two-barred Crossbill

♂

Corn Bunting   *Miliaria calandra*   L 18 cm

Identified by size, 'lark-coloured' plumage, lack of white on tail, and powerful bill. Tied to open cultivated terrain, where in many places it is common and easy to see; often perches on telephone wires and roadside fences. Song a fast chipping followed by a grating or 'glass-splintering' jangle with 3−4 convolutions, 'tük-tük-tük trirililirirililee. Male flies to and from songpost (or while singing) with rapid shallow wingbeats and dangling legs. During non-breeding season in flocks, often together with Yellowhammers. Contact call a low but very hard 'tik'; simple call a soft rolling 'dchrrut', when agitated also a creaky 'zieh...tzek'. Rather local in Britain, on downland and extensive arable with hedgerows. Decreasing in N and NW Europe.

Yellow-breasted Bunting   *Emberiza aureola*   L 15 cm

Male unmistakable: liver-brown breast-band and white carpal area distinguish it from Black-headed Bunting. Female has strikingly contrasting head pattern and streaked mantle, unstreaked yellow belly and white wingbar. 1st-summer male variable, sometimes almost exactly like female. Juv./1st-winter on autumn passage (Aug) straw-coloured below, with broad creamy supercilium, prominent wingbars and dark-streaked rump. Birds in female-type plumage typically have two pale lines (braces) on mantle. Sings frequently. Song is a quiet jingle, varyingly put together and most like Ortolan Bunting's, but often has something of Reed Bunting's slightly 'hiccuping' notes; it often consists of 3 or 4 sections, e.g. 'tse tuee-tuee, tsiu-tsiu, zeeu' or 'tsiu-tsiu-tsiu, vüe-vüe, tsia-tsia, trip-trip'. Call a short piercing 'tsik' or 'tsee'. Breeds in rank, often marshy meadowland, dryer marsh and bogs with a profuse element of willow, birch or alder. Migrates to SE Asia in Aug, returning at beginning of Jun. Vagrant to Britain, mainly in north and east, mostly in Aug−Oct.

Pine Bunting   *Emberiza leucocephalos*   L 16.5 cm

Vagrant from Siberia. Very like Yellowhammer in behaviour, build and basic pattern but lacks yellow in plumage. Male easily identified by white and liver-brown markings and dark-marked throat. Female more grey-brown and rusty toned than 1st-winter female Yellowhammer (which can lack obvious yellow tones), but has sharper blackish streaking on crown and on malar stripe down towards upper breast. Voice as Yellowhammer's. Breeds in similar habitat to Yellowhammer and hybridisation occurs in one area in W Siberia (a hybrid has been recorded also in England, in Suffolk in Apr 1982). Extremely rare vagrant to NW Europe, mostly autumn−winter.

Black-faced Bunting   *Emberiza spodocephala*   L 14 cm

Very rare vagrant from Siberia, mainly in autumn. Male has grey hood and breast with black mask (lores), with sulphur-yellow and faintly streaked belly. 1st-winter males usually have more banded head pattern. Female very dull, brown and streaked, has grey rump and white-streaked vent. Bill relatively long, culmen straight (cf. Reed Bunting). Call a sharp 'tzick'.   *Ill. p.533*

Corn Bunting

Yellow-breasted Bunting

Pine Bunting ♂

Corn Bunting

Yellow-breasted
Bunting

♂

2nd-cal ♂

♀

Yellowhammer   *Emberiza citrinella*   L 16.5 cm

A large, elongated and long-tailed bunting with yellow on head and with rusty-red rump. In fresh winter plumage the visible yellow is reduced by grey-green feather-tips. Female often has pale yellow or sometimes buffish-yellow colour and more streaked breast. 1st-winter female lacks yellow, is predominantly grey-buff with olive-brown markings. Forages by hopping on ground, often in crouched and attenuated posture. Song characteristic, with six fast, high and often insect-like chirping notes followed by a drawn-out melancholy final note, 'tzi-tzi-tzi-tzi-tzi-tzi tzuuh'. When flushed gives a short 'tsik', sometimes followed by a dry rolling 'prüllüllü...'. Call a rasping 'dzüh', short or somewhat drawn-out, when more committed a double-call 'tscheet-schrüt', often accompanied by tail jerk. Occurs commonly in open country with hedges, gardens, juniper slopes, thorny scrub etc. Mainly resident, in winter visiting farmyards and stubble. Northernmost populations move south end Sep–Oct, some perhaps wintering in Britain.

Cirl Bunting   *Emberiza cirlus*   L 16.5 cm

Male unmistakable, with black throat and stripy head. Female very like female Yellowhammer, but generally has more straggly breast markings, more diluted yellow or yellow-grey colour below and olive-grey to brown-grey rump; safest distinguishing mark is the grey-toned rump, though may have rusty-brown tinge to uppertail-coverts. Recalls Yellowhammer in habits but associated more with timbered terrain, e.g. gardens, plantations, lines of roadside trees and woodland edges, and often harder to locate. In autumn and winter also on open fields and arable. Replaces Yellowhammer in large parts of Mediterranean. Song a drawn-out, wooden rattle very like Lesser Whitethroat's, 'zee tetetetetet', also a faster, higher, dry trill. Call a slightly drawn-out 'zeeh' and in flight a very sharp 'zit', 'zitit' or trisyllabic 'zit it it', sometimes almost vowel-less. Rare, local, in Britain.

Ortolan Bunting   *Emberiza hortulana*   L 16.5 cm

In N Europe most easily confused with Yellowhammer, but recognised by olive-toned head with distinct sulphur-yellow eye-ring and drooping moustache together with brownish-pink tone to bill (blue-grey on Yellowhammer). Has yellow-pink or peach-coloured belly, on male contrasting clearly with grey breast. 1st-winter on autumn passage has more streaked breast, but eye-ring and bill colour diagnostic. Song has an attractive ringing, Great Tit-like first section and a descending, more melancholy second part: e.g. 'tsie-tsie-tsie-tsie, truh-truh-truh'. Call a short 'chip', from migrants more of a 'sie' followed by a short 'plit' in regular alternating sequence; also has a rather Bullfinch-like 'cheu'. Occurs in open agricultural country with scattered trees, copses and rows of trees, in thorny scrub, in rank meadowland with willows, birches and other trees, often near wetlands. Migrates to tropical Africa Aug–Sep, returning Apr–May. Scarce migrant in Britain.

Yellowhammer

Cirl Bunting

Ortolan Bunting

Yellowhammer ♀ ♂

Cirl Bunting ♀ ♂

♂

Ortolan Bunting ♀

Rock Bunting   *Emberiza cia*   *L 16 cm*

Male has uniform rusty-brown tone to body and grey head with distinct black stripes. Female less brightly coloured and sometimes quite unassuming. Relatively common in mountain districts, often on rocky slopes with scrub. Often flies up from roadside verges, when rusty-red rump and white-edged tail are characteristic. Song relatively long, fast and high-ringing, recalls Dunnock or Treecreeper, e.g. 'zit ziterit zit zit ziterit zit'. Commonest calls a sharp 'tsee' or 'zie' and a short 'tüp', on rising a variable 'chelut', 'chit vit' or slightly vibrant 'chee dee dee'; also utters a rolling 'kierrrr'. Feeds on insects and seeds. Resident or partial migrant, moves to lower regions in winter. Very rare vagrant to Britain.

Cretzschmar's Bunting   *Emberiza caesia*   *L 15.5 cm*

Resembles Ortolan Bunting, which also breeds in Greece and Turkey, but is smaller, more rusty-toned and has blue-grey (not olive-green) head with rusty-coloured (not yellow-white) throat and submoustachial stripe. Female less brightly coloured and has streaked crown. 1st-winter very like 1st-winter Ortolan, but more rusty-toned on especially mantle, back and rump, never olive-toned. Song variable, like Ortolan's but often harsher in tone and shorter, sometimes seems cut short, e.g. 'tsee tsee tsee tsee tsuuh'. Call/flight call variable, e.g. a rather harsh, sometimes grating 'zie' or 'chit' combined with a 'tyüf' or nasal, almost House Sparrow-like 'dyeu'. Relatively common on dry, rocky slopes with scrub, often near gardens and smaller cultivations. Migrates mostly Aug, returning Apr.

Grey-necked Bunting   *Emberiza buchanani*   *L 16 cm*

Like a pale and less patterned Cretzschmar's Bunting; mantle/scapulars with little streaking but with contrasting red-brown lower scapular feathers. Has whitish eye-ring, throat and submoustachial stripe, grey on breast confined to breast-sides, centre of breast and rest of underparts have a rusty-pink colour often with admixed white fringes (looks untidy), belly and vent/undertail-coverts pale yellow-buff. Sexes fairly similar. Song resembles Ortolan Bunting's, e.g. 'sti-sti-stüe ste-stüe'. Occurs in easternmost Turkey and further eastwards on sparsely vegetated rocky slopes and plateaux usually above 2000 m. Migrates southeast, returning end Apr.

House Bunting   *Emberiza striolata*   *L 14 cm*

Like a very small Rock Sparrow at first sight: grey, streaked head and rusty-brown body. Bill bicoloured, black upper mandible and rusty-yellow lower. Female has more brownish-grey head with less-defined streaking. In Middle East and Arabian Peninsula race *striolata*, has more heavily marked scapulars, paler belly and more pronounced stripes on face. Song Chaffinch-like but weaker and higher-pitched. In N Africa (*saharae*) common by or in villages and cultivations. Very fearless.

Rock Bunting

Cretzschmar's Bunting

Grey-necked Bunting

House Bunting

Rock Bunting ♂ ♀

♀ 1st-winter

Cretzschmar's Bunting

Grey-necked Bunting ♂ ♀

Ortolan Bunting ♂

♀ ♂

House Bunting

Black-headed Bunting ♀   Cinereous Bunting   Rock Bunting ♂

Red-headed Bunting *Emberiza bruniceps*   *L 17 cm*

Very like Black-headed Bunting in behaviour, habits and voice. Male has intense brownish-red face and breast, yellow belly and dark-streaked moss-green back. Female and juv. very like Black-headed but lack rusty-brown tones on mantle and rump, more olive-grey in tone. Breeds in open cultivated country and on shrub steppe. Replaces Black-headed in C Asia, nearest breeders north of Caspian Sea.

Black-headed Bunting *Emberiza melanocephala*   *L 17 cm*

An obviously large bunting which attracts attention through its song and its bright colours. Female has pale yellow or yellow-grey underparts and usually dark olive-grey 'hood', in summer sometimes greyish-black crown and with rusty-brown centres to mantle and rump feathers. Some (mainly 2nd-cal-year) females are pale grey-buff, but always have yellow vent, pale eye-ring and are not very streaked. Lacks white tail markings. Song a variable but characteristic verse, usually introduced by short harsh notes and ending with a few mellow notes with a distinctive tinny ring, e.g. 'tzi zia zia zia zerlee zerlee zerlee' or 'pzt pzt pzt pzt pzt pzt chirri chirri chirrli chürrlü chürrlü'. Call a lively 'pyiup' and a 'tyilp'; flight call usually a sombre 'dripping' 'pchlü' or 'plüt', not unlike some of the Goldfinch's deeper flight calls. A characteristic bird of open bushy country such as olive groves, gardens and alongside arable fields, cultivations and roadsides. Migrates southeast as early as Aug, returning end of Apr to early May. Vagrant to Britain, mostly May–Jun but also Jul–Oct.

Cinereous Bunting *Emberiza cineracea*   *L 16.5 cm*

Male is very pale, and on rising looks washed-out with conspicuous white markings in tail. Female darker and duller in colour (often olive-grey) but with a greenish-yellow tinge mainly on throat, has brown-grey rump and pale eye-ring. Juv./1st-winters and 1st-summer female warmer brown, but differ from Ortolan and Cretzschmar's Buntings in greyish (not pale buffy-pink) bill. Song is a simple, high ringing verse, often composed of 5–6 short syllables in 2 or 3 sections, e.g. 'dreep dreep dreep dreep drüe drüeh'. Call a metallic 'kyip' and a 'tyeeh' with clear brassy tone. Rare and local. Mainly on grassy hills with boulders.

Red-headed Bunting   Black-headed Bunting   Cinereous Bunting

♀

Red-headed Bunting ♂

♀ 2nd-cal

♂

Black-headed Bunting

♀ 1st-winter

♀

♂

Cinereous Bunting

♀ 1st-winter

Yellowhammer

♂ winter

Cirl Bunting
♀ winter

Cirl Bunting
♂ winter

Ortolan Bunting
1st-winter

**Yellow-breasted
Bunting** juv

Corn Bunting winter

♀ winter

Pine Bunting

♂ 1st-winter

♀ winter

Black-faced Bunting

♂ 1st-winter

Yellow-browed Bunting
juv

Yellow-browed Bunting *Emberiza chrysophrys* L 14 cm

Vagrant from Siberia. Size of Rustic Bunting, with big conical bill and distinctly patterned head. Spring male has black hood with broad yellowish supercilium starting just in front of eye and white crown-stripe. On female and in fresh winter plumage, ear-coverts are brown and supercilium begins at bill-join and is bright yellow at front but becoming whiter to rear. Has a prominent pale spot on rear ear-coverts and black-streaked malar stripe. Underparts without yellow or rusty tones but distinctly dark-streaked. Call a sharp 'tzit' like Rustic Bunting's. Recorded only a few times in W Europe (Oct). *Ill. p.533*

Rustic Bunting *Emberiza rustica* L 15 cm

Size of Reed Bunting, but often gives a more 'rustic' impression owing to the contrastingly marked head and the relatively sturdier bill. Has coarsely demarcated liver-brown to rusty-red blotches on breast and flanks. In winter plumage sexes are rather alike and easy to confuse with Reed Bunting. Distinguished from latter by longer bill with straight culmen, pale spot on rear ear-coverts, more peaked head profile with straighter forehead, and reddish-brown breast and flank markings (blackish on Reed and Little Buntings). Song is high and clear, but with a rather melancholy ring, and syllables vary greatly, often short, e.g. 'stülee vülee vülee vultee'; most recalls an abbreviated Dunnock's song. Call a hard 'tzit' or 'tsik' like Song Thrush; anxiety call at nest a soft drawn-out 'tsie' like Penduline Tit. Breeds relatively commonly in rather swampy coniferous or mixed forest, usually at thinly wooded bog edges. Feeds on seeds, in breeding season insects also. Migrates southeast end Aug–Sep, returning May. Rare vagrant to Britain, mostly Sep–Nov.

Little Bunting *Emberiza pusilla* L 13 cm

Slightly smaller than Reed Bunting, and with slightly longer bill with straighter culmen. In summer plumage usually rusty-coloured on cheeks, crown and chin, with conspicuous yellow-white eye-ring. In winter plumage more like Reed Bunting, but with more rusty-brown ear-coverts, prominent eye-ring and cold brown lesser coverts (in contrast to rusty-coloured on Reed Bunting). The dark lower border to ear-coverts does not extend forward to bill (on Reed Bunting forms a blackish moustachial stripe). Song not unlike Rustic Bunting's but more 'bitty' and slightly ticking in character, something between Reed and Rustic's, and can in a way recall a section from Tree Pipit's song: often 3–4 sections can be distinguished, such as 'titititi-chup chup-sturriep' or 'pie pie-sturi sturi-tulee-tchee'. Call a metallic piercing 'tsik' or 'tik'. Breeds in swampy, thin birch or spruce forest with understorey of dwarf birch, also in areas with willows and often near water. Very rare breeder in Norway/Sweden, more widespread in Finland. Feeds on seeds and insects, especially caterpillars. Migrates southeast in Sep–Oct, returning in May. Rare vagrant to Britain, mostly Sep–Oct, exceptionally also Nov–May.

Rustic Bunting

Little Bunting

Rustic Bunting ♀

♂

Little Bunting ♂

♀

Pallas's Reed Bunting

♂

♀ 1st-winter

Pallas's Reed Bunting   *Emberiza pallasi*   L 13 cm

Breeds in E Siberia, recorded only a few times in Europe. Much smaller and somewhat longer-tailed than Reed Bunting. Bill more conical, with straight culmen and paler lower mandible. Plumage generally paler, less rusty, and has distinctly paler rump. Spring male almost black-and-white in pattern, with double white wingbar and whitish rump. Winter-plumaged male and females have two distinct buff-white wingbars (on Reed entire covert fringes incl. tip are rufous); rump is paler, more greyish-white or buff-white, often unstreaked on ad. whereas birds in 1st-winter plumage normally have streaked rump; have less pronounced supercilium behind eye and often a clearly demarcated dark spot on rear ear-coverts (Reed usually has a border around entire ear-coverts). Juv. has blackish streaks on breast, female and 1st-winter pale rusty-brown streaks. Lesser coverts (carpal) are grey or brown-grey and not rufous as on Reed, though this difficult to see in field. Little Bunting, which is closer in size, always has obvious eye-ring, a distinct rusty-buff to reddish-brown tone to cheeks and prominent pale supercilium. Call very unlike Reed's, a clear 'tchi-ulp', rather like House Sparrow's.

Reed Bunting   *Emberiza schoeniclus*   L 15.5 cm

Male unmistakable: black head, white collar and drooping moustache. Female variable, usually with broad blackish malar stripe, dark brown cheeks and grey tone to neck-side. In winter plumage in autumn sexing and ageing difficult: typical are distinct buff supercilium and submoustachial stripe, and uniformly brown to grey-buff cheeks framed by dark border which at lower edge reaches bill-join (moustachial stripe). Never has prominent pale spot on rear ear-coverts like Rustic Bunting. Culmen convex or slightly arched, bill appears shorter and stubbier than on Rustic and Little Buntings. Scapulars and wing often have rich rusty tone, lesser coverts are uniform rufous. Rump and uppertail-coverts have grey ground colour but feathers are often rusty-coloured towards tip. Breeds commonly at most wetlands with rushes or reeds and osiers, in

Britain also in dryer sites (e.g. young conifers), its thin indrawn 'tseeu' often revealing its presence. Perches on top of reeds or plants, often jerks tail and dives down when danger threatens. Song varies in construction, but is slow and chipping or 'hiccuping' with a faster final whirr. Migrants give a low harsh and nasal 'chup'. On migration and in winter often in small groups, incl. on fields and grassy areas far from water (even visits birdtables). British residents augmented by visitors from N and E Europe, Sep—May.

♀

Reed Bunting

♂

♂ early spring

♀ winter

Little Bunting
winter

Rustic Bunting
winter

♀ winter

Lapland Bunting   *Calcarius lapponicus*   L 16 cm

A big, rather heavy bunting which is easy to recognise during breeding season. Female relatively distinctive, with clear-cut dark markings on head, fox-red nape, and buff-yellow bill with dark tip. In winter plumage in autumn, male's black markings as well as the red nape are only faintly discernible beneath the pale fringes. In 1st-winter plumage has a brownish-yellow tinge over entire head (chiefly females). A striking feature on autumn birds (most obvious on males) is the brownish-red greater coverts framed by broad, whitish wingbars. On the breeding grounds the males often perch prominently on the top of dwarf birches, willows or on rocks and are then easy to see. On migration and in winter, however, the birds are highly terrestrial and run rapidly in hunched posture through low vegetation on stubblefields, coastal meadows and pastures which they then frequent. Commonest flight call a hard rippling 'prrrrt', usually preceded by a nasal 'tew'. On breeding grounds also gives a softer ringing 'dyuee' followed by 2-second pause and then 'triü', in regular slow alternating sequence. Song has a lively and clear ring, resembles both Snow Bunting's and Shore Lark's but is usually more 'intricate' in structure, e.g. 'prriteeh-trilillilli-chirreecheeree'. Sings from low perch or in song flight. Occurs commonly on arctic tundra and in Scandinavian mountains, most abundantly around tree line in areas with low bush vegetation and often beside bogs and willows by watercourses. Often nests in small colonies. Feeds largely on various seeds, but young are reared on insects. Migrates mainly southeast in Sep–Oct. In Britain an uncommon passage and winter visitor, mainly on east coast, mostly Sep–May; has nested Scotland.

Snow Bunting   *Plectrophenax nivalis*   L 16–17 cm

Easily recognised by white wing markings. Plumage varies considerably, however, and imm. females (1st- and 2nd-cal-years) have only very little grey-white, on secondaries and lesser coverts. In winter plumage has long buffish-ochre fringes. Summer plumage is acquired mainly through loss of fringes: pale fringes wear and drop off, exposing dark or white 'cores' of feathers. Juv. gives a dull greyish impression and its mouse-grey head and clear buffish eye-ring recall Ortolan Bunting. Song very like Lapland Bunting's, varies considerably but is usually simpler, e.g. 'techutee-teelee' or as one, repeated tinkling note 'teelu-teelu-teelu-tetwee'. Song flight as Lapland Bunting's. Call sometimes virtually identical with Lapland's, 'chuh', but the following 'ripple' has a pleasantly ringing tone, 'prillillillee' like a Curlew Sandpiper; also a clear 'teeu' and a rasping 'trrree'. Very much a species of high mountains, breeding in stony terrain high up in the lichen region, though on arctic coast also side by side with Lapland Bunting down to sea level. Food as Lapland Bunting's. Arrives at breeding sites in Mar–Apr, southward passage recorded in North Sea area mainly in Oct–Nov. Winters on extensive plains, and in NW Europe on shores and coastal meadows and moors. Mainly a winter visitor to Britain Oct–Apr, but small numbers breed in N Scotland.

Lapland Bunting

Snow Bunting

Lapland Bunting

Snow Bunting

Little Bunting winter

Reed Bunting
♀ winter

♂ winter

Rustic Bunting

♀ winter

♀ winter

Lapland Bunting

♂ winter

ad ♂ winter

♀ 1st-winter

♀ winter

Snow Bunting

♂ winter

♀ winter

♀ juv

Vireos and wood-warblers

Vagrants from N America. Resemble European warblers in behaviour. All are extremely rare and appear mainly in autumn from end of Sep and in Oct in association with westerly winds, but there are also a few spring records. Almost all the records are from England and Ireland with the focal point in the southwest and especially the Isles of Scilly, with some also from Iceland. Shown here are species found more than 3 times. Number of published records up to 1989 is also given. A further ten or so species have been recorded.

Red-eyed Vireo   *Vireo olivaceus*   L 14 cm

Size of Great Tit, hops about in horizontal posture in foliage. Red iris on ad., brown on 1st-cal-year. Call a discordant, rather whining nasal 'cher'. British and Irish records are concentrated within period 21 Sep−19 Oct. 67 records.

Black-and-white Warbler   *Mniotilta varia*   L 13 cm

Feeding habits recall treecreepers'. Male has less buff tones and more prominent black streaks on breast and flanks in summer, with black on throat and ear-coverts. Call a sharp 'peet' and a thin Treecreeper-like 'seeh'. 13 records.

Northern Parula   *Parula americana*   L 11.5 cm

Size of Chiffchaff. Female lacks red spots on breast and is darker overall, with more green above. Often clambers rather tit-like on branches. Call a sharp 'chip'. 19 records.

Yellow-rumped Warbler   *Dendroica coronata*   L 14 cm

Long-tailed, yellow rump and large white ovals on outer tail feathers, yellow patch on breast-side. Call a sharp metallic 'chek' (not like Lesser Whitethroat). Recorded also on European mainland and Madeira. 24 records, of which 7 from Iceland.

Blackpoll Warbler   *Dendroica striata*   L 13 cm

1st-cal-year autumn unassuming, streaked, with two white wingbars and white patches on outer tail feathers. Call a loud clicking, a thin 'seet' and a sharp 'ztreex' with Yellowhammer quality. Records almost exclusively from Oct. 33 records.

American Redstart   *Setophaga ruticilla*   L 13 cm

Fairly small but long-tailed. Takes insects in air. Adult male black with orange-red markings on breast-sides, wing and tail. Female and 1st-winter male brownish-green above, with yellow wingbar of varying extent. Call a high explosive 'tzip'. 11 records.

Ovenbird   *Seiurus aurocapillus*   L 15 cm

Terrestrial, moves jerkily (creeps) on ground in shelter of vegetation, like a rounded short-tailed Tree Pipit. Eye-ring conspicuous. Call a clucking 'chuk'. 4 records.

Northern Waterthrush   *Seiurus noveboracensis*   L 14.5 cm

Often by water, rocks rear body and bobs like Dipper. Call a penetrating sharp 'chip' or 'chük'. 8 records.

Common Yellowthroat   *Geothlypis trichas*   L 13 cm

Small, short-winged, often cocks tail, moves about mostly low down in brush and marsh vegetation. Male has black eye-mask (mostly concealed in 1st-winter plumage). Call a loud hard 'chek'. 3 records.

Red-eyed Vireo
1st-winter

Black-and-white Warbler
♀ winter

Northern Parula
♂ 1st-winter

Yellow-rumped Warbler
winter

Blackpoll Warbler
winter

American Redstart
♀/1st-cal ♂ winter

Ovenbird
winter

Common Yellowthroat
♀ 1st winter

Northern Waterthrush
winter

N American tanagers, finches, sparrows and orioles

Number of published records in Europe up to and including 1989 is given. Most are from England and Ireland.

Scarlet Tanager   *Piranga olivacea*   L 18 cm

Large-billed, rather finch-like, moves about in trees and taller bushes. Summer-plumaged male scarlet-red with black wings, in winter plumage yellow-green with contrasting dark wings; female has greenish-brown wings and is duller in colour. 1st-winter male like female but with some black wing coverts. Call 'chip-purr', with dry rattle at end. 9 records, mostly in Oct.

Song Sparrow   *Zonotrichia melodia*   L 16 cm

A robust sparrow with long rounded tail, which is 'pumped out' when it flies away. Head looks markedly stripy and has heavy malar stripe and breast streaking which forms a patch in centre of breast. Typical call a peculiar hollow 'chimp'. 7 records, all in spring.

White-throated Sparrow   *Zonotrichia albicollis*   L 17 cm

Size of Yellowhammer, with heavier bill. White throat, and crown with broad blackish and pale stripes (white or buff on some and on 1st-winter). Call a loud 'chink' and a high lisping 'tseehp'. 29 records, most from spring.

Dark-eyed Junco   *Junco hyemalis*   L 16 cm

Unmistakable; in flight shows conspicuous whitish outer tail feathers. Call a short and sharp 'tzit' or 'tzit-it-it' on rising. 18 records, most in winter–spring.

Rose-breasted Grosbeak   *Pheucticus ludovicianus*   L 20 cm

Slightly bigger than Hawfinch. Summer-plumaged male black-and-white with rosy breast. In autumn (1st cal-year) brown and buff, dark-streaked and with characteristic broadly striped head pattern and male usually with white wing markings. Male has rosy underwings. Flight call a very high-pitched, slightly creaking 'eenk'. 32 records, with marked concentration in Oct.

Indigo Bunting   *Passerina cyanea*   L 14 cm

Linnet-sized with rather large bill. Male indigo-blue, in winter plumage the blue partly concealed by cinnamon-brown fringes. 1st-summer male often not in full ad. plumage and with brownish flight feathers. Female rather like female Scarlet Rosefinch, but lacks prominent streaking and is warmer brown. Call a sharp 'tsik'. 14 records.

Bobolink   *Dolichonyx oryzivorus*   L 18 cm

Size of Corn Bunting, with distinctive pointed tail feathers. In winter plumage straw-yellow with dark-streaked buff mantle and broad dark lateral crown-stripes and broad supercilium. Male in summer mostly black with white shoulders and rump and with yellow-buff nape. Flight call a clear 'pink'. Frequents tall grass, maize fields, reeds etc. 18 records, mostly in Sep–Oct.

Northern Oriole   *Icterus galbula*   L 22 cm

Size of a Starling, with long tail and conical bill. Summer-plumaged male bright orange and black with white wingbars; in winter plumage less colourful, but often with an intense brownish-orange tone. Female in winter often more subdued, but has un-streaked yellow to yellowish-buff underparts and bold pale wingbars. Call a slightly nasal wheezy 'veeht'. 21 records, mostly mid Sep–Oct.

Scarlet Tanager
♂ 1st-winter

Dark-eyed Junco

White-throated Sparrow

Rose-breasted Grosbeak
♂ 1st-winter

♀ winter

♂ winter

Indigo Bunting

Bobolink
1st-winter

Northern Oriole
♀/1st-cal ♂ winter

Bibliography

A selection of works recommended for those with specialist interest, dealing with birds occurring in Europe and the W Palearctic.

Ahlström, P., Colston, P., & Lewington, I. 1991. *The Rare Birds of Britain and Europe.* London.

Bannerman, D.A. & W.M. 1971. *Handbook of the Birds of Cyprus and Migrants of the Middle East.*

Bannerman, D.A., & Lodge, G.E. 1953-63. *The Birds of the British Isles.* 12 vols. London.

Bardarson, H.R. 1986. *Birds of Iceland.* Reykjavik.

Blædel, N., et al. 1959-67. *Nordens fåglar i färg.* 7 vols. Malmö.

Campbell, B., & Lack, E. (eds.) 1985. *A Dictionary of Birds.* Calton.

Chandler, R.J. 1989. *North Atlantic Shorebirds.* London.

Cramp, S. (chief ed.) 1977-. *The Birds of the Western Palearctic.* vols. 1-5. Oxford. Further vols. in prep.

Curry-Lindahl, K. (ed.) et al. 1959-62. *Våra fåglar i Norden.* 4 vols. 2nd edition. Stockholm.

Delin, H., & Svensson, L. 1988. *A Photographic Guide to the Birds of Britain and Europe.* London.

Dementiev, G.P., & Gladkov, N.A. et al. 1951-54. *Birds of the Soviet union.* 6 vols. Moscow. (Israel Progr. for Sci. Transl., Jerusalem, 1966-70.)

Dymond, J.N., Fraser, P.A., & Gantlett, S.J.M. 1989. *Rare Birds in Britain and Ireland.* Calton.

Etchécopar, R.D., & Hüe, F. 1967. *The Birds of North Africa.* Edinburgh.

Farrand, J., Jr (ed.) et al. 1983. *The Audubon Society Master Guide to Birding.* 3 vols. New York.

Ferguson-Lees, J., Willis, I., & Sharrock, J.T.R. 1983. *The Shell Guide to the Birds of Britain and Ireland.* London.

Fjeldså, J. 1977. *Guide to the Young of European Precocial Birds.* Tisvilde.

Flint, V.E. et al. 1984. *A Field Guide to the Birds of the USSR.* Princeton.

Forsman, D. 1984. *Rovfågelsguiden.* Helsinki.

Fransson, T., & Staav, R. 1987. *Nordens fåglar.* Stockholm.

Fry, C.H. 1992. *Kingfishers, Bee-eaters and Rollers.* London.

Génsbøl, B. 1986. *Collins Guide to the Birds of Prey of Britain and Europe.* London.

Géroudet, P. 1947-57. *La vie des oiseaux.* 6 vols. Neuchâtel and Paris.

Glutz von Blotzheim, U.N. (chief ed.), Bauer, K., & Bezzel, E. 1966-. *Handbuch der Vögel Mitteleuropas.* vols. 1-11. Wiesbaden. Further vols. in prep.

Grant, P.J. 1986. *Gulls: a guide to identification.* 2nd edition. Calton.

Haftorn, S. 1971. *Norges fugler.* Trondheim.

Harris. A., Tucker, L., & Vinicombe, K. 1989. *The Macmillan Field Guide to Bird Identification.* London.

Harrison, C. 1982. *An Atlas of the Birds of the Western Palaearctic.* London.

Harrison, P. 1987. *Seabirds of the World: a photographic guide.* London.

Harrison, P. 1991. *Seabirds: an identification guide.* Revised edition. London.

Hayman, P., Marchant, A.J., & Prater, A.H. 1986. *Shorebirds: an identification guide to the waders of the world.* London.

Heinzel, H., Fitter, R., & Parslow, J. 1985. *The Birds of Britain and Europe with North Africa and the Middle East.* Revised edition. London.

Hollom, P.A.D. 1980. *The Popular Handbook of Rarer British Birds.* 2nd edition. London.

Hollom, P.A.D., Porter, R.F., Christensen, S., & Willis, I. 1988. *Birds of the Middle East and North Africa.* Calton.

Hüe, F., & Etchécopar, R.D. 1971. *Les oiseaux du Proche et du moyen Orient de la Méditerranée aux contreforts de l'Himalaya.* Paris.

Joensen, A.H. 1966. *Fuglene på Færøerne.* Copenhagen.

King, B.F., Dickinson, E.C., & Woodcock, M.W. 1975. *A Field Guide to the Birds of South-East Asia.* London.

Lack, P. (ed.) 1986. *The Atlas of Wintering Birds in Britain and Ireland.* Calton.

Lekagul, B., & Round, P.D. 1991. *A Guide to the Birds of Thailand.* Bangkok.

Madge, S., & Burn, H. 1988. *Wildfowl: an identification guide to the ducks, geese and swans of the world.* London.

National Geographic Society. 1983. *Field Guide to the Birds of North America.* Washington.

Parmenter, T., & Byers, C. 1991. *A Guide to the Warblers of the Western Palearctic.* Uxbridge.

Paz, U. 1987. *The Birds of Israel.* London.

Peterson, R.T., Mountfort, G., & Hollom, P.A.D. 1985. *Field Guide to the Birds of Britain and Europe.* London.

Pforr, M., & Limbrunner, A. 1981-82. *The Breeding Birds of Europe.* 2 vols. London.

Porter, R.F., et al. 1981. *Flight Identification of European Raptors.* 3rd edition. Calton.

Sharrock, J.T.R. (ed.) 1980. *The Atlas of Breeding Birds in Britain and Ireland.* 3rd edition. Calton.

Sonobe, K., Washburn Robinson, J. (eds.), et al. 1982. *A Field Guide to the Birds of Japan.* Tokyo.

Svensson, L. 1992. *Identification Guide to European Passerines.* 4th edition. Stockholm.

Sveriges Ornitologiska Förening. 1990. *Sveriges fåglar.* Stockholm.

Vaurie, C. 1959. *The Birds of the Palearctic Fauna.* 2 vols. London.

Witherby, H.F., Jourdain, F.C.R., Ticehurst, N.F., & Tucker, B.W. 1938-41. *The Handbook of British Birds.* 5 vols. London.

Voous, K.H. 1960. *Atlas of European Birds.* London.

Voous, K.H. 1977. *List of Recent Holarctic Bird Species. Ibis* suppl., London.

Base references for maps

The distribution maps are based on the following literature; and also on unpublished information supplied by Klaus Malling Olsen (Denmark), George I. Handrinos (Greece) and Iztok Geister (Yugoslavia), to all of whom thanks are due.

Anon. 1978-90. European news. *Brit. Birds* 71-82.

Bentz, P.-G., & Génsbøl, B. 1988. *Norsk fuglehandbok.* Oslo.

Bloch, D., & Sørensen, S. 1984. *Yvirlit yvir Føroya'fuglar.* Torshavn.

Cramp, S. (chief ed.) 1977-88. *The Birds of the Western Palearctic.* vols. 1-5. Oxford.

Dybbro, T. 1976. *De danske ynglefugles udbredelse.* Copenhagen.

Ferrer, X., Martinex i Vilalta, A., & Muntaner, J. (eds.) 1986. *Historia natural dels Paisos Catalans.* Barcelona.

Flint, P.R., & Stewart, P.F. 1983. *The Birds of Cyprus.* London.

Flint, V.E., Boehme, R.L., Kostin, Y.V., & Kuznetsov, A.A. 1984. *A Field Guide to the Birds of the USSR.* Princeton.

Geister, I. 1989. *Slovenskij prispevek kevropskemu ornitoloskemu atlasu za obduje 1979-1988.* Ljubljana.

Goodman, S.M. & Meininger, P.L. (eds.) 1989. *The Birds of Egypt.* Oxford.

Green, A.A. 1984. The avifauna of the Alf Jawr, Northwest Saudi Arabia. *Sandgrouse* 6: 48-58.

Harrison, C. 1982. An Atlas of the Birds of the Western Palearctic. London.

Harrison, P. 1985. *Seabirds: an identification guide.* 2nd edition. London.

Hollom, P.A.D., Porter, R.F., Christensen, S., & Willis, I. 1988. *Birds of the Middle East and North Africa.* Calton.

Hyytiä, K., Kellomäki, E., & Koistinen, J. (eds.) 1983. *Suomen lintuatlas.* Helsinki.

Il'cev, V.D. (chief ed.) 1985-89. *Handbuch der Vögel der Sowjetunion.* vols. 1 & 4. Wittenberg Lutherstadt.

Jennings, M.C. 1981. *The Birds of Saudi Arabia: a checklist.* Cambridge.

Klafs, G., & Stübs, J. 1987. *Die Vogelwelt Mecklenburgs.* Jena.

Koskimies, P. 1989. *Distribution and Numbers of Finnish Breeding Birds.* Helsinki.

Lack, P. (ed.) 1986. *The Atlas of Wintering Birds in Britain and Ireland.* Calton.

Mikkola, H. 1983. *Owls of Europe.* Calton.

Nikene, J. 1989. *Latvian Breeding Bird Atlas 1980-1984.* Riga.

Paz, U. 1987. *The Birds of Israel.* London.

Pforr, M., & Limbrunner, A. 1982. *The Breeding Birds of Europe.* vol. 2. London.

Rutschke, E. 1987. *Die Wildgänse Europas.* Berlin.

Schifferli, A., Géroudet, P., & Winkler, R. (eds.) 1980. *Verbreitungsatlas der Brutvögel der Schweiz.* Sempach.

Sharrock, J.T.R. (ed.) 1976. *The Atlas of Breeding Birds in Britain and Ireland.* Calton.

SOF. 1990. *Sveriges fåglar.* 2nd edition. Stockholm.

SOVON. 1987. *Atlas van de Nederlandse vogels.* Arnhem.

Štastný, K., Randík, A., & Hudec, K. 1987. *Atlas hnizdniho rozšířeni ptáku v ČSSR 1973/77.* Prague.

Telleria, J.L. (ed.) 1988. *Invernada de Aves en la Peninsula Iberica.* Madrid.

Thomsen, P., & Jacobsen, P. 1979. *The Birds of Tunisia.* Copenhagen.

Tomialojć, L. 1990. *Ptaki Polski.* Warsaw.

Wallace, D.I.M. 1985. The breeding birds of the Azraq Oasis and its desert surround, Jordan, in the mid-1960s. *Sandgrouse* 7: 1-10.

Sound recordings

Andersson, B., & Svensson, L. 1990. *Fågelsång i Sverige.* CD and cassette plus booklet.

Chappuis, C. *Oiseaux de France.* Rouen.

Chappuis, C. 1989. *Sounds of Migrant and Wintering Birds.*

Hazevoet, K. (ed.), et al. *Nederlandse Vogels.* 6 vols. Cassettes published by Nederlandse Vereniging tot Bescherming van Vogels. Zeist.

Kettle, R. (ed.) 1987. *British Bird Songs and Calls.* 2 cassettes. National Sound Archive, London.

Lewis, V. 1984. *A Sound Guide to the British Warblers, . . .Finches, . . . Thrushes, . . .Tits, . . . Hawks & Falcons, . . .Breeding Waders.* 6 cassettes.

Mild, K. 1987. *Soviet Bird Songs.* 2 cassettes. Stockholm.

Mild, K. 1990. *Bird Songs of Israel and the Middle East.* 2 cassettes and booklet. Stockholm.

Paatela, J. *Laulava lintu kirja.* W. Söderström, Helsinki.

Palmér, S., & Boswall, J. 1970-73. *A Field Guide to the Bird Songs of Britain and Europe.* RFLP 5001-5015. Sveriges Radio, Stockholm. Cassette version 1981, revised and expanded.

Roché, J.C., et al. 1965-67. *Guide sonore des oiseaux d'Europe.* Jean Claude Roché, Institut Echo.

Roché, J.C. 1990. *Tous les oiseaux d'Europe.* 4 CDs plus booklet. Sittelle. La Mure.

Schubert, M. *Stimmen der Vögel Mitteleuropas, I-IV,* Eterna. VEB Deutsche Schallplatten, Berlin.

Schubert, M. *Stimmen der Vögel, VII: Vogelstimmen Südosteuropas, 1-2.* Eterna. VEB Deutsche Schallplatten, Berlin.

Schubert, M. *Stimmen der Vögel Zentralasiens.* Eterna. VEB Deutsche Schallplatten, Berlin.

Shove, L., et al. *British Birds Series.* London.

Svensson, L. 1984. *Soviet Birds.* 90-min. cassette. Stockholm.

Wahlström, S. *Våra svenska fåglar i ton.* AB Svensk Litteratur, Stockholm.

Wahlström, S. *Fåglar i vår närhet, Fågelsjön, Skogsfåglar, Fjäll-och kustfåglar.* Cassettes published by Sveriges Ornitologiska Förening.

Veprintsev, B.N., et al. *Naturens Röster.* Union Studio of Disc Recording, Moscow.

A wide selection of bird recordings is available from WildSounds, PO Box 309, West Byfleet, Surrey KY14 7YA.

Ornithological journals and societies

A large number of journals dealing with various aspects of birds are published in Europe by birdwatching and bird-conservation societies or by private organisations. Listed below is a selection of journals in N and W Europe in which field identification, morphology, faunistics and bird conservation form a major part of the contents, along with societies to which those interested can turn for further information.

Belgium
Le Gerfaut, Institut Royal des Sciences Naturelles de Belgique, 31 rue Vantier, 1040 Bruxelles.

Britain and Ireland
British Birds, Dr J.T.R. Sharrock (ed.), Fountains, Park Lane, Blunham, Bedford MK44 3NJ.

Birding World, S.J.M. Gantlett (ed.), Tickers, High Street, Cley-next-the-Sea, Holt, Norfolk NR25 7RZ.

Birds, **The Royal Society for the Protection of Birds,** The Lodge, Sandy, Bedfordshire SG19 2DL.

Bird Study, **The British Trust for Ornithology,** The Nunnery, Nunnery Place, Thetford, Norfolk IP24 2PU.

The Ibis, **British Ornithologists' Union,** c/o The Zoological Society of London, Regent's Park, London NW1 4RV.

Scottish Birds, **Scottish Ornithologists' Club,** 21 Regent Terrace, Edinburgh EH7 5BT.

Irish Birds, **Irish Wildbird Conservancy,** Ruttledge House, 8 Longford Place, Monkstown, Co. Dublin, Ireland.

Sandgrouse (birds of the Middle East), **The Ornithological Society of the Middle East,** c/o The Lodge, Sandy, Bedfordshire SG19 2DL.

Denmark
Fugle, Dansk Ornitologisk Forenings Tidsskrift, **Dansk Ornitologisk Forening,** Vesterbrogade 140, DK-1620 Copenhagen.

Finland
Linnut, **Association of Ornithological Societies in Finland,** Box 17, SF-1801, Heinola.

France
L'Oiseau et la Revue Française d'Ornithologie, **Société Ornithologique de France,** 55 rue de Buffon, 75005 Paris Vᵉ.

Alauda, Société d'Etudes Ornithologiques, Ecole Normale Supérieure, Laboratoire de Zoologie, 46 rue d'Ulm, 75230 Paris Cedex 05.

Germany
Die Vogelwarte, Helgoland, 23 Wilhemshaven.

Journal für Ornithologie, **Deutsche Ornithologen-Gesellschaft,** Gsteigstrasse 43, 81 Garmisch-Partenkirchen.

Limicola, Peter H. Barthel (ed.), Thieplatz 6A, D-3410 Northeim 6A.

Netherlands
Ardea, postbus 9201, 6800 HB Arnhem.

Limosa, Boomgaardweg 44, 3984 KK Odijk.

Nederlandse Ornithologische Unie, PO Box 4766, 1009 AT Amsterdam.

Dutch Birding, Postbus 75611, 1070 AP Amsterdam.

Norway
Vår Fuglefauna, **Norsk Ornitologisk Forening,** PO Box 2207, N-7001 Trondheim.

Cinclus, Svein Haftorn (ed.), Vetenskapsmuseet, Erling Skakkes gate 47C, N-7013 Trondheim.

Poland
Ornithological Section of the Polish Zoological Society, Sienkiew 21, PL-50335 Wrocklaw.

Acta Ornithologica, Polska Akademic Nauk, Instytut Zoologiczny, Warsaw.

Sweden
Vår Fågelvärld, Anders Wirdheim (ed.), Genvägen 4, S-302 40 Halmstad.

Sveriges Ornitologiska Förening, Box 14219, S-10440 Stockholm.

Ornis Scandinavica, Hans Källander (ed.), Ekologihuset, S-223 62 Lund.

Index

Accentor, Alpine **380**
  Black-throated **382**
  Radde's **382**
  Siberian **382**
Accipiter brevipes **136**
  gentilis **134**
  nisus **134**
Acrocephalus aedon **430**
  agricola **430**
  arundinaceus **426**
  dumetorum **428**
  melanopogon **424**
  paludicola **426**
  palustris **428**
  schoenobaenus **426**
  scirpaceus **428**
  stentoreus **430**
Actitis hypoleucos **244**
  macularia **248**
Aegithalos caudatus **468**
Aegolius funereus **322**
Aix galericulata **96**
  sponsa **96**
Alaemon alaudipes **360**
Alauda arvensis **350**
  gulgula **350**
Albatross, Black-browed **52**
  Wandering **52**
Alca torda **294**
Alcedo atthis **334**
Alectoris barbara **178**
  chukar **176**
  graeca **176**
  rufa **178**
Alle alle **296**
Alopochen aegyptiacus **86**
Amandava amandava **502**
Ammomanes cincturus **360**
  deserti **360**
Ammoperdix griseogularis
  176
  heyi **176**
Anas acuta **92**
  americana **88**
  clypeata **92**
  crecca **94**
  cyanoptera **96**
  discors **96**
  falcata **96**
  formosa **96**
  penelope **88**
  platyrhynchos **90**
  querquedula **94**
  rubripes **96**

  strepera **90**
Anser albifrons **80**
  anser **80**
  brachyrhynchus **78**
  caerulescens **82**
  erythropus **80**
  fabalis **78**
  indicus **82**
Anthropoides virgo **190**
Anthus campestris **372**
  cervinus **368**
  godlewskii **370**
  gustavi **370**
  hodgsoni **370**
  novaeseelandiae **370**
  petrosus **366**
  pratensis **368**
  rubescens **366**
  similis **370**
  spinoletta **366**
  trivialis **368**
Apus affinis **331**
  apus **332**
  caffer **331**
  melba **332**
  pallidus **332**
Aquila chrysaetos **146**
  clanga **150**
  heliaca **148**
  nipalensis **148**
  pomarina **150**
  rapax **148**
Ardea cinerea **68**
  purpurea **68**
Ardeola ralloides **64**
Arenaria interpres **214**
Asio capensis **312**
  flammeus **312**
  otus **314**
Athene noctua **324**
Auk, Little **296**
Avadavat **502**
Avocet **196**
Aythya affinis **104**
  collaris **104**
  ferina **100**
  fuligula **102**
  marila **102**
  nyroca **100**

Babbler, Arabian **475**
  Fulvous **475**
Bartramia longicauda **230**
Bee-eater **336**

  Blue-cheeked **336**
  Little Green **336**
Bittern **60**
  American **60**
  Little **62**
Blackbird **416**
Blackcap **442**
Blackstart **392**
Bluetail, Red-flanked **388**
Bluethroat **388**
Bobolink **544**
Bombycilla garrulus **378**
Bonasa bonasia **174**
Booby, Brown **52**
Botaurus lentiginosus **60**
  stellaris **60**
Brambling **504**
Branta bernicla **84**
  canadensis **82**
  leucopsis **84**
  ruficollis **82**
Bubo bubo **314**
Bubulcus ibis **64**
Bucanetes githagineus **518**
Bucephala albeola **114**
  clangula **116**
  islandica **115**
Bufflehead **114**
Bulbul, Common **476**
  Yellow-vented **476**
Bullfinch **512**
Bulweria bulwerii **44**
Bunting, Black-faced **524**
  Black-headed **530**
  Cinereous **530**
  Cirl **526**
  Corn **524**
  Cretzschmar's **528**
  Grey-necked **528**
  House **528**
  Indigo **544**
  Lapland **538**
  Little **534**
  Ortolan **526**
  Pallas's Reed **536**
  Pine **524**
  Red-headed **530**
  Reed **536**
  Rock **528**
  Rustic **534**
  Snow **538**
  Yellow-breasted **524**
  Yellow-browed **534**
Burhinus oedicnemus **194**

Bushchat, see Robin,
  Rufous Bush
Bustard, Great **190**
  Houbara **192**
  Little **192**
Buteo buteo **138**
  lagopus **140**
  rufinus **140**
Butorides striatus **60**
Buzzard **138**
  Honey **138**
  Long-legged **140**
  Rough-legged **140**

Calandrella brachydactyla
  354
  rufescens **354**
Calcarius lapponicus **538**
Calidris acuminata **230**
  alba **214**
  alpina **218**
  bairdii **228**
  canutus **216**
  ferruginea **216**
  fuscicollis **228**
  maritima **220**
  mauri **224**
  melanotos **230**
  minuta **222**
  minutilla **226**
  pusilla **224**
  ruficollis **224**
  subminuta **226**
  temminckii **222**
Calonectris diomedea **46**
Canary **507**
Capercaillie **172**
Caprimulgus aegyptius **330**
  europaeus **328**
  nubicus **330**
  ruficollis **328**
Carduelis cannabina **516**
  carduelis **512**
  chloris **510**
  flammea **514**
  flavirostris **516**
  hornemanni **514**
  spinus **510**
Carpodacus erythrinus **516**
  rubicilla **518**
  synoicus **518**
Catharus fuscescens **410**
  guttatus **410**
  minimus **410**
  ustulatus **410**
Cepphus grylle **296**

Cercomela melanura **392**
Cercotrichas galactotes **386**
Certhia brachydactyla **472**
  familiaris **472**
Ceryle alcyon **334**
  rudis **334**
Cettia cetti **424**
Chaffinch **504**
Charadrius alexandrinus
  200
  asiaticus **202**
  dubius **200**
  hiaticula **200**
  leschenaultii **202**
  mongolus **202**
  morinellus **204**
  vociferus **206**
Chersophilus duponti **352**
Chettusia gregaria **210**
  leucura **210**
Chiffchaff **450**
Chlamydotis undulata **192**
Chlidonias hybridus **292**
  leucopterus **292**
  niger **292**
Chordeiles minor **330**
Chough **490**
  Alpine **490**
Chrysolophus amherstiae
  181
  pictus **181**
Chukar **176**
Ciconia ciconia **70**
  nigra **70**
Cinclus cinclus **378**
Circaetus gallicus **154**
Circus aeruginosus **133**
  cyaneus **128**
  macrourus **128**
  pygargus **128**
Cisticola juncidis **424**
Clamator glandarius **310**
Clangula hyemalis **110**
Coccothraustes
  coccothraustes **506**
Coccyzus americanus **311**
  erythrophthalmus **311**
Columba livia **304**
  oenas **302**
  palumbus **302**
  trocaz **304**
Coot **186**
  Crested **188**
Coracias garrulus **338**
Cormorant **54**
  Pygmy **56**

Corncrake **182**
Corvus corax **492**
  corone **494**
  frugilegus **494**
  monedula **492**
  rhipidurus **492**
  ruficollis **492**
Coturnix coturnix **182**
Courser, Cream-coloured
  198
crake, Baillon's **184**
  Little **184**
  Spotted **184**
Crane **190**
  Demoiselle **190**
Crex crex **182**
Crossbill **521**
  Parrot **521**
  Scottish **521**
  Two-barred **521**
Crow, Carrion **494**
Cuckoo **308**
  Black-billed **311**
  Great Spotted **310**
  Oriental **308**
  Yellow-billed **311**
Cuculus canorus **308**
  saturatus **308**
Curlew **234**
  Slender-billed **234**
Cursorius cursor **198**
Cyanopica cyana **490**
Cygnus columbianus **76**
  cygnus **76**
  olor **76**

Delichon urbica **364**
Dendrocopos leucotos **346**
  major **346**
  medius **344**
  minor **348**
  syriacus **344**
Dendroica coronata **542**
  striata **542**
Diomedea exulans **52**
  melanophris **52**
Dipper **378**
Diver, Black-throated **32**
  Great Northern **34**
  Red-throated **32**
  White-billed **36**
Dolichonyx oryzivorus **544**
Dotterel **204**
Dove, Collared **304**
  Laughing **306**
  Namaqua **306**

Rock **304**
Rufous Turtle **306**
Stock **302**
Turtle **306**
Dowitcher, Long-billed **248**
    Short-billed **248**
Dryocopus martius **341**
Duck, American Black **96**
    Falcated **96**
    Ferruginous **100**
    Harlequin **110**
    Long-tailed **110**
    Marbled **98**
    Ring-necked **104**
    Ruddy **98**
    Tufted **102**
    White-headed **98**
    Wood **96**
Dunlin **218**
Dunnock **380**

Eagle, Bonelli's **152**
    Booted **152**
    Golden **146**
    Imperial **148**
    Lesser Spotted **150**
    Pallas's Fish **144**
    Short-toed **154**
    Spotted **150**
    Steppe **148**
    Tawny **148**
    White-tailed **144**
Egret, Cattle **64**
    Great White **66**
    Little **66**
Egretta alba **66**
    garzetta **66**
    gularis **64**
Eider **108**
    King **106**
    Spectacled **108**
    Steller's **106**
Elanus caeruleus **121**
Emberiza aureola **524**
    bruniceps **530**
    buchanani **528**
    caesia **528**
    chrysophrys **534**
    cia **528**
    cineracea **530**
    cirlus **526**
    citrinella **526**
    hortulana **526**
    leucocephalos **524**
    melanocephala **530**

    pallasi **536**
    pusilla **534**
    rustica **534**
    schoeniclus **536**
    spodocephala **524**
    striolata **528**
Eremalauda dunni **360**
Eremophila alpestris **358**
    bilopha **359**
Erithacus rubecula **384**
Estrila astrild **502**
Euodice malabarica **502**

Falco biarmicus **162**
    cherrug **162**
    columbarius **160**
    concolor **158**
    eleonorae **158**
    naumanni **158**
    pelegrinoides **160**
    peregrinus **160**
    rusticolus **164**
    subbuteo **156**
    tinnunculus **156**
    vespertinus **156**
Falcon, Barbary **160**
    Eleonora's **158**
    Gyr **164**
    Red-footed **156**
    Sooty **158**
Ficedula albicollis **456**
    hypoleuca **456**
    parva **458**
    semitorquata **456**
Fieldfare **416**
Finch, Citril **508**
    Crimson-winged **518**
    Desert **518**
    Snow **502**
    Trumpeter **518**
Firecrest **454**
Flamingo, Greater **75**
Flycatcher, Brown **458**
    Collared **456**
    Pied **456**
    Red-breasted **458**
    Semi-collared **456**
    Spotted **458**
Francolin, Black **176**
    Double-spurred **178**
Francolinus bicalcaratus **178**
    francolinus **176**
Fratercula arctica **296**
Fregata magnificens **52**
Freira **44**

Frigatebird, Magnificent **52**
Fringilla coelebs **504**
    montifringilla **504**
Fulica atra **186**
    cristata **188**
Fulmar **44**
Fulmarus glacialis **44**

Gadwall **90**
Galerida cristata **352**
    theklae **352**
Gallinago gallinago **252**
    media **252**
    stenura **250**
Gallinula chloropus **186**
Gallinule, Purple **188**
Gannet **52**
Garganey **94**
Garrulus glandarius **488**
Gavia adamsii **36**
    arctica **32**
    immer **34**
    stellata **32**
Gelochelidon nilotica **282**
Geothlypis trichas **542**
Geronticus eremita **72**
Glareola nordmanni **198**
    pratincola **198**
Glaucidium passerinum **322**
Godwit, Bar-tailed **236**
    Black-tailed **236**
Goldcrest **454**
Goldeneye **116**
    Barrow's **115**
Goldfinch **512**
Gon-gon **44**
Goosander **118**
Goose, Bar-headed **82**
    Barnacle **84**
    Bean **78**
    Brent **84**
    Canada **82**
    Egyptian **86**
    Greylag **80**
    Lesser White-fronted **80**
    Pink-footed **78**
    Red-breasted **82**
    Snow **82**
    White-fronted **80**
Goshawk **134**
    Dark Chanting **136**
Grackle, Tristram's **486**
Grebe, Black-necked **42**
    Little Crested **40**
    Little **42**
    Pied-billed **40**

Red-necked **40**
Slavonian **42**
Greenfinch **510**
Greenshank **242**
Grosbeak, Pine **520**
Rose-breasted **544**
Grouse, Black **172**
Caucasian Black **175**
Hazel **174**
Red **170**
Guillemot **294**
Black **296**
Brünnich's **294**
Gull, Audouin's **272**
Black-headed **264**
Bonaparte's **268**
Common **266**
Franklin's **268**
Glaucous **274**
Great Black-backed **276**
Great Black-headed **272**
Herring **274**
Iceland **274**
Ivory **270**
Laughing **268**
Lesser Black-backed **276**
Little **264**
Mediterranean **262**
Ring-billed **268**
Ross's **270**
Sabine's **270**
Slender-billed **262**
Yellow-legged **274**
Gypaetus barbatus **124**
Gyps fulvus **126**
Gyrfalcon **164**

Haematopus ostralegus **194**
Halcyon smyrnensis **334**
Haliaeetus albicilla **144**
leucoryphus **144**
Harrier, Hen **128, 130**
Marsh **133**
Montagu's **128, 130**
Pallid **128, 130**
Hawfinch **506**
Hemipode, Andalusian **188**
Heron, Green-backed **60**
Grey **68**
Night **62**
Purple **68**
Squacco **64**
Western Reef **64**
Hieraaetus fasciatus **152**
pennatus **152**
Himantopus himantopus **196**

Hippolais caligata **430**
icterina **434**
languida **432**
olivetorum **432**
pallida **432**
polyglotta **434**
Hirundapus caudacutus **331**
Hirundo daurica **364**
rustica **364**
Histrionicus histrionicus **110**
Hobby **156**
Hoopoe **338**
Hoplopterus indicus **210**
spinosus **212**
Hydrobates pelagicus **50**
Hylocichla mustelina **410**

Ibis, Bald **72**
Glossy **72**
Icterus galbula **544**
Irania gutturalis **386**
Ixobrychus minutus **62**

Jackdaw **492**
Jay **488**
Siberian **487**
Junco, Dark-eyed **544**
Junco hyemalis **544**
Jynx torquilla **340**

Kestrel **156**
Lesser **158**
Killdeer **206**
Kingfisher **334**
Belted **334**
Pied **334**
White-breasted **334**
Kite, Black **122**
Black-shouldered **121**
Red **122**
Kittiwake **266**
Knot **216**

Lagopus lagopus **168, 170**
mutus **168**
Lammergeier **124**
Lanius collurio **478**
excubitor **480**
isabellinus **478**
minor **478**
nubicus **482**
senator **482**
Lanner **162**
Lapwing **212**
Lark, Bar-tailed **360**
Bimaculated **356**
Black **359**

Calandra **356**
Crested **352**
Desert **360**
Dunn's **360**
Dupont's **352**
Hoopoe **360**
Lesser Short-toed **354**
Shore **358**
Short-toed **354**
Sky **350**
Small, see Skylark, Oriental
Temminck's Horned **359**
Thekla **352**
Thick-billed **360**
White-winged **359**
Wood **350**
Larus argentatus **274**
atricilla **268**
audouinii **272**
cachinnans **274**
canus **266**
delawarensis **268**
fuscus **276**
genei **262**
glaucoides **274**
hyperboreus **274**
ichthyaetus **272**
marinus **276**
melanocephalus **262**
minutus **264**
philadelphia **268**
pipixcan **268**
ridibundus **264**
sabini **270**
Limicola falcinellus **218**
Limnodromus griseus **248**
scolopaceus **248**
Limosa lapponica **236**
limosa **236**
Linnet **516**
Locustella certhiola **422**
fluviatilis **420**
lanceolata **422**
luscinioides **420**
naevia **420**
Loxia curvirostra **521**
leucoptera **521**
pytyopsittacus **521**
scotica **521**
Lullula arborea **350**
Luscinia calliope **386**
luscinia **384**
megarhynchos **384**
svecica **388**
Lymnocryptes minimus **252**

Magpie **488**
  Azure-winged **490**
Mallard **90**
Mandarin **96**
Marmaronetta angustirostris
  98
Martin, Brown-throated
  Sand **362**
  Crag **362**
  House **364**
  Rock **362**
  Sand **362**
Melanitta fusca **112**
  nigra **112**
  perspicillata **114**
Melanocorypha bimaculata
  356
  calandra **356**
  leucoptera **359**
  yeltoniensis **359**
Melierax metabates **136**
Merganser, Red-breasted
  118
Mergus albellus **116**
  merganser **118**
  serrator **118**
Merlin **160**
Merops apiaster **336**
  orientalis **336**
  superciliosus **336**
Micropalama himantopus
  228
Miliaria calandra **524**
Milvus migrans **122**
  milvus **122**
Mniotilta varia **542**
Monticola saxatilis **408**
  solitarius **408**
Montifringilla nivalis **502**
Moorhen **186**
Motacilla alba **372**
  cinerea **374**
  citreola **377**
  flava **374**
Muscicapa dauurica **458**
  striata **458**

Nectarinia osea **476**
Neophron percnopterus
  124
Netta rufina **100**
Nighthawk, Common **330**
Nightingale **384**
  Thrush **384**
Nightjar **328**
  Egyptian **330**

Nubian **330**
Red-necked **328**
Nucifraga caryocatactes
  488
Numenius arquata **234**
  phaeopus **234**
  tenuirostris **234**
Nutcracker **488**
Nuthatch **472**
  Algerian **470**
  Corsican **470**
  Great Rock **470**
  Krüper's **470**
  Rock **470**
Nyctea scandiaca **316**
Nycticorax nycticorax **62**

Oceanites oceanicus **50**
Oceanodroma castro **50**
  leucorhoa **50**
Oenanthe cypriaca **404**
  deserti **400**
  finschii **402**
  hispanica **400**
  isabellina **398**
  leucopyga **406**
  leucura **402**
  lugens **404**
  moesta **406**
  monacha **404**
  oenanthe **396**
  pleschanka **402**
  xanthroprymna **406**
Oenas capensis **306**
Onychognathus tristramii
  486
Oriole, Golden **486**
  Northern **544**
Oriolus oriolus **486**
Osprey **155**
Otis tarda **190**
Otus brucei **324**
  scops **324**
Ouzel, Ring **415**
Ovenbird **542**
Owl, Barn **312**
  Eagle **314**
  Great Grey **320**
  Hawk **317**
  Hume's Tawny **318**
  Little **324**
  Long-eared **314**
  Marsh **312**
  Pygmy **322**
  Scops **324**
  Short-eared **312**

Snowy **316**
Striated Scops **324**
Tawny **318**
Tengmalm's **322**
Ural **320**
Oxyura jamaicensis **98**
  leucocephala **98**
Oystercatcher **194**

Pagophila eburnea **270**
Pandion haliaetus **155**
Panurus biarmicus **460**
Parakeet, Ring-necked **311**
Partridge, Barbary **178**
  Grey **180**
  Red-legged **178**
  Rock **176**
  Sand **176**
Parula, Northern **542**
Parula americana **542**
Parus ater **466**
  caeruleus **466**
  cinctus **462**
  cristatus **464**
  cyanus **468**
  lugubris **462**
  major **466**
  montanus **464**
  palustris **464**
Passer domesticus **496**
  hispaniolensis **498**
  moabiticus **500**
  montanus **496**
  simplex **500**
Passerina cyanea **544**
Pelagodroma marina **50**
Pelecanus crispus **58**
  onocrotalus **58**
  rufescens **58**
Pelican, Dalmatian **58**
  Pink-backed **58**
  White **58**
Perdix perdix **180**
Peregrine **160**
Perisoreus infaustus **487**
Pernis apivorus **138**
Petrel, Bulwer's **44**
  Soft-plumaged **44**
  see also Storm-petrel
Petronia brachydactyla **500**
  petronia **498**
  xanthocollis **500**
Phalacrocorax aristotelis **54**
  carbo **54**
  pygmeus **56**
Phalarope, Grey **254**

Red-necked 254
Wilson's 254
Phalaropus fulicarius 254
   lobatus 254
   tricolor 254
Phasianus colchicus 182
Pheasant 182
   Golden 181
   Lady Amherst's 181
Pheucticus ludovicianus
   544
Philomachus pugnax 232
Phoenicopterus ruber 75
Phoenicurus erythrogaster
   392
   moussieri 392
   ochruros 390
   phoenicurus 390
Phylloscopus bonelli 448
   borealis 452
   collybita 450
   fuscatus 450
   humei 454
   inornatus 454
   proregulus 454
   schwarzi 450
   sibilatrix 449
   trochiloides 452
   (t.) nitidus 452
   (t.) plumbeitarsus 452
   trochilus 450
Pica pica 488
Picoides tridactylus 348
Picus canus 342
   vaillantii 342
   viridis 342
Pigeon, Feral, see Dove,
   Rock
   Long-toed 304
   Wood 302
Pinicola enucleator 520
Pintail 92
Pipit, Blyth's 370
   Buff-bellied 366
   Long-billed 370
   Meadow 368
   Olive-backed 370
   Pechora 370
   Red-throated 368
   Richard's 370
   Rock 366
   Tawny 372
   Tree 368
   Water 366
Piranga olivacea 544
Platalea leucorodia 72

Plectrophenax nivalis 538
Plegadis falcinellus 72
Plover, American Golden
   206
   Caspian 202
   Golden 208
   Greater Sand 202
   Grey 208
   Kentish 200
   Little Ringed 200
   Red-wattled 210
   Ringd 200
   Sociable 210
   Spur-winged 212
   White-tailed 210
Pluvialis apricaria 208
   dominica 206
   fulva 206
   squatarola 208
Pochard 100
   Red-crested 100
Podiceps auritus 42
   cristatus 40
   grisegena 40
   nigricollis 42
Podilymbus podiceps 40
Polysticta stelleri 106
Porphyrio porphyrio 188
Porzana carolina 184
   parva 184
   porzana 184
   pusilla 184
Pratincole, Black-winged
   198
   Collared 198
Prinia gracilis 422
Prunella atrogularis 382
   collaris 380
   modularis 380
   montanella 382
   ocularis 382
Psittacula krameri 311
Ptarmigan 168
Pterocles alchata 300
   coronatus 299
   lichtensteinii 299
   orientalis 300
   senegallus 299
Pterodroma (mollis) feae 44
   (m.) madeira 44
Ptyonoprogne fuligula 362
   rupestris 362
Puffin 296
Puffinus assimilis 48
   gravis 46
   griseus 46

   puffinus 48
   yelkouan 48
Pycnonotus barbatus 476
   xanthopygos 476
Pyrrhocorax graculus 490
   pyrrhocorax 490
Pyrrhula pyrrhula 512

Quail 182

Rail, Water 186
Rallus aquaticus 186
Raven 492
   Brown-necked 492
   Fan-tailed 492
Razorbill 294
Recurvirostra avosetta 196
Redpoll 514
   Arctic 514
Redshank 240
   Spotted 240
Redstart 390
   American 542
   Black 390
   Güldenstädt's 392
   Moussier's 392
Redwing 418
Regulus ignicapillus 454
   regulus 454
Rhamphocoris clotbey 360
Rhodopechys sanguinea
   518
Rhodospiza obsoleta 518
Rhodostethia rosea 270
Riparia paludicola 362
   riparia 362
Rissa tridactyla 266
Robin 384
   Rufous Bush 386
   White-throated 386
Roller 338
Rook 494
Rosefinch, Great 518
   Scarlet 516
   Sinai 518
Rubythroat, Siberian 386
Ruff 232

Saker 162
Sanderling 214
Sandgrouse, Black-bellied
   300
   Crowned 299
   Lichtenstein's 299
   Pallas's 300
   Pin-tailed 300

Spotted **299**
Sandpiper, Baird's **228**
  Broad-billed **218**
  Buff-breasted **230**
  Common **244**
  Curlew **216**
  Green **244**
  Least **226**
  Marsh **246**
  Pectoral **230**
  Purple **220**
  Semipalmated **224**
  Sharp-tailed **230**
  Solitary **244**
  Spotted **248**
  Stilt **228**
  Terek **246**
  Upland **230**
  Western **224**
  White-rumped **228**
  Wood **242**
Sapsucker, Yellow-bellied **344**
Saxicola maura **394**
  rubetra **394**
  torquata **394**
Scaup **102**
  Lesser **104**
Scolopax rusticola **250**
Scoter, Common **112**
  Surf **114**
  Velvet **112**
Scotocerca inquieta **422**
See-see **176**
Seiurus aurocapillus **542**
  noveboracensis **542**
Serin **508**
  Red-fronted **508**
  Tristram's **507**
Serinus canaria **507**
  citrinella **508**
  pusillus **508**
  serinus **508**
  syriacus **507**
Setophaga ruticilla **542**
Shag **54**
Shearwater, Cory's **46**
  Great **46**
  Little **48**
  Manx **48**
  Sooty **46**
  Yelkouan **48**
Shelduck **86**
  Ruddy **86**
Shorelark **358**
Shoveler **92**

Shrike, Black-headed Bush **476**
  Great Grey **480**
  Isabelline **478**
  Lesser Grey **478**
  Masked **482**
  Red-backed **478**
  Woodchat **482**
Silverbill, Indian **502**
Siskin **510**
Sitta europaea **472**
  krueperi **470**
  ledanti **470**
  neumayer **470**
  tephronota **470**
  whiteheadi **470**
Skua, Arctic **257**
  Great **256**
  Long-tailed **257**
  Pomarine **256**
Skylark **350**
  Oriental **350**
Smew **116**
Somateria fischeri **108**
  mollissima **108**
  spectabilis **106**
Snipe **252**
  Great **252**
  Jack **252**
  Pintail **250**
Snowcock, Caspian **175**
  Caucasian **175**
Sora **184**
Sparrow, Dead Sea **500**
  Desert **500**
  House **496**
  Pale Rock **500**
  Rock **498**
  Spanish **498**
  Tree **496**
  White-throated **500**
  Yellow-throated **500**
Sparrowhawk **134**
  Levant **136**
Sphyrapicus varius **344**
Spoonbill **72**
Starling **484**
  Rose-coloured **484**
  Spotless **484**
Stercorarius longicaudus **257**
  parasiticus **257**
  pomarinus **256**
  skua **256**
Sterna albifrons **286**
  anaethetus **290**

  bengalensis **290**
  bergii **290**
  caspia **286**
  dougallii **284**
  elegans **290**
  forsteri **290**
  fuscata **290**
  hirundo **284**
  maxima **290**
  paradisaea **284**
  sandvicensis **282**
Stilt, Black-winged **196**
Stint, Little **222**
  Long-toed **226**
  Red-necked **224**
  Temminck's **394**
Stonechat **394**
  Siberian (Eastern) **394**
Stone-curlew **194**
Stork, Black **70**
  White **70**
Storm-petrel, British **50**
  Leach's **50**
  Madeiran **50**
  White-faced **50**
  Wilson's **50**
Streptopelia decaocto **304**
  orientalis **306**
  senegalensis **306**
  turtur **306**
Strix aluco **318**
  butleri **318**
  nebulosa **320**
  uralensis **320**
Sturnus roseus **484**
  unicolor **484**
  vulgaris **484**
Sula bassana **52**
  leucogaster **52**
Sunbird, Palestine **476**
Surnia ulula **317**
Swallow **364**
  Red-rumped **364**
Swan, Bewick's **76**
  Mute **76**
  Whooper **76**
Swift **332**
  Alpine **332**
  Little **331**
  Needle-tailed **331**
  Pallid **332**
  White-rumped **331**
Sylvia atricapilla **442**
  borin **400**
  cantillans **438**
  communis **440**

conspicillata **438**
curruca **440**
deserticola **436**
hortensis **444**
leucomelaena **442**
melanocephala **444**
melanothorax **446**
mystacea **446**
nana **438**
nisoria **442**
rueppelli **444**
sarda **436**
undata **436**
Syrrhaptes paradoxus **300**

Tachybaptus ruficollis **42**
Tadorna ferruginea **86**
tadorna **86**
Tanager, Scarlet **544**
Tarsiger cyanurus **388**
Tchagra senegala **476**
Teal **94**
  Baikal **96**
  Blue-winged **96**
  Cinnamon **96**
  Green-winged **96**
Tern, Arctic **284**
  Black **292**
  Bridled **290**
  Caspian **286**
  Common **284**
  Crested **290**
  Elegant **290**
  Forster's **290**
  Gull-billed **282**
  Lesser Crested **290**
  Little **196**
  Roseate **284**
  Royal **290**
  Sandwich **282**
  Sooty **290**
  Whiskered **292**
  White-winged Black **292**
Tetrao mlokosiewiczi **175**
  tetrix **172**
  urogallus **172**
Tetraogallus caspius **175**
  caucasicus **175**
Tetrax tetrax **192**
Thrush, Black-throated **414**
  Blue Rock **408**
  Dusky **414**
  Eye-browed **414**
  Grey-cheeked **410**
  Hermit **410**
  Mistle **418**

Naumann's **414**
  Rock **408**
  Siberian **414**
  Song **418**
  Swainson's **410**
  Whie's **414**
  Wood **410**
Tichodroma muraria **474**
Tit, Azure **468**
  Bearded **460**
  Blue **466**
  Coal **466**
  Crested **464**
  Great **466**
  Long-tailed **468**
  Marsh **464**
  Penduline **460**
  SIberian **462**
  Sombre **462**
  Willow **464**
Treecreeper **472**
  Short-toed **472**
Tringa erythropus **240**
  flavipes **248**
  glareola **242**
  melanoleuca **248**
  nebularia **242**
  ochropus **244**
  solitaria **244**
  stagnatilis **246**
  totanus **240**
Troglodytes troglodytes **380**
Tryngites subruficollis **230**
Turdoides fulvus **475**
  squamiceps **475**
Turdus merula **416**
  migratorius **410**
  naumanni **414**
  obscurus **414**
  philomelos **418**
  pilaris **416**
  ruficollis **414**
  torquatus **415**
  viscivorus **418**
Turnix sylvatica **188**
Turnstone **214**
Twite **516**
Tyto alba **312**

Upupa epops **338**
Uria aalge **294**
  lomvia **294**

Vanellus vanellus **212**
Veery **410**
Vireo, Red-eyed **542**
Vireo olivaceus **542**

Vulture, Bearded, see
  Lammergeier
  Black **126**
  Egyptian **124**
  Griffon **126**

Wagtail, Citrine **377**
  Grey **374**
  Pied **372**
  Yellow **374**
Wallcreeper **474**
Warbler, Aquatic **426**
  Arabian **442**
  Arctic **452**
  Barred **442**
  Black-and-white **542**
  Blackpoll **542**
  Blyth's Reed **428**
  Bonelli's **448**
  Booted **430**
  Cetti's **424**
  Clamorous Reed **430**
  Cyprus **446**
  Dartford **436**
  Desert **438**
  Dusky **450**
  Fan-tailed **424**
  Garden **440**
  Graceful **422**
  Grasshopper **420**
  Great Reed **426**
  Green **452**
  Greenish **452**
  Hume's Yellow-browed
    454
  Icterine **434**
  Lanceolated **422**
  Marmora's **436**
  Marsh **428**
  Melodious **434**
  Ménétries's **446**
  Moustached **424**
  Olivaceous **432**
  Olive-tree **432**
  Orphean **444**
  Paddyfield **430**
  Pallas's **454**
  Pallas's Grasshopper **422**
  Radde's **450**
  Reed **428**
  River **420**
  Rüppell's **444**
  Sardinian **444**
  Savi's **420**
  Scrub **422**
  Sedge **426**

Spectacled **438**
Subalpine **438**
Thick-billed **430**
Tristram's **436**
Two-barred Greenish **452**
Upcher's **432**
Willow **450**
Wood **449**
Yellow-browed **454**
Yellow-rumped **542**
Waterthrush, Northern **542**
Waxbill, Common **502**
Waxwing **378**
Wheatear, Black **402**
Black-eared **400**
Cyprus Pied **404**
Desert **400**
Finsch's **402**
Hooded **404**

Isabelline **398**
Mourning **404**
Northern **397**
Pied **402**
Red-rumped **406**
Red-tailed **406**
White-crowned Black **406**
Whimbrel **234**
Whinchat **394**
Whitethroat **440**
Lesser **440**
Wigeon **88**
American **88**
Woodcock **250**
Woodlark **350**
Woodpecker, Black **341**
Great Spotted **346**
Green **342**
Grey-headed **342**

Lesser Spotted **348**
Levaillant's Green **342**
Middle Spotted **344**
Syrian **344**
Three-toed **348**
White-backed **346**
Woodpigeon **302**
Wren **380**
Wryneck **340**

Xenus cinereus **246**

Yellowlegs, Greater **248**
Lesser **248**
Yellowhammer **526**
Yellowthroat, Common **542**

Zonotrichia albicollis **544**
Zonotrichia melodia **544**
Zoothera dauma **414**
sibirica **414**